MY DOUBLE LIFE

MY DOUBLE LIFE

The Memoirs of
Sarah Bernhardt

PETER OWEN · LONDON

ISBN 0 7206 0502 4

392997/04/1

PETER OWEN LIMITED
73 Kenway Road London SW5 0RE

Translated from the French *Ma Double Vie*
and first published in England 1907
This edition © Peter Owen Ltd 1977

Printed in Great Britain by
Redwood Burn Limited, Trowbridge & Esher

CONTENTS

CONTENTS

I

CHILDHOOD

My mother was fond of travelling : she would go from Spain to England, from London to Paris, from Paris to Berlin, and from there to Christiania ; then she would come back, embrace me, and set out again for Holland, her native country. She used to send my nurse clothing for herself and cakes for me. To one of my aunts she would write : " Look after little Sarah; I shall return in a month's time." A month later she would write to another of her sisters : "Go and see the child at her nurse's ; I shall be back in a couple of weeks."

My mother's age was nineteen ; I was three years old, and my two aunts were seventeen and twenty years of age; another aunt was fifteen, and the eldest was twenty-eight; but the last one lived at Martinique, and was the mother of six children. My grandmother was blind, my grandfather dead, and my father had been in China for the last two years. I have no idea why he had gone there.

My youthful aunts always promised to come to see me, but rarely kept their word. My nurse hailed from Brittany, and lived near Quimperlé, in a little white house with a low thatched roof, on which wild gilly-flowers grew. That was the first flower which charmed my eyes as a child, and I have loved it ever since. Its leaves are heavy and sad-looking, and its petals are made of the setting sun.

Brittany is a long way off, even in our epoch of velocity! In those days it was the end of the world. Fortunately my nurse was, it appears, a good, kind woman, and, as her own child had died, she had only me to love. But she loved after the manner of poor people, when she had time.

One day, as her husband was ill, she went into the field to

help gather in potatoes ; the over-damp soil was rotting them, and there was no time to be lost. She left me in charge of her husband, who was lying on his Breton bedstead suffering from a bad attack of lumbago. The good woman had placed me in my high chair, and had been careful to put in the wooden peg which supported the narrow table for my toys. She threw a faggot in the grate, and said to me in Breton language (until the age of four I only understood Breton), "Be a good girl, Milk Blossom." That was my only name at the time. When she had gone, I tried to withdraw the wooden peg which she had taken so much trouble to put in place. Finally I succeeded in pushing aside the little rampart. I wanted to reach the ground, but—poor little me!—I fell into the fire, which was burning joyfully.

The screams of my foster-father, who could not move, brought in some neighbours. I was thrown, all smoking, into a large pail of fresh milk. My aunts were informed of what had happened : they communicated the news to my mother, and for the next four days that quiet part of the country was ploughed by stage-coaches which arrived in rapid succession. My aunts came from all parts of the world, and my mother, in the greatest alarm, hastened from Brussels, with Baron Larrey, one of her friends, who was a young doctor, just beginning to acquire celebrity, and a house surgeon whom Baron Larrey had brought with him. I have been told since that nothing was so painful to witness and yet so charming as my mother's despair. The doctor approved of the "mask of butter," which was changed every two hours.

Dear Baron Larrey ! I often saw him afterwards, and now and again we shall meet him in the pages of my Memoirs. He used to tell me in such charming fashion how those kind folks loved Milk Blossom. And he could never refrain from laughing at the thought of that butter. There was butter everywhere, he used to say : on the bedsteads, on the cupboards, on the chairs, on the tables, hanging up on nails in bladders. All the neighbours used to bring butter to make masks for Milk Blossom.

Mother, adorably beautiful, looked like a Madonna, with her golden hair and her eyes fringed with such long lashes that they made a shadow on her cheeks when she looked down.

She distributed money on all sides. She would have given her golden hair, her slender white fingers, her tiny feet, her life itself, in order to save her child. And she was as sincere in her despair and her love as in her unconscious forgetfulness. Baron Larrey returned to Paris, leaving my mother, Aunt Rosine, and the surgeon with me. Forty-two days later, mother took back in triumph to Paris the nurse, the foster-father, and me, and installed us in a little house at Neuilly, on the banks of the Seine. I had not even a scar, it appears. My skin was rather too bright a pink, but that was all. My mother, happy and trustful once more, began to travel again, leaving me in care of my aunts.

Two years were spent in the little garden at Neuilly, which was full of horrible dahlias growing close together and coloured like wooden balls. My aunts never came there. My mother used to send money, bon-bons, and toys. The foster-father died, and my nurse married a concierge, who used to pull open the door at 65 Rue de Provence.

Not knowing where to find my mother, and not being able to write, my nurse—without telling any of my friends—took me with her to her new abode.

The change delighted me. I was five years old at the time, and I remember the day as if it were yesterday. My nurse's abode was just over the doorway of the house, and the window was framed in the heavy and monumental door. From outside I thought it was beautiful, and I began to clap my hands on reaching the house. It was towards five o'clock in the evening, in the month of November, when everything looks grey. I was put to bed, and no doubt I went to sleep at once, for there end my recollections of that day.

The next morning there was terrible grief in store for me. There was no window in the little room in which I slept, and I began to cry, and escaped from the arms of my nurse, who was dressing me, so that I could go into the adjoining room. I ran to the round window, which was an immense " bull's-eye " above the doorway. I pressed my stubborn brow against the glass, and began to scream with rage on seeing no trees, no box-weed, no leaves falling, nothing, nothing but stone—cold, grey, ugly stone—and panes of glass opposite me. " I want to go away ! I don't want to stay here ! It is all black, black ! It is ugly !

I want to see the ceiling of the street!" and I burst into tears. My poor nurse took me up in her arms, and, folding me in a rug, took me down into the courtyard. "Lift up your head, Milk Blossom, and look! See—there is the ceiling of the street!"

It comforted me somewhat to see that there was some sky in this ugly place, but my little soul was very sad. I could not eat, and I grew pale and became anæmic, and should certainly have died of consumption if it had not been for a mere chance, a most unexpected incident. One day I was playing in the courtyard with a little girl, called Titine, who lived on the second floor, and whose face or real name I cannot recall, when I saw my nurse's husband walking across the courtyard with two ladies, one of whom was most fashionably attired. I could only see their backs, but the voice of the fashionably attired lady caused my heart to stop beating. My poor little body trembled with nervous excitement.

"Do any of the windows look on to the courtyard?" she asked.

"Yes, Madame, those four," he replied, pointing to four open ones on the first floor.

The lady turned to look at them, and I uttered a cry of joy.

"Aunt Rosine! Aunt Rosine!" I exclaimed, clinging to the skirts of the pretty visitor. I buried my face in her furs, stamping, sobbing, laughing, and tearing her wide lace sleeves in my frenzy of delight. She took me in her arms and tried to calm me, and questioning the concierge, she stammered out to her friend: "I can't understand what it all means! This is little Sarah! My sister Youle's child!"

The noise I made had attracted attention, and people opened their windows. My aunt decided to take refuge in the concierge's lodge, in order to come to an explanation. My poor nurse told her about all that had taken place, her husband's death, and her second marriage. I do not remember what she said to excuse herself. I clung to my aunt, who was deliciously perfumed, and I would not let go of her. She promised to come the following day to fetch me, but I did not want to stay any longer in that dark place. I asked to start at once with my nurse. My aunt stroked my hair gently, and spoke to her friend in a language I did not understand. She tried in vain to explain something to me; I do not know what it was, but I insisted that I wanted to go away with her at once. In a gentle, tender, caressing voice, but without any real affection, she said all kinds of pretty things, stroked me with her gloved hands, patted my frock, which was turned up, and made any amount of charming, frivolous little gestures, but all without any real feeling. She then went away, at her friend's entreaty, after emptying her purse in my nurse's hands. I rushed towards the door, but the husband of my nurse, who had opened it for her, now closed it again. My nurse was crying, and, taking me in her arms, she opened the window, saying to me, " Don't cry, Milk Blossom. Look at your pretty aunt ; she will come back again, and then you can go away with her." Great tears rolled down her calm, round, handsome face. I could see nothing but the dark, black hole which remained there immutable behind me, and in a fit of despair I rushed out to my aunt, who was just getting into a carriage. After that I knew nothing more ; everything seemed dark, there was a noise in the distance. I could hear voices far, far away. I had managed to escape from my poor nurse, and had fallen down on the pavement in front of my aunt. I had broken my arm in two places, and injured my left knee-cap. I only came to myself again a few hours later, to find that I was in a beautiful, wide bed which smelt very nice. It stood in the middle of a large room, with two lovely windows, which made me very joyful, for I could see the ceiling of the street through them.

My mother, who had been sent for immediately, came to take care of me, and I saw the rest of my family, my aunts and my cousins. My poor little brain could not understand why all these people should suddenly be so fond of me, when I had passed so many days and nights only cared for by one single person.

As I was weakly, and my bones small and friable, I was two years recovering from this terrible fall, and during that time was nearly always carried about. I will pass over these two years of my life, which have left me only a vague memory of being petted and of a chronic state of torpor.

II

AT BOARDING SCHOOL

ONE day my mother took me on her knees and said to me, "You are a big girl now, and you must learn to read and write." I was then seven years old, and could neither read, write, nor count, as I had been five years with the old nurse and two years ill. "You must go to school," continued my mother, playing with my curly hair, "like a big girl." I did not know what all this meant, and I asked what a school was.

"It's a place where there are many little girls," replied my mother.

"Are they ill?" I asked.

"Oh no! They are quite well, as you are now, and they play together, and are very gay and happy."

I jumped about in delight, and gave free vent to my joy, but on seeing tears in my mother's eyes I flung myself in her arms.

"But what about you, Mamma?" I asked. "You will be all alone, and you won't have any little girl."

She bent down to me and said : "God has told me that He will send me some flowers and a little baby."

My delight was more and more boisterous. "Then I shall have a little brother!" I exclaimed, "or else a little sister. Oh no, I don't want that; I don't like little sisters."

Mamma kissed me very affectionately, and then I was dressed, I remember, in a blue corded velvet frock, of which I was very proud. Arrayed thus in all my splendour, I waited impatiently for Aunt Rosine's carriage, which was to take us to Auteuil.

It was about three when she arrived. The housemaid had gone on about an hour before, and I had watched with delight my little trunk and my toys being packed into the carriage. The maid climbed up and took the seat by the driver, in spite of my mother protesting at first against this. When my aunt's magnificent equipage arrived, mamma was the first to get in, slowly and calmly. I got in when my turn came, giving myself airs, because the concierge and some of the shopkeepers were watching. My aunt then sprang in lightly, but by no means calmly, after giving her orders in English to the stiff, ridiculous-looking coachman, and handing him a paper on which the address was written. Another carriage followed ours, in which thrèe men were seated: Régis L——, a friend of my father's, General de P——, and an artist, named Fleury, I think, whose pictures of horses and sporting subjects were very much in vogue just then.

I heard on the way that these gentlemen were to make arrangements for a little dinner near Auteuil, to console mamma for her great trouble in being separated from me. Some other guests were to be there to meet them. I did not pay very much attention to what my mother and my aunt said to each other. Sometimes when they spoke of me they talked either English or German, and smiled at me affectionately. The long drive was greatly appreciated by me, for with my face pressed against the window and my eyes wide open I gazed out eagerly at the grey muddy road, with its ugly houses on each side, and its bare trees. I thought it was all very beautiful, because it kept changing.

The carriage stopped at 18 Rue Boileau, Auteuil. On the iron gate was a long, dark signboard, with gold letters. I looked up at it, and mamma said, "You will be able to read that soon, I hope." My aunt whispered to me, "Boarding School, Madame Fressard," and very promptly I said to mamma, "It says 'Boarding School, Madame Fressard.'"

Mamma, my aunt, and the three gentlemen laughed heartily at my assurance, and we entered the house. Madame Fressard came forward to meet us, and I liked her at once. She was of medium height, rather stout, and her hair turning grey, à la Sévigné. She had beautiful large eyes, rather like George Sand's, and very white teeth, which showed up all the more as her complexion was rather tawny. She looked healthy, spoke kindly; her hands were plump and her fingers long. She took my hand gently in hers, and half kneeling, so that her face was level with mine, she said in a musical voice, "You won't be afraid of me, will you, little girl?" I did not answer, but my face flushed as red as a cockscomb. She asked me several questions, but I refused to reply. They all gathered round me. "Speak, child—— Come, Sarah, be a good girl—— Oh, the naughty little child!"

It was all in vain. I remained perfectly mute. The customary round was then made, to the bed-rooms, the dining-hall, the class-rooms, and the usual exaggerated compliments were paid. "How beautifully it is all kept! How spotlessly clean everything is!" and a hundred stupidities of this kind about the comfort of these prisons for children. My mother went aside with Madame Fressard, and I clung to her knees so that she could not walk. "This is the doctor's prescription," she said, and then followed a long list of things that were to be done for me.

Madame Fressard smiled rather ironically. "You know, Madame," she said to my mother, "we shall not be able to curl her hair like that."

"And you certainly will not be able to uncurl it," replied my mother, stroking my head with her gloved hands. "It's a regular wig, and they must never attempt to comb it until it has been well brushed. They could not possibly get the knots out otherwise, and it would hurt her too much. What do you give the children at four o'clock?" she asked, changing the subject.

"Oh, a slice of bread and just what the parents leave for them."

"There are twelve pots of different kinds of jam," said my mother, "but she must have jam one day, and chocolate another, as she has not a good appetite, and requires change of food. I have brought six pounds of chocolate." Madame Fressard smiled in a good-natured but rather ironical way. She picked up a packet of the chocolate and looked at the name of the maker.

"Ah! from Marquis's! What a spoiled little girl it is!" She patted my cheek with her white fingers, and then as her eyes fell on a large jar she looked surprised. "That's cold cream," said my mother. "I make it myself, and I should like my little girl's face and hands to be rubbed with it every night when she goes to bed."

"But——" began Madame Fressard.

"Oh, I'll pay double laundry expenses for the sheets," interrupted my mother impatiently. (Ah, my poor mother!

I remember quite well that my sheets were changed once a month, like those of the other pupils.)

The farewell moment came at last, and every one gathered round mamma, and finally carried her off, after a great deal of kissing and with all kinds of consoling words. " It will be so good for her—it is just what she needs—you'll find her quite changed when you see her again "—&c. &c.

The General, who was very fond of me, picked me up in his arms and tossed me in the air.

" You little chit," he said ; " they are putting you into barracks, and you'll have to mind your behaviour ! "

I pulled his long moustache, and he said, winking, and look-ing in the direction of Madame Fressard, who had a slight moustache, " You mustn't do that to the lady, you know ! "

My aunt laughed heartily, and my mother gave a little stifled laugh, and the whole troop went off in a regular whirlwind of rustling skirts and farewells, whilst I was taken away to the cage where I was to be imprisoned.

I spent two years at this pension. I was taught reading, writing, and reckoning. I also learnt a hundred new games. I learnt to sing *rondeaux* and to embroider handkerchiefs for my mother. I was relatively happy there, as we always went out somewhere on Thursdays and Sundays, and this gave me the sensation of liberty. The very ground in the street seemed to me quite different from the ground of the large garden belonging to the pension. Besides, there were little festivities at Madame Fressard's which used to send me into raptures. Mlle. Stella Colas, who had just made her *début* at the Théâtre Français, came sometimes on Thursdays and recited poetry to us. I could never sleep a wink the night before, and in the morning I used to comb my hair carefully and get ready, my heart beating fast with excitement, in order to listen to something I did not understand at all, but which nevertheless left me spell-bound. Then, too, there was quite a legend attached to this pretty girl. She had flung herself almost under the horses' feet as the Emperor was driving along, in order to attract his attention and obtain the pardon of her brother, who had conspired against his sovereign.

Mlle. Stella Colas had a sister at Madame Fressard's, and this sister, Clothilde, is now the wife of M. Pierre Merlou, Under

Secretary of State in the Treasury Department. Stella was slight and fair, with blue eyes that were rather hard but expressive. She had a deep voice, and when this pale, fragile girl began to recite Athalie's Dream, it thrilled me through and through. How many times, seated on my child's bed, did I practise saying in a low voice, " *Tremble, fille digne de moi* "—I used to twist my head on my shoulders, swell out my cheeks, and commence :

" *Tremble—trem-ble—trem-em-ble——* "

But it always ended badly, and I would begin again very quietly, in a stifled voice, and then unconsciously speak louder ; and my companions, roused by the noise, were amused at my attempts, and roared with laughter. I would then rush about to the right and left, giving them kicks and blows, which they returned with interest.

Madame Fressard's adopted daughter, Mlle. Caroline (whom I chanced to meet a long time after, married to the celebrated artist, Yvon), would then appear on the scene. Angry and implacable, she would give us all kinds of punishments for the following day. As for me, I used to get locked up for three days : that was followed by my being detained on the first day we were allowed out. And in addition I would receive five strokes with a ruler on my fingers. Ah! those ruler strokes of Mlle. Caroline's! I reproached her about them when I met her again twenty-five years later. She used to make us put all our fingers round the thumb and hold our hands straight out to her, and then bang came her wide ebony ruler. She used to give us a cruelly hard, sharp blow which made the tears spurt to our eyes. I took a dislike to Mlle. Caroline. She was beautiful, but with the kind of beauty I did not care for. She had a very white complexion, and very black hair, which she wore in waved *bandeaux*. When I saw her a long time afterwards, one of my relatives brought her to my house and said, " I am sure you will not recognise this lady, and yet you know her very well." I was leaning against the large mantelpiece in the hall, and I saw this tall woman, still beautiful, but rather provincial-looking, coming through the first drawing-room. As she descended the three steps into the hall the light fell on her protruding forehead, framed on each side with the hard, waved *bandeaux*.

"Mademoiselle Caroline!" I exclaimed, and with a furtive, childish movement I hid my two hands behind my back. I never saw her again, for the grudge I had owed her from my childhood must have been apparent under my politeness as hostess.

As I said before, I was not unhappy at Madame Fressard's, and it seemed quite natural to me that I should stay there until I was quite a grown-up girl. My uncle, Félix Faure, who has entered the Carthusian monastery, had stipulated that his wife, my mother's sister, should often take me out. He had a very fine country place at, Neuilly, with a stream running through the grounds, and I used to fish there for hours, together with my two cousins, a boy and girl.

These two years of my life passed peacefully, without any other events than my terrible fits of temper, which upset the whole pension and always left me in the infirmary for two or three days. These outbursts of temper were like attacks of madness.

One day Aunt Rosine arrived suddenly to take me away altogether. My father had written giving orders as to where I was to be placed, and these orders were imperative. My mother was travelling, so she had sent word to my aunt, who had hurried off at once, between two dances, to carry out the instructions she had received.

The idea that I was to be ordered about, without any regard to my own wishes or inclinations, put me into an indescribable rage. I rolled about on the ground, uttering the most heart-rending cries. I yelled out all kinds of reproaches, blaming mamma, my aunts, and Madame Fressard for not finding some way to keep me with her. The struggle lasted two hours, and while I was being dressed I escaped twice into the garden and attempted to climb the trees and to throw myself into the pond, in which there was more mud than water.

Finally, when I was completely exhausted and subdued, I was taken off, sobbing, in my aunt's carriage.

I stayed three days at her house, as I was so feverish that my life was said to be in danger.

My father used to come to my aunt Rosine's, who was then living at 6 Rue de la Chaussée d'Antin. He was on friendly terms with Rossini, who lived at No. 4 in the same street. He often brought him in, and Rossini made me laugh with his clever stories and comic grimaces.

My father was as "handsome as a god," and I used to look at him with pride. I did not know him well, as I saw him so rarely, but I loved him for his seductive voice and his slow, gentle gestures. He commanded a certain respect, and I noticed that even my exuberant aunt calmed down in his presence.

I had recovered, and Dr. Monod, who was attending me, said that I could now be moved without any fear of ill effects.

We had been waiting for my mother, but she was ill at Haarlem. My aunt offered to accompany us if my father would take me to the convent, but he refused, and I can hear him now with his gentle voice saying :

"No ; her mother will take her to the convent. I have written to the Faures, and the child is to stay there a fortnight."

My aunt was about to protest, but my father replied :

"It's quieter there, my dear Rosine, and the child needs tranquillity more than anything else."

I went that very evening to my aunt Faure's. I did not care much for her, as she was cold and affected, but I adored my uncle. He was so gentle and so calm, and there was an infinite charm in his smile. His son was as turbulent as I was myself, adventurous and rather hare-brained, so that we always liked being together. His sister, an adorable, Greuze-like girl, was reserved, and always afraid of soiling her frocks and even her pinafores. The poor child married Baron Cerise, and died during her confinement, in the very flower of youth and beauty, because her timidity, her reserve, and narrow education had made her refuse to see a doctor when the intervention of a medical man was absolutely necessary. I was very fond of her, and her death was a great grief to me. At present I never see the faintest ray of moonlight without its evoking a pale vision of her.

I stayed three weeks at my uncle's, roaming about with my cousin and spending hours lying down flat, fishing for cray-fish in the little stream that ran through the park. This park was immense, and surrounded by a wide ditch. How many times I used to have bets with my cousins that I would jump that ditch ! The bet was sometimes three sheets of paper, or five pins, or perhaps my two pancakes, for we used to have pancakes every Tuesday. And after the bet I jumped, more often than not falling into the ditch and splashing about in the green water, screaming because I was afraid of the frogs, and yelling with terror when my cousins pretended to rush away.

When I returned to the house my aunt was always watching anxiously at the top of the stone steps for our arrival. What a lecture I had, and what a cold look.

"Go upstairs and change your clothes, Mademoiselle," she would say, "and then stay in your room. Your dinner will be sent to you there without any dessert."

As I passed the big glass in the hall I caught sight of myself, looking like a rotten tree stump, and I saw my cousin making signs, by putting his hand to his mouth, that he would bring me some dessert.

His sister used to go to his mother, who fondled her and seemed to say, "Thank Heaven you are not like that little Bohemian!" This was my aunt's stinging epithet for me in moments of anger. I used to go up to my room with a heavy heart, thoroughly ashamed and vexed, vowing to myself that I would never again jump the ditch, but on reaching my room I used to find the gardener's daughter there, a big, awkward, merry girl, who used to wait on me.

"Oh, how comic Mademoiselle looks like that!" she would say, laughing so heartily that I was proud of looking comic, and I decided that when I jumped the ditch again I would get weeds and mud all over me. When I had undressed and washed I used to put on a flannel gown and wait in my room until my dinner came. Soup was sent up, and then meat, bread, and water. I detested meat then, just as I do now, and threw it out of the window after cutting off the fat, which I put on the rim of my plate, as my aunt used to come up unexpectedly.

"Have you eaten your dinner, Mademoiselle?" she would ask.

"Yes, Aunt," I replied.

"Are you still hungry?"

"No, Aunt."

"Write out 'Our Father' and the 'Creed' three times, you little heathen." This was because I had not been baptized. A quarter of an hour later my uncle would come upstairs.

"Have you had enough dinner?" he would ask.

"Yes, Uncle," I replied.

" Did you eat your meat ? "

" No ; I threw it out of the window.   I don't like meat."

" You told your aunt an untruth, then."

" No ; she asked me if I had eaten my dinner, and I answered that I had, but I did not say that I had eaten my meat."

" What punishment has she given you ? "

" I am to write out ' Our Father ' and the ' Creed ' three times before going to bed."

" Do you know them by heart ? "

" No, not very well ; I make mistakes always."

And the adorable man would then dictate to me " Our Father " and the " Creed," and I copied it in the most devoted way, as he used to dictate with deep feeling and emotion.   He was religious, very religious indeed, this uncle of mine, and after the death of my aunt he became a Carthusian monk.   As I write these lines, ill and aged as he is, and bent with pain, I know he is digging his own grave, weak with the weight of the spade, imploring God to take him, and thinking sometimes of me, of his little Bohemian.   Ah, the dear, good man, it is to him that I owe all that is best in me.   I love him devotedly and have the greatest respect for him.   How many times in the difficult phases of my life I have thought of him and consulted his ideas, for I never saw him again, as my aunt quarrelled purposely with my mother and me.   He was always fond of me, though, and has told his friends to assure me of this.   Occasionally, too, he has sent me his advice, which has always been very straightforward and full of indulgence and common sense.

Recently I went to the country where the Carthusians have taken refuge.   A friend of mine went to see my uncle, and I wept on hearing the words he had dictated to be repeated to me.

To return to my story.   After my uncle's visit, Marie, the gardener's daughter, came to my room, looking quite indifferent, but with her pockets stuffed with apples, biscuits, raisins, and nuts.   My cousin had sent me some dessert, but she, the good-hearted girl, had cleared all the dessert dishes.   I told her to sit down and crack the nuts, and I would eat them when I had finished my " Lord's Prayer " and " Creed."   She sat down on the floor, so that she could hide everything quickly under the table in case my aunt returned. But my aunt did not come again, as she and her daughter used to spend their evenings at the piano, whilst my uncle taught his son mathematics.

Finally, my mother wrote to say that she was coming. There was great excitement in my uncle's house, and my little trunk was packed in readiness.

The Grand-Champs Convent, which I was about to enter, had a prescribed uniform, and my cousin, who loved sewing, marked all my things with the initials S. B. in red cotton. My uncle gave me a silver spoon, fork, and goblet, and these were all marked 32, which was the number under which I was registered there. Marie gave me a thick woollen muffler in shades of violet, which she had been knitting for me in secret for several days. My aunt put round my neck a little scapulary which had been blessed, and when my mother and father arrived everything was ready.

A farewell dinner was given, to which two of my mother's friends, Aunt Rosine, and four other members of the family were invited.

I felt very important. I was neither sad nor gay, but had just this feeling of importance which was quite enough for me. Every one at table talked about me ; my uncle kept stroking my hair, and my cousin from her end of the table threw me kisses. Suddenly my father's musical voice made me turn towards him.

"Listen to me, Sarah," he said. "If you are very good at the convent, I will come in four years and fetch you away, and you shall travel with me and see some beautiful countries."

"Oh, I will be good !" I exclaimed ; "I'll be as good as Aunt Henriette ! "

This was my aunt Faure. Everybody smiled.

After dinner, the weather being very fine, we all went out to stroll in the park. My father took me with him, and talked to me very seriously. He told me things that were sad, which I had never heard before. I understood, although I was so young, and my eyes filled with tears. He was sitting on an old bench and I was on his knee, with my head resting on his shoulder. I listened to all he said and cried silently, my childish mind disturbed by his words. Poor father! I was never, never to see him again.

III

CONVENT LIFE

I DID not sleep well that night, and the following morning at eight o'clock we started by diligence for Versailles. I can see Marie now, great big girl as she then was, in tears. All the members of the family were assembled at the top of the stone steps. There was my little trunk, and then a wooden case of games which my mother had brought, and a kite that my cousin had made, which he gave me at the last moment, just as the carriage was starting. I can still see the large white house, which seemed to get smaller and smaller the farther we drove away from it. I stood up, with my father holding me, and waved his blue silk muffler which I had taken from his neck. After this I sat down in the carriage and fell asleep, only rousing up again when we were at the heavy-looking door of the Grand-Champs Convent. I rubbed my eyes and tried to collect my thoughts. I then jumped down from the diligence and looked curiously around me. The paving-stones of the street were round and small, with grass growing everywhere. There was a wall, and then a great gateway surmounted by a cross, and nothing behind it, nothing whatever to be seen. To the left there was a house, and to the right the Satory barracks. Not a sound to be heard—not a footfall, not even an echo.

"Oh, Mamma," I exclaimed, "is it inside there I am to go? Oh no! I would rather go back to Madame Fressard's!"

My mother shrugged her shoulders and pointed to my father, thus explaining that she was not responsible for this step. I rushed to him, and he took me by the hand as he rang the bell. The door opened, and he led me gently in, followed by my mother and Aunt Rosine.

The courtyard was large and dreary-looking, but there were buildings to be seen, and windows from which children's faces were gazing curiously at us. My father said something to the nun who came forward, and she took us into the parlour. This was large, with a polished floor, and was divided by an enormous black grating which ran the whole length of the room. There were benches covered with red velvet by the wall, and a few chairs and armchairs near the grating. On the walls were a portrait of Pius IX., a full length one of St. Augustine, and one of Henri V. My teeth chattered, for it seemed to me that I remembered reading in some book the description of a prison, and that it was just like this. I looked at my father and my mother, and began to distrust them. I had so often heard that I was ungovernable, that I needed an iron hand to rule me, and that I was the devil incarnate in a child. My aunt Faure had so often repeated, "That child will come to a bad end, she has such mad ideas," &c. &c. "Papa, papa!" I suddenly cried out, seized with terror; "I won't go to prison. This is a prison, I am sure. I am frightened—oh, I am so frightened!"

On the other side of the grating a door had just opened, and I stopped to see who was coming. A little round, short woman made her appearance and came up to the grating. Her black veil was lowered as far as her mouth, so that I could scarcely see anything of her face. She recognised my father, whom she had probably seen before, when matters were being arranged. She opened a door in the grating, and we all went through to the other side of the room. On seeing me pale and my terrified eyes full of tears, she gently took my hand in hers and, turning her back to my father, raised her veil. I then saw the sweetest and merriest face imaginable, with large child-like blue eyes, a turn-up nose, a laughing mouth with full lips and beautiful, strong, white teeth. She looked so kind, so energetic, and so happy that I flung myself at once into her arms. It was Mother St. Sophie, the Superior of the Grand-Champs Convent.

"Ah, we are friends now, you see," she said to my father, lowering her veil again. What secret instinct could have told this woman, who was not coquettish, who had no looking-glass and never troubled about beauty, that her face was fascinating and that her bright smile could enliven the gloom of the convent?

" We will now go and see the house," she said.

We at once started, she and my father each holding one of my hands. Two other nuns accompanied us, one of whom was the Mother Prefect, a tall, cold woman with thin lips, and the other Sister Séraphine, who was as white and supple as a spray of lily of the valley. We entered the building, and came first to the large class-room in which all the pupils met on Thursdays at the lectures, which were nearly always given by Mother St. Sophie. Most of them did needlework all day long ; some worked at tapestry, others embroidery, and still others decalcography.

The room was very large, and on St. Catherine's Day and other holidays we used to dance there. It was in this room, too, that once a year the Mother Superior gave to each of the sisters the *sou* which represented her annual income. The walls were adorned with religious engravings and with a few oil paintings done by the pupils. The place of honour, though, belonged to St. Augustine. A magnificent large engraving depicted the conversion of this saint, and oh, how often I have looked at that engraving. St. Augustine has certainly caused me very much emotion and greatly disturbed my childish heart. Mamma admired the cleanliness of the refectory. She asked to see which would be my seat at table, and when this was shown to her she objected strongly to my having that place.

" No," she said ; " the child has not a strong chest, and she would always be in a draught. I will not let her sit there."

My father agreed with my mother, and insisted on a change being made. It was therefore decided that I should sit at the end of the room, and the promise given was faithfully kept.

When mamma saw the wide staircase leading to the dormitories she was aghast. It was very, very wide, and the steps were low and easy to mount, but there were so many of them before one reached the first floor. For a few seconds mamma hesitated and stood there gazing at them, her arms hanging down in despair.

"Stay down here, Youle," said my aunt, " and I will go up."

" No, no," replied my mother in a sorrowful voice. " I must see where the child is to sleep—she is so delicate."

My father helped her, and indeed almost carried her up, and we then went into one of the immense dormitories. It was very much like the dormitory at Madame Fressard's, but a great deal larger, and there was a tiled floor without any carpet.

" Oh, this is quite impossible!" exclaimed mamma. "The child cannot sleep here; it is too cold ; it would kill her."

The Mother Superior, St. Sophie, gave my mother a chair and tried to soothe her. She was pale, for her heart was already very much affected.

" We will put your little girl in this dormitory, Madame," she said, opening a door that led into a room with eight beds. The floor was of polished wood, and this room, adjoining the infirmary, was the one in which delicate or convalescent children slept. Mamma was reassured on seing this, and we then went down and inspected the grounds. There were three woods, the " Little Wood," the " Middle Wood," and the " Big Wood," and then there was an orchard that stretched along as far as the eye could see. In this orchard was the building where the poor children lived. They were taught gratis, and every week they helped with the laundry for the convent.

The sight of these immense woods, with swings, hammocks, and a gymnasium, delighted me, for I thought I should be able to roam about at pleasure there. Mother St. Sophie explained to us that the Little Wood was reserved for the older pupils, and the Middle Wood for the little ones, whilst the Big Wood was for the whole convent on holidays. Then after telling us about the collecting of the chestnuts and the gathering of the acacia, Mother St. Sophie informed us that every child could have a small garden, and that sometimes two or three of them had a larger one.

" Oh, can I have a garden of my own?" I exclaimed—"a garden all to myself?"

" Yes, one of your own."

The Mother Superior called the gardener, Père Larcher, the only man, with the exception of the chaplain, who was on the convent staff.

" Père Larcher," said the kind woman, " here is a little girl who wants a beautiful garden. Find a nice place for it."

" Very good, Reverend Mother," answered the honest fellow, and I saw my father slip a coin into his hand, for which the man thanked him in an embarrassed way.

It was getting late, and we had to separate. I remember

quite well that I did not feel any grief, as I was thinking of nothing but my garden. The convent no longer seemed to me like a prison, but like paradise. I kissed my mother and my aunt. Papa drew me to him and held me a moment in a close embrace. When I looked at him I saw that his eyes were full of tears. I did not feel at all inclined to cry, and I gave him a hearty kiss and whispered, " I am going to be very, very good and work well, so that I can go with you at the end of four years." I then went towards my mother, who was giving Mother St. Sophie the same instructions she had given to Madame Fressard about cold cream, chocolate, jam, &c. &c. Mother St. Sophie wrote down all these instructions, and it is only fair to say that she carried them out afterwards most scrupulously.

When my parents had gone I felt inclined to cry, but the Mother Superior took me by the hand and, leading me to the Middle Wood, showed me where my garden would be. That was quite enough to distract my thoughts, for we found Père Larcher there marking out my piece of ground in a corner of the wood. There was a young birch tree against the wall. The corner was formed by the joining of two walls, one of which bounded the railway line on the left bank of the river which cuts the Satory woods in two. The other wall was that of the cemetery. All the woods of the convent were part of the beautiful Satory forest.

They had all given me money, my father, my mother, and my aunt. I had altogether about forty or fifty francs, and I wanted to give all to Père Larcher for buying seed. The Mother Superior smiled, and sent for the Mother Treasurer and Mother St. Appoline. I had to hand all my money over to the former, with the exception of twenty sous which she left me, saying, " When that is all gone, little girl, come and get some more from me."

Mother St. Appoline, who taught botany, then asked me what kind of flowers I wanted. What kind of flowers! Why, I wanted every sort that grew. She at once proceeded to give me a botany lesson by explaining that all flowers did not grow at the same season. She then asked the Mother Treasurer for some of my money, which she gave to Père Larcher, telling him to buy me a spade, a rake, a hoe, and a watering-can, some seeds and a few plants, the names of which she wrote down for him. I was delighted, and I then went with Mother St. Sophie to the refectory to have dinner. On entering the immense room I stood still for a second, amazed and confused. More than a hundred girls were assembled there, standing up for the benediction to be pronounced. When the Mother Superior appeared, every one bowed respectfully, and then all eyes were turned on me. Mother St. Sophie took me to the seat which had been chosen for me at the end of the room, and then returned to the middle of the refectory. She stood still, made the sign of the cross, and in an audible voice pronounced the benediction. As she left the room every one bowed again, and I then found myself alone, quite alone, in this cage of little wild animals. I was seated between two little girls of from ten to twelve years old, both as dusky as two young moles. They were twins from Jamaica, and their names were Dolores and Pepa Cardaños. They had only been in the convent two months, and appeared to be as timid as I was. The dinner was composed of soup made of everything, and of veal with haricot beans. I detested soup, and I have always had a horror of veal. I turned my plate over when the soup was handed round, but the nun who waited on us turned it round again and poured the hot soup in, regardless of scalding me.

" You must eat your soup," whispered my right hand neighbour, whose name was Pepa.

" I don't like that sort and I don't want any," I said aloud. The inspectress was passing by just at that moment.

" You must eat your soup, Mademoiselle," she said.

" No, I don't like that sort of soup," I answered.

She smiled, and said in a gentle voice, " We must like everything. I shall be coming round again just now. Be a good girl and take your soup."

I was getting into a rage, but Dolores gave me her empty plate and ate up the soup for me. When the inspectress came round again she expressed her satisfaction. I was furious, and put my tongue out, and this made all the table laugh. She turned round, and the pupil who sat at the end of the table and was appointed to watch over us, because she was the eldest, said to her in a low voice, " It's the new girl making grimaces." The inspectress moved away again, and when the veal was

served my portion found its way to the plate of Dolores. I
wanted to keep the haricot beans, though, and we almost came
to a quarrel over them. She gave way finally, but with the veal
she dragged away a few beans which I tried to keep on my
plate.

An hour later we had evening prayers, and afterwards all
went up to bed. My bed was placed against the wall, in which
there was a niche for the statue of the Virgin Mary. A lamp
was always kept burning in the niche, and the oil for it was
provided by the children who had been ill and were grateful for
their recovery. Two tiny flower-pots were placed at the foot of
the little statue. The pots were of terra-cotta and the flowers
of paper. I made paper flowers very well, and I at once decided
that I would make all the flowers for the Virgin Mary. I fell
asleep, to dream of garlands of flowers, of haricot beans, and of
distant countries, for the twins from Jamaica had made an impression on my mind.

The awakening was cruel. I was not accustomed to get up
so early. Daylight was scarcely visible through the opaque
window-panes. I grumbled as I dressed, for we were allowed a
quarter of an hour, and it always took me a good half-hour to
comb my hair. Sister Marie, seeing that I was not ready, came
towards me, and before I knew what she was going to do
snatched the comb violently out of my hand.

" Come, come," she said ; " you must not dawdle like this."
She then planted the comb in my mop of hair and tore out a
handful of it. Pain, and anger at seeing myself treated in this
way, threw me immediately into one of my fits of rage which
always terrified those who witnessed them. I flung myself upon
the unfortunate sister, and with feet, teeth, hands, elbows, head,
and indeed all my poor little body, I hit and thumped, yelling
at the same time. All the pupils, all the sisters, and indeed
every one, came running to see what was the matter. The
sisters made the sign of the cross, but did not venture to
approach me. The Mother Prefect threw some holy water over
me to exorcise the evil spirit. Finally the Mother Superior
arrived on the scene. My father had told her of my fits of wild
fury, which were my only serious fault, and my state of health was
quite as much responsible for them as the violence of my disposition. She approached me as I was still clutching Sister Marie,

though I was exhausted by this struggle with the poor woman, who, although tall and strong, only tried to ward off my blows without retaliating, endeavouring to hold first my feet and then my hands.

I looked up on hearing Mother St. Sophie's voice. My eyes were bathed in tears, but nevertheless I saw such an expression of pity on her sweet face that, without altogether letting go, I ceased fighting for a second, and all trembling and ashamed, said very quickly, " She commenced it. She snatched the comb out of my hand like a wicked woman, and tore out my hair. She was rough and hurt me. She is a wicked, wicked woman." I then burst into sobs, and my hands loosed their hold. The next thing I knew was that I found myself lying on my little bed, with Mother St. Sophie's hand on my forehead and her kind, deep voice lecturing me gently. All the others had gone, and I was quite alone with her and the Holy Virgin in the niche. From that day forth Mother St. Sophie had an immense influence over me. Every morning I went to her, and Sister Marie, whose forgiveness I had been obliged to ask before the whole convent, combed my hair out in her presence. Seated on a little stool, I listened to the book that the Mother Superior read to me or to the instructive story she told me. Ah, what an adorable woman she was, and how I love to recall her to my memory !

I adored her as a child adores the being who has entirely won its heart, without knowing, without reasoning, without even being aware that it was so, but I was simply under the spell of an infinite fascination. Since then, however, I have understood and admired her, realising how unique and radiant a soul was imprisoned under the thick-set exterior and happy face of that holy woman. I have loved her ever since for all that she awakened within me of nobleness. I love her for the letters which she wrote to me, letters that I often read over and over again. I love her also because, imperfect as I am, it seems to me that I should have been one hundred times more so had I not known and loved that pure creature.

Once only did I see her severe and felt that she was suddenly angry. In the little room used as a parlour, leading into her cell, there was a portrait of a young man, whose handsome face was stamped with a certain nobility.

" Is that the Emperor ? " I asked her,

"No," she answered, turning quickly towards me; "it is the King; it is Henri V."

It was only later on that I understood the meaning of her emotion. All the convent was royalist, and Henri V. was their recognised sovereign. They all had the most utter contempt for Napoleon III., and on the day when the Prince Imperial was baptized there was no distribution of bon-bons for us, and we were not allowed the holiday that was accorded to all the colleges, boarding-schools, and convents. Politics were a dead letter to me, and I was happy at the convent, thanks to Mother St. Sophie.

Then, too, I was a favourite with my schoolfellows, who frequently did my compositions for me. I did not care for any studies, except geography and drawing. Arithmetic drove me wild, spelling plagued my life out, and I thoroughly despised the piano. I was very timid, and quite lost my head when questioned unexpectedly.

I had a passion for animals of all kinds. I used to carry about with me, in small cardboard boxes or cages that I manufactured myself, adders, of which our woods were full, crickets that I found on the leaves of the tiger lilies, and lizards. The latter nearly always had their tails broken, as, in order to see if they were eating, I used to lift the lid of the box a little, and on seeing this the lizards rushed to the opening. I shut the box very quickly, red with surprise at such assurance, and *crac!* in a twinkling, either at right or left, there was nearly always a tail caught. This used to grieve me for hours, and whilst one of the sisters was explaining to us, by figures on the blackboard, the metric system, I was wondering, with my lizard's tail in my hand, how I could fasten it on again. I had some *toc-marteau* (death watches) in a little box, and five spiders in a cage that Père Larcher had made for me with some wire netting. I used, very cruelly, to give flies to my spiders, and they, fat and well fed, would spin their webs. Very often during recreation a whole group of us, ten or twelve little girls, would stand round, with a cage on a bench or tree stump, and watch the wonderful work of these little creatures. If one of my schoolfellows cut herself I used to go at once to her, feeling very proud and important: "Come at once," I would say, "I have some fresh spider-web, and I will wrap your finger

in it." Provided with a little thin stick, I would take the
web and wrap it round the wounded finger. "And now,
my lady spiders, you must begin your work again," and, active
and minute, *mesdames* 'he spiders began their spinning once
more.

I was looked upon as a little authority, and was made umpire
in questions that had to be decided. I used to receive orders
for fashionable trousseaux, made of paper, for dolls. It was
quite an easy thing for me in those days to make long ermine
cloaks with fur tippets and muff, and this filled my little
playfellows with admiration. I charged for my *trousseaux*,
according to their importance, two pencils, five *tête-de-mort*
nibs, or a couple of sheets of white paper. In short, I became
a personality, and that sufficed for my childish pride. I did not
learn anything, and I received no distinctions. My name was
only once on the honour list, and that was not as a studious
pupil, but for a courageous deed. I had fished a little girl out
of the big pool. She had fallen in whilst trying to catch frogs.
The pool was in the large orchard, on the poor children's side of
the grounds. As a punishment for some misdeed, which I do
not remember, I had been sent away for two days among
the poor children. This was supposed to be a punishment, but
I delighted in it. In the first place, I was looked upon by them as a
"young lady." Then I used to give the day pupils a few sous
to bring me, on the sly, a little moist sugar. During recreation
I heard some heartrending shrieks, and, rushing to the pool
from whence they came, I jumped into the water without
reflecting. There was so much mud that we both sank in it.
The little girl was only four years old, and so small that she
kept disappearing. I was over ten at that time. I do not
know how I managed to rescue her, but I dragged her out of
the water with her mouth, nose, ears, and eyes all filled with
mud. I was told afterawrds that it was a long time before
she was restored to consciousness. As for me, I was carried
away with my teeth chattering, nervous and half fainting.
I was very feverish afterwards, and Mother St. Sophie herself
sat up with me. I overheard her words to the doctor:

"This child," she said, "is one of the best we have here,
She will be perfect when once she has received the holy
hrism."

This speech made such an impression on me that from that day forth mysticism had great hold on me. I had a very vivid imagination and was extremely sensitive, and the Christian legend took possession of me, heart and soul. The Son of God became the object of my worship and the Mother of the Seven Sorrows my ideal.

IV

MY DÉBUT

An event, very simple in itself, was destined to disturb the silence of our secluded life and to attach me more than ever to my convent, where I wanted to remain for ever.

The Archbishop of Paris, Monseigneur Sibour, was paying a round of visits to some of the communities, and ours was among the chosen ones. The news was told us by Mother St. Alexis, the *doyenne*, the most aged member of the community, who was so tall, so thin, and so old that I never looked upon her as a human being or as a living being. It always seemed to me as though she were stuffed, and as though she moved by machinery. She frightened me, and I never consented to go near her until after her death.

We were all assembled in the large room which we used on Thursdays. Mother St. Alexis, supported by two lay sisters, stood on the little platform, and in a voice that sounded far, far off announced to us the approaching visit of Monseigneur. He was to come on St. Catherine's Day, just a fortnight after the speech of the Reverend Mother.

Our peaceful convent was from thenceforth like a bee-hive into which a hornet had entered. Our lesson hours were curtailed, so that we might have time to make festoons of roses and lilies. The wide, tall arm-chair of carved wood was uncushioned, so that it might be varnished and polished. We made lamp-shades covered with crystalline. The grass was pulled up in the court-yard—and I cannot tell what was not done in honour of this visitor.

Two days after the announcement made by Mother St. Alexis, the programme of the *fête* was communicated to us by Mother St. Sophie. The youngest of the nuns was to read a few words of welcome to Monseigneur. This was the delightful Sister

Séraphine.   After that Marie Buguet was to play a pianoforte solo by Henri Herz.   Marie de Lacour was to sing a song by Louise Puget, and then a little play in three scenes was to be given, entitled *Tobit Recovering his Eyesight.*   It had been written by Mother St. Thérèse.   I have now before me the little manuscript, all yellow with age and torn, and I can only just make out the sense of it and a few of the phrases.   Scene I. Tobias's farewell to his blind father.   He vows to bring back to him the ten talents lent to Gabael, one of his relatives. Scene II.   Tobias, asleep on the banks of the Tigris, is being watched over by the Angel Raphael.   Struggle with a monster fish which had attacked Tobias whilst he slept.   When the fish is killed the angel advises Tobias to take its heart, its liver, and its gall, and to preserve these religiously.   Scene III. Tobias's return to his blind father.   The angel tells him to rub the old man's eyes with the entrails of the fish.   The father's eyesight is restored, and when Tobit begs the Angel Raphael to accept some reward, the latter makes himself known, and, in a song to the glory of God, vanishes to heaven.

The little play was read to us by Mother St. Thérèse, one Thursday, in the large assembly room.   We were all in tears at the end, and Mother St. Thérèse was obliged to make a great effort in order to avoid committing, if only for a second, the sin of pride.

I wondered anxiously what part I should take in this religious comedy, for, considering that I was now treated as a little personage, I had no doubt that some *rôle* would be given to me. The very thought of it made me tremble beforehand.   I began to get quite nervous ; my hands became quite cold, my heart beat furiously, and my temples throbbed.   I did not approach, but remained sulkily seated on my stool when Mother St. Thérèse said in her calm voice :

" Young ladies, please pay attention, and listen to your names and the different parts :

Tobit	Eugénie Charmel
Tobias	Amélie Pluche
Gabael	Renée d'Arville
The Angel Raphael . .	Louise Buguet
Tobias's mother . . .	Eulalie Lacroix
Tobias's sister . . .	Virginie Depaul."

I had been listening, although pretending not to, and I was stupefied, amazed, and furious. Mother St. Thérèse then added. "Here are your manuscripts, young ladies," and a manuscript of the little play was handed to each pupil chosen to take part in it.

Louise Buguet was my favourite playmate, and I went up to her and asked her to let me see her manuscript, which I read over enthusiastically.

"You'll make me rehearse, when I know my part, won't you?" she asked, and I answered, "Yes, certainly."

"Oh, how frightened I shall be!" she said.

She had been chosen for the angel, I suppose, because she was as pale and sweet as a moonbeam. She had a soft, timid voice, and sometimes we used to make her cry, as she was so pretty then. The tears used to flow limpid and pearl-like from her grey, questioning eyes.

She began at once to learn her part, and I was like a shepherd's dog going from one to another among the chosen ones. It had really nothing to do with me, but I wanted to be "in it." The Mother Superior passed by, and as we all curtseyed to her she patted my cheek.

"We thought of you, little girl," she said, "but you are so timid when you are asked anything."

"Oh, that's when it is history or arithmetic," I said. "This is not the same thing, and I should not have been afraid."

She smiled distrustfully and moved on. There were rehearsals during the next week. I asked to be allowed to take the part of the monster, as I wanted to have some *rôle* in the play at any cost. It was decided, though, that César, the convent dog, should be the fish monster.

A competition was opened for the fish costume. I went to an endless amount of trouble cutting out scales from cardboard that I had painted, and sewing them together afterwards. I made some enormous gills, which were to be glued on to César. My costume was not chosen; it was passed over for that of a stupid, big girl whose name I cannot remember. She had made a huge tail of kid and a mask with big eyes and gills, but there were no scales, and we should have to see César's shaggy coat. I nevertheless turned my attention to Louise Buguet's costume, and worked at it with two of the lay sisters, Sister St. Cécile and Sister St. Jeanne, who had charge of the linen room.

At the rehearsals not a word could be extorted from the Angel Raphael. She stood there stupefied on the little platform, tears dimming her beautiful eyes. She brought the whole play to a standstill, and kept appealing to me in a weeping voice. I prompted her, and, getting up, rushed to her, kissed her, and whispered her whole speech to her. I was beginning to be " in it " myself at last.

Finally, two days before the great solemnity, there was a dress rehearsal. The angel looked lovely, but, immediately on entering, she sank down on a bench, sobbing out in an imploring voice :

" Oh no ; I shall never be able to do it, never ! "

" Quite true, she never will be able to," sighed Mother St. Sophie.

Forgetting for the moment my little friend's grief, and wild with joy, pride, and assurance, I ran up to the platform and bounded on to the form on which the Angel Raphael had sunk down weeping.

" Oh, Mother, I know her part. Shall I take her place for the rehearsal ? "

" Yes, yes ! " exclaimed voices from all sides.

" Oh yes, you know it so well," said Louise Buguet, and she wanted to put her band on my head.

" No, let me rehearse as I am, first," I answered.

They began the second scene again, and I came in carrying a long branch of willow.

"Fear nothing, Tobias," I commenced. " I will be your guide. I will remove from your path all thorns and stones. You are overwhelmed with fatigue. Lie down and rest, for I will watch over you."

Whereupon Tobias, worn out, lay down by the side of a strip of blue muslin, about five yards of which, stretched out and winding about, represented the Tigris.

I then continued with a prayer to God whilst Tobias fell asleep. César next appeared as the Monster Fish, and the audience trembled with fear. César had been well taught by the gardener. Père Larcher, and he advanced slowly from under the blue muslin, He was wearing his mask, representing the head of a fish. Two enormous nut-shells for his eyes had been painted white, and a hole pierced through them, so that the dog could see. The mask was fastened with wire to his collar, which also supported two gills as large as palm leaves. César, sniffing the ground, snorted and growled, and then leaped wildly on to Tobias, who with his cudgel slew the monster at one blow. The dog fell on his back with his four paws in the air, and then rolled over on to his side, pretending to be dead.

There was wild delight in the house, and the audience clapped and stamped. The younger pupils stood up on their stools and shouted, " Good César! Clever César! Oh, good dog, good dog!" The sisters, touched by the efforts of the guardian of the convent, shook their heads with emotion. As for me, I quite forgot that I was the Angel Raphael, and I stooped down and stroked César affectionately. " Ah, how well he has acted his part!" I said, kissing him and taking one paw and then the other in my hand, whilst the dog, motionless, continued to be dead.

The little bell was rung to call us to order. I stood up again, and, accompanied by the piano, we burst into a hymn of praise, a duet to the glory of God, who had just saved Tobias from the fearful monster.

After this the little green serge curtain was drawn, and I was surrounded, petted, and praised. Mother St. Sophie came up on to the platform and kissed me affectionately. As to Louise Buguet, she was now joyful again and her angelic face beamed.

" Oh, how well you knew the part!" she said. " And then, too, every one can hear what you say. Oh, thank you so much!" She kissed me and I hugged her with all my might. At last I was in it!

The third scene began. The action took place in Father Tobit's house. Gabael, the Angel, and young Tobias were holding the entrails of the fish in their hands and looking at them. The Angel explained how they must be used for rubbing the blind father's eyes. I felt rather sick, for I was holding in my hand a skate's liver and the heart and gizzard of a fowl. I had never touched such things before, and every now and then the nausea overcame me and the tears rose to my eyes.

Finally the blind father came in, led by Tobias's sister. Gabael knelt down before the old man and gave him the ten silver talents, telling him, in a long recital, of Tobias's exploits in

Medea. After this Tobias advanced, embraced his father, and then rubbed his eyes with the skate's liver.

Eugénie Charmel made a grimace, but after wiping her eyes she exclaimed:

"I can see, I can see. Oh! God of goodness, God of mercy! I can see, I can see!"

She came forward with outstretched arms, her eyes open, in an ecstatic attitude, and the whole little assembly, so simpleminded and loving, wept.

All the actors except old Tobit and the Angel sank on their knees and gave praise to God, and at the close of this thanksgiving the public, moved by religious sentiment and discipline repeated, Amen!

Tobias's mother then approached the Angel and said, "Oh, noble stranger, take up your abode from henceforth with us. You shall be our guest, our son, our brother!"

I advanced, and in a long speech of at least thirty lines made known that I was the messenger of God, that I was the Angel Raphael. I then gathered up quickly the pale blue tarlatan, which was being concealed for a final effect, and veiled myself in cloudy tissue which was intended to simulate my flight heavenwards. The little green serge curtain was then closed on this apotheosis.

Finally the solemn day arrived.

I was so feverish with expectation that I could not sleep the last three nights.

The dressing bell was rung for us earlier than usual, but I was already up and trying to smooth my rebellious hair, which I brushed with a wet brush by way of making it behave better.

Monseigneur was to arrive at eleven o'clock in the morning. We therefore lunched at ten, and were then drawn up in the principal courtyard. Only Mother St. Alexis, the eldest of the nuns, was in front, and Mother St. Sophie just behind her. The chaplain was a little distance away from the two Superiors. Then came the other nuns, and behind them the girls, and then all the little children. The lay sisters and the servants were also there. We were all dressed in white, with the respective colours of our various classes.

The bell rang out a peal. The large carriage entered the

first courtyard. The gate of the principal courtyard was then opened, and Monseigneur appeared on the carriage steps which the footman lowered for him. Mother St. Alexis advanced and, bending down, kissed the episcopal ring. Mother St. Sophie, the Superior, who was younger, knelt down to kiss the ring. The signal was then given to us, and we all knelt to receive the benediction of Monseigneur. When we looked up again the big gate was closed, and Monseigneur had disappeared, conducted by the Mother Superior. Mother St. Alexis was exhausted, and went back to her cell.

In obedience to the signal given we all rose from our knees. We then went to the chapel, where a short Mass was celebrated, after which we had an hour's recreation. The concert was to commence at half-past one. The recreation hour was devoted to preparing the large room and to getting ready to appear before Monseigneur. I wore the angel's long robe, with a blue sash round my waist and two paper wings fastened on with narrow blue straps that crossed over each other in front. Round my head was a band of gold braid fastening behind. I kept mumbling my " part," for in those days we did not know the word *rôle*. People are more familiar with the stage now-adays, but at the convent we always said " part," and years afterwards I was surprised, the first time I played in England, to hear a young English girl say, " Oh, what a fine part you had in *Hernani!* "

The room looked beautiful, oh, so beautiful ! There were festoons of green leaves, with paper flowers at intervals, every-where. Then there were little lustres hung about with gold cord. A wide piece of red velvet carpet was laid down from the door to Monseigneur's arm-chair, upon which were two cushions of red velvet with gold fringe.

I thought all these horrors very fine, very beautiful !

The concert began, and it seemed to me that everything went very well. Monseigneur, however, could not help smiling at the sight of César, and it was he who led the applause when the dog died. It was César, in fact, who made the greatest success, but we were nevertheless sent for to appear before Monseigneur Sibour. He was certainly the kindest and most charming of prelates, and on this occasion he gave to each of us a consecrated medal,

When my turn came he took my hand in his and said, " It is you, my child, who are not baptized, is it not ? "

" Yes, Reverend Father, yes, Monseigneur," I replied in confusion.

" She is to be baptized this spring," said the Mother Superior. " Her father is coming back specially from a very distant country."

She and Monseigneur then said a few words to each other in a very low voice.

" Very well ; if I can, I will come again for the ceremony," said the Archbishop aloud. I was trembling with emotion and pride as I kissed the old man's ring. I then ran away to the dormitory and cried for a long time. I was found there later on, fast asleep from exhaustion.

From that day forth I was a better child, more studious and less violent. In my fits of anger I was calmed by the mention of Monseigneur Sibour's name, and reminded of his promise to come for my baptism.

Alas ! I was not destined to have that great joy. One morning in January, when we were all assembled in the chapel for Mass, I was surprised and had a foreboding of coming evil as I saw the Abbé Lethurgi go up into the pulpit before commencing the Mass. He was very pale, and I turned instinctively to look at the Mother Superior. She was seated in her regular place. The almoner then began, in a voice broken with emotion, to tell us of the murder of Monseigneur Sibour.

Murdered ! A thrill of horror went through us, and a hundred stifled cries, forming one great sob, drowned for an instant the priest's voice. Murdered ! The word seemed to sting me personally even more than the others. Had I not been, for one instant, the favourite of the kind old man ? It was as though the murderer, Verger, had struck at me too, in my grateful love for the prelate, in my little fame, of which he had now robbed me. I burst into sobs, and the organ, accompanying the prayer for the dead, increased my grief, which became so intense that I fainted. It was from this moment that I was taken with an ardent love for mysticism. It was fortified by the religious exercises, the dramatic effect of our worship, and the gentle encouragement, both fervent and sincere, of those who were educating me. They were very fond of me, and I adored them, so that even now the very memory of them, fascinating and restful as it is, thrills me with affection.

The time appointed for my baptism drew near, and I grew more and more excitable. My nervous attacks were more and more frequent—fits of tears for no reason at all, and fits of terror without any cause. Everything seemed to take strange proportions as far as I was concerned. One day one of my little friends dropped a doll that I had lent her (for I played with dolls until I was over thirteen). I began to tremble all over, as I adored that doll, which had been given to me by my father.

"You have broken my doll's head, you naughty girl!" I exclaimed. "You have hurt my father!"

I would not eat anything afterwards, and in the night I woke up in a great perspiration, with haggard eyes, sobbing, "Papa is dead! Papa is dead!"

Three days later my mother came. She asked to see me in the parlour, and, making me stand in front of her, she said, "My poor little girl, I have something to tell you that will cause you great sorrow. Papa is dead."

"I know," I said, "I know"; and the expression in my eyes, my mother frequently told me afterwards, was such that she trembled a long time for my reason.

I was very sad and not at all well. I refused to learn anything, except catechism and scripture, and I wanted to be a nun.

My mother had succeeded in arranging that my two sisters should be baptized with me—Jeanne, who was then six years old, and Régina, who was not three, but who had been taken as a boarder at the convent with the idea that her presence might cheer me up a little.

I was isolated for a week before my baptism and for a week afterwards, as I was to be confirmed one week after the event.

My mother, Aunt Rosine Berendt and Aunt Henriette Faure, my godfather Régis, Monsieur Meydieu, Jeanne's godfather, and General Polhes, Régina's godfather, the godmothers of my two sisters and my various cousins, all came, and revolutionised the convent. My mother and my aunts were in fashionable mourning attire. Aunt Rosine had put a spray of lilac in her bonnet, "to enliven her mourning," as she said. It was a strange expression, but I have certainly heard it since used by other people besides her.

I had never before felt so far away from all these people who had come there on my account. I adored my mother, but with a touching and fervent desire to leave her, never to see her again, to sacrifice her to God. As to the others, I did not see them. I was very grave and rather moody. A short time previously a nun had taken the veil at the convent, and I could think of nothing else.

This baptismal ceremony was the prelude to my dream. I could see myself like the novice who had just been admitted as a nun. I pictured myself lying down on the ground covered over with the heavy black cloth with its white cross, and four massive candlesticks placed at the four corners of the cloth, and I planned to die under this cloth. How I was to do this I do not know. I did not think of killing myself, as I knew that would be a crime. But I made up my mind to die like this, and my ideas galloped along, so that I saw in my imagination the horror of the sisters and heard the cries of the pupils, and was delighted at the emotion which I had caused.

After the baptismal ceremony my mother wished to take me away with her. She had rented a small house with a garden in the Boulevard de la Reine, at Versailles, for my holidays, and she had decorated it with flowers for this *fête* day, as she wanted to celebrate the baptism of her three children. She was very gently told that, as I was to be confirmed in a week's time, I was now to be isolated until then. My mother cried, and I can remember now, to my sorrow, that it did not make me sad to see her tears, but quite the contrary.

When every one had gone and I went into the little cell in which I had been living for the last week and wherein I was to live for another week, I fell on my knees in a state of exaltation and offered up to God my mother's sorrow. "You saw, O Lord God, that mamma cried, and that it did not affect me!" Poor child that I was, I imagined in my wild exaggeration of everything that what was expected from me was the renunciation of all affection, devotion, and pity.

The following day Mother St. Sophie lectured me gently about my wrong comprehension of religious duties, and she told me that when once I was confirmed she should give me a fortnight's holiday, to go and make my mother forget her sorrow and disappointment.

My confirmation took place with the same pompous ceremonial. All the pupils, dressed in white, carried wax tapers. For the whole week I had refused to eat. I was pale and had grown thinner, and my eyes looked larger from my perpetual transports, for I went to extremes in everything.

Baron Larrey, who came with my mother to my confirmation, asked for a month's holiday for me to recruit, and this was granted.

Accordingly we started, my mother, Madame Guérard, her son Ernest, my sister Jeanne, and I, for Cauterets in the Pyrénées.

The movement, the packing of the trunks, parcels, and packages, the railway, the diligence, the scenery, the crowds and the general disturbance cured me of my nerves and my mysticism. I clapped my hands, laughed aloud, flung myself on mamma and nearly stifled her with kisses. I sang hymns at the top of my voice; I was hungry and thirsty, so I ate, drank, and in a word, lived.

V

THE SOLDIER'S SHAKO

CAUTERETS at that time was not what it is now. It was an abominable but charming little hole of a place, with plenty of verdure, very few houses, and a great many huts belonging to the mountain people. There were plenty of donkeys to be hired, that took us up the mountains by extraordinary paths.

I adore the sea and the plain, but I neither care for mountains nor for forests. Mountains seem to crush me and forests to stifle me. I must, at any cost, have the horizon stretching out as far as the eye can see and skies to dream about.

I wanted to go up the mountains, so that they should lose their crushing effect. And consequently we went up always higher and higher.

Mamma used to stay at home with her sweet friend, Madame Guérard. She used to read novels whilst Madame Guérard embroidered. They would sit there together without speaking, each dreaming her own dream, seeing it fade away, and beginning it over again. The old servant, Marguerite, was the only domestic mamma had brought with her, and she used to accompany us. Gay and daring, she always knew how to make the men laugh with her prattle, the sense and crudeness of which I did not understand until much later. She was the life of the party always. As she had been with us from the time we were born, she was very familiar, and sometimes objectionably so ; but I would not let her have her own way with me, though, and I used to answer her back in most cutting fashion. She took her revenge in the evening by giving us a dish of sweets for dinner that I did not like.

I began to look better for the change, and although still very religious, my mysticism was growing calmer. As I could not exist, however, without a passion of some kind, I began to get very fond of goats, and I asked mamma quite seriously whether I might become a goat-herd.

"I would rather you were that than a nun," she replied ; and then she added, " We will talk about it later on."

Every day I brought down with me from the mountain another little kid. We had seven of them, when my mother interfered and put a stop to my zeal.

Finally, it was time to return to the convent. My holiday was over, and I was quite well again.

I was to go back to work once more. I accepted the situation willingly, to the great surprise of mamma, who loved travelling, but detested the actual moving from one place to another.

I was delighted at the idea of the re-packing of the parcels and trunks, of being seated in things that moved along, of seeing again all the villages, towns, people, and trees, which changed all the time. I wanted to take my goats with me, but my mother nearly had a fit.

" You are mad ! " she exclaimed. " Seven goats in a train and in a carriage ! Where could you put them ? No, a hundred times no ! "

She finally consented to my taking two of them and a blackbird that one of the mountaineers had given me. And so we returned to the convent.

I was received there with such sincere joy that I felt very happy again immediately. I was allowed to keep my two goats there, and to have them out at playtime. We had great fun with them : they used to butt us and we used to butt them, and we laughed, frolicked, and were very foolish. And yet I was nearly fourteen at this time ; but I was very puny and childish.

I stayed at the convent another ten months without learning anything more. The idea of becoming a nun always haunted me, but I was no longer mystic.

My godfather looked upon me as the greatest dunce of a child, I worked, though, during the holidays, and I used to have lessons with Sophie Croizette, who lived near to our country house. This gave a slight impetus to me in my studies, but it was only slight. Sophie was very gay, and what we liked best was to go to the museum, where her sister Pauline, who was later on to become Madame Carolus Duran, was copying pictures by the great masters.

Pauline was as cold and calm as Sophie was charming talkative, and noisy. Pauline Croizette was beautiful, but I liked Sophie better—she was more gracious and pretty. Madame Croizette, their mother, always seemed sad and resigned. She had given up her career very early. She had been a dancer at the opera in St. Petersburg, and had been very much adored and flattered and spoiled. I fancy it was the birth of Sophie that had compelled her to leave the stage. Her money had then been injudiciously invested, and she had been ruined. She was very distinguished-looking; her face had a kind expression; there was an infinite melancholy about her, and people were instinctively drawn towards her. Mamma and she had made each other's acquaintance while listening to the music in the park at Versailles, and for some time we saw a great deal of one another.

Sophie and I had some fine games in that magnificent park. Our greatest joy, though, was to go to Madame Masson's in the Rue de la Gare. Madame Masson had a curiosity shop. Her daughter Cécile was a perfect little beauty. We three used to delight in changing the tickets on the vases, snuff-boxes, fans, and jewels, and then when poor M. Masson came back with a rich customer—for Masson the antiquary enjoyed a world-wide reputation—Sophie and I used to hide so that we should see his fury. Cécile, with an innocent air, would be helping her mother, and glancing slyly at us from time to time.

The whirl of life separated me brusquely from all these people whom I loved, and an incident, trivial in itself, caused me to leave the convent earlier than my mother wished.

It was a *fête* day, and we had two hours for recreation. We were marching in procession along the wall which skirts the railway on the left bank of the Seine, and as we were burying my pet lizard we were chanting the "De Profundis." About twenty of my little playfellows were following me, when suddenly a soldier's shako fell at my feet.

"What's that?" called out one of the girls.

"A soldier's shako."

"Did it come from over the wall?"

"Yes, yes. Listen. There's a quarrel going on!"

We were suddenly silent, listening with all our ears.

" Don't be stupid! It's idiotic! It's the Grand-Champs Convent! "

" How am I to get my shako back? "

These were the words we overheard, and then, as a soldier suddenly appeared astride on our wall, there were shrieks from the terrified children and angry exclamations from the nuns. In a second we were all about twenty yards away from the wall, like a group of frightened sparrows flying off to land a little farther away, inquisitive, and very much on the alert.

" Have you seen my shako, young ladies? " called out the unfortunate soldier, in a beseeching tone.

" No, no! " I cried, hiding it behind my back.

" Oh no! " echoed the other girls, with peals of laughter, and in the most tormenting, insolent, jeering way we continued shouting " No, no! " running backwards all the time in obedience to the sisters, who, veiled and hidden behind the trees, were in despair.

We were only a few yards from the huge gymnasium. I climbed up breathless at full speed, and reached the wide plank at the top ; when there I unfastened the rope ladder, but, as I could not raise the wooden ladder, by which I had ascended, up to me, I unfastened the rings. The wooden ladder fell and broke, making a great noise. I then stood up wickedly triumphant on the plank, calling out, " Here is your shako, but you won't get it now! " I put it on my head and walked up and down, as no one could get to me there, for I had pulled up the rope ladder. I suppose my first idea had just been to have a little fun, but the girls had laughed and clapped, and my strength had held out better than I had hoped, so that my head was turned, and nothing could stop me then.

The young soldier was furious. He jumped down from the wall and rushed in my direction, pushing the girls out of his way. The sisters, beside themselves, ran to the house calling for help. The chaplain, the Mother Superior, Father Larcher, and every one else came running out. I believe the soldier swore like a trooper, and it was really quite excusable. Mother St. Sophie from below besought me to come down and to give up the shako.

The soldier tried to get up to me by means of the trapeze and the gymnasium rope.

His useless efforts delighted all the pupils, whom the sisters had in vain tried to send away. Finally the sister who was door-keeper sounded the alarm bell, and five minutes later the soldiers from the Satory barracks arrived, thinking that a fire had broken out. When the officer in command was told what was the matter, he sent back his men and asked to see the Mother Superior. He was brought to Mother St. Sophie, whom he found under the gymnasium, crying with shame and impotence. He ordered the soldier to return immediately to the barracks. He obeyed after clenching his fist at me, but on looking up he could not help laughing. His shako came down to my eyes, and was only prevented by my ears, which were bent over, from covering my face.

I was furious and wildly excited with the turn my joke had taken.

"There it is, your shako!" I called out, and I flung it violently over the wall which skirted the gymnasium and formed the boundary to the cemetery.

"Oh, the young plague!" muttered the officer, and then, apologising to the nuns, he saluted them and went away, accompanied by Father Larcher.

As for me, I felt like a fox with its tail cut.

I refused to come down immediately.

"I shall come down when every one has gone away," I exclaimed.

All the classes received punishments.

I was left alone. The sun had set. The silence in the cemetery terrified me. The dark trees took mournful or threatening shapes. The moisture from the wood fell like a mantle over my shoulders, and seemed to get heavier every moment. I felt abandoned by every one, and I began to cry.

I was angry with myself, with the soldier, with Mother St. Sophie, with the pupils who had excited me by their laughter, with the officer who had humiliated me, and with the sister who had sounded the alarm bell.

Then I began to think about getting down the rope ladder which I had pulled up on to the plank. Very clumsily, trembling with fear at the least sound, listening eagerly all the time, and with eyes looking to the right and left, I was an enormous time, and was very much afraid of unhooking the rings. Finally I managed to unroll it, and I was just about to put my foot on the first step when the barking of César alarmed me. He was tearing along from the wood. The sight of the dark shadow on the gymnasium appeared to the faithful dog to bode no good. He was furious, and began to scratch the thick wooden posts.

" Why, César, don't you know your friend ? " I said very gently. He growled in reply, and in a louder voice I said, " Fie, César, bad César ; you ought to be ashamed ! Fancy barking at your friend ! "

He now began to howl, and I was seized with terror. I pulled the ladder up again, and sat down at the top. César lay down under the gymnasium, his tail straight out, his ears pricked up, his coat bristling, growling in a sullen way. I appealed to the Holy Virgin to help me. I prayed fervently, vowed to say three supplementary *Aves*, three *Credos*, and three *Paters* every day.

When I was a little calmer I called out in a subdued voice, " César ! my dear César, my beautiful César ! You know I am the Angel Raphael ! " Ah, much César cared for him. He considered my presence, alone, at so late an hour in the garden and on the gymnasium quite incomprehensible. Why was I not in the refectory ? Poor César, he went on growling, and I was getting very hungry, and began to think things were most unjust. It was true that I had been to blame for taking the soldier's shako, but after all, he had commenced. Why had he thrown his shako over the wall ? My imagination now came to my aid, and in the end I began to look upon myself as a martyr. I had been left to the dog, and he would eat me. I was terrified at the dead people behind me, and every one knew I was very nervous. My chest too was delicate, and there I was, exposed to the biting cold with no protection whatever. I began to think about Mother St. Sophie, who evidently no longer cared for me, as she was deserting me so cruelly. I lay with my face downwards on the plank, and gave myself up to the wildest despair, calling my mother, my father, and Mother St. Sophie, sobbing, wishing I could die there and then——Between my sobs I suddenly heard my name pronounced by a voice. I got up, and, peering through the gloom, caught a glimpse of my beloved Mother St. Sophie. She was there, the dear

saint, and had never left her rebellious child.   Concealed behind
the statue of St. Augustine, she had been praying whilst awaiting the end of this crisis, which in her simplicity she had
believed might prove fatal to my reason and perhaps to my
salvation.   She had sent every one away and remained there
alone, and she too had not dined.   I came down and threw
myself, repentant and wretched, into her motherly arms.   She
did not say a word to me about the horrible incident, but took
me quickly back to the convent.   I was all damp with the icy
evening dew, my cheeks were feverish, and my hands and feet
frozen.

I had an attack of pleurisy after this, and was twenty-three
days between life and death.   Mother St. Sophie never left
me an instant.   The sweet Mother blamed herself for my
illness, declaring as she beat her breast that she had left me
outside too long.

"It's my fault!   It's my fault!" she kept exclaiming.

My aunt Faure came to see me nearly every day.   My mother
was in Scotland, and came back by short stages.   My aunt Rosine
was at Baden-Baden, ruining the whole family with a new
"system."   "I am coming.   I am coming," she kept saying, when
she wrote to ask how I was.   Dr. Despagne and Dr. Monod,
who had been called in for a consultation, did not think there was
any hope.   Baron Larrey, who was very fond of me, came often.
He had a certain influence over me, and I willingly obeyed him.
My mother arrived a short time before my convalescence, and
did not leave me again.   As soon as I could be moved she
took me to Paris, promising to send me back to the convent
when I was quite well.

It was for ever, though, that I had left my dear convent, but
it was not for ever that I left Mother St. Sophie.   I seemed
to take something of her away with me.   For a long time
she was part of my life, and even to-day, when she has
been dead for years, she haunts my mind, bringing back to
me the simple thoughts of former days and making the simple
flowers of yore bloom again.

Life for me then commenced in earnest.

The cloister life is a life for every one.   There may be
a hundred or a thousand individuals there, but every one lives a
life which is the same and the only life for all.   The rumour of

the outside world dies away at the heavy cloister gate. The sole ambition is to sing more loudly than the others at vespers, to take a little more of the form, to be at the end of the table, to be on the list of honour. When I was told that I was not to go back to the convent, it was to me as though I was to be thrown into the sea when I could not swim.

I besought my godfather to let me go back to the convent. The dowry left to me by my father was ample enough for the dowry of a nun. I wanted to take the veil. "Very well," replied my godfather; "you can take the veil in two years' time, but not before. In the meantime learn all that you do not yet know (and that means everything) from the governess your mother has chosen for you."

That very day an elderly unmarried lady, with soft, grey, gentle eyes, came and took possession of my life, my mind, and my conscience for eight hours every day. Her name was Mlle. de Brabender, and she had educated a grand duchess in Russia. She had a sweet voice, an enormous sandy moustache, a grotesque nose, but a way of walking, of expressing herself, and of bowing which simply commanded deference. She lived at the convent in the Rue Notre Dame des Champs, and this was why, in spite of my mother's entreaties, she refused to come and remain with us.

She soon won my affection, and I learnt quite easily with her everything that she wanted me to learn. I worked eagerly, for my dream was to return to the convent, not as a pupil, but as a teaching sister.

VI

THE FAMILY COUNCIL AND MY FIRST VISIT
TO A THEATRE

I AROSE one September morning, my heart leaping with some remote joy. It was eight o'clock. I pressed my forehead against the window-panes and gazed out, looking at I know not what. I had been roused with a start in the midst of some fine dream, and I had rushed towards the light in the hope of finding in the infinite space of the grey sky the luminous point that would explain my anxious and blissful expectation. Expectation of what? I could not have answered that question then, any more than I can now after much reflection. I was on the eve of my fifteenth birthday, and I was in a state of expectation as to the future of my life. That particular morning seemed to me to be the precursor of a new era. I was not mistaken, for on that September day my fate was settled for me.

Hypnotised by what was taking place in my mind, I remained with my forehead pressed against the window-pane, gazing through the halo of vapour formed by my breath at houses, palaces, carriages, jewels, and pearls passing along in front of me—oh, what a number of pearls there were! There were princes and kings, too; yes, I could even see kings! Oh! how fast one's imagination travels, and its enemy, reason, always allows it to roam on alone. In my fancy I proudly rejected the princes, I rejected the kings, refused the pearls and the palaces, and declared that I was going to be a nun, for in the infinite grey sky I had caught a glimpse of the convent of Grand-Champs, of my white bed-room, and of the small lamp that swung to and fro above the little Virgin all decorated with flowers by us. The king offered me a throne, but I preferred the throne of our Mother Superior, and I entertained a vague

ambition to occupy it some far-off day in the distant future; the
king was heart-broken and dying of despair.   Yes, *mon Dieu!*
I preferred to the pearls that were offered me by princes the
pearls of the rosary I was telling with my fingers; and no
costume could compete in my mind with the black barège veil
that fell like a soft shadow over the snowy-white cambric that
encircled the beloved faces of the nuns of Grand-Champs.   I do
not know how long I had been dreaming thus when I heard my
mother's voice asking our old servant Marguerite if I were
awake.   With one bound I was back in bed, and I buried my
face under the sheet.   Mamma half opened the door very gently,
and I pretended to wake up.

"How lazy you are to-day!" she said.   I kissed her, and
answered in a coaxing tone, "It is Thursday, and I have no
music lesson."

"And are you glad?" she asked.

"Oh yes," I replied promptly.

My mother frowned; she adored music, and I hated the piano.
She was so fond of music that although she was then nearly
thirty, she took lessons herself in order to encourage me to
practise.   What horrible torture it was!   I used, very wickedly,
to do my utmost to set my mother and my music mistress at
variance.   They were both of them as short-sighted as possible.
When my mother had practised a new piece three or four days,
she knew it by heart and played it fairly well, to the astonishment of Mlle. Clarisse, my insufferable old teacher, who held
the music in her hand and read every note with her nose nearly
touching the page.   One day I heard, with joy, a quarrel
beginning between mamma and this disagreeable Mlle. Clarisse.

"There, that's a quaver!"

"No, there's no quaver!"

"This is a flat!"

"No, you forget the sharp!   How absurd you are, Mademoiselle!" added my mother, perfectly furious.

A few minutes later my mother went to her room, and Mlle.
Clarisse departed, muttering as she left.

As for me, I was choking with laughter in my bed-room, for
one of my cousins, who was a good musician, had helped me to
add sharps, flats, and quavers, and we had done it with such care
that even a trained eye would have had difficulty in discerning

the fraud immediately. As Mlle. Clarisse had been sent off, I had no lesson that day. Mamma gazed at me a long time with her mysterious eyes, the most beautiful eyes I have ever seen in my life, and then she said, speaking very slowly :

" After luncheon there is to be a family council."

I felt myself turning pale.

" All right," I answered. " What frock am I to put on, Mamma ? " I said this merely for the sake of saying something, and to keep myself from crying.

" Put your blue silk on ; you look more staid in that."

Just at this moment my sister Jeanne opened the door boisterously, and with a burst of laughter jumped on to my bed and, slipping under the sheets, called out, " I'm there ! "

Marguerite had followed her into the room, panting and scolding. The child had escaped from her just as she was about to bathe her, and had announced, " I'm going into my sister's bed."

Jeanne's mirth at this moment, which I felt was a very serious one for me, made me burst out crying and sobbing. My mother, not understanding the reason of this grief, shrugged her shoulders, told Marguerite to fetch Jeanne's slippers, and taking the little bare feet in her hands, kissed them tenderly.

I sobbed more bitterly than ever. It was very evident that mamma loved my sister more than me, and this preference, which did not trouble me in an ordinary way, hurt me sorely now.

Mamma went away quite out of patience with me. I fell asleep in order to forget, and was roused by Marguerite, who helped me to dress, as otherwise I should have been late for luncheon. The guests that day were Aunt Rosine, Mlle. de Brabender, my governess (a charming creature, whom I have always regretted), my godfather, and the Duc de Morny, a great friend of my godfather and of my mother. The luncheon was a mournful meal for me, as I was thinking all the time about the family council. Mlle. de Brabender, in her gentle way and with her affectionate words, insisted on my eating. My sister burst out laughing when she looked at me.

" Your eyes are as little as that," she said, putting her small thumb on the tip of her forefinger ; " and it serves you right, because you've been crying, and Mamma doesn't like any one to cry. Do you, Mamma ? "

"What have you been crying about?" asked the Duc de Morny. I did not answer, in spite of the friendly nudge Mlle. de Brabender gave me with her sharp elbow. The Duc de Morny always awed me a little. He was gentle and kind, but he was a great quiz. I knew, too, that he occupied a high place at court, and that my family considered his friendship a great honour.

"Because I told her that after luncheon there was to be a family council on her behalf," said my mother, speaking slowly. "At times it seems to me that she is quite idiotic. She quite disheartens me."

"Come, come," exclaimed my godfather, and Aunt Rosine said something in English to the Duc de Morny which made him smile shrewdly under his thin moustache. Mlle. de Brabender scolded me in a low voice, and her scoldings were like words from heaven. When at last luncheon was over, mamma told me, as she passed, to pour out the coffee. Marguerite helped me to arrange the cups, and I went into the drawing-room. Maître C——, the notary from Hàvre, whom I detested, was already there. He represented the family of my father, who had died at Pisa in a way which had never been explained, but which seemed mysterious. My childish hatred was instinctive, and I learnt later on that this man had been my father's bitter enemy. He was very, very ugly, this notary; his whole face seemed to have moved up higher. It was as though he had been hanging by his hair for a long time, and his eyes, his mouth, his cheeks, and his nose had got into the habit of trying to reach the back of his head. He ought to have had a joyful expression, as so many of his features turned up, but instead of this his face was smooth and sinister-looking. He had red hair planted in his head like couch grass, and on his nose he wore a pair of gold-rimmed spectacles. Oh, the horrible man! What a torturing nightmare the very memory of him is, for he was the evil genius of my father, and his hatred now pursued me. My poor grandmother, since the death of my father, never went out, but spent her time mourning the loss of her beloved son who had died so young. She had absolute faith in this man, who besides was the executor of my father's will. He had the control of the money that my dear father had left me. I was not to receive it until the day of my marriage, but my mother was to use the interest for my education. My uncle, Félix Faure, was also there. Seated near the fireplace, buried in an arm-chair, M. Meydieu pulled out his watch in a querulous way. He was an old friend of the family, and he always called me *ma fil*, which annoyed me greatly, as did his familiarity. He considered me stupid, and when I handed him his coffee he said in a jeering tone: "And it is for you, *ma fil*, that so many honest people have been hindered in their work. We have plenty of other things to attend to, I can assure you, than to discuss the fate of a little brat like you. Ah, if it had been her sister there would have been no difficulty," and with his benumbed fingers he patted Jeanne's head as she remained on the floor plaiting the fringe of the sofa upon which he was seated.

When the coffee had been drunk, the cups carried away and my sister also, there was a short silence.

The Duc de Morny rose to take his leave, but my mother begged him to stay. "You will be able to advise us," she urged, and the Duc took his seat again near my aunt, with whom it seemed to me he was carrying on a slight flirtation.

Mamma had moved nearer to the window, her embroidery frame in front of her, and her beautiful clear-cut profile showing to advantage against the light. She looked as though she had nothing to do with what was about to be discussed.

The hideous notary had risen.

My uncle had drawn me near to him. My godfather Régis seemed to be the exact counterpart of M. Meydieu. They both of them had the same *bourgeois* mind, and were equally stubborn and obstinate. They were both devoted to whist and good wine, and they both agreed that I was thin enough for a scarecrow. The door opened, and a pale, dark-haired woman entered, a most poetical-looking and charming creature. It was Madame Guérard, "the lady of the upstairs flat," as Marguerite always called her. My mother had made friends with her in rather a patronising way certainly, but Madame Guérard was devoted to me, and endured the little slights to which she was treated very patiently for my sake. She was tall and slender as a lath, very compliant and demure. She lived in the flat above, and had come down without a hat; she was wearing an indoor gown of indienne with a design of little brown leaves.

M. Meydieu muttered something, I did not catch what. The

abominable notary made a very curt bow to Madame Guérard. The Duc de Morny was very gracious, for the new-comer was so pretty. My godfather merely bent his head, as Madame Guérard was nothing to him. Aunt Rosine glanced at her from head to foot. Mlle. de Brabender shook hands cordially with her, for Madame Guérard was fond of me.

My uncle, Félix Faure, gave her a chair, and asked her to sit down, and then inquired in a kindly way about her husband, a *savant*, with whom my uncle collaborated sometimes for his book, "The Life of St. Louis."

Mamma had merely glanced across the room without raising her head, for Madame Guérard did not prefer my sister to me.

"Well, as we have come here on account of this child," said my godfather, looking at his watch, "we must begin and discuss what is to be done with her."

I began to tremble, and drew closer to *mon petit Dame* (as I had always called Madame Guérard from my infancy) and to Mlle. de Brabender. They each took my hand by way of encouraging me.

"Yes," continued M. Meydieu, with a laugh; "it appears you want to be a nun."

"Ah, indeed," said the Duc de Morny to Aunt Rosine.

"Sh!" she retorted, with a laugh. Mamma sighed, and held her wools up close to her eyes to match them.

"You have to be rich, though, to enter a convent," grunted the Hâvre notary, "and you have not a sou." I leaned towards Mlle. de Brabender and whispered, "I have the money that papa left."

The horrid man overheard.

"Your father left some money to get you married," he said.

"Well, then, I'll marry the *bon Dieu*," I answered, and my voice was quite resolute now. I turned very red, and for the second time in my life I felt a desire and a strong inclination to fight for myself. I had no more fear, as every one had gone too far and provoked me too much. I slipped away from my two kind friends, and advanced towards the other group.

"I will be a nun, I will!" I exclaimed. "I know that papa left me some money so that I should be married, and I know that the nuns marry the Saviour. Mamma says she does not care, it is all the same to her, so that it won't be vexing her

at all, and they love me better at the convent than you do
here ! "

"My dear child," said my uncle, drawing me towards him,
"your religious vocation appears to me to be more a wish to
love——"

"And to be loved," murmured Madame Guérard in a very
low voice.

Every one glanced at mamma, who shrugged her shoulders
lightly. It seemed to me as though the glance they all gave
her was a reproachful one, and I felt a pang of remorse at once.
I went across to her, and, throwing my arms round her neck,
said :

"You don't mind my being a nun, do you ? It won't make
you unhappy, will it ? "

Mamma stroked my hair, of which she was very proud.

"Yes, it would make me unhappy. You know very well that,
after your sister, I love you better than any one else in the
world."

She said this very slowly in a gentle voice. It was like the
sound of a little waterfall as it flows down, babbling and clear,
from the mountain, dragging with it the gravel, and gradually
increasing in volume with the thawed snow until it sweeps
along rocks and trees in its course. This was the effect my
mother's clear drawling voice had upon me at that moment. I
rushed back impulsively to the others, who were all speechless at
this unexpected and spontaneous burst of eloquence. I went
from one to the other, explaining my decision, and giving reasons
which were certainly no reasons at all. I did my utmost to get
some one to support me in the matter. Finally the Duc de
Morny was bored, and rose to go.

"Do you know what you ought to do with this child?" he said.
"You ought to send her to the Conservatoire." He then patted
my cheek, kissed my aunt's hand, and bowed to all the others.
As he bent over my mother's hand I heard him say to her, "You
would have made a bad diplomatist; but follow my advice,
and send her to the Conservatoire."

He then took his departure, and I gazed at every one in
perfect anguish.

The Conservatoire ! What was it ? What did it mean ?

I went up to my governess, Mlle. de Brabender. Her lips

were firmly pressed together, and she looked shocked, just as she did sometimes when my godfather told some story that she did not approve at table. My uncle, Félix Faure, was gazing at the floor in an absent-minded way ; the notary had a spiteful look in his eyes, my aunt was holding forth in a very excited manner, and M. Meydieu kept shaking his head and muttering, " Perhaps—yes—who knows ?—hum—hum ! " Madame Guérard was very pale and sad, and she looked at me with infinite tenderness.

What could this Conservatoire be ? The word uttered so carelessly seemed to have entirely disturbed the equanimity of all present. Each one of them seemed to me to have a different impression about it, but none looked pleased. Suddenly in the midst of the general embarrassment my godfather exclaimed brutally :

" She is too thin to make an actress."

" I won't be an actress ! " I exclaimed.

" You don't know what an actress is," said my aunt.

" Oh yes, I do. Rachel is an actress."

" You know Rachel ? " asked mamma, getting up.

" Oh yes ; she came to the convent once to see little Adèle Sarony. She went all over the convent and into the garden, and she had to sit down because she could not get her breath. They fetched her something to bring her round, and she was so pale, oh, so pale. I was very sorry for her, and Sister St. Appoline told me what she did was killing her, for she was an actress ; and so I won't be an actress—I won't ! "

I had said all this in a breath, with my cheeks on fire and my voice hard.

I remembered all that Sister St. Appoline had told me, and Mother St. Sophie, too. I remembered also that when Rachel had gone out of the garden, looking very pale, and holding a lady's arm for support, a little girl had put her tongue out at her. I did not want people to put out their tongues at me when I was grown up.

Conservatoire ! That word alarmed me. He wanted me to be an actress, and he had now gone away, so that I could not talk things over with him. He went away smiling and tranquil, after caressing me in the usual friendly way. He had gone, caring little about the scraggy child whose future had been discussed.

" Send her to the Conservatoire ! "

And that sentence, uttered carelessly, had come like a bomb into my life.

I, the dreamy child, who that morning was ready to repulse princes and kings ; I, whose trembling fingers had that morning told over chaplets of dreams, who only a few hours ago had felt my heart beating with emotion hitherto unknown to me ; I, who had got up expecting some great event to take place— was to see everything disappear, thanks to that phrase as heavy as lead and as deadly as a bullet.

" Send her to the Conservatoire ! "

And I divined that this phrase was to be the sign-post of my life. All those people had gathered together at the turning of the cross roads. " Send her to the Conservatoire ! " I wanted to be a nun, and this was considered absurd, idiotic, un-reasonable. " Send her to the Conservatoire ! " had opened out a field for discussion, the horizon of a future. My uncle Félix Faure and Mlle. Brabender were the only ones against this idea. They tried in vain to make my mother understand that with the 100,000 francs that my father had left me I might marry. But mother replied that I had declared I had a horror of marriage, and that I should wait until I was of age to go into a convent.

" Under these conditions," she said, " Sarah will never have her father's money."

" No, certainly not," put in the notary.

" Then," continued my mother, " she would enter the convent as a servant, and I will not have that ! My money is an annuity, so that I cannot leave anything to my children. I therefore want them to have a career of their own."

My mother was now exhausted with so much talking, and lay back in an arm-chair. I got very much excited, and my mother asked me to go away.

Mlle. de Brabender and Madame Guérard were arguing in a low voice, and I thought of the aristocratic man who had just left us. I was very angry with him, for this idea of the Conservatoire was his.

Mlle. de Brabender tried to console me. Madame Guérard said that this career had its advantages. Mlle. de Brabender considered that the convent would have a great fascination for so dreamy a nature as mine. The latter was very religious and a great church-goer, *mon petit Dame* was a pagan in the purest acceptation of that word, and yet the two women got on very well together, thanks to their affectionate devotion to me.

Madame Guérard adored the proud rebelliousness of my nature, my pretty face, and the slenderness of my figure; Mlle. de Brabender was touched by my delicate health. She endeavoured to comfort me when I was jealous at not being loved as much as my sister, but what she liked best about me was my voice. She always declared that my voice was modulated for prayers, and my delight in the convent appeared to her quite natural. She loved me with a gentle pious affection, and Madame Guérard loved me with bursts of paganism. These two women, whose memory is still dear to me, shared me between them, and made the best of my good qualities and my faults. I certainly owe to both of them this study of myself and the vision I have of myself.

The day was destined to end in the strangest of fashions. Madame Guérard had gone back to her apartment upstairs, and I was lying back on a little cane arm-chair which was the most ornamental piece of furniture in my room. I felt very drowsy, and was holding Mlle. de Brabender's hand in mine, when the door opened and my aunt entered, followed by my mother. I can see them now, my aunt in her dress of puce silk trimmed with fur, her brown velvet hat tied under her chin with long, wide strings, and mamma, who had taken off her dress and put on a white woollen dressing-gown. She always detested keeping on her dress in the house, and I understood by her change of costume that every one had gone and that my aunt was ready to leave. I got up from my arm-chair, but mamma made me sit down again.

" Rest yourself thoroughly," she said, " for we are going to take you to the theatre this evening, to the Français." I felt sure that this was just a bait, and I would not show any sign of pleasure, although in my heart I was delighted at the idea of going to the Français. The only theatre I knew anything of was the Robert Houdin, to which I was taken sometimes with my sister, and I fancy that it was for her benefit we went, as I was really too old to care for that kind of performance.

"Will you come with us?" mamma said, turning to Mlle. de Brabender.

"Willingly, Madame," replied this dear creature. "I will go home and change my dress."

My aunt laughed at my sullen looks.

"Little fraud," she said, as she went away; "you are hiding your delight. Ah well, you will see some actresses to-night."

"Is Rachel going to act?" I asked.

"Oh no ; she is ill."

My aunt kissed me and went away, saying she should see me again later on, and my mother followed her out of the room. Mlle. de Brabender then hurriedly prepared to leave me. She had to go home to dress and to say that she would not be in until quite late, for in her convent special permission had to be obtained when one wished to be out later than ten at night. When I was alone I swung myself backwards and forwards in my arm-chair, which, by the way, was anything but a rocking-chair. I began to think, and for the first time in my life my critical comprehension came to my aid. And so all these serious people had been inconvenienced, the notary fetched from Hâvre, my uncle dragged away from working at his book, the old bachelor M. Meydieu disturbed in his habits and customs, my godfather kept away from the Stock Exchange, and that aristocratic and sceptical Duc de Morny cramped up for two hours in the midst of our *bourgeois* surroundings, and all to end in this decision, *She shall be taken to the theatre.* I do not know what part my uncle had played in this burlesque plan, but I doubt whether it was to his taste. All the same, I was glad to go to the theatre ; it made me feel more important. That morning on waking up I was quite a child, and now events had taken place which had transformed me into a young girl. I had been discussed by every one, and I had expressed my wishes, without any result, certainly, but all the same I had expressed them, and now it was deemed necessary to humour and indulge me in order to win me over. They could not force me into agreeing to what they wanted me to do. My consent was necessary, and I felt so joyful and so proud about it that I was quite touched and almost ready to yield. I said to myself that it would be better to hold my own and let them ask me again.

After dinner we all squeezed into a cab, mamma, my god-father, Mlle. de Brabender, and I.   My godfather made me a present of some white gloves.

On mounting the steps at the Théâtre Français I trod on a lady's dress.   She turned round and called me a "stupid child."   I moved back hastily, and came into collision with a very stout old gentleman, who gave me a rough push forward.

When once we were all installed in a box facing the stage, mamma and I in the first row, with Mlle. de Brabender behind me, I felt more reassured.   I was close against the partition of the box, and I could feel Mlle. de Brabender's sharp knees through the velvet of my chair.   This gave me confidence, and I leaned against the back of the chair purposely to feel the support of those two knees.

When the curtain slowly rose I thought I should have fainted.   It was as though the curtain of my future life were being raised.   These columns (*Britannicus* was being played) were to be my palaces, the borders above were to be my skies, and those boards were to bend under my frail weight.   I heard nothing of *Britannicus*, for I was far, far away, at Grand-Champs, in my dormitory there.

"Well, what do you think of it?" asked my godfather when the curtain fell.   I did not answer, and he laid his hand on my head and turned my face round towards him.   I was crying, and big tears were rolling slowly down my cheeks, those tears that come without any sobs and without any hope of ever ceasing.

My godfather shrugged his shoulders, and getting up, left the box, banging the door after him.   Mamma, losing all patience with me, proceeded to review the house through her opera-glasses.

Mlle. de Brabender passed me her handkerchief, for I had dropped mine and dared not pick it up.

*   *   *   *   *

The curtain had been raised for the second piece, *Amphytrion*, and I made an effort to listen, for the sake of pleasing my governess, who was so gentle and conciliating.   I can only remember one thing, and that is that Alcmène seemed to be so unhappy that I burst into loud sobs, and that the whole house, very much amused, looked at our box. My mother, greatly annoyed, took me out, and Mlle. de Brabender went with us. My godfather was furious, and muttered, " She ought to be shut up in a convent and left there. Good heavens, what a little idiot the child is ! " This was the *début* of my artistic career.

VII

MY CAREER—FIRST LESSONS

I WAS beginning to think, though, of my new career. Books were sent to me from all quarters : Racine, Corneille, Molière, Casimir Delavigne, &c. I opened them, but, as I did not understand them at all, I quickly closed them again, and read my little Lafontaine, which I loved passionately. I knew all his fables, and one of my delights was to make a bet with my god-father or with M. Meydieu, our learned and tiresome friend. I used to bet that they would not recognise all the fables if I began with the last verse and went backwards to the first one, and I often won the bet.

A line from my aunt arrived one day, telling my mother that M. Auber, who was then director of the Conservatoire, was expecting us the next day at nine in the morning. I was about to put my foot in the stirrup. My mother sent me with Madame Guérard. M. Auber received us very affably, as the Duc de Morny had spoken to him of me. I was very much impressed by him, with his refined face and white hair, his ivory complexion and magnificent black eyes, his fragile and distinguished look, his melodious voice and the celebrity of his name. I scarcely dared answer his questions. He spoke to me very gently, and told me to sit down.

" You are very fond of the stage ? " he began.

" Oh, no, Monsieur," I answered.

This unexpected reply amazed him. He looked at Madame Guérard from under his heavy eyelids, and she at once said : " No, she does not care for the stage ; but she does not want to marry, and consequently she will have no money, as her father left her a hundred thousand francs which she can only get on her wedding-day. Her mother, therefore, wants her to have some profession, for Madame Bernhardt has only an annuity, a fairly good one, but it is only an annuity, and so she will not be able to leave her daughters anything. On that account she wants Sarah to become independent. She would like to enter a convent."

" But that is not an independent career, my child," said Auber slowly. " How old is she ? " he asked.

" Fourteen and a half," replied Madame Guérard.

" No," I exclaimed, " I am nearly fifteen."

The kind old man smiled.

" In twenty years from now," he said, " you will insist less upon the exact figures," and, evidently thinking the visit had lasted long enough, he rose.

" It appears," he said to Madame Guérard, " that this little girl's mother is very beautiful ? "

" Oh, very beautiful," she replied.

" You will please express my regret to her that I have not seen her, and my thanks for her having been so charmingly replaced." He thereupon kissed Madame Guérard's hand, and she coloured slightly. This conversation remained engraved on my mind. I remember every word of it, every movement and every gesture of M. Auber's, for this little man, so charming and so gentle, held my future in his transparent-looking hand. He opened the door for us and, touching me on my shoulder, said : " Come, courage, little girl. Believe me, you will thank your mother some day for driving you to it. Don't look so sad. Life is well worth beginning seriously, but gaily."

I stammered out a few words of thanks, and just as I was making my exit a fine-looking woman knocked against me. She was heavy and extremely bustling, though, and M. Auber bent his head towards me and said quietly :

" Above all things, don't let yourself get stout like this singer. Stoutness is the enemy of a woman and of an artist."

The man-servant was now holding the door open for us, and as M. Auber returned to his visitor I heard him say :

" Well, most ideal of women ? "

I went away rather astounded, and did not say a word in the carriage. Madame Guérard told my mother about our interview, but she did not even let her finish, and only said, " Good, good ; thank you."

As the examination was to take place a month after this visit, it became necessary to prepare for it. My mother did not know any theatrical people. My godfather advised me to learn *Phèdre*, but Mlle. de Brabender objected, as she thought it a little offensive, and refused to help me if I chose that. M. Meydieu, our old friend, wanted me to work at Chimène in *Le Cid*, but first he declared that I clenched my teeth too much for it. It was quite true that I did not make the *o* open enough and did not roll the *r* sufficiently either. He wrote a little note-book for me, which I am copying textually, as my poor dear Guérard religiously kept everything concerning me, and she gave me, later on, a quantity of papers which are useful now.

The following is our odious friend's work :

" Every morning instead of *do . . re . . mi . . .* practise *te . . de . . de . .*, in order to learn to vibrate. . . .

" Before breakfast repeat forty times over, *Un-très-gros-rat-dans-un-très-gros-trou*, in order to vibrate the *r*.

" Before dinner repeat forty times : *Combien ces six saucisses-ci ? C'est six sous, ces six saucisses-ci. Six sous ces six saucisses-ci ? Six sous ceux-ci ! Six sous ceux-là ; six sous ces six saucissons-ci !* in order to learn not to whizz the *s*.

" At night, when going to bed, repeat twenty times : *Didon dina, dit-on, du dos d'un dodu dindon*.

" And twenty times : *Le plus petit papa, petit pipi, petit popo, petit pupu.* Open the mouth square for the *d* and pout for the *p*."

He gave this piece of work quite seriously to Mlle. de Brabender, who quite seriously wanted me to practise it. My governess was charming, and I was very fond of her, but I could not help yelling with laughter when, after making me go through the *te de de* exercise, which went fairly well, and then the *très gros rat*, &c., she started on the *saucisson* (sausages) ! Ah, no. There was a cacophony of hisses in her toothless mouth, enough to make all the dogs in Paris howl. And when she began with the *Didon*, accompanied by the *plus petit papa*, I thought my dear governess was losing her reason. She half closed her eyes, her face was red, her moustache bristled up, she put on a sentencious, hurried manner ; her mouth widened out and looked like the slit in a money-box, or else it was creased up into a little ring, and she purred and hissed and chirped and fooled without ceasing. I flung myself exhausted into my wicker chair, choking with laughter, and great tears poured from my eyes. I stamped on the floor, flung my arms out right and left until they were tired, and rocked myself backwards and forwards, pealing with laughter.

My mother, attracted by the noise I was making, half opened the door. Mlle. de Brabender explained to her very gravely that she was showing me M. Meydieu's method. My mother expostulated with me, but I would not listen to anything, as I was nearly beside myself with laughter. She then took Mlle. de Brabender away and left me alone, for she feared that I should finish with hysterics. When once I was by myself I began to calm down. I closed my eyes and thought of my convent again. The *te de de* got mixed up in my enervated brain with the " Our Father," which I used to have to repeat some days fifteen or twenty times as a punishment. Finally I came to myself again, got up, and after bathing my face in cold water went to my mother, whom I found playing whist with my governess and godfather. I kissed Mlle. de Brabender, and she returned my kiss with such indulgent kindness that I felt quite embarrassed by it.

Ten days passed by, and I did none of M. Meydieu's exercises, except the *te de de* at the piano. My mother came and woke me every morning for this, and it drove me wild. My godfather made me learn *Aricie*, but I understood nothing of what he told me about the verses. He considered, and explained to me, that poetry must be said with an intonation, and that all the value of it resided in the rhyme. His theories were boring to listen to and impossible to execute. Then I could not understand Aricie's character, for it did not seem to me that she loved Hippolyte at all, and she appeared to me to be a scheming flirt. My godfather explained to me that in olden times this was the way people loved each other, and when I remarked that Phèdre appeared to love in a better way than that, he took me by the chin and said : " Just look at this naughty child. She is pretending not to understand, and would like us explain to her. . . ."

This was simply idiotic. I did not understand, and had not asked anything, but this man had a *bourgeois* mind, and was sly and lewd. He did not like me because I was thin, but he was interested in me because I was going to be an actress. That word evoked for him the weak side of our art. He did not see the beauty, the nobleness of it, nor yet its beneficial power.

I could not fathom all this at that time, but I did not feel at ease with this man, whom I had seen from my childhood and who was almost like a father to me. I did not want to continue learning *Aricie*. In the first place, I could not talk about it with my governess, as she would not discuss the piece at all.

I then learnt *L'Ecole des Femmes*, and Mlle. de Brabender explained Agnès to me. The dear, good lady did not see much in it, for the whole story appeared to her of childlike simplicity, and when I said the lines, " He has taken from me, he has taken from me the ribbon you gave me," she smiled in all confidence when Meydieu and my godfather laughed heartily.

VIII

THE CONSERVATOIRE

Finally the examination day arrived. Every one had given me advice, but no one any real helpful counsel. It had not occurred to any one that I ought to have had a professional to prepare me for my examination. I got up in the morning with a heavy heart and an anxious mind. My mother had had a black silk dress made for me. It was slightly low-necked, and was finished with a gathered berthe. The frock was rather short, and showed my drawers. These were trimmed with embroidery, and came down to my brown kid boots. A white guimpe emerged from my black bodice and was fastened round my throat, which was too slender. My hair was parted on my forehead and then fell as it liked, for it was not held by pins or ribbons. I wore a large straw hat, although the season was rather advanced. Every one came to inspect my dress, and I was turned round and round twenty times at least. I had to make my curtsey for every one to see. Finally I seemed to give general satisfaction. *Mon petit Dame* came downstairs, with her grave husband, and kissed me. She was deeply affected. Our old Marguerite made me sit down, and put before me a cup of cold beef tea, which she had simmered so carefully for a long time that it was then a delicious jelly ; I swallowed it in a second. I was in a great hurry to start. On rising from my chair, I moved so brusquely that my dress caught on to an invisible splinter of wood, and was torn. My mother turned to a visitor, who had arrived about five minutes before and had remained in contemplative admiration ever since.

" There," she said to him in a vexed tone, " that is a proof of what I told you. All your silks tear with the slightest movement."

"Oh no," replied our visitor quickly ; "I told you that this one was not well dressed, and let you have it at a low price on that account."

He who spoke was a young Jew, not ugly. He was a Dutchman—shy, tenacious, but never violent. I had known him from my childhood. His father, who was a friend of my grandfather's on my mother's side, was a rich tradesman and the father of a tribe of children. He gave each of his sons a small sum of money, and sent them out to make their fortune where they liked. Jacques, the one of whom I am speaking, came to Paris. He had commenced by selling Passover cakes, and as a boy had often brought me some of them to the convent, together with the dainties that my mother sent me. Later on, my surprise was great on seeing him offer my mother rolls of oil-cloth such as is used for tablecloths for early breakfast. I remember one of those cloths the border of which was formed of medallions representing the French kings. It was from that oil-cloth that I learned my history best. For the last month he had owned quite an elegant vehicle, and he sold "silks that were not well dressed." At present he is one of the leading jewellers of Paris.

The slit in my dress was soon mended, and, knowing now that the silk was not well dressed, I treated it with respect, Well, finally we started, Mlle. de Brabender, Madame Guérard, and I, in a carriage that was only intended for two persons ; and I was glad that it was so small, for I was close to two people who were fond of me, and my silk frock was spread carefully over their knees.

When I entered the waiting-room that leads into the recital hall of the Conservatoire, there were about fifteen young men and twenty girls there. All these girls were accompanied by their mother, father, aunt, brother, or sister. There was an odour of pomade and vanilla that made me feel sick.

When we were shown into this room I felt that every one was looking at me, and I blushed to the back of my head. Madame Guérard drew me gently along, and I turned to take Mlle. de Brabender's hand. She came shyly forward, blushing more and still more confused than I was. Every one looked at her, and I saw the girls nudge each other and nod in her direction.

One of them got suddenly up and moved across to her

E

mother. " Oh, mercy, look at that old sight !" she said.
My poor governess felt most uncomfortable, and I was furious,
I thought she was a thousand times nicer than all those fat,
dressed-up, common-looking mothers.   Certainly she was
different from other people in her appearance, for Mlle. de
Brabender was wearing a salmon-coloured dress and an Indian
shawl, drawn tightly across her shoulders and fastened with a
very large cameo brooch.   Her bonnet was trimmed with
ruches, so close together that it looked like a nun's head-gear.
She certainly was not at all like these dreadful people in whose
society we found ourselves, and among whom there were not
more than ten exceptions.   The young men were standing in
compact groups near the windows.   They were laughing and,
I expect, making remarks in doubtful taste.

The door opened and a girl with a red face, and a young
man perfectly scarlet, came back after acting their scene.   They
each went to their respective friends and then chattered away,
finding fault with each other.   A name was called out :
Mlle. Dica Petit, and I saw a tall, fair, distinguished-looking
girl move forward without any embarrassment.   She stopped
on her way to kiss a pretty woman, stout, with a pink and white
complexion, and very much dressed up.

" Don't be afraid, mother dear," she said, and then she added
a few words in Dutch before disappearing, followed by a young
man and a very thin girl who were to perform with her.

This was explained to me by Léautaud, who called over the
names of the pupils and took down the names of those who were
up to pass their examination and those who were to act with
them and give them the cues.   I knew nothing of all this, and
wondered who was to give me the cues for Agnès.   He
mentioned several young men, but I interrupted him.

" Oh no," I said ; " I will not ask any one.   I do not know
any of them, and I will not ask."

" Well, then, what will you recite, Mademoiselle ? " asked
Léautaud, with the most *fouchtre* accent possible.

" I will recite a fable," I replied.

He burst out laughing as he wrote down my name and the
title, *Deux Pigeons*, which I gave him.   I heard him still laughing under his heavy moustache as he continued his round.   He
then went back into the Conservatoire, and I began to get

feverish with excitement, so much so that Madame Guérard was anxious about me, as my health unfortunately was very delicate. She made me sit down, and then she put a few drops of eau-de-Cologne behind my ears.

" There, that will teach you to wink like that ! " were the words I suddenly heard, and a girl with the prettiest face imaginable had her ears boxed soundly. Nathalie Mauvoy's mother was correcting her daughter. I sprang up, trembling with fright and indignation; I was as angry as a young turkey-cock. I wanted to go and box the horrible woman's ears in return, and then to kiss the pretty girl who had been insulted in this way, but I was held back firmly by my two guardians.

Dica Petit now returned, and this caused a diversion in the waiting-room. She was radiant and quite satisfied with herself. Oh, very well satisfied indeed ! Her father held out a little flask to her in which was some kind of cordial, and I should have liked some of it too, for my mouth was dry and burning. Her mother then put a little woollen square over her chest before fastening her coat for her, and then all three of them went away. Several other girls and young men were called before my turn came.

Finally the call of my name made me jump as a sardine does when pursued by a big fish. I tossed my head to shake my hair back, and *mon petit Dame* stroked my badly dressed silk. Mlle. de Brabender reminded me about the *o* and the *a*, the *r*, the *p*, and the *t*, and I then went alone into the hall. I had never been alone an hour in my life. As a little child I was always clinging to the skirts of my nurse ; at the convent I was always with one of my friends or one of the sisters; at home either with Mlle. de Brabender or Madame Guérard, or if they were not there in the kitchen with Marguerite. And now there I was alone in that strange-looking room, with a platform at the end, a large table in the middle, and, seated round this table, men who either grumbled, growled, or jeered. There was only one woman present, and she had a loud voice. She was holding an eyeglass, and as I entered she dropped it and looked at me through her opera-glass. I felt every one's gaze on my back as I climbed up the few steps on to the platform. Léautaud bent forward and whispered, " Make your bow and commence, and then stop when the chairman rings." I looked at the chairman, and saw that it was M. Auber. I had forgotten that he was director of the Conservatoire, just as I had forgotten everything else. I at once made my bow and began :

> *Deux pigeons s'aimaient d'amour tendre,*
> *L'un d'eux s'ennuyant* . . .

A low, grumbling sound was heard, and then a " ventriloquist " muttered, " It isn't an elocution class here. What an idea to come here reciting fables ! "

It was Beauvallet, the deafening tragedian of the Comédie Française. I stopped short, my heart beating wildly.

" Go on, my child," said a man with silvery hair. This was Provost.

" Yes, it won't be as long as a scene from a play," exclaimed Augustine Brohan, the one woman present.

I began again :

> *Deux pigeons s'aimaient d'amour tendre,*
> *L'un d'eux s'ennuyant au logis*
> *Fut assez* . . .

" Louder, my child, louder," said a little man with curly white hair, in a kindly tone. This was Samson.

I stopped again, confused and frightened, seized suddenly with such a foolish fit of nervousness that I could have shouted or howled. Samson saw this, and said to me, " Come, come ; we are not ogres ! " He had just been talking in a low voice with Auber.

" Come now, begin again," he said, " and speak up."

" Ah no," put in Augustine Brohan, " if she is to begin again it will be longer than a scene ! " This speech made all the table laugh, and that gave me time to recover myself. I thought all these people unkind to laugh like this at the expense of a poor little trembling creature who had been delivered over to them, bound hand and foot.

I felt, without exactly defining it, a slight contempt for these pitiless judges. Since then I have very often thought of that trial of mine, and I have come to the conclusion that individuals who are kind, intelligent, and compassionate become less estimable when they are together. The feeling of personal irresponsibility arouses their evil instincts, and the fear of ridicule chases away their good ones.

When I had recovered my will power I began my fable again, determined not to mind what happened. My voice was more liquid on account of the emotion, and the desire to make myself heard caused it to be more resonant.

There was silence, and before I had finished my fable the little bell rang. I bowed and came down the few steps from the platform, thoroughly exhausted. M. Auber stopped me as I was passing by the table.

"Well, little girl," he said, "that was very good indeed. M. Provost and M. Beauvallet both want you in their class."

I recoiled slightly when he told me which was M. Beauvallet, for he was the "ventriloquist" who had given me such a fright.

"Well, which of these two gentlemen should you prefer?" he asked.

I did not utter a word, but pointed to M. Provost.

"That's all right. Get your handkerchief out, my poor Beauvallet, and I shall entrust this child to you, my dear Provost."

I understood, and, wild with joy, I exclaimed, "Then I have passed?"

"Yes, you have passed; and there is only one thing I regret, and that is that such a pretty voice should not be for music."

I did not hear anything else, for I was beside myself with joy. I did not stay to thank any one, but bounded to the door.

"*Mon petit Dame*! Mademoiselle, I have passed!" I exclaimed, and when they shook hands and asked me no end of questions I could only reply, "Oh, it's quite true. I have passed, I have passed!"

I was surrounded and questioned.

"How do you know that you have passed? No one knows beforehand."

"Yes, yes; I know, though. Monsieur Auber told me. I am to go into Monsieur Provost's class. Monsieur Beauvallet wanted me, but his voice is too loud for me!"

A disagreeable girl exclaimed, "Can't you stop that? And so they all want you!" A pretty girl, who was too dark, though, for my taste, came nearer and asked me gently what I had recited.

"The fable of the 'Two Pigeons,'" I replied.

She was surprised, and so was every one; while, as for me, I was wildly delighted to surprise them all. I tossed my hat on my head, shook my frock out, and, dragging my two friends along, ran away dancing. They wanted to take me to the confectioner's to have something, but I refused. We got into a cab, and I should have liked to push that cab along myself. I fancied I saw the words, "I have passed," written up over all the shops.

When, on account of the crowded streets, the cab had to stop, it seemed to me that the people stared at me, and I caught myself tossing my head, as though telling them all that it was quite true I had passed my examination. I never thought any more about the convent, and only experienced a feeling of pride at having succeeded in my first venturesome enterprise. Venturesome, but the success had only depended on me. It seemed to me as though the cabman would never arrive at 265 Rue St. Honoré. I kept putting my head out of the window, and saying, "Faster, cabby, faster, please!"

At last we reached the house, and I sprang out of the cab and hurried along to tell the good news to my mother. On the way I was stopped by the daughter of the hall-porter. She was a corset-maker, and worked in a little room on the top floor of the house which was opposite our dining-room, where I used to do my lessons with my governess, so that I could not help seeing her ruddy, wide-awake face constantly. I had never spoken to her, but I knew who she was.

"Well, Mademoiselle Sarah, are you satisfied?" she called out.

"Oh yes, I have passed," I answered, and I could not resist stopping a minute in order to enjoy the astonishment of the hall-porter family. I then hurried on, but on reaching the courtyard came to a dead stand, anger and grief taking possession of me, for there I beheld my *petit dame*, her two hands forming a trumpet, her head thrown back, shouting to my mother, who was leaning out of the window, "Yes, yes; she has passed!"

I gave her a thump with my clenched hand and began to cry with rage, for I had prepared a little story for my mother, ending up with the joyful surprise. I had intended putting on a very sad look on arriving at the door, and pretending to be broken-hearted and ashamed. I felt sure she would say, "Oh, I am not surprised, my poor child, you are so foolish!" and then I should have thrown my arms round her neck and said, "It isn't true, it isn't true; I have passed!" I had pictured to myself her face brightening up, and then old Marguerite and my godfather laughing heartily and my sisters dancing with joy, and here was Madame Guérard sounding her trumpet and spoiling all the effects that I had prepared so well.

I must say that the kind woman continued as long as she lived, that is the greater part of my life, to spoil all my effects. It was all in vain that I made scenes; she could not help herself. Whenever I related an adventure and wanted it to be very effective, she would invariably burst into fits of laughter before the end of it. If I told a story with a very lamentable ending, which was to be a surprise, she would sigh, roll her eyes, and murmur, "Oh dear, oh dear!" so that I always missed the effect I was counting on. All this used to exasperate me to such a degree that before beginning a story or a game I used to ask her to go out of the room, and she would get up and go, laughing at the idea of the blunder she would make if there.

Abusing Guérard, I went upstairs to my mother, whom I found at the open door. She kissed me affectionately, and on seeing my sulky face asked if I was not satisfied.

"Yes," I replied; "but I am furious with Guérard. Be nice, mamma, and pretend you don't know. Shut the door, and I will ring."

She did this, and I rang the bell. Marguerite opened the door, and my mother came and pretended to be astonished. My sisters, too, arrived, and my godfather and my aunt. When I kissed my mother, exclaiming, "I have passed!" every one shouted with joy, and I was gay again. I had made my effect, anyhow. It was "the career" taking possession of me unawares. My sister Régina, whom the sisters would not have in the convent, and so had sent home, began to dance a jig. She had learnt this in the country when she had been put out to nurse, and upon every occasion she danced it, finishing always with this couplet :

Mon p'tit ventr' éjouis toi
Tout ce ze gagn' est pou' toi . . .

Nothing could be more comic than this chubby child, with her serious air. Régina never laughed, and only a suspicion of a smile ever played over her thin lips and her mouth, which was too small. Nothing could be more comic than to see her, looking grave and rough, dancing the jig.

She was funnier than ever that day, as she was excited by the general joy. She was four years old, and nothing ever embarrassed her. She was both timid and bold. She detested society and people generally, and when she was made to go into the dining-room she embarrassed people by her crude remarks, which were most odd, by her rough answers, and her kicks and blows. She was a terrible child, with silvery hair, dark complexion, blue eyes, too large for her face, and thick lashes which made a shadow on her cheeks when she lowered the lids and joined her eyebrows when her eyes were open. She would be four or five hours sometimes without uttering a word, without answering any question she was asked, and then she would jump up from her little chair, begin to sing as loud as she could, and dance the jig. On this day she was in a good temper, for she kissed me affectionately and opened her thin lips to smile. My sister Jeanne kissed me and made me tell her about my examination. My godfather gave me a hundred francs, and Meydieu, who had just arrived to find out the result, promised to take me the next day to Barbédienne's to choose a clock for my room, as that was one of my dreams.

IX

A MARRIAGE PROPOSAL AND EXAMINATIONS—
THE CONSERVATOIRE

An evolution took place in me from that day. For rather
a long time my soul remained child-like, but my mind discerned
life more distinctly. I felt the need of creating a personality for
myself. That was the first awakening of my will. I wanted to
be some one. Mlle. de Brabender declared to me that this
was pride. It seemed to me that it was not quite that, but
I could not then define what the sentiment was which imposed
this wish on me. I did not understand until a few months later
why I wished to be some one.

A friend of my godfather's made me an offer of marriage.
This man was a rich tanner and very kind, but so dark and with
such long hair and such a beard that he disgusted me. I refused
him, and my godfather then asked to speak to me alone. He
made me sit down in my mother's boudoir, and said to me : " My
poor child, it is pure folly to refuse Monsieur Bed——. He has
sixty thousand francs a year and expectations." It was the first
time I had heard this use of the word, and when the meaning
was explained to me I wondered if that was the right thing to
say on such an occasion.

" Why, yes," replied my godfather ; " you are idiotic with
your romantic ideas. Marriage is a business affair, and must be
considered as such. Your future father- and mother-in-law will
have to die, just as we shall, and it is by no means disagreeable
to know that they will leave two million francs to their son, and
consequently to you, if you marry him."

" I shall not marry him, though."

" Why ? "

" Because I do not love him."

"But you never love your husband before——" replied my practical adviser. "You can love him after."

"After what?"

"Ask your mother. But listen to me now, for it is not a question of that. You must marry. Your mother has a small income which your father left her, but this income comes from the profits of the manufactory, which belongs to your grand-mother, and she cannot bear your mother, who will therefore lose that income, and then she will have nothing, and three children on her hands. It is that accursed lawyer who is arranging all this. The whys and wherefores would take too long to explain. Your father managed his business affairs very badly. You must marry, therefore, if not for your own sake, for the sake of your mother and sisters. You can then give your mother the hundred thousand francs your father left you, which no one else can touch. Monsieur Bed—— will settle three hundred thousand francs on you. I have arranged everything, so that you can give this to your mother if you like, and with four hundred thousand francs she will be able to live very well."

I cried and sobbed, and asked to have time to think it over. I found my mother in the dining-room.

"Has your godfather told you?" she asked gently, in rather a timid way.

"Yes, mother, yes; he has told me. Let me think it over, will you?" I said, sobbing; as I kissed her neck lingeringly. I then locked myself in my bedroom, and for the first time for many days I regretted my convent. All my childhood rose up before me, and I cried more and more, and felt so unhappy that I wished I could die. Gradually, however, I began to get calm again, and realised what had happened and what my godfather's words meant. Most decidedly I did not want to marry this man. Since I had been at the Conservatoire I had learnt a few things vaguely, very vaguely, for I was never alone, but I understood enough to make me not want to marry without being in love. I was, however, destined to be attacked in a quarter from which I should not have expected it. Madame Guérard asked me to go up to her room to see the embroidery she was doing on a frame for my mother's birthday.

My astonishment was great to find M. Bed—— there. He

begged me to change my mind. He made me very wretched, for he pleaded with tears in his eyes.

" Do you want a larger marriage settlement ? " he asked. " I would make it five hundred thousand francs."

But it was not that at all, and I said in a very low voice, " I do not love you, Monsieur."

" If you do not marry me, Mademoiselle," he said, " I shall die of grief.

I looked at him, and repeated to myself the words " die of grief." I was embarrassed and desperate, but at the same time delighted, for he loved me just as a man does in a play. Phrases that I had read or heard came to my mind vaguely, and I repeated them without any real conviction, and then left him without the slightest coquetry.

M. Bed—— did not die. He is still living, and has a very important financial position. He is much nicer now than when he was so black, for at present he is quite white.

Well, I had just passed my first examination with remarkable success, particularly in tragedy.

M. Provost, my professor, had not wanted me to compete in *Zaïre*, but I had insisted. I thought that scene with Zaïre and her brother Néréstan very fine, and it suited me. But when Zaïre, overwhelmed with her brother's reproaches, falls on her knees at his feet, Provost wanted me to say the words, "Strike, I tell you! I love him!" with violence, and I wanted to say them gently, perfectly resigned to a death that was almost certain. I argued about it for a long time with my professor, and finally I appeared to give in to him during the lesson. But on the day of the competition I fell on my knees before Néréstan with a sob so real, my arms outstretched, offering my heart, so full of love, to the deadly blow that I expected, and I murmured with such tenderness, " Strike, I tell you! I love him!" that the whole house burst into applause and repeated the outburst twice over.

The second prize for tragedy was awarded me, to the great dissatisfaction of the public, as it was thought that I ought to have had the first prize. And yet it was only just that I should have the second, on account of my age and the short time I had been studying. I had a first accessit or comedy in *La fausse Agnès*.

I felt, therefore, that I had the right to refuse. My future lay open before me, and consequently my mother would not be in want if she should lose her present income. A few days later M. Régnier, professor at the Conservatoire and secretary of the Comédie Française, came to ask my mother whether she would allow me to play in a piece of his at the Vaudeville. The piece was *Germaine,* and the managers would give me twenty-five francs for each performance. I was amazed at the sum. Seven hundred and fifty francs a month for my first appearance! I was wild with joy. I besought my mother to accept the offer made by the Vaudeville, and she told me to do as I liked in the matter.

I asked M. Camille Doucet, director of the Fine Arts Department, to be so good as to receive me, and, as my mother always refused to accompany me, Madame Guérard went with me. My little sister Régina begged me to take her, and very unwisely I consented. We had not been in the director's office more than five minutes before my sister, who was only six years old, began to climb on to the furniture. She jumped on to a stool, and finally sat down on the floor, pulling towards her the paper basket, which was under the desk, and proceeded to spread about all the torn papers which it contained. On seeing this Camille Doucet mildly observed that she was not a very good little girl. My sister, with her head in the basket, answered in her husky voice, "If you bother me, Monsieur, I shall tell every one that you are there to give out holy water that is poison. My aunt says so." My face turned purple with shame, and I stammered out, "Please do not believe that, Monsieur Doucet. My little sister is telling an untruth."

Régina sprang to her feet, and clenching her little fists, rushed at me like a little fury. "Aunt Rosine never said that?" she exclaimed. "You are telling an untruth. Why, she said it to Monsieur de Morny, and he answered——"

I had forgotten this, and I have forgotten what the Duc de Morny answered, but, beside myself with anger, I put my hand over my sister's mouth and took her quickly away. She howled like a polecat, and we rushed like a hurricane through the waiting-room, which was full of people.

I then gave way to one of those violent fits of temper to which I had been subject in my childhood. I sprang into the first cab that passed the door, and, when once in the cab, struck my sister with such fury that Madame Guérard was alarmed, and protected her with her own body, receiving all the blows I gave with my head, arms, and feet, for in my anger, grief, and shame I flung myself about to right and left. My grief was all the more profound from the fact that I was very fond of Camille Doucet. He was gentle and charming, affable and kind-hearted. He had refused my aunt something she had asked for, and, unaccustomed to being refused anything, she had a spite against him. This had nothing to do with me, though, and I wondered what Camille Doucet would think. And then, too, I had not asked him about the Vaudeville.

All my fine dreams had come to nothing. And it was this little monster, who looked as fair and as white as a seraph, who had just shattered my first hopes. Huddled up in the cab, an expression of fear on her self-willed looking face and her thin lips compressed, she was gazing at me under her long lashes with half-closed eyes.

On reaching home I told my mother all that had happened, and she declared that my little sister should have no dessert for two days. Régina was greedy, but her pride was greater than her greediness. She turned round on her little heels and, dancing her jig, began to sing, "My little stomach isn't at all pleased," until I wanted to rush at her and shake her.

A few days later, during my lessons, I was told that the Ministry refused to allow me to perform at the Vaudeville.

M. Régnier told me how sorry he was, but he added in a kindly tone :

"Oh, but, my dear child, the Conservatoire thinks a lot of you. Therefore you need not worry too much."

"I am sure that Camille Doucet is at the bottom of it," I said.

"No, he certainly is not," answered M. Régnier. "Camille Doucet was your warmest advocate ; but the Minister will not upon any account hear of anything that might be detrimental to your *début* next year."

I at once felt most grateful to Camille Doucet for his kindness in bearing no ill-will after my little sister's stupid behaviour. I began to work again with the greatest zeal, and did not miss a single lesson. Every morning I went to the Conservatoire with my governess. We started early, as I preferred walking to taking the omnibus, and I kept the franc which my mother gave me every morning, sixty centimes of which was for the omnibus, and forty for cakes. We were to walk home always, but every other day we took a cab with the two francs I had saved for this purpose. My mother never knew about this little scheme, but it was not without remorse that my kind Brabender consented to be my accomplice.

As I said before, I did not miss a lesson, and I even went to the deportment class, at which poor old M. Elie, duly curled, powdered, and adorned with lace frills, presided. This was the most amusing lesson imaginable. Very few of us attended this class, and M. Elie avenged himself on us for the abstention of the others. At every lesson each one of us was called forward. He addressed us by the familiar term of *thou*, and considered us as his property. There were only five or six of us, but we all had to go on the stage. He always stood up with his little black stick in his hand. No one knew why he had this stick.

" Now, young ladies," he would say, " the body thrown back, the head up, on tip-toes. That's it. Perfect! One, two, three, march ! "

And we marched along on tip-toes with heads up and eyelids drawn over our eyes as we tried to look down in order to see where we were walking. We marched along like this with all the stateliness and solemnity of camels ! He then taught us to make our exit with indifference, dignity, or fury, and it was amusing to see us going towards the doors either with a lagging step, or in an animated or hurried way, according to the mood in which we were supposed to be. Then we heard " Enough ! Go ! Not a word ! " For M. Elie would not allow us to murmur a single word. " Everything," he used to say, " is in the look, the gesture, the attitude ! " Then there was what he called " *l'assiette*," which meant the way to sit down in a dignified manner, to let one's self fall into a seat wearily, or the " *assiette*," which meant " I am listening, Monsieur ; say what you wish." Ah, that was distractingly complicated, that way of sitting down. We had to put everything into it : the desire to know what was going to be said to us, the fear of hearing it, the determination to go away, the will to stay. Oh, the tears that this " *assiette* " cost me. Poor old M. Elie! I do not bear him any ill-will, but I did my utmost later on to forget everything he had taught me, for nothing could have been more useless than those deportment lessons. Every human being moves about according to his or her proportions. Women who are too tall take long strides, those who stoop walk like the Eastern women; stout women walk like ducks, short-legged ones trot; very small women skip along, and the gawky ones walk like cranes. Nothing can be changed, and the deportment class has very wisely been abolished. The gesture must depict the thought, and it is harmonious or stupid according to whether the artist is intelligent or dull. On the stage one needs long arms; it is better to have them too long than too short. An artiste with short arms can never, never make a fine gesture. It was all in vain that poor Elie told us this or that. We were always stupid and awkward, whilst he was always comic, oh, so comic, poor old man!

I also took fencing-lessons. Aunt Rosine put this idea into my mother's head. I had a lesson once a week from the famous Pons. Oh, what a terrible man he was! Brutal, rude, and always teasing; he was an incomparable fencing-master, but he disliked giving lessons to " brats " like us, as he called us. He was not rich, though, and I believe, but am not sure of it, that this class had been organised for him by a distinguished patron of his. He always kept his hat on, and this horrified Mlle. de Brabender. He smoked his cigar, too, all the time, and this made his pupils cough, as they were already out of breath from the fencing exercise. What torture those lessons were! He sometimes brought with him friends of his, who delighted in our awkwardness. This gave rise to a scandal, as one day one of these gay spectators made a most violent remark about one of the male pupils named Châtelain, and the latter turned round quickly and gave him a blow in the face. A skirmish immediately occurred, and Pons, on endeavouring to intervene, received a blow or two himself. This made a great stir, and from that day forth visitors were not allowed to be present at the lesson. I obtained my mother's authorisation to discontinue attending the class, and this was a great relief to me.

I very much preferred Régnier's lessons to any others. He was gentle, had nice manners, and taught us to be natural in what we recited, but I certainly owe all that I know to the variety of instruction which I had, and which I followed up in the most devoted way.

Provost taught a broad style, with diction somewhat pompous but sustained. He specially emphasised freedom of gesture and inflexion. Beauvallet, in my opinion, did not teach anything that was any good. He had a deep, effective voice, but that he could not give to any one. It was an admirable instrument, but it did not give him any talent. He was awkward in his gestures; his arms were too short and his face common. I detested him as a professor.

Samson was just the opposite. His voice was not strong, but piercing. He had a certain acquired distinction, but was very correct. His method was simplicity. Provost emphasised breadth, Samson exactitude, and he was very particular about the finals. He would not allow us to drop the voice at the end of the phrase. Coquelin, who is one of Régnier's pupils, I believe, has a great deal of Samson's style, although he has retained the essentials of his first master's teaching. As for me, I remember my three professors, Régnier, Provost, and Samson, as though I had heard them only yesterday.

The year passed by without any great change in my life, but two months before my second examination I had the misfortune to have to change my professor. Provost was taken ill, and I went into Samson's class. He counted very much on me, but he was authoritative and persistent. He gave me two very bad parts in two very bad pieces: Hortense in *L'Ecole des Viellards*, by Casimir Delavigne, for comedy, and *La Fille du Cid* for tragedy. This piece was also by Casimir Delavigne. I did not feel at all in my element in these two *rôles*, both of which were written in hard, emphatic language. The examination day arrived, and I did not look at all nice. My mother had insisted on my having my hair done by her hairdresser, and I had cried and sobbed on seeing this "Figaro" make partings all over my head in order to separate my rebellious mane. Idiot that he was, he had suggested this style to my mother, and my head was in his stupid hands for more than hour and a half, for he never before had to deal with a mane like mine. He kept mopping his forehead every five minutes and muttering, "What hair! Good Heavens, it is horrible; just like tow! It might be the hair of a white negress!" Turning to my mother, he suggested that my head should be entirely shaved and the hair then trained as it grew again. "I will think about it," replied my mother in an absent-minded way. I turned my head so abruptly to look at her when she said this that the curling irons burnt my forehead. The man was using the irons to *uncurl* my hair. He considered that it curled naturally in such a disordered style that he must get the natural curl out of it and then wave it, as this would be more becoming to the face.

"Mademoiselle's hair is stopped in its growth by this extreme curliness. All the Tangier girls and negresses have hair like this. As Mademoiselle is going on to the stage, she would look better if she had hair like Madame," he said, bowing with respectful admiration to my mother, who certainly had the most beautiful hair imaginable. It was fair, and so long that when standing up she could tread on it and bend her head forward. It is only fair to say, though, that my mother was very short.

Finally I was out of the hands of this wretched man, and was nearly dead with fatigue after an hour and a half's brushing, combing, curling, hair-pinning, with my head turned from left to right and from right to left, &c. &c. I was completely disfigured at the end of it all, and did not recognise myself. My hair was drawn tightly back from my temples, my ears were very visible and stood out, looking positively bold in their bareness, whilst on the top of my head was a parcel of little sausages arranged near each other to imitate the ancient diadem.

I looked perfectly hideous. My forehead, which I always saw more or less covered with a golden fluff of hair, seemed to me immense, implacable.

I did not recognise my eyes, accustomed as I was to see them shadowed by my hair. My head weighed two or three pounds. I was accustomed to fasten my hair as I still do, with two hair-pins, and this man had put five or six packets in it, and all this was heavy for my poor head.

I was late, and so I had to dress very quickly. I cried with anger, and my eyes looked smaller, my nose larger, and my veins swelled. The climax was when I had to put my hat on. It would not go on the packet of sausages, and my mother wrapped my head up in a lace scarf and hurried me to the door.

F

On arriving at the Conservatoire, I hurried with *mon petit Dame* to the waiting-room, whilst my mother went direct to the theatre. I tore off the lace which covered my hair, and, seated on a bench, after relating the Odyssey of my hair-dressing, I gave my head up to my companions. All of them adored and envied my hair, because it was so soft and light and golden· They were all sorry for me in my misery, and were touched by my ugliness. Their mothers, however, were brimming over with joy in their own fat.

The girls began to take out my hair-pins, and one of them, Marie Lloyd, whom I liked best, took my head in her hands and kissed it affectionately.

" Oh, your beautiful hair, what have they done to it ? " she exclaimed, pulling out the last of the hair-pins. This sympathy made me once more burst into tears.

Finally I stood up, triumphant, without any hair-pins and without any sausages. But my poor hair was very heavy with the pomade the wretched man had put on it, and it was full of the partings he had made for the creation of the sausages. It fell now in mournful-looking, greasy flakes round my face.

I shook my head for five minutes in mad rage. I then succeeded in making the hair more loose, and I put it up as well as I could with a couple of hair-pins.

The competition had commenced, and I was the tenth on the list. I could not remember what I had to say. Madame Guérard moistened my temples with cold water, and Mlle. de Brabender, who had only just arrived, did not recognise me, and looked about for me everywhere. She had broken her leg nearly three months before, and had to hobble about on a crutch-stick, but she had resolved to come.

Madame Guérard was just beginning to tell her about the drama of the hair when my name echoed through the room : " Mademoiselle Chara Bernhardt ! " It was Léautaud, who later on was prompter at the Comédie Française, and who had a strong accent peculiar to the natives of Auvergne. " Mademoiselle Chara Bernhardt ! " I heard again, and then I sprang up without an idea in my mind and without uttering a word. I looked round for my partner who was to give me my cues, and together we made our entry.

I was surprised at the sound of my voice, which I did not

recognise. I had cried so much that it had affected my voice, and I spoke through my nose.

I heard a woman's voice say, " Poor child ; she ought not to have been allowed to compete. She has an atrocious cold, her nose is running and her face is swollen."

I finished my scene, made my bow, and went away in the midst of very feeble and spiritless applause. I walked like a somnambulist, and on reaching Madame Guérard and Mlle. de Brabender fainted away in their arms. Some one went to the hall in search of a doctor, and the rumour that " the little Bernhardt had fainted" reached my mother. She was sitting far back in a box, feeling bored to death. When I came to myself again I opened my eyes and saw my mother's pretty face, with tears hanging on her long lashes. I laid my head against hers and cried quietly, but this time the tears were refreshing, not salt ones that burnt my eyelids.

I stood up, shook out my dress, and looked at myself in the greenish mirror. I was certainly less ugly now, for my face was rested, my hair was once more soft and fluffy, and altogether there was a general improvement in my appearance.

The tragedy competition was over, and the prizes had been awarded. I had nothing at all, but mention was made of my last year's second prize. I felt confused, but it did not cause me any disappointment, as I quite expected things to be like this. Several persons had protested in my favour. Camille Doucet, who was a member of the jury, had pleaded a long time. He wanted me to have a first prize in spite of my bad recitation. He said that my examination results ought to be taken into account, and they were excellent ; and then, too, I had the best class reports. Nothing, however, could overcome the bad effect produced that day by my nasal voice, my swollen face, and my heavy flakes of hair. After half an hour's interval, during which I drank a glass of port wine and ate cakes, the signal was given for the comedy competition. I was fourteenth on the list for this, so that I had ample time to recover. My fighting instinct now began to take possession of me, and a sense of injustice made me feel rebellious. I had not deserved my prize that day, but it seemed to me that I ought to have received it nevertheless.

I made up my mind that I would have the first prize for

comedy, and with the exaggeration that I have always put into everything I began to get excited, and I said to myself that if I did not get the first prize I must give up the idea of the stage as a career. My mystic love and weakness for the convent came back to me more strongly than ever. I decided that I would enter the convent if I did not get the first prize. And the most foolish illogical strife imaginable was waged in my weak girl's brain. I felt a genuine vocation for the convent when distressed about losing the prize, and a genuine vocation for the theatre when I was hopeful about winning the prize.

With a very natural partiality, I discovered in myself the gift of absolute self-sacrifice, renunciation, and devotion of every kind—qualities which would win for me easily the post of Mother Superior in the Grand-Champs Convent. Then with the most indulgent generosity I attributed to myself all the necessary gifts for the fulfiment of my other dream, namely, to become the first, the most celebrated, and the most envied of actresses. I told off on my fingers all my qualities: grace, charm, distinction, beauty, mystery, piquancy.

Oh yes, I found I had all these, and when my reason and my honesty raised any doubt or suggested a " but " to this fabulous inventory of my qualities, my combative and paradoxical ego at once found a plain, decisive answer which admitted of no further argument.

It was under these special conditions and in this frame of mind that I went on to the stage when my turn came. The choice of my *rôle* for this competition was a very stupid one. I had to represent a married woman who was " reasonable " and very much inclined to argue, and I was a mere child, and looked much younger than my years. In spite of this I was very brilliant; I argued well, was very gay, and made an immense success. I was transfigured with joy and wildly excited, so sure I felt of a first prize.

I never doubted for a moment but that it would be awarded to me unanimously. When the competition was over, the committee met to discuss the awards, and in the meantime I asked for something to eat. A cutlet was brought from the pastry-cook's patronised by the Conservatoire, and I devoured it, to the great joy of Madame Guérard and Mlle. de Brabender, for I detested meat, and always refused to eat it.

The members of the committee at last went to their places in the large box, and there was silence in the theatre. The young men were called first on the stage. There was no first prize awarded to them. Parfouru's name was called for the second prize for comedy. Parfouru is known to-day as M. Paul Porel, director of the Vaudeville Theatre and Réjane's husband. After this came the turn of the girls.

I was in the doorway, ready to rush up to the stage. The words " First prize for comedy " were uttered, and I made a step forward, pushing aside a girl who was a head taller than I was. " First prize for comedy awarded unanimously to Mademoiselle Marie Lloyd." The tall girl I had pushed aside now went forward, slender and radiant, towards the stage.

There were a few protestations, but her beauty, her distinction, and her modest charm won the day with every one, and Marie Lloyd was cheered. She passed me on her return, and kissed me affectionately. We were great friends, and I liked her very much, but I considered her a nullity as a pupil. I do not remember whether she had received any prize the previous year, but certainly no one expected her to have one now. I was simply petrified with amazement.

" Second prize for comedy: Mademoiselle Bernhardt." I had not heard, and was pushed forward by my companions. On reaching the stage I bowed, and all the time I could see hundreds of Marie Lloyds dancing before me. Some of them were making grimaces at me, others were throwing me kisses ; some were fanning themselves, and others bowing. They were very tall, all these Marie Lloyds, too tall for the ceiling, and they walked over the heads of all the people and came towards me, stifling me, crushing me, so that I could not breathe. My face, it seems, was whiter than my dress.

On leaving the stage I went and sat down on the bench without uttering a word, and looked at Marie Lloyd, who was being made much of, and who was greatly complimented by every one. She was wearing a pale blue tarlatan dress, with a bunch of forget-me-nots in the bodice and another in her black hair. She was very tall, and her delicate white shoulders emerged modestly from her dress, which was cut very low . . . but in her case this was without danger. Her refined face, with its somewhat proud expression, was charming and very beautiful.

Although very young, she had more of a woman's fascination than any of us. Her large brown eyes shone with dilating pupils ; her small round mouth gave a sly little smile at the corners, and her wonderfully shaped nose had quivering nostrils. The oval of her beautiful face was intercepted by two little pearly, transparent ears of the most exquisite shape. She had a long, flexible white neck, and the pose of her head was charming. It was a beauty prize that the jury had conscientiously awarded to Marie Lloyd.

She had come on to the stage gay and fascinating in her *rôle* of Célimène, and in spite of the monotony of her delivery, the carelessness of her elocution, the impersonality of her acting, she had carried off all the votes because she was the very personification of Célimène, that coquette of twenty years of age who was so unconsciously cruel.

She had realised for every one the ideal dreamed of by Molière. All these thoughts shaped themselves later on in my brain, and this first lesson, which was so painful at the time, was of great service to me in my career. I never forgot Marie Lloyd's prize, and every time that I have had a *rôle* to create, the personage always appears before me dressed from head to foot, walking, bowing, sitting down, getting up.

But that is but the vision of a second ; my mind has been thinking of the soul that is to govern this personage. When listening to an author reading his work, I try to define the intention of his idea, in my desire to identify myself with that intention. I have never played an author false with regard to his idea. And I have always tried to represent the personage according to history, whenever it is a historical personage, and as the novelist describes it if an invented personage.

I have sometimes tried to compel the public to return to the truth and to destroy the legendary side of certain personages whom history, with all its documents, now represents to us as they were in reality, but the public never followed me. I soon realised that legend remains victorious in spite of history. And this is perhaps an advantage for the mind of the people. Jesus, Joan of Arc, Shakespeare, the Virgin Mary, Mahomet, and Napoleon I. have all entered into legend.

It is impossible now for our brain to picture Jesus and the Virgin Mary accomplishing humiliating human functions. They lived the life that we are living. Death chilled their sacred limbs, and it is not without rebellion and grief that we accept this fact. We start off in pursuit of them in an ethereal heaven, in the infinite of our dreams. We cast aside all the failings of humanity in order to leave them, clothed in the ideal, seated on a throne of love. We do not like Joan of Arc to be the rustic, bold peasant girl, repulsing violently the hardy soldier who wants to joke with her, the girl sitting astride her big Percheron horse like a man, laughing readily at the coarse jokes of the soldiers, submitting to the lewd promiscuities of the barbarous epoch in which she lived, and having on that account all the more merit in remaining the heroic virgin.

We do not care for such useless truths. In the legend she is a fragile woman guided by a divine soul. Her girlish arm which holds the heavy banner is supported by an invisible angel. In her childish eyes there is something from another world, and it is from this that all the warriors drew strength and courage. It is thus that we wish it to be, and so the legend remains triumphant.

X

MY FIRST ENGAGEMENT AT THE COMÉDIE FRANÇAISE

BUT to return to the Conservatoire. Nearly all the pupils had gone away, and I remained quiet and embarrassed on my bench. Marie Lloyd came and sat down by me.

" Are you unhappy ? " she asked.

" Yes," I answered. " I wanted the first prize, and you have it. It is not fair."

" I do not know whether it is fair or not," answered Marie Lloyd, " but I assure you that it is not my fault."

I could not help laughing at this.

" Shall I come home with you to luncheon ? " she asked, and her beautiful eyes grew moist and beseeching. She was an orphan and unhappy, and on this day of triumph she felt the need of a family. My heart began to melt with pity and affection. I threw my arms round her neck, and we all four went away together—Marie Lloyd, Madame Guérard, Mlle. de Brabender, and I. My mother had sent me word that she had gone on home.

In the cab my " don't care " character won the day once more, and we chattered about every one. " Oh, how ridiculous such and such a person was ! " " Did you see her mother's bonnet ? " " And old Estebenet ; did you see his white gloves ? He must have stolen them from some policeman ! " And hereupon we laughed like idiots, and then began again. " And that poor Châtelain had had his hair curled ! " said Marie Lloyd. " Did you see his head ? "

I did not laugh any more, though, for this reminded me of how my own hair had been uncurled, and it was thanks to that I had not won the first prize for tragedy.

Sarah Bernhardt with her mother.

At the time of leaving the Conservatoire.

On reaching home we found my mother, my aunt, my god-father, our old friend Meydieu, Madame Guérard's husband, and my sister Jeanne with her hair all curled. This gave me a pang, for she had straight hair and it had been curled to make her prettier, although she was charming without that, and the curl had been taken out of my hair, so that I had looked uglier.

My mother spoke to Marie Lloyd with that charming and distinguished indifference peculiar to her. My godfather made a great fuss of her, for success was everything to this *bourgeois*. He had seen my young friend a hundred times before, and had not been struck by her beauty nor yet touched by her poverty, but on this particular day he assured us that he had for a long time predicted Marie Lloyd's triumph. He then came to me, put his two hands on my shoulders, and held me facing him. " Well, you were a failure," he said. " Why persist now in going on the stage? You are thin and small, your face is pretty enough when near, but ugly in the distance, and your voice does not carry ! "

" Yes, my dear girl," put in M. Meydieu, " your god-father is right. You had better marry the miller who proposed, or that imbecile of a Spanish tanner who lost his brainless head for the sake of your pretty eyes. You will never do anything on the stage ! You'd better marry."

M. Guérard came and shook hands with me. He was a man of nearly sixty years of age, and Madame Guérard was under thirty. He was melancholy, gentle, and timid : he had been awarded the red ribbon of the Legion of Honour, and he wore a long, shabby frock coat, used aristocratic gestures, and was private secretary to M. de la Tour Desmoulins, a prominent deputy at the time. M. Guérard was a well of science, and I owe much to his kindness. My sister Jeanne whispered to me, " Sister's godfather said when he came in that you looked as ugly as possible." Jeanne always spoke of my godfather in this way. I pushed her away, and we sat down to table. All through the meal my one wish was to go back to the convent. I did not eat much, and directly after luncheon was so tired that I had to go to bed.

When once I was alone in my room between the sheets, with tired limbs, my head heavy, and my heart oppressed with keeping back my sighs, I tried to consider my wretched situation ; but sleep, the great restorer, came to the rescue, and I was very soon slumbering peacefully. When I woke I could not collect my thoughts at first. I wondered what time it was, and looked at my watch. It was just ten, and I had been asleep since three o'clock in the afternoon. I listened for a few minutes, but everything was silent in the house. On a table near my bed was a small tray on which were a cup of chocolate and a cake. A sheet of writing paper was placed upright against the cup. I trembled as I took it up, for I never received any letters. With great difficulty, by my night-light, I managed to read the following words, written by Madame Guérard : " When you had gone to sleep the Duc de Morny sent word to your mother that Camille Doucet had just assured him that you were to be engaged at the Comédie Française. Do not worry any more, therefore, my dear child, but have faith in the future.—Your *petit Dame*."

I pinched myself to make sure that I was really awake. I got up and rushed to the window. I looked out, and the sky was black. Yes, it was black to every one else, but starry to me. The stars were shining, and I looked for my own special one, and chose the largest and brightest.

I went back towards my bed and amused myself with jumping on to it, holding my feet together. Each time I missed I laughed like a lunatic. I then drank my chocolate, and nearly choked myself devouring my cake.

Standing up on my bolster, I then made a long speech to the Virgin Mary at the head of my bed. I adored the Virgin Mary, and I explained to her my reasons for not being able to take the veil, in spite of my vocation. I tried to charm and persuade her, and I kissed her very gently on her foot, which was crushing the serpent. Then in the darkness I tried to find my mother's portrait. I could scarcely see this, but I threw kisses to it. I then took up again the letter from *mon petit Dame*, and went to sleep with it clasped in my hand. I do not remember what my dreams were.

The next day every one was very kind to me. My godfather, who arrived early, nodded his head in a contented way.

" She must have some fresh air," he said. " I will treat you to a landau."

The drive seemed to me delicious, for I could dream to my heart's content, as my mother disliked talking when in a carriage.

Two days later our old servant Marguerite, breathless with excitement, brought me a letter. On the corner of the envelope there was a large stamp, around which stood the magic words " Comédie Française." I glanced at my mother, and she nodded as a sign that I might open the letter, after blaming Marguerite for handing it to me before obtaining her permission to do so.

"It is for to-morrow, to-morrow!" I exclaimed. " I am to go there to-morrow! Look—read it!"

My sisters came rushing to me and seized my hands. I danced round with them, singing, "It's for to-morrow! It's for to-morrow!" My younger sister was eight years old, but I was only six that day. I went upstairs to the flat above to tell Madame Guérard. She was just soaping her children's white frocks and pinafores. She took my face in her hands and kissed me affectionately. Her two hands were covered with a soapy lather, and left a snowy patch on each side of my head. I rushed down-stairs again like this, and went noisily into the drawing-room. My godfather, M. Meydieu, my aunt, and my mother were just beginning a game of whist. I kissed each of them, leaving a patch of soap-suds on their faces, at which I laughed heartily. But I was allowed to do anything that day, for I had become a personage.

The next day, Tuesday, I was to go to the Théâtre Français at one o'clock to see M. Thierry, who was then director.

What was I to wear? That was the great question. My mother had sent for the milliner, who arrived with various hats. I chose a white one trimmed with pale blue, a white *bavolet* and blue strings. Aunt Rosine had sent one of her dresses for me, for my mother thought all my frocks were too childish. Oh, that dress! I shall see it all my life. It was hideous, cabbage-green, with black velvet put on in a Grecian pattern. I looked like a monkey in that dress. But I was obliged to wear it. Fortunately, it was covered by a mantle of black *gros-grain* stitched all round with white. It was thought better for me to be dressed like a grown-up person, and all my clothes were only suitable for a school-girl. Mlle. de Brabender gave me a handkerchief that she had embroidered, and Madame Guérard a

sunshade.   My mother gave me a very pretty turquoise
ring.

Dressed up in this way, looking pretty in my white hat, uncomfortable in my green dress, but comforted by my mantle, I
went, the following day, with Madame Guérard to M. Thierry's.
My aunt lent me her carriage for the occasion, as she thought
it would look better to arrive in a private carriage.   Later on I
heard that this arrival in my own carriage, with a footman,
made a very bad impression.   What all the theatre people
thought I never cared to consider, and it seems to me that my
extreme youth must really have protected me from all suspicion.

M. Thierry received me very kindly, and made a little non-
sensical speech.   He then unfolded a paper which he handed to
Madame Guérard, asking her to read it and then to sign it.
This paper was my contract, and *mon petit Dame* explained
that she was not my mother.

"Ah," said M. Thierry, getting up, "then will you take it
with you and have it signed by Mademoiselle's mother?"

He then took my hand.   I felt an instinctive horror at his,
for it was flabby, and there was no life or sincerity in its grasp.
I quickly took mine away and looked at him.   He was plain,
with a red face and eyes that avoided one's gaze.   As I was
going away I met Coquelin, who, hearing I was there, had
waited to see me.   He had made his *début* a year before with
great success.

"Well, it's settled then!" he said gaily.

I showed him the contract and shook hands with him.   I
went quickly down the stairs, and just as I was leaving the
theatre found myself in the midst of a group in the doorway.

"Are you satisfied?" asked a gentle voice which I recognised
as M. Doucet's.

"Oh yes, Monsieur; thank you so much," I answered.

"But my dear child, I have nothing to do with it," he
said.

"Your competition was not at all good, but nevertheless
we feel sure of you," put in M. Régnier, and then turning to
Camille Doucet he asked, "What do you say, Excellency?"

"I think that this child will be a very great artist," he
replied.

There was a silence for a moment.

MY FIRST ENGAGEMENT 93

" Well, you have got a fine carriage! " exclaimed Beauvallet rudely. He was the first tragedian of the Comédie, and the most uncouth man in France or anywhere else.

" This carriage belongs to Mademoiselle's aunt," remarked Camille Doucet, shaking hands with me gently.

" Oh—well, I am glad to hear that," answered the tragedian.

I then stepped into the carriage which had caused such a sensation at the theatre, and drove away. On reaching home I took the contract to my mother. She signed it without reading it.

I made my mind resolutely to be some one *quand-même*.

A few days after my engagement at the Comédie Française my aunt gave a dinner-party. Among her guests were the Duc de Morny, Camille Doucet and the Minister of Fine Arts, M. de Walewski, Rossini, my mother, Mlle. de Brabender, and I. During the evening a great many other people came. My mother had dressed me very elegantly, and it was the first time I had worn a really low dress. Oh, how uncomfortable I was! Every one paid me great attention. Rossini asked me to recite some poetry, and I consented willingly, glad and proud to be of some little importance. I chose Casimir Delavigne's poem, " *L'Ame du Purgatoire*." " That should be spoken with music as an accompaniment," exclaimed Rossini when I came to an end. Every one approved this idea, and Walewski said : " Mademoiselle will begin again, and you could improvise, *cher maître*."

There was great excitement, and I at once began again. Rossini improvised the most delightful harmony, which filled me with emotion. My tears flowed freely without my being conscious of them, and at the end my mother kissed me, saying : " This is the first time that you have really moved me."

As a matter of fact, she adored music, and it was Rossini's improvisation that had moved her.

The Comte de Kératry, an elegant young hussar, was also present. He paid me great compliments, and invited me to go and recite some poetry at his mother's house.

My aunt then sang a song which was very much in vogue, and made a great success. She was coquettish and charming, and just a trifle jealous of this insignificant niece who had taken up the attention of her adorers for a few minutes.

When I returned home I was quite another being. I sat down, dressed as I was, on my bed, and remained for a long time deep in thought. Hitherto all I had known of life had been through my family and my work. I had now just had a glimpse of it through society, and I was struck by the hypocrisy of some of the people and the conceit of others. I began to wonder uneasily what I should do, shy and frank as I was. I thought of my mother. She did not do anything, though she was indifferent to everything. I thought of my aunt Rosine, who, on the contrary, liked to mix in everything.

I remained there looking down on the ground, my head in a whirl, and feeling very anxious, and I did not go to bed until I was thoroughly chilled.

The next few days passed by without any particular events. I was working hard at Iphigénie, as M. Thierry had told me that I was to make my *début* in that *rôle*.

At the end of August I received a notice requesting me to attend the rehearsal of *Iphigénie*. Oh, that first notice, how it made my heart beat. I could not sleep at night, and daylight did not come quickly enough for me. I kept getting up to look at the time. It seemed to me that the clock had stopped. I had dozed, and I fancied it was the same time as before. Finally a streak of light coming through my window-panes was, I thought, the triumphant sun illuminating my room. I got up at once, pulled back the curtains, and mumbled my *rôle* while dressing.

I thought of my rehearsing with Madame Devoyod, the leading *tragédienne* of the Comédie Française, with Maubant, with—— I trembled as I thought of all this, for Madame Devoyod was said to be anything but indulgent. I arrived for the rehearsal an hour before the time. The stage manager, Davenne, smiled and asked me whether I knew my *rôle*. "Oh yes," I exclaimed with conviction. "Come and rehearse it. Would you like to?" and he took me to the stage.

I went with him through the long corridor of busts which leads from the green-room to the stage. He told me the names of the celebrities represented by these busts. I stood still a moment before that of Adrienne Lecouvreur.

"I love that artiste," I said.

"Do you know her story?" he asked.

" Yes ; I have read all that has been written about her."

" That's right, my child," said the worthy man. " You ought to read all that concerns your art. I will lend you some interesting books."

He took me towards the stage. The mysterious gloom, the scenery reared up like fortifications, the bareness of the floor, the endless number of weights, ropes, trees, borders, battens overhead, the yawning house completely dark, the silence, broken by the creaking of the floor, and the vault-like chill that one felt—all this together awed me. It did not seem to me as if I were entering the brilliant ranks of living artistes who every night won the applause of the house by their merriment or their sobs. No, I felt as though I were in the tomb of dead glories, and the stage seemed to me to be getting crowded with the illustrious shadows of those whom the stage manager had just mentioned. With my highly strung nerves, my imagination, which was always evoking something, now saw them advance towards me stretching out their hands. These spectres wanted to take me away with them. I put my hands over my eyes and stood still.

" Are you not well ? " asked M. Davenne.

" Oh yes, thank you ; it was just a little giddiness."

His voice had chased away the spectres, and I opened my eyes and paid attention to the worthy man's advice. Book in hand, he explained to me where I was to stand, and my changes of place, &c. He was rather pleased with my way of reciting, and he taught me a few of the traditions. At the line,

Eurybate à l'autel, conduisez la victime,

he said, " Mademoiselle Favart was very effective there."

The artistes gradually began to arrive, grumbling more or less. They glanced at me, and then rehearsed their scenes without taking any notice of me at all.

I felt inclined to cry, but I was more vexed than anything else. I heard three coarse words used by one or another of the artistes. I was not accustomed to this somewhat brutal language. At home every one was rather timorous. At my aunt's people were a trifle affected, whilst at the convent, it is unnecessary to say, I had never heard a word that was out of place. It is true that I had been through the Conservatoire, but I had not cultivated any of the pupils with the exception of Marie Lloyd and Rose Baretta, the elder sister of Blanche Baretta, who is now a Sociétaire of the Comédie Française.

When the rehearsal was over it was decided that there should be another one at the same hour the following day in the public *foyer*.

The costume-maker came in search of me, as she wanted to try on my costume. Mlle. de Brabender, who had arrived during the rehearsal, went up with me to the costume-room. She wanted my arms to be covered, but the costume-maker told her gently that this was impossible in tragedy.

A dress of white woollen material was tried on me. It was very ugly, and the veil was so stiff that I refused it. A wreath of roses was tried on, but this too was so unsightly that I refused to wear it.

" Well, then, Mademoiselle," said the costume-maker dryly, " you will have to get these things and pay for them yourself, as this is the costume supplied by the Comédie."

" Very well," I answered, blushing ; " I will get them myself."

On returning home I told my mother my troubles, and, as she was always very generous, she promptly bought me a veil of white barège that fell in beautiful, large, soft folds, and a wreath of hedge roses which at night looked very soft and white. She also ordered me buskins from the shoemaker employed by the Comédie.

The next thing to think about was the make-up box. For this my mother had recourse to the mother of Dica Petit, my fellow student at the Conservatoire. I went with Madame Dica Petit to M. Massin, a manufacturer of these make-up boxes. He was the father of Léontine Massin, another Conservatoire pupil.

We went up to the sixth floor of a house in the Rue Réaumur, and on a plain-looking door read the words *Massin, manufacturer of make-up boxes*. I knocked, and a little hunchback girl opened the door. I recognised Léontine's sister, as she had come several times to the Conservatoire.

" Oh," she exclaimed, " what a surprise for us ! Titine," she then called out, " here is Mademoiselle Sarah !"

Léontine Massin came running out of the next room. She was a pretty girl, very gentle and calm in demeanour. She threw her arms round me, exclaiming, " How glad I am to see you ! And so you are going to make your début at the Comédie. I saw it in the papers."

I blushed up to my ears at the idea of being mentioned in the papers.

"I am engaged at the Variétés," she said, and then she talked away at such a rate that I was bewildered. Madame Petit did not enter into all this, and tried in vain to separate us. She had replied by a nod and an indifferent "Thanks" to Léontine's inquiries about her daughter's health. Finally, when the young girl had finished saying all she had to say, Madame Petit remarked :

"You must order your box. We have come here for that, you know."

"Oh you will find my father in his workshop at the end of the passage, and if you are not very long I shall still be here. I am going to rehearsal at the Variétés later on."

Madame Petit was furious, for she did not like Léontine Massin.

"Don't wait, Mademoiselle," she said ; "it will be impossible for us to stay afterwards."

Léontine was annoyed, and, shrugging her shoulders, turned her back on my companion. She then put her hat on, kissed me, and bowing gravely to Madame Petit, said : "I hope, Madame 'Gros-tas,' I shall never see you again." She then ran off, laughing merrily. I heard Madame Petit mutter a few disagreeable words in Dutch, but the meaning of them was only explained to me later on. We then went to the work-shop, and found old Massin at his bench, planing some small planks of white wood. His hunch-back daughter kept coming in and out, humming gaily all the time. The father was glum and harsh, and had an anxious look. As soon as we had ordered the box we took our leave. Madame Petit went out first ; Léontine's sister held me back by the hand and said quietly, "Father is not very polite, but it is because he is jealous. He wanted my sister to be at the Théâtre Français."

I was rather disturbed by this confidence, and I had a vague idea of the painful drama which was acting so differently on the various members of this humble home.

XI

MY DÉBUT AT THE HOUSE OF MOLIÈRE, AND MY FIRST DEPARTURE THEREFROM

On September 1, 1862, the day I was to make my *début*, I was in the Rue Duphot looking at the theatrical posters. They used to be put up then at the corner of the Rue Duphot and the Rue St. Honoré. On the poster of the Comédie Française I read the words "*Début of Mlle. Sarah Bernhardt.*" I have no idea how long I stood there, fascinated by the letters of my name, but I remember that it seemed to me as though every person who stopped to read the poster looked at me afterwards, and I blushed to the very roots of my hair.

At five o'clock I went to the theatre. I had a dressing-room on the top floor which I shared with Mlle. Coblentz. This room was on the other side of the Rue de Richelieu, in a house rented by the Comédie Française. A small covered bridge over the street served as a passage and means of communication for us to reach the Comédie.

I was a tremendously long time dressing, and did not know whether I looked nice or not. *Mon petit Dame* thought I was too pale, and Mlle. de Brabender considered that I had too much colour. My mother was to go direct to her seat in the theatre, and Aunt Rosine was away in the country.

When the call-boy announced that the play was about to begin, I broke into a cold perspiration from head to foot, and felt ready to faint. I went downstairs trembling, tottering, and my teeth chattering. When I arrived on the stage the curtain was rising. That curtain which was being raised so slowly and solemnly was to me like the veil being torn which was to let me have a glimpse of my future. A deep gentle voice made me turn round. It was Provost, my first professor, who had come to encourage me. I greeted him warmly, so glad was I to see him again. Samson was there, too ; I believe that he was playing that night in one of Molière's comedies. The two men were very different. Provost was tall, his silvery hair was blown about, and he had a droll face. Samson was small, precise, dainty ; his shiny white hair curled firmly and closely round his head. Both men had been moved by the same sentiment of protection for the poor, fragile, nervous girl, who was nevertheless so full of hope. Both of them knew my zeal for work, my obstinate will, which was always struggling for victory over my physical weakness. They knew that my motto " *Quand-même* " had not been adopted by me merely by chance, but that it was the outcome of a deliberate exercise of will power on my part. My mother had told them how I had chosen this motto at the age of nine, after a formidable leap over a ditch which no one could jump and which my young cousin had dared me to attempt. I had hurt my face, broken my wrist, and was in pain all over. Whilst I was being carried home I exclaimed furiously, " Yes, I would do it again, *quand-même*, if any one dared me again. And I will always do what I want to do all my life." In the evening of that day my aunt, who was grieved to see me in such pain, asked me what would give me any pleasure. My poor little body was all bandaged, but I jumped with joy at this, and quite consoled, I whispered in a coaxing way, " I should like to have some writing-paper with a motto of my own."

My mother asked me rather slyly what my motto was. I did not answer for a minute, and then, as they were all waiting quietly, I uttered such a furious " *Quand-même* " that my Aunt Faure started back exclaiming, " What a terrible child ! "

Samson and Provost reminded me of this story in order to give me courage, but my ears were buzzing so that I could not listen to them. Provost heard my " cue " on the stage, and pushed me gently forward. I made my entry and hurried towards Agamemnon, my father. I did not want to leave him again, as I felt I must have some one to hold on to. I then rushed to my mother, Clytemnestra . . . I stammered . . . and on leaving the stage I rushed up to my room and began to undress.

Madame Guérard was terrified, and asked me if I was mad.

I had only played one act, and there were four more. I realised then that it would really be dangerous to give way to my nerves. I had recourse to my own motto, and, standing in front of the glass gazing into my own eyes, I ordered myself to be calm and to conquer myself, and my nerves, in a state of confusion, yielded to my brain. I got through the play, but was very insignificant in my part.

The next morning my mother sent for me early. She had been looking at Sarcey's article in *L'Opinion Nationale*, and she now read me the following lines : " Mlle. Bernhardt who made her *début* yesterday in the *rôle* of Iphigénie, is a tall, pretty girl with a slender figure and a very pleasing expression ; the upper part of her face is remarkably beautiful. Her carriage is excellent, and her enunciation is perfectly clear. This is all that can be said for her at present."

" The man is an idiot," said my mother, drawing me to her. " You were charming."

She then prepared a little cup of coffee for me, and made it with cream. I was happy, but not completely so.

When my godfather arrived in the afternoon he exclaimed, " Good heavens ! My poor child, what thin arms you have ! "

As a matter of fact, people had laughed, and I had heard them, when stretching out my arms towards Eurybate. I had said the famous line in which Favart had made her " effect " that was now a tradition. I certainly had made no " effect," unless the smiles caused by my long, thin arms can be reckoned as such.

My second appearance was in *Valérie*, when I did make some slight success.

My third appearance at the Comédie resulted in the following *boutade* from the pen of the same Sarcey :

L'Opinion Nationale, September 12 : " The same evening *Les Femmes Savantes* was given. This was Mlle. Bernhardt's third *début*, and she assumed the *rôle* of Henriette. She was just as pretty and insignificant in this as in that of Junie [he had made a mistake, as it was Iphigénie I had played] and of Valérie, both of which *rôles* had been entrusted to her previously. This performance was a very poor affair, and gives rise to reflections by no means gay. That Mlle. Bernhardt should be insignificant does not much matter. She is a *débutante*, and among the number presented to us it is only natural that some should be failures. The pitiful part is, though, that the comedians playing with her were not much better than she was, and they are Sociétaires of the Théâtre Français. All that they had more than their young comrade was a greater familiarity with the boards. They are just as Mlle. Bernhardt may be in twenty years' time, if she stays at the Comédie Française."

I did not stay there, though, for one of those nothings which change a whole life changed mine. I had entered the Comédie expecting to remain there always. I had heard my godfather explain to my mother all about the various stages of my career.

"The child will have so much during the first five years," he said, "and so much afterwards, and then at the end of thirty years she will have the pension given to Sociétaires—that is, if she ever becomes a Sociétaire." He appeared to have his doubts about that.

My sister Régina was the cause (though quite involuntarily this time) of the drama which made me leave the Comédie. It was Molière's anniversary, and all the artistes of the Français salute the bust of the great writer, according to the tradition of the theatre. It was to be my first appearance at a " ceremony," and my little sister, on hearing me tell about it at home, besought me to take her to it.

My mother gave me permission to do so, and our old Marguerite was to accompany us. All the members of the Comédie were assembled in the *foyer*. The men and women, dressed in different costumes, all wore the famous doctor's cloak. The signal was given that the ceremony was about to commence, and every one hurried along the corridor of the busts. I was holding my little sister's hand, and just in front of us was the very fat and very solemn Madame Nathalie. She was a Sociétaire of the Comédie, old, spiteful, and surly.

Régina, in trying to avoid the train of Marie Roger's cloak, stepped on to Nathalie's, and the latter turned round and gave the child such a violent push that she was knocked against a column on which was a bust. Régina screamed out, and as she turned back to me I saw that her pretty face was bleeding.

"You miserable creature!" I called out to the fat woman, and as she turned round to reply I slapped her in the face. She proceeded to faint; there was a great tumult, and an uproar of indignation, approval, stifled laughter, satisfied revenge, pity for the poor child from those artistes who were mothers, &c. &c. Two groups were formed, one around the wretched Nathalie, who was still in her swoon, and the other around little Régina. And the different aspect of these two groups was rather strange. Around Nathalie were cold, solemn-looking men and women, fanning the fat, helpless lump with their handkerchiefs or fans. A young but severe-looking Sociétaire was sprinkling her with drops of water. Nathalie, on feeling this, roused up suddenly, put her hands over her face, and muttered in a far-away voice, " How stupid! You'll spoil my make-up! "

The younger men were stooping over Régina, washing her pretty face, and the child was saying in her broken voice, " I did not do it on purpose, sister, I am certain I didn't. She's an old cow, and she just kicked for nothing at all! " Régina was a fair-haired seraph, who might have made the angels envious, for she had the most ideal and poetical beauty—but her language was by no means choice, and nothing in the world could change it. Her coarse speech made the friendly group burst out laughing, while all the members of the enemy's camp shrugged their shoulders. Bressant, who was the most charming of the comedians and a general favourite, came up to me and said :

" We must arrange this little matter, dear Mademoiselle, for Nathalie's short arms are really very long. Between ourselves, you were a trifle hasty, but I like that, and then that child is so droll and so pretty," he added, pointing to my little sister.

The house was stamping with impatience, for this little scene had caused twenty minutes' delay, and we were obliged to go on to the stage at once. Marie Roger kissed me, saying, " You are a plucky little comrade! " Rose Baretta drew me to her, murmuring, " How dared you do it! She is a Sociétaire! "

As for me, I was not very conscious as to what I had done, but my instinct warned me that I should pay dearly for it.

The following day I received a letter from the manager asking me to call at the Comédie at one o'clock, about a matter concerning me privately. I had been crying all night long, more through nervous excitement than from remorse, and I was particularly annoyed at the idea of the attacks I should have to endure from my own family. I did not let my mother see the letter, for from the day that I had entered the Comédie I had been emancipated. I received my letters now direct, without her supervision, and I went about alone.

At one o'clock precisely I was shown into the manager's office. M. Thierry, his nose more congested than ever, and his eyes more crafty, preached me a deadly sermon, blamed my want of discipline, absence of respect, and scandalous conduct, and finished his pitiful harangue by advising me to beg Madame Nathalie's pardon.

" I have asked her to come," he added, " and you must apologise to her before three Sociétaires, members of the committee. If she consents to forgive you, the committee will then consider whether to fine you or to cancel your engagement."

I did not reply for a few minutes. I thought of my mother in distress, my godfather laughing in his *bourgeois* way, and my Aunt Faure triumphant, with her usual phrase, " That child is terrible ! " I thought too of my beloved Brabender, with her hands clasped, her moustache drooping sadly, her small eyes full of tears, so touching in their mute supplication. I could hear my gentle, timid Madame Guérard arguing with every one, so courageous was she always in her confidence in my future.

" Well, Mademoiselle ? " said M. Thierry curtly.

I looked at him without speaking, and he began to get impatient.

" I will go and ask Madame Nathalie to come here," he said, " and I beg you will do your part as quickly as possible, for I have other things to attend to than to put your blunders right."

" Oh no, do not fetch Madame Nathalie," I said at last. " I shall not apologise to her. I will leave ; I will cancel my engagement at once."

He was stupefied, and his arrogance melted away in pity for the ungovernable, wilful child, who was about to ruin her whole future for the sake of a question of self-esteem. He was at once gentler and more polite. He asked me to sit down, which he had not hitherto done, and he sat down himself opposite to me, and spoke to me gently about the advantages of the Comédie, and of the danger that there would be for me in leaving that illustrious theatre, which had done me the honour of admitting me. He gave me a hundred other very good, wise reasons which softened me. When he saw the effect he had made he wanted to send for Madame Nathalie, but I roused up then like a little wild animal.

"Oh, don't let her come here; I should box her ears again!" I exclaimed.

"Well then, I must ask your mother to come," he said.

My mother would never come," I said.

"Then I will go and call on her," he remarked.

"It will be quite useless," I persisted. "My mother has emancipated me, and I am quite free to lead my own life. I alone am responsible for all that I do."

"Well then, Mademoiselle, I will think it over," he said, rising, to show me that the interview was at an end. I went back home, determined to say nothing to my mother; but my little sister when questioned about her wound had told everything in her own way, exaggerating, if possible, the brutality of Madame Nathalie and the audacity of what I had done. Rose Baretta, too, had been to see me, and had burst into tears, assuring my mother that my engagement would be cancelled. The whole family was very much excited and distressed when I arrived, and when they began to argue with me it made me still more nervous. I did not take calmly the reproaches which one and another of them addressed to me, and I was not at all willing to follow their advice. I went to my room and locked myself in.

The following day no one spoke to me, and I went up to Madame Guérard to be comforted and consoled.

Several days passed by, and I had nothing to do at the theatre. Finally one morning I received a notice requesting me to be present at the reading of a play,—*Dolorès*, by M. Bouilhet. This was the first time I had been asked to attend the reading of a new piece. I was evidently to have a *rôle* to "create." All my sorrows were at once dispersed like a cloud of butterflies. I told my mother of my joy, and she naturally concluded that as I was asked to attend a reading my engagement was not to be cancelled, and I was not to be asked again to apologise to Madame Nathalie.

I went to the theatre, and to my utter surprise I received from M. Davennes the *rôle* of Dolorès, the chief part in Bouilhet's play. I knew that Favart, who should have had this *rôle*, was not well; but there were other artistès, and I could not get over my joy and surprise. Nevertheless, I felt somewhat uneasy. A terrible presentiment has always warned me of any troubles about to come upon me.

I had been rehearsing for five days, when one morning on going upstairs I suddenly found myself face to face with Nathalie, seated under Gérôme's portrait of Rachel, known as "the red pimento." I did not know whether to go downstairs again or to pass by. My hesitation was noticed by the spiteful woman.

"Oh, you can pass, Mademoiselle," she said. "I have forgiven you, as I have avenged myself. The *rôle* that you like so much is not going to be for you after all."

I went by without uttering a word. I was thunderstruck by her speech, which I guessed would prove true.

I did not mention this incident to any one, but continued rehearsing. It was on Tuesday that Nathalie had spoken to me, and on Friday I was disappointed to hear that Davennes was not there, and that there was to be no rehearsal. Just as I was getting into my cab the hall-porter ran out to give me a letter from Davennes. The poor man had not ventured to come himself and give me the news, which he was sure would be so painful to me.

He explained to me in his letter that on account of my extreme youth—the importance of the *rôle*—such responsibility for my young shoulders—and finally that as Madame Favart had recovered from her illness, it was more prudent that, &c. &c." I finished reading the letter through blinding tears, but very soon anger took the place of grief. I rushed back again and sent my name in to the manager's office. He could not see me just then, but I said I would wait. After one hour, thoroughly impatient, taking no notice of the office-boy and the secretary, who wanted to prevent my entering, I opened the door of M. Thierry's office and walked in. All that despair, anger against injustice, and fury against falseness could inspire me with I let him have, in a stream of eloquence only interrupted by my sobs. The manager gazed at me in bewilderment. He could not conceive of such daring and such violence in a girl so young.

When at last, thoroughly exhausted, I sank down in an arm-chair, he tried to calm me, but all in vain.

" I will leave at once," I said.   " Give me back my contract and I will send you back mine."

Finally, tired of argument and persuasion, he called his secretary and gave him the necessary orders, and the latter soon brought in my contract.

" Here is your mother's signature, Mademoiselle.   I leave you free to bring it me back within forty-eight hours.   After that time if I do not receive it I shall consider that you are no longer a member of the theatre.   But believe me, you are acting unwisely.   Think it over during the next forty-eight hours."

I did not answer, but went out of his office.   That very evening I sent back to M. Thierry the contract bearing his signature, and tore up the one with that of my mother.

I had left Molière's Theatre, and was not to re-enter it until twelve years later.

XII

AT THE GYMNASE THEATRE—A TRIP TO SPAIN

THIS proceeding of mine was certainly violently decisive, and it completely upset my home life. I was not happy from this time forth amongst my own people, as I was continually being blamed for my violence. Irritating remarks with a double meaning were constantly being made by my aunt and my little sister. My godfather, whom I had once for all requested to mind his own business, no longer dared to attack me openly ; but he influenced my mother against me. There was no longer any peace for me except at Madame Guérard's, and so I was constantly with her. I enjoyed helping her in her domestic affairs. She taught me to make cakes, chocolate, and scrambled eggs. All this gave me something else to think about, and I soon recovered my gaiety.

One morning there was something very mysterious about my mother. She kept looking at the clock, and seemed uneasy because my godfather, who lunched and dined with us every day, had not arrived.

"It's very strange," my mother said, "for last night after whist he said he should be with us this morning before luncheon. It's very strange indeed ! "

She was usually calm, but she kept coming in and out of the room, and when Marguerite put her head in at the door to ask whether she should serve the luncheon, my mother told her to wait.

Finally the bell rang, startling my mother and Jeanne. My little sister was evidently in the secret.

"Well, it's settled ! " exclaimed my godfather, shaking the snow from his hat. " Here, read that, you self-willed girl."

He handed me a letter stamped with the words " Théâtre du

Gymnase." It was from Montigny, the manager of the theatre, to M. de Gerbois, a friend of my godfather's whom I knew very well. The letter was very friendly, as far as M. de Gerbois was concerned, but it finished with the following words, " I will engage your *protégée* in order to be agreeable to you . . . but she appears to me to have a vile temper."

I blushed as I read these lines, and I thought my godfather was wanting in tact, as he might have given me real delight and avoided hurting my feelings in this way, but he was the clumsiest-minded man that ever lived. My mother seemed very much pleased, so I kissed her pretty face and thanked my god-father. Oh, how I loved kissing that pearly face, which was always so cool and always slightly dewy. When I was a little child I used to ask her to play at butterfly on my cheeks with her long lashes, and she would put her face close to mine and open and shut her eyes, tickling my cheeks whilst I lay back breathless with delight.

The following day I went to the Gymnase. I was kept wait-ing for some little time, together with about fifty other girls. M. Monval, a cynical old man who was stage manager and almost general manager, then interviewed us. I liked him at first, because he was like M. Guérard, but I very soon disliked him. His way of looking at me, of speaking to me, and of taking stock of me generally roused my ire at once. I answered his questions curtly, and our conversation, which seemed likely to take an aggressive turn, was cut short by the arrival of M. Montigny, the manager.

" Which of you is Mademoiselle Sarah Bernhardt ? " he asked.

I at once rose, and he continued, " Will you come into my office, Mademoiselle ? "

Montigny had been an actor, and was plump and good-humoured. He appeared to be somewhat infatuated with his own personality, with his ego, but that did not matter to me.

After some friendly conversation, he preached a little to me about my outburst at the Comédie. and made me a great many promises about the *rôles* I should have to play. He prepared my contract, and gave it me to take home for my mother's signature and that of my family council.

" I am emancipated," I said to him, " so that my own signature is all that is required.

"Oh, very good," he said; "but what nonsense to have emancipated a self-willed girl. Your parents did not do you a good turn by that."

I was just on the point of replying that what my parents chose to do did not concern him, but I held my peace, signed the contract, and hurried home feeling very joyful.

Montigny kept his word at first. He let me understudy Victoria Lafontaine, a young artist very much in vogue just then, who had the most delightful talent. I played in *La maison sans enfants*, and I took her *rôle* at a moment's notice in *Le démon du jeu*, a piece which made a great success. I was fairly good in both plays, but Montigny, in spite of my entreaties, never came to see me in them, and the spiteful stage manager played me no end of tricks. I used to feel a sullen anger stirring within me, and I struggled with myself as much possible to keep my nerves calm.

One evening, on leaving the theatre, a notice was handed to me requesting me to be present at the reading of a play the following day. Montigny had promised me a good part, and I fell asleep that night lulled by fairies, who carried me off into the land of glory and success. On arriving at the theatre I found Blanche Pierson and Céline Montalant already there— two of the prettiest creatures that God has been pleased to create, the one as fair as the rising sun, and the other as dark as a starry night, for she was brilliant-looking in spite of her black hair. There were other women there, too—very, very pretty ones.

The play to be read was entitled *Un mari qui lance sa femme*, and it was by Raymond Deslandes. I listened to it without any great pleasure, and I thought it stupid. I waited anxiously to see what *rôle* was to be given to me, and I discovered this only too soon. It was a certain Princess Dimchinka, a frivolous, foolish, laughing individual, who was always eating or dancing. I did not like the part at all. I was very inexperienced on the stage, and my timidity made me rather awkward. Besides, I had not worked for three years with such persistency and conviction in order to create the *rôle* of an idiotic woman in an imbecile play. I was in despair, and the wildest ideas came into my head. I wanted to give up the stage and go into business. I spoke of this to our old family friend, Meydieu, who was so unbearable.

He approved of my idea, and wanted me to take a shop—a confectioner's—on the Boulevard des Italiens. This became a fixed idea with the worthy man. He loved sweets himself, and he knew lots of recipes for various sorts of sweets that were not generally known, and which he wanted to introduce. I remember one kind that he wanted to call "*bonbon nègre*." It was a mixture of chocolate and essence of coffee rolled into grilled licorice root. It was like black *praliné*, and was extremely good. I was very persistent in this idea at first, and went with Meydieu to look at a shop, but when he showed me the little flat over it where I should have to live, it upset me so much that I gave up for ever the idea of business.

I went every day to the rehearsal of the stupid piece, and was bad-tempered all the time. Finally the first performance took place, and my part was neither a success nor a failure. I simply was not noticed, and at night my mother remarked, "My poor child, you were ridiculous in your Russian princess *rôle*, and I was very much grieved!"

I did not answer at all, but I should honestly have liked to kill myself. I slept very badly that night, and towards six in the morning I rushed up to Madame Guérard. I asked her to give me some laudanum, but she refused. When she saw that I really wanted it, the poor dear woman understood my design. "Well, then," I said, "swear by your children that you will not tell any one what I am going to do, and then I will not kill myself." A sudden idea had just come into my mind, and, without going further into it, I wanted to carry it out at once. She promised, and I then told her that I was going at once to Spain, as I had longed to see that country for a long time.

"Go to Spain!" she exclaimed. "With whom and when?"

"With the money I have saved," I answered. "And this very morning. Every one is asleep at home. I shall go and pack my trunk, and start at once with you!"

"No, no, I cannot go," exclaimed Madame Guérard, nearly beside herself. "There is my husband to think of, and my children."

Her little girl was scarcely two years old at that time.

"Well, then, *mon petit Dame*, find me some one to go with me."

"I do not know any one," she answered, crying in her excitement. "My dear little Sarah give up such an idea, I beseech you."

But by this time it was a fixed idea with me, and I was very determined about it. I went downstairs, packed my trunk, and then returned to Madame Guérard. I had wrapped up a pewter fork in paper, and this I threw against one of the panes of glass in a skylight window opposite. The window was opened abruptly, and the sleepy, angry face of a young woman appeared. I made a trumpet of my two hands and called out :

"Caroline, will you start with me at once for Spain ?" The bewildered expression on the woman's face showed that she had not comprehended, but she replied at once, "I am coming, Mademoiselle." She then closed her window, and ten minutes later Caroline was tapping at the door. Madame Guérard had sunk down aghast in an arm-chair.

M. Guérard had asked several times from his bedroom what was going on.

"Sarah is here," his wife had replied. "I will tell you later on."

Caroline did dressmaking by the day at Madame Guérard's, and she had offered her services to me as lady's maid. She was agreeable and rather daring, and she now accepted my offer at once. But as it would not do to arouse the suspicions of the concierge, it was decided that I should take her dresses in my trunk, and that she should put her linen into a bag to be lent by *mon petit Dame*.

Poor dear Madame Guérard had given in. She was quite conquered, and soon began to help in my preparations, which certainly did not take me long.

But I did not know how to get to Spain.

"You go through Bordeaux," said Madame Guérard.

"Oh no," exclaimed Caroline ; "my brother-in-law is a skipper, and he often goes to Spain by Marseilles."

I had saved nine hundred francs, and Madame Guérard lent me six hundred. It was perfectly mad, but I felt ready to conquer the universe, and nothing would have induced me to abandon my plan. Then, too, it seemed to me as though I had been wishing to see Spain for a long time. I had got it into my head that my Fate willed it, that I must obey my star, and a hundred other ideas, each one more foolish than the other, strengthened me in my plan. I was destined to act in this way, I thought.

I went downstairs again. The door was still ajar. With Caroline's help I carried the empty trunk up to Madame Guérard's, and Caroline emptied my wardrobe and drawers, and then packed the trunk. I shall never forget that delightful moment. It seemed to me as though the world was about to be mine. I was going to start off with a woman to wait on me. I was about to travel alone, with no one to criticise what I decided to do. I should see an unknown country about which I had dreamed, and I should cross the sea. Oh, how happy I was! Twenty times I must have gone up and down the staircase which separated our two flats. Every one was asleep in my mother's flat, and the rooms were so disposed that not a sound of our going in and out could reach her.

My trunk was at last closed, Caroline's valise fastened, and my little bag crammed full. I was quite ready to start, but the fingers of the clock had moved along by this time, and to my horror I discovered that it was eight o'clock. Marguerite would be coming down from her bedroom at the top of the house to prepare my mother's coffee, my chocolate, and bread and milk for my sisters. In a fit of despair and wild determination I kissed Madame Guérard with such violence as almost to stifle her, and rushed once more to my room to get my little Virgin Mary, which went with me everywhere. I threw a hundred kisses to my mother's room, and then, with wet eyes and a joyful heart, went downstairs. *Mon petit Dame* had asked the man who polished the floors to take the trunk and the valise down, and Caroline had fetched a cab. I went like a whirlwind past the concierge's door. She had her back turned towards me and was sweeping the floor. I sprang into the cab, and the driver whipped up his horse. I was on my way to Spain. I had written an affectionate letter to my mother begging her to forgive me and not to be grieved. I had written a stupid letter of explanation to Montigny, the manager of the Gymnase Theatre. The letter did not explain anything, though. It was written by a child whose brain was certainly a little affected, and I finished up with these words : " Have pity on a poor, crazy girl ! "

Sardou told me later on that he happened to be in Montigny's office when he received my letter.

"The conversation was very animated, and when the door opened Montigny exclaimed in a fury, 'I had given orders that I was not to be disturbed!' He was somewhat appeased, however, on seeing old Monval's troubled look, and he knew something urgent was the matter. 'Oh, what's happened now?' he asked, taking the letter that the old stage manager held out to him. On recognising my paper, with its grey border, he said, 'Oh, it's from that mad child! Is she ill?'

" 'No,' said Monval; 'she has gone to Spain.'

" 'She can go to the deuce!' exclaimed Montigny. 'Send for Madame Dieudonnée to take her part. She has a good memory, and half the *rôle* must be cut. That will settle it.'

" 'Any trouble for to-night?' I asked Montigny.

" 'Oh, nothing,' he answered; 'it's that little Sarah Bernhardt who has cleared off to Spain!'

" 'That girl from the Français who boxed Nathalie's ears?'

" 'Yes.'

" 'She's rather amusing.'

" 'Yes, but not for her managers,' remarked Montigny, continuing immediately afterwards the conversation which had been interrupted."

This is exactly as Victorien Sardou related the incident.

*　　　*　　　*　　　*　　　*

On arriving at Marseilles, Caroline went to get information about the journey. The result was that we embarked on an abominable trading-boat, a dirty coaster, smelling of oil and stale fish, a perfect horror.

I had never been on the sea, so I fancied that all boats were like this one, and that it was no good complaining. After six days of rough sea we landed at Alicante. Oh, that landing, how well I remember it! I had to jump from boat to boat, from plank to plank, with the risk of falling into the water a hundred times over, for I am naturally inclined to dizziness, and the little gangways, without any rails, rope, or anything, thrown across from one boat to another and bending under my light weight seemed to me like mere ropes stretched across space.

Exhausted with fatigue and hunger, I went to the first hotel recommended to us. Oh, what a hotel it was! The house itself was built of stone, with low arcades. Rooms on the first floor

H

were given to me.   Certainly the owners of these hotel people
had never had two ladies in their house before.   The bedroom
was large, but with a low ceiling.   By way of decoration there
were enormous fish bones arranged in garlands caught up by the
heads of fish.   By half shutting one's eyes this decoration
might be taken for delicate sculpture of ancient times.   In
reality, however, it was merely composed of fish-bones.

I had a bed put up for Caroline in this sinister-looking room.
We pulled the furniture across against the doors, and I did not
undress, for I could not venture on those sheets.   I was accustomed to fine sheets perfumed with iris, for my pretty little
mother, like all Dutch women, had a mania for linen and cleanliness, and she had inculcated me with this harmless mania.

It was about five in the morning when I opened my eyes, no
doubt instinctively, as there had been no sound to rouse me.
A door, leading I did not know where, opened, and a man
looked in.   I gave a shrill cry, seized my little Virgin Mary,
and waved her about, wild with terror.

Caroline roused up with a start, and courageously rushed to
the window.   She threw it up, screaming, " Fire ! Thieves !
Help ! "

The man disappeared, and the house was soon invaded by the
police.   I leave it to be imagined what the police of Alicante
forty years ago were like.   I answered all the questions asked
me by a vice-consul, who was an Hungarian and spoke
French.   I had seen the man, and he had a silk handkerchief on
his head.   He had a beard, and on his shoulder a *poncho*, but
that was all I knew.   The Hungarian vice-consul, who, I
believe, represented France, Austria, and Hungary, asked me
the colour of the brigand's beard, silk handkerchief, and *poncho*.
It had been too dark for me to distinguish the colours exactly.
The worthy man was very much annoyed at my answer.   After
taking down a few notes he remained thoughtful for a moment
and then gave orders for a message to be taken to his home.   It
was to ask his wife to send a carriage, and to get a room ready
in order to receive a young foreigner in distress.   I prepared to
go with him, and after paying my bill at the hotel we started
off in the worthy Hungarian's carriage, and I was welcomed by
his wife with the most touching cordiality.   I drank the coffee
with thick cream which she poured out for me, and during

breakfast told her who I was and where I was going. She then told me in return that her father was an important manufacturer of cloth, that he was from Bohemia, and a great friend of my father's. She took me to the room that had been prepared for me, made me go to bed, and told me that while I was asleep she would write me some letters of introduction for Madrid.

I slept for ten hours without waking, and when I roused up was thoroughly rested in mind and body. I wanted to send a telegram to my mother, but this was impossible, as there was no telegraph at Alicante. I wrote a letter, therefore, to my poor dear mother, telling her that I was in the house of friends of my father, &c. &c.

The following day I started for Madrid with a letter for the landlord of the Hôtel de la Puerta del Sol. Nice rooms were given to us, and I sent messengers with the letters from Madame Rudcowitz. I spent a fortnight in Madrid, and was made a great deal of and generally fêted. I went to all the bull-fights, and was infatuated with them. I had the honour of being invited to a great *corrida* given in honour of Victor Emmanuel, who was just then the guest of the Queen of Spain. I forgot Paris, my sorrows, disappointments, ambitions and everything else, and I wanted to live in Spain. A telegram sent by Madame Guérard made me change all my plans. My mother was very ill, the telegram informed me. I packed my trunk and wanted to start off at once, but when my hotel bill was paid I had not a *sou* to pay for the railway journey. The landlord of the hotel took two tickets for me, prepared a basket of provisions, and gave me two hundred francs at the station, telling me that he had received orders from Madame Rudcowitz not to let me want for anything. She and her husband were certainly most delightful people.

My heart beat fast when I reached my mother's house in Paris. *Mon petit Dame* was waiting for me downstairs in the concierge's room. She was very excited to see me looking so well, and kissed me with her eyes full of tears of joy. The concierge and family poured forth their compliments. Madame Guérard went upstairs before me to inform my mother of my arrival, and I waited a moment in the kitchen and was hugged by our old servant Marguerite.

My sisters both came running in. Jeanne kissed me, then turned me round and examined me. Régina, with her hands behind her back, leaned against the stove gazing at me furiously.

"Well, won't you kiss me, Régina?" I asked, stooping down to her.

"No, don't like you," she answered. "You've went off without me. Don't like you now." She turned away brusquely to avoid my kiss, and knocked her head against the stove.

Finally Madame Guérard appeared again, and I went with her. Oh, how repentant I was, and how deeply affected. I knocked gently at the door of the room, which was hung with pale blue rep. My mother looked very white, lying in her bed. Her face was thinner, but wonderfully beautiful. She stretched out her arms like two wings, and I rushed forward to this white, loving nest. My mother cried silently, as she always did. Then her hands played with my hair, which she let down and combed with her long, taper fingers. Then we asked each other a hundred questions. I wanted to know everything, and she did too, so that we had the most amusing duet of words, phrases, and kisses. I found that my mother had had a rather severe attack of pleurisy, that she was now getting better, but was not yet well. I therefore took up my abode again with her, and for the time being went back to my old bed-room. Madame Guérard had told me in a letter that my grandmother on my father's side had at last agreed to the proposal made by my mother. My father had left a certain sum of money which I was to have on my wedding-day. My mother, at my request, had asked my grandmother to let me have half this sum, and she had at last consented, saying that she should use the interest of the other half, but that this latter half would always be at my disposal if I changed my mind and consented to marry.

I was therefore determined to live my life as I wished, to go away from home and be quite independent. I adored my mother, but our ideas were altogether different. Besides, my godfather was perfectly odious to me, and for years and years he had been in the habit of lunching and dining with us every day, and of playing whist every evening. He was always hurting my feelings in one way or another. He was a very rich old bachelor, with no near relatives. He adored my mother, but she had always refused to marry him. She had put up with him at first, because he was a friend of my father's. After my father's death she had continued to put up with him, because she was then accustomed to him, until finally she quite missed him when he was ill or travelling. But, placid as she was, my mother was authoritative, and could not endure any kind of constraint. She therefore rebelled against the idea of another master. She was very gentle but determined, and this determination of hers ended sometimes in the most violent anger. She used then to turn very pale, and violet rings would come round her eyes, her lips would tremble, her teeth chatter, her beautiful eyes take a fixed gaze, the words would come at intervals from her throat, all chopped up—hissing and hoarse. After this she would faint; and the veins of her throat would swell, and her hands and feet turned icy cold. Sometimes she would be uncon-cious for hours, and the doctors told us that she might die in one of these attacks, so that we did all in our power to avoid these terrible accidents. My mother knew this, and rather took advantage of it, and, as I had inherited this tendency to fits of rage from her, I could not and did not wish to live with her. As for me, I am not placid. I am active and always ready for fight, and what I want I always want immediately. I have not the gentle obstinacy peculiar to my mother. The blood begins to boil under my temples before I have time to control it. Time has made me wiser in this respect, but not sufficiently so. I am aware of this, and it causes me to suffer.

I did not say anything about my plans to our dear invalid, but I asked our old friend Meydieu to find me a flat. The old man, who had tormented me so much during my childhood, had been most kind to me ever since my *début* at the Théâtre Français, and, in spite of my row with Nathalie, and my escapade when at the Gymnase, he was now ready to see the best in me. When he came to see us the day after my return home, I remained talking with him for a time in the drawing-room, and confided my intentions to him. He quite approved, and said that my intercourse with my mother would be all the more agreeable because of this separation.

XIII

FROM THE PORTE ST. MARTIN THEATRE TO THE ODÉON

I took a flat in the Rue Duphot, quite near to my mother, and Madame Guérard undertook to have it furnished for me. As soon as my mother was well again, I talked to her about it, and I was not long in making her agree with me that it was really better I should live by myself and in my own way. When once she had accepted the situation everything went along satisfactorily. My sisters were present when we were talking about it. Jeanne was close to my mother, and Régina, who had refused to speak to me or look at me ever since my return three weeks ago, suddenly jumped on to my lap.

"Take me with you this time!" she exclaimed suddenly. "I will kiss you, if you will."

I glanced at my mother, rather embarrassed.

"Oh, take her," she said, "for she is unbearable."

Régina jumped down again and began to dance a jig, muttering the rudest, silliest things at the same time. She then nearly stifled me with kisses, sprang on to my mother's arm-chair, and kissed her hair, her eyes, her cheeks, saying :

"You are glad I am going, aren't you? You can give everything to your Jenny!"

My mother coloured slightly, but as her eyes fell on Jeanne her expression changed and a look of unspeakable affection came over her face. She pushed Régina gently aside, and the child went on with her jig.

"We two will stay together," said my mother, leaning her head back on Jeanne's shoulder, and she said this quite unconsciously, just in the same way as she had gazed at my sister. I was perfectly stupefied, and closed my eyes so that I should not see. I could only hear my little sister dancing her jig and emphasising every stamp on the floor with the words, " And we two as well ; we two, we two ! "

It was a very painful little drama that was stirring our four hearts in this little *bourgeois* home, and the result of it was that I settled down finally with my little sister in the flat in the Rue Duphot. I kept Caroline with me, and engaged a cook. *Mon petit Dame* was with me nearly all day, and I dined every evening with my mother.

I was still on good terms with an actor of the Porte Saint Martin Theatre, who had been appointed stage manager there, Marc Fournier being at that time manager of the theatre. A piece entitled *La biche au bois* was then being given. It was a spectacular play, and was having a great success. A delightful actress from the Odéon Theatre, Mlle. Debay, had been engaged for the principal *rôle*. She played tragedy princesses most charmingly. I often had tickets for the Porte Saint Martin, and I thoroughly enjoyed *La biche au bois*. Madame Ulgade sang admirably in her *rôle* of the young prince, and amazed me. Mariquita charmed me with her dancing. She was delightful and so animated in her dances, so characteristic, and always so full of distinction. Thanks to old Josse, I knew every one.

But to my surprise and terror, one evening towards five o'clock, on arriving at the theatre to get the tickets for our seats, he exclaimed on seeing me :

" Why here is our Princess, our little *biche au bois*. Here she is ! It is the Providence that watches over theatres who has sent her."

I struggled like an eel caught in a net, but it was all in vain. M. Marc Fournier, who could be very charming, gave me to understand that I should be rendering him a great service and would " save " the receipts. Josse, who guessed what my scruples were, exclaimed :

" But, my dear child, it will still be your high art, for Mademoiselle Debay from the Odéon Theatre plays this *rôle* of Princess, and Mademoiselle Debay is the first artiste at the Odéon and the Odéon is an imperial theatre, so that it cannot be any disgrace after your studies."

Mariquita, who had just arrived, also persuaded me, and

Madame Ulgade was sent for to rehearse the duos, for I was to
sing. Yes, and I was to sing with a veritable artiste, one who
was considered to be the first artiste of the Opéra Comique.

There was but little time to spare. Josse made me rehearse
my rôle, which I almost knew, as I had seen the piece often and
I had an extraordinary memory. The minutes flew, soon running
into quarters of an hour, and these quarters of an hour made
half-hours, and then entire hours. I kept looking at the clock,
the large clock in the manager's room, where Madame Ulgade
was making me rehearse. She thought my voice was pretty,
but I kept singing out of tune, and she helped me along and
encouraged me all the time.

I was dressed up in Mlle. Debay's clothes, and the curtain
was raised. Poor me! I was more dead than alive, but my
courage returned after a triple burst of applause for the couplet
which I sang on waking in very much the same way as I should
have murmured a series of Racine's lines.

When the performance was over Marc Fournier offered me,
through Josse, a three years' engagement, but I asked to be
allowed to think it over. Josse had introduced me to a
dramatic author, Lambert Thiboust, a charming man who was
certainly not without talent. He thought I was just the ideal
actress for his heroine in La bergère d'Ivry, but M. Faille, an old
actor, who had just become manager of the Ambigu Theatre,
was not the only person to consult, for a certain M. de Chilly
had some interest in the theatre. De Chilly had made his name
in the rôle of Rodin in Le Juif errant, and after marrying a
rather wealthy wife, had left the stage, and was now interested
in the business side of theatrical affairs. He had, I think, just
given the Ambigu up to Faille.

De Chilly was then helping on a charming girl named Laurence
Gérard. She was gentle and very bourgeoise, rather pretty, but
without any real beauty or grace.

Faille told Lambert Thiboust that he was negotiating with
Laurence Gérard, but that he was ready to do as the author
wished in the matter. The only thing he stipulated was that
he should hear me before deciding. I was willing to humour
the poor fellow, who must have been as poor a manager as he
had been an artiste. I gave a short performance for him at
the Ambigu Theatre. The stage was only lighted by the

wretched *servante*, a little transportable lamp. About a yard in front of me I could see M. Faille balancing himself on his chair, one hand on his waistcoat and the fingers of the other hand in his enormous nostrils. This disgusted me horribly. Lambert Thiboust was seated near him, his handsome face smiling as he looked at me encouragingly.

I had selected *On ne badine pas avec l'amour* ; I did not want to recite verse, because I was to perform in a play in prose. I believe I was perfectly charming, and Lambert Thiboust thought so too, but when I had finished poor Faille got up in a clumsy, pretentious way, said something in a low voice to the author, and took me to his office.

" My child." remarked the worthy but stupid manager, " you are no good on the stage ! "

I resented this, but he continued :

" Oh no, no good," and as the door then opened he added, pointing to the new-comer, " here is M. de Chilly, who was also listening to you, and he will say just the same as I say."

M. de Chilly nodded and shrugged his shoulders.

" Lambert Thiboust is mad," he remarked. " No one ever saw such a thin shepherdess ! "

He then rang the bell and told the boy to show in Mlle. Laurence Gérard. I understood. and, without taking leave of the two boors, I left the room.

My heart was heavy, though, as I went back to the *foyer*, where I had left my hat. There I found Laurence Gérard, but she was fetched away the next moment. I was standing near her, and as I looked in the glass I was struck by the contrast between us. She was plump, with a wide face and magnificent black eyes ; her nose was rather *canaille*, her mouth heavy, and there was a very ordinary look about her generally. I was fair, slight, and frail-looking, like a reed, with a long, pale face, blue eyes, a rather sad mouth and a general look of distinction. This hasty vision consoled me for my failure, and then, too, I felt that this Faille was a nonentity and that de Chilly was common.

I was destined to meet with them both again later in my life : Chilly soon after, as manager at the Odéon, and Faille twenty years later, in such a wretched condition that the tears came to my eyes when he appeared before me and begged me to play for his benefit.

"Oh, I beseech you," said the poor man.   " You will be the only attraction at this performance, and I have only you to count on for the receipts."

I shook hands with him.   I do not know whether he remembered our first interview and my "*audition*," but I who remembered it well only hope that he did not.

Five days later Mlle. Debay was well again, and took her *rôle* as usual.

Before accepting an engagement at the Porte Saint Martin, I wrote to Camille Doucet. The following day I received a letter asking me to call at the Ministry. It was not without some emotion that I went to see this kind man again. He was standing up waiting for me when I was ushered into the room.   He held out his hands to me, and drew me gently towards him.

" Oh, what a terrible child ! " he said, giving me a chair. " Come now, you must be calmer.   It will never do to waste all these admirable gifts in voyages, escapades, and boxing people's ears."

I was deeply moved by his kindness, and my eyes were full of regret as I looked at him.

"Now, don't cry, my dear child ; don't cry.   Let us try and find out how we are to make up for all this folly."

He was silent for a moment, and then, opening a drawer, he took out a letter.   " Here is something which will perhaps save us," he said.

It was a letter from Duquesnel, who had just been appointed manager of the Odéon Theatre in conjunction with Chilly.

" They ask me for some young artistes to make up the Odéon company.   Well, we must attend to this." He got up, and, accompanying me to the door, said as I went away, " We shall succeed."

I went back home and began at once to rehearse all my *rôles* in Racine's plays.   I waited very anxiously for several days, consoled by Madame Guérard, who succeeded in restoring my confidence.   Finally I received a letter, and went at once to the Ministry.   Camille Doucet received me with a beaming expression on his face.

"It's settled," he said. "Oh, but it has not been easy, though," he added. "You are very young, but very celebrated already for your headstrong character. But I have pledged my word that you will be as gentle as a young lamb."

"Yes, I will be gentle, I promise," I replied, "if only out of gratitude. But what am I to do?"

"Here is a letter for Félix Duquesnel," he replied; "he is expecting you."

I thanked Camille Doucet heartily, and he then said, "I shall see you again, less officially, at your aunt's on Thursday. I have received an invitation this morning to dine there, so you will be able to tell me what Duquesnel says."

It was then half-past ten in the morning. I went home to put some pretty clothes on. I chose a dress the underskirt of which was of canary yellow, the dress being of black silk with the skirt scalloped round, and a straw conical-shaped hat trimmed with corn, and black ribbon velvet under the chin. It must have been delightfully mad looking. Arrayed in this style, feeling very joyful and full of confidence, I went to call on Félix Duquesnel. I waited a few moments in a little room, very artistically furnished. A young man appeared, looking very elegant. He was smiling and altogether charming. I could not grasp the fact that this fair-haired, gay young man would be my manager.

After a short conversation we agreed on every point we touched.

"Come to the Odéon at two o'clock," said Duquesnel, by way of leave-taking, "and I will introduce you to my partner. I ought to say it the other way round, according to society etiquette," he added, laughing, "but we are talking *théâtre*" (shop).

He came a few steps down the staircase with me, and stayed there leaning over the balustrade to wish me good-bye.

At two o'clock precisely I was at the Odéon, and had to wait an hour. I began to grind my teeth, and only the remembrance of my promise to Camille Doucet prevented me from going away.

Finally Duquesnel appeared and took me across to the manager's office.

"You will now see the other ogre," he said, and I pictured to

myself the other ogre as charming as his partner. I was therefore greatly disappointed on seeing a very ugly little man, whom
I recognised as Chilly.

He eyed me up and down most impolitely, and pretended not
to recognise me. He signed to me to sit down, and without a
word handed me a pen and showed me where to sign my name
on the paper before me. Madame Guérard interposed, laying
her hand on mine.

" Do not sign without reading it," she said.

" Are you Mademoiselle's mother ? " he asked, looking
up.

" No," she said, " but it is just as though I were."

" Well, yes, you are right. Read it quickly," he continued,
" and then sign or leave it alone, but be quick."

I felt the colour coming into my face, for this man was odious.
Duquesnel whispered to me, " There's no ceremony about him,
but he's a good fellow ; don't take offence."

I signed my contract and handed it to his ugly partner.

"You know," he remarked, "He is responsible for you. I
should not upon any account have engaged you."

" And if you had been alone, Monsieur," I answered, " I should
not have signed, so we are quits."

I went away at once, and hurried to my mother's to tell her,
for I knew this would be a great joy for her. Then, that very
day, I set off with *mon petit Dame* to buy everything necessary
for furnishing my dressing-room.

The following day I went to the convent in the Rue Notre
Dame-des-Champs to see my dear governess, Mlle. de Brabender.
She had been ill with acute rheumatism in all her limbs for
the last thirteen months. She had suffered so much that she
looked like a different person. She was lying in her little
white bed, a little white cap covering her hair ; her big nose
was drawn with pain, her washed-out eyes seemed to have no
colour in them. Her formidable moustache alone bristled up
with constant spasms of pain. Besides all this she was so
strangely altered that I wondered what had caused the
change. I went nearer, and, bending down, kissed her gently.
I then gazed at her so inquisitively that she understood instinctively. With her eyes she signed to me to look on the table
near her, and there in a glass I saw all my dear old friend's

teeth. I put the three roses I had brought her in the glass, and, kissing her again, I asked her forgiveness for my impertinent curiosity. I left the convent with a very heavy heart, for the Mother Superior told me in the garden that my beloved Mlle. de Brabender could not live much longer. I therefore went every day for a time to see my gentle old governess, but as soon as the rehearsals commenced at the Odéon my visits had to be less frequent.

One morning about seven o'clock a message came from the convent to fetch me in great haste, and I was present at the dear woman's death-agony. Her face lighted up at the supreme moment with such a holy look that I suddenly longed to die. I kissed her hands, which were holding the crucifix, and they had already turned cold. I asked to be allowed to be there when she was placed in her coffin. On arriving at the convent the next day, at the hour fixed, I found the sisters in such a state of consternation that I was alarmed. What could have happened, I wondered? They pointed to the door of the cell, without uttering a word. The nuns were standing round the bed, on which was the most extraordinary looking being imaginable. My poor governess, lying rigid on her deathbed, had a man's face. Her moustache had grown longer, and she had a beard nearly half an inch long. Her moustache and beard were sandy, whilst the long hair framing her face was white. Her mouth, without the support of the teeth, had sunk in so that her nose fell on the sandy moustache. It was like a terrible and ridiculous-looking mask, instead of the sweet face of my friend. It was the mask of a man, whilst the little delicate hands were those of a woman.

There was an awe-struck expression in the eyes of the nuns, in spite of the assurance of the nurse who had dressed the poor dead body, and had declared to them that the body was that of a woman. But the poor little sisters were trembling and crossing themselves all the time.

The day after this dismal ceremony I made my *début* at the Odéon in *Le jeu de l'amour et du hasard*. I was not suited for Marivaux's plays, as they require a certain coquettishness and an affectation which were not then and still are not among my qualities. Then, too, I was rather too slight, so that I made no success at all. Chilly happened to be passing along the corridor, just as Duquesnel was talking to me and encouraging me. Chilly pointed to me and remarked :

" *Une flûte pour les gens du monde, il n'y a même pas de mie.*"

I was furious at the man's insolence, and the blood rushed to my face, but I saw through my half-closed eyes Camille Doucet's face, that face always so clean shaven and young-look-ing under his crown of white hair. I thought it was a vision of my mind, which was always on the alert, on account of the promise I had made. But no, it was he himself, and he came up to me.

" What a pretty voice you have !" he said. " Your second appearance will be such a pleasure for us ! "

This man was always courteous, but truthful. This *début* of mine had not given him any pleasure, but he was counting on my next appearance, and he had spoken the truth. I had a pretty voice, and that was all that any one could say from my first trial.

I remained at the Odéon, and worked very hard. I was ready to take any one's place at a moment's notice, for I knew all the *rôles*. I made some success, and the students had a pre-dilection for me. When I came on to the stage I was always greeted by applause from these young men. A few old sticklers used to turn towards the pit and try and command silence, but no one cared a straw for them.

Finally my day of triumph dawned. Duquesnel had the happy idea of putting *Athalie* on again, with Mendelssohn's choruses.

Beauvallet, who had been odious as a professor, was charming as a comrade. By special permission from the Ministry he was to play Joad. The *rôle* of Zacharie was assigned to me. Some of the Conservatoire pupils were to take the spoken choruses, and the female pupils who studied singing undertook the musical part. The rehearsals were so bad that Duquesnel and Chilly were in despair.

Beauvallet, who was more agreeable now, but not choice in his language, muttered some terrible words. We began over and over again, but it was all to no purpose. The spoken choruses were simply abominable. When suddenly Chilly exclaimed :

" Well, let the young one say all the spoken choruses. They will be right enough with her pretty voice! "

Duquesnel did not utter a word, but he pulled his moustache to hide a smile. Chilly was coming round to his *protégée* after all. He nodded his head in an indifferent way, in answer to his partner's questioning look, and we began again, I reading all the spoken choruses. Every one applauded, and the conductor of the orchestra was delighted, for the poor man had suffered enough. The first performance was a veritable little triumph for me! Oh, quite a little one, but still full of promise for my future. The audience, charmed with the sweetness of my voice and its crystal purity, encored the part of the spoken choruses, and I was rewarded by three rounds of applause.

At the end of the act Chilly came to me and said, " *Thou* art adorable! " His *thou* rather annoyed me, but I answered mischievously, using the same form of speech :

" *Thou* findest me fatter? "

He burst into a fit of laughter, and from that day forth we both used the familiar *thou* and became the best friends imaginable.

Oh, that Odéon Theatre! It is the theatre I loved most. I was very sorry to leave it, for every one liked each other there, and every one was gay. The theatre is a little like the continuation of school. The young artistes came there, and Duquesnel was an intelligent manager, and very polite and young himself. During rehearsal we often went off, several of us together, to play ball in the Luxembourg, during the acts in which we were not " on." I used to think of my few months at the Comédie Française. The little world I had known there had been stiff, scandal-mongering, and jealous. I recalled my few months at the Gymnase. Hats and dresses were always discussed there, and every one chattered about a hundred things that had nothing to do with art.

At the Odéon I was happy. We thought of nothing but putting plays on, and we rehearsed morning, afternoon, and at all hours, and I liked that very much.

For the summer I had taken a little house in the Villa Montmorency at Auteuil. I went to the theatre in a *petit duc*, which I drove myself. I had two wonderful ponies that Aunt

Rosine had given to me because they had very nearly broken her neck by taking fright at St. Cloud at a whirligig of wooden horses. I used to drive at full speed along the quays, and in spite of the atmosphere brilliant with the July sunshine, and the gaiety of everything outside, I always ran up the cold, cracked steps of the theatre with veritable joy, and rushed up to my dressing-room, wishing every one I passed good morning on my way. When I had taken off my coat and gloves I went on to the stage, delighted to be once more in that infinite darkness with only a poor light (a *servante* hanging here and there on a tree, a turret, a wall, or placed on a bench) thrown on the faces of the artistes for a few seconds.

There was nothing more vivifying for me than that atmosphere, full of microbes, nothing more gay than that obscurity, and nothing more brilliant than that darkness.

One day my mother had the curiosity to come behind the scenes. I thought she would have died with horror and disgust. " Oh, you poor child," she murmured, " how can you live in that ! " When once she was outside again she began to breathe freely, taking long gasps several times. Oh yes, I could live in it, and I really only lived well in it. Since then I have changed a little, but I still have a great liking for that gloomy workshop in which we joyous lapidaries of art cut the precious stones supplied to us by the poets.

The days passed by, carrying away with them all our little disappointed hopes, and fresh days dawned bringing fresh dreams, so that life seemed to me eternal happiness. I played in turn in *Le Marquis de Villemer* and *François le Champi*. In the former I took the part of the foolish baroness, an expert woman of thirty-five years of age. I was scarcely twenty-one myself, and I looked seventeen. In the second piece I played Mariette, and made a great success.

Those rehearsals of the *Marquis de Villemer* and *François le Champi* have remained in my memory as so many exquisite hours. Madame George Sand was a sweet, charming creature, extremely timid. She did not talk much, but smoked all the time. Her large eyes were always dreamy, and her mouth, which was rather heavy and common, had the kindest expression. She had perhaps had a medium-sized figure, but she was no longer upright. I used to watch her with the most romantic affection, for had she not been the heroine of a fine love romance !

I used to sit down by her, and when I took her hand in mine I held it as long as possible. Her voice, too, was gentle and fascinating.

Prince Napoleon, commonly known as " Plon-Plon," often used to come to George Sand's rehearsals. He was extremely fond of her. The first time I ever saw that man I turned pale, and felt as though my heart had stopped beating. He looked so much like Napoleon I. that I disliked him for it. By resembling him it seemed to me that he made him seem less far away, and brought him nearer to every one.

Madame Sand introduced me to him, in spite of my wishes. He looked at me in an impertinent way : he displeased me. I scarcely replied to his compliments, and went closer to George Sand.

" Why, she is in love with you ! " he exclaimed, laughing.

George Sand stroked my cheek gently.

" She is my little Madonna," she answered ; " do not torment her."

I stayed with her, casting displeased and furtive glances at the Prince. Gradually, though, I began to enjoy listening to him, for his conversation was brilliant, serious, and at the same time witty. He sprinkled his discourses and his replies with words that were a trifle crude, but all that he said was interesting and instructive. He was not very indulgent, though, and I have heard him say base, horrible things about little Thiers which I believe had little truth in them. He drew such an amusing portrait one day of that agreeable Louis Bouilhet, that George Sand, who liked him, could not help laughing, although she called the Prince a bad man. He was very unceremonious, too, but at the same time he did not like people to be wanting in respect to him. One day an artiste, named Paul Deshayes, who was playing in *François le Champi*, came into the green-room. Prince Napoleon, Madame George Sand, the curator of the library, whose name I have forgotten, and myself were there. This artiste was common, and something of an anarchist. He bowed to Madame Sand, and addressing the Prince, said :

" You are sitting on my gloves, sir."

I

The Prince scarcely moved, pulled the gloves out, and, throwing them on the floor, remarked, " I thought this seat was clean."

The actor coloured, picked up the gloves, and went away, murmuring some revolutionary threat.

I played the part of Hortense in *Le testament de César*, by Girodot, and of Anna Danby in Alexandre Dumas's *Kean*. On the evening of the first performance of the latter piece[1] the audience was most aggravating. Dumas *père* was quite out of favour on account of a private matter that had nothing to do with art. Politics for some time past had been exciting every one, and the return of Victor Hugo from exile was very much desired. When Dumas entered his box he was greeted by yells. The students were there in full force, and they began shouting for *Ruy Blas*. Dumas rose and asked to be allowed to speak. " My young friends," he began, as soon as there was silence. " We are quite willing to listen," called out some one, " but you must be alone in your box."

Dumas protested vehemently. Several persons in the orchestra took his side, for he had invited a lady into his box, and whoever that lady might be, no one had any right to insult her in so outrageous a manner. I had never yet witnessed a scene of this kind. I looked through the hole in the curtain, and was very much interested and excited. I saw our great Dumas, pale with anger, clenching his fists, shouting, swearing, and storming. Then suddenly there was a burst of applause. The woman had disappeared from the box. She had taken advantage of the moment when Dumas, leaning well over the front of the box, was answering, " No, no, this lady shall not leave the box ! "

Just at this moment she slipped away, and the whole house, delighted, shouted, " Bravo ! " Dumas was then allowed to continue, but only for a few seconds. Cries of " *Ruy Blas ! Ruy Blas !* Victor Hugo ! Hugo ! " could then be heard again in the midst of an infernal uproar. We had been ready to commence the play for an hour, and I was greatly excited. Chilly and Duquesnel then came to us on the stage.

" *Courage, mes enfants*, for the house has gone mad," they said. " We will commence anyhow, let what will happen."

1 February 18, 1868.

"I'm afraid I shall faint," I said to Duquesnel. My hands were as cold as ice, and my heart was beating wildly. "What am I to do," I asked him, "if I get too frightened?"

"There's nothing to be done," he replied. "Be frightened, but go on playing, and don't faint upon any account!"

The curtain was drawn up in the midst of a veritable tempest, bird cries, cat-calls, and a heavy rhythmical refrain of "*Ruy Blas! Ruy Blas!* Victor Hugo! Victor Hugo!"

My turn came. Berton *père*, who was playing Kean, had been received badly. I was wearing the eccentric costume of an Englishwoman in the year 1820. As soon as I appeared I heard a burst of laughter, and I stood still, rooted to the spot in the doorway. At the very same instant the cheers of my dear friends the students drowned the laughter of the aggravators. This gave me courage, and I even felt a desire to fight. But it was not necessary, for after the second endlessly long harangue, in which I give an idea of my love for Kean, the house was delighted, and gave me an ovation.

"Ignotus" wrote the following paragraph in the *Figaro*:

"Mlle. Sarah Bernhardt appeared wearing an eccentric costume which increased the tumult, but her rich voice, that astonishing voice of hers, appealed to the public, and she charmed them like a little Orpheus."

After *Kean* I played in *La loterie du mariage*. When we were rehearsing the piece, Agar came up to me one day, in the corner where I usually sat. I had a little arm-chair there from my dressing-room, and put my feet up on a straw chair. I liked this place, because there was a little gas-burner there, and I could work whilst waiting for my turn to go on the stage. I loved embroidery and tapestry work. I had a quantity of different kinds of fancy work commenced, and could take up one or the other as I felt inclined.

Madame Agar was an admirable creature. She had evidently been created for the joy of the eyes. She was a brunette, tall, pale, with large, dark, gentle eyes, a very small mouth with full rounded lips, which went up at the corners with an imperceptible smile. She had exquisite teeth, and her head was covered with thick, glossy hair. She was the living incarnation of one of the most beautiful types of ancient Greece. Her pretty hands were long and rather soft, whilst her slow and rather heavy walk

completed the illusion. She was the great *tragédienne* of the
Odéon Theatre. She approached me, with her measured tread,
followed by a young man of from twenty-four to twenty-six
years of age.

" Well, my dear," she said, kissing me, " there is a chance for
you to make a poet happy ! " She then introduced François
Coppée. I invited the young man to sit down, and then I
looked at him more thoroughly. His handsome face, emaciated
and pale, was that of the immortal Bonaparte. A thrill of
emotion went through me, for I adore Napoleon I.

" Are you a poet, Monsieur ? " I asked.

" Yes, Mademoiselle."

His voice, too, trembled, for he was still more timid than I
was.

" I have written a little piece," he continued, " and Mlle.
Agar is sure that you will play it with her."

" Yes, my dear," put in Agar, " you are going to play it for
him. It is a little masterpiece, and I am sure you will make a
gigantic success."

" Oh, and you too. You will be so beautiful in it ! " said the
poet, gazing rapturously at Agar.

I was called on to the stage just at this moment, and on
returning a few minutes later I found the young poet talking in
a low voice to the beautiful *tragédienne*. I coughed, and Agar,
who had taken my arm-chair, wanted to give it me back. On
my refusing it she pulled me down on to her lap. The young
man drew up his chair and we chatted away together, our three
heads almost touching. It was decided that after reading the
piece I should show it to Duquesnel, who alone was capable of
judging poetry, and that we should then get permission from
both managers to play it at a benefit that was to take place
after our next production.

The young man was delighted, and his pale face lighted up
with a grateful smile as he shook hands excitedly. Agar walked
away with him as far as the little landing which projected over
the stage. I watched them as they went, the magnificent statue-
like woman and the slender outline of the young writer. Agar
was perhaps thirty-five at that time. She was certainly very
beautiful, but to me there was no charm about her, and I could
not understand why this poetical Bonaparte was in love with

this matronly woman. It was as clear as daylight that he was, and she too appeared to be in love. This interested me infinitely. I watched them clasp each other's hands, and then, with an abrupt and almost awkward movement, the young poet bent over the beautiful hand he was holding and kissed it fervently.

Agar came back to me with a faint colour in her cheeks. This was rare with her, for she had a marble-like complexion. " Here is the manuscript ! " she said, giving me a little roll of paper.

The rehearsal was over, and I wished Agar good-bye, and on my way home read the piece. I was so delighted with it that I drove straight back to the theatre to give it to Duquesnel at once. I met him coming downstairs.

" Do come back again, please ! " I exclaimed.

" Good heavens, my dear girl, what is the matter ? " he asked. " You look as though you have won a big lottery prize."

" Well, it is something like that," I said, and entering his office, I produced the manuscript.

" Read this, please," I continued.

" I'll take it with me," he said.

" Oh no, read it here at once ! " I insisted. " Shall I read it to you ? "

" No, no," he replied ; " your voice is treacherous. It makes charming poetry of the worst lines possible. Well, let me have it," he continued, sitting down in his arm-chair. He began to read whilst I looked at the newspapers.

" It's delicious ! " he soon exclaimed. " It's a perfect master-piece."

I sprang to my feet in joy.

" And you will get Chilly to accept it ? "

" Oh yes, you can make your mind easy. But when do you want to play it ? "

" Well, the author seems to be in a great hurry," I said, " and Agar too."

" And you as well," he put in, laughing, " for this is a *rôle* that just suits your fancy."

" Yes, my dear ' *Duq*,' " I acknowledged. " I too want it put on at once. Do you want to be very nice ? " I added. " If so, let us have it for the benefit of Madame —— in a fortnight from now. That would not make any difference to other arrangements, and our poet would be so happy."

"Good!" said Duquesnel, "I will settle it like that. What about the scenery, though?" he muttered meditatively, biting his nails, which were then his favourite meal when disturbed in his mind.

I had already thought that out, so I offered to drive him home, and on the way I put my plan before him.

We might have the scenery of *Jeanne de Ligneris*, a piece that had been put on and taken off again immediately, after being jeered at by the public. The scenery consisted of a superb Italian park, with flowers, statues, and even a flight of steps. As to costumes, if we spoke of them to Chilly, no matter how little they might cost he would shriek, as he had done in his *rôle* of Rodin. Agar and I would supply our own costumes.

When I arrived at Duquesnel's house, he asked me to go in and discuss the costumes with his wife. I accepted his invitation, and, after kissing the prettiest face one could possibly dream of, I told its owner about our plot. She approved of everything, and promised to begin at once to look out for pretty designs for our costumes. Whilst she was talking I compared her with Agar. Oh, how much I preferred that charming head, with its fair hair, those large, limpid eyes, and the face, with its two little pink dimples. Her hair was soft and light, and formed a halo round her forehead. I admired, too, her delicate wrists, finishing with the loveliest hands imaginable, hands that were later on quite famous.

On leaving my two friends I drove straight to Agar's to tell her what had happened. She kissed me over and over again, and a cousin of hers, a priest, who happened to be there, appeared to be very delighted with my story. He seemed to know about everything. Presently there was a timid ring at the bell, and François Coppée was announced.

"I am just going away," I said to him, as I met him in the doorway and shook hands. "Agar will tell you everything."

XIV

LE PASSANT—AT THE TUILERIES—FIRE IN
MY FLAT

THE rehearsals of *Le Passant* commenced very soon after this, and were delightful, for the timid young poet was a most interesting and intelligent talker.

The first performance took place as arranged, and *Le Passant* was a veritable triumph. The whole house cheered over and over again, and Agar and myself had eight curtain calls. We tried in vain to bring the author forward, as the audience wished to see him. François Coppée was not to be found. The young poet, hitherto unknown, had become famous within a few hours. His name was on all lips. As for Agar and myself, we were simply overwhelmed with praise, and Chilly wanted to pay for our costumes. We played this one-act piece more than a hundred times consecutively to full houses.

We were asked to give it at the Tuileries, and at the house of Princess Mathilde.

Oh, that first performance at the Tuileries! It is stamped on my brain for ever, and with my eyes shut I can see every detail again even now. It had been arranged between Duquesnel and the official sent from the Court that Agar and I should go to the Tuileries to see the room where we were to play, in order to have it arranged according to the requirements of the piece. Count de Laferrière was to introduce me to the Emperor, who would then introduce me to the Empress Eugénie. Agar was to be introduced by Princess Mathilde, to whom she was then sitting as Minerva.

M. de Laferrière came for me at nine o'clock in a state carriage, and Madame Guérard accompanied me.

M. de Laferrière was a very agreeable man, with rather stiff

manners.   As we were turning round the Rue Royale the
carriage had to draw up an instant, and General Fleury approached us.   I knew him, as he had been introduced to me by
Morny.   He spoke to us, and Comte de Laferrière explained
where we were going.   As he left us he said to me, " Good luck ! "
Just at that moment a man who was passing by took up the
words and called out, " Good luck, perhaps, but not for long,
you crowd of good-for-nothings ! "

On arriving at the Palace we all three got out of the carriage,
and were shown into a small yellow drawing-room on the ground
floor.

" I will go and inform his Majesty that you are here," said
M. de Laferrière, leaving us.

When alone with Madame Guérard I thought I would rehearse
my three curtseys.

" *Mon petit Dame*," I said, " tell me whether they are right."

I made the curtseys, murmuring, " Sire . . . Sire . . ."   I
began over again several times, looking down at my dress as
I said " Sire . . ." when suddenly I heard a stifled laugh.

I stood up quickly, furious with Madame Guérard, but
I saw that she too was bent over in a half circle.   I turned
round quickly, and behind me—was the Emperor.   He
was clapping his hands silently and laughing quietly, but still
he *was* laughing.   My face flushed, and I was embarrassed, for
I wondered how long he had been there.   I had been curtseying
I do not know how many times, trying to get my reverence
right, and saying, " There . . . that's too low. . . There ; is
that right, Guérard ? "

" Good Heavens ! " I now said to myself.   " Has he heard it
all ? "

In spite of my confusion, I now made my curtsey again, but
the Emperor said, smiling :

" Oh ! no ; it could not be better than it was just now.
Save them for the Empress, who is expecting you."

Oh, that " just now."   I wondered when it had been ?

I could not question Madame Guérard, as she was following
at some distance with M. de Laferrière.   The Emperor
was at my side, talking to me of a hundred things, but I could
only answer in an absent-minded way, on account of that " just
now."

I liked him much better thus, quite near, than in his portraits. He had such fine eyes, which he half closed whilst looking through his long lashes. His smile was sad and rather mocking. His face was pale and his voice faint, but seductive.

We found the Empress seated in a large arm-chair. Her body was sheathed in a grey dress, and seemed to have been moulded into the material. I thought her very beautiful. She too was more beautiful than her portraits. I made my three curtseys under the laughing eyes of the Emperor. The Empress spoke, and the spell was then broken. That rough, hard voice coming from that brilliant woman gave me a shock.

From that moment I felt ill at ease with her, in spite of her graciousness and her kindness. As soon as Agar arrived and had been introduced, the Empress had us conducted to the large drawing-room, where the performance was to take place. The measurements were taken for the platform, and there was to be the flight of steps where Agar had to pose as the unhappy courtesan cursing mercenary love and longing for ideal love.

This flight of steps was quite a problem. They were supposed to represent the first three steps of a huge flight leading up to a Florentine palace, and had to be half hidden in some way. I asked for some shrubs, flowers and plants, which I arranged along the three steps.

The Prince Imperial, who had come in, was then about thirteen years of age. He helped me to arrange the plants, and laughed wildly when Agar mounted the steps to try the effect. He was delicious, with his magnificent eyes with heavy lids like those of his mother, and with his father's long eyelashes. He was witty like the Emperor, whom people surnamed " Louis the Imbecile," and who certainly had the most refined, subtle, and at the same time the most generous wit.

We arranged everything as well as we could, and it was decided that we should return two days later for a rehearsal before their Majesties.

How gracefully the Prince Imperial asked permission to be present at the rehearsal! His request was granted, and the Empress then took leave of us in the most charming manner, but her voice was very ugly. She told the two ladies who were

with her to give us wine and biscuits, and to show us over the
Palace if we wished to see it. I did not care much about this,
but *mon petit Dame* and Agar seemed so delighted at the offer
that I gave in to them.

I have regretted ever since that I did so, for nothing could
have been uglier than the private rooms, with the exception of
the Emperor's study and the staircases. This inspection of the
Palace bored me terribly. A few of the pictures consoled me,
and I stayed some time gazing at Winterhalter's portrait
representing the Empress Eugénie. She looked beautiful, and
I thanked Heaven that the portrait could not speak, for it
served to explain and justify the wonderful good luck of her
Majesty.

The rehearsal took place without any special incident. The
young Prince did his utmost to prove to us his gratitude and
delight, for we had made it a dress rehearsal on his account,
as he was not to be present at the *soirée*. He sketched my
costume, and intended to have it copied for a *bal déguisé* which
was to be given for the Imperial child. Our performance was
in honour of the Queen of Holland, accompanied by the Prince
of Orange, commonly known in Paris as " Prince Citron."

A rather amusing incident occurred during the evening. The
Empress had remarkably small feet, and in order to make them
look still smaller she encased them in shoes that were too narrow.
She looked wonderfully beautiful that night, with her pretty
sloping shoulders emerging from a dress of pale blue satin
embroidered with silver. On her lovely hair she was wearing a
little diadem of turquoises and diamonds, and her small feet
were on a cushion of silver brocade. All through Coppée's
piece my eyes wandered frequently to this cushion, and I saw
the two little feet moving restlessly about. Finally I saw one
of the shoes pushing its little brother very, very gently, and
then I saw the heel of the Empress come out of its prison. The
foot was then only covered at the toe, and I was very anxious to
know how it would get back, for under such circumstances the
foot swells, and cannot go into a shoe that is too narrow.
When the piece was over we were recalled twice, and as it was
the Empress who started the applause, I thought she was
putting off the moment for getting up, and I saw her pretty
little sore foot trying in vain to get back into its shoe. The

curtains were drawn, and as I had told Agar about the cushion drama, we watched through them its various phases.

The Emperor rose, and every one followed his example. He offered his arm to the Queen of Holland, but she looked at the Empress, who had not yet risen. The Emperor's face lighted up with that smile which I had already seen. He said a word to General Fleury, and immediately the generals and other officers on duty, who were seated behind the sovereigns, formed a rampart between the crowd and the Empress. The Emperor and the Queen of Holland then passed on, without appearing to have noticed her Majesty's distress, and the Prince of Orange, with one knee on the ground, helped the beautiful sovereign to put on her Cinderella-like slipper. I saw that the Empress leaned more heavily on the Prince's arm than she would have liked, for her pretty foot was evidently rather painful.

We were then sent for to be complimented, and we were surrounded and fêted so much that we were delighted with our evening.

After *Le Passant* and the prodigious success of that adorable piece, a success in which Agar and I had our share, Chilly thought more of me, and began to like me. He insisted on paying for our costumes, which was great extravagance for him. I had become the adored queen of the students, and I used to receive little bouquets of violets, sonnets, and long, long poems—too long to read. Sometimes on arriving at the theatre as I was getting out of my carriage I received a shower of flowers which simply covered me, and I was delighted, and used to thank my worshippers. The only thing was that their admiration blinded them, so that when in some pieces I was not so good, and the house was rather chary of applause, my little army of students would be indignant and would cheer wildly, without rhyme or reason. I can understand quite well that this used to exasperate the regular subscribers of the Odéon, who were very kindly disposed towards me nevertheless, as they too used to spoil me, but they would have liked me to be more humble and meek, and less headstrong. How many times one or another of these old subscribers would come and give me a word of advice. "Mademoiselle, you were charming in *Junie*," one of them observed; "but you bite your lips, and the Roman women never did that!"

"My dear girl," another said, "you were delicious in *François le Champi*, but there is not a single Breton woman in the whole of Brittany with her hair curled."

A professor from the Sorbonne said to me one day rather curtly, "It is a want of respect, Mademoiselle, to turn your back on the public!"

"But, Monsieur," I replied, "I was accompanying an old lady to a door at the back of the stage. I could not walk along with her backwards."

"The artistes we had before you, Mademoiselle, who were quite as talented as you, if not more so, had a way of going across the stage without turning their back on the public."

And he turned quickly on his heel and was going away, when I stopped him.

"Monsieur, will you go to that door, through which you intended to pass, without turning your back on me?"

He made an attempt, and then, furious, turned his back on me and disappeared, slamming the door after him.

I lived some time at 16 Rue Auber, in a flat on the first floor, which was rather a nice one. I had furnished it with old Dutch furniture which my grandmother had sent me. My godfather advised me to insure against fire, as this furniture, he told me, constituted a small fortune. I decided to follow his advice, and asked *mon petit Dame* to take the necessary steps for me. A few days later she told me that some one would call about it on the 12th.

On the day in question, towards two o'clock, a gentleman called, but I was in an extremely nervous condition, and said: "No, I must be left alone to-day. I do not wish to see any one."

I had refused to be disturbed, and had shut myself up in my bedroom in a frightfully depressed state.

That same evening I received a letter from the fire insurance company, La Foncière, asking which day their agent might call to have the agreement signed. I replied that he might come on Saturday.

On Friday I was so utterly wretched that I sent to ask my mother to come and lunch with me. I was not playing that day, as I never used to perform on Tuesdays and Fridays, days on which répertoire plays only were given. As I was playing every other day in new pieces, it was feared that I should be over-tired.

My mother on arriving thought I looked very pale.

"Yes," I replied. "I do not know what is the matter with me, but I am in a very nervous state and most depressed."

The governess came to fetch my little boy, to take him out for a walk, but I would not let him go.

"Oh no!" I exclaimed. "The child must not leave me to-day. I am afraid of something happening."

What happened was fortunately of a less serious nature than, with my love for my family, I was dreading.

I had my grandmother living with me at that time, and she was blind. It was the grandmother who had given me most of my furniture. She was a spectral-looking woman, and her beauty was of a cold, hard type. She was very tall indeed, six feet, but she looked like a giantess. She was thin and very upright, and her long arms were always stretched in front of her, feeling for all the objects in her way, so that she might not knock herself, although she was always accompanied by the nurse whom I had engaged for her. Above this long body was her little face, with two immense pale blue eyes, which were always open, even when asleep at night. She was generally dressed from head to foot in grey, and this neutral colour gave something unreal to her general appearance.

My mother, after trying to comfort me, went away about two o'clock. My grandmother, seated opposite me in her large Voltaire armchair, questioned me:

"What are you afraid of?" she asked. "Why are you so mournful? I have not heard you laugh all day."

I did not answer, but looked at my grandmother. It seemed to me that the trouble I was dreading would come through her.

"Are you not there?" she insisted.

"Yes, I am here," I answered; "but please do not talk to me."

She did not utter another word, but with her two hands on her lap sat there for hours. I sketched her strange, fatidical face.

It began to grow dusk, and I thought I would go and dress, after being present at the meal taken by my grandmother and the child. My friend Rose Baretta was dining with me that evening, and I had also invited a most charming and witty man,

Charles Haas. Arthur Meyer came too. He was a young journalist already very much in vogue. I told them about my forebodings with regard to that day, and begged them not to leave me before midnght.

"After that," I said, "it will not be to-day, and the wicked spirits who are watching me will have missed their chance."

They agreed to humour my fancy, and Arthur Meyer, who was to have gone to some first night at one of the theatres, remained with us. Dinner was more animated than luncheon had been, and it was nine o'clock when we left the table. Rose Baretta sang us some delightful old songs. I went away for a minute to see that all was right in my grandmother's room. I found my maid with her head wrapped up in cloths soaked in sedative water. I asked what was the matter, and she said that she had a terrible headache. I told her to prepare my bath and everything for me for the night, and then to go to bed. She thanked me, and obeyed.

I went back to the drawing-room, and, sitting down to the piano, played "Il Bacio," Mendelssohn's "Bells," and Weber's "Last Thought." I had not come to the end of this last melody when I stopped, suddenly hearing in the street cries of "Fire! Fire!"

"'They are shouting 'Fire!'" exclaimed Arthur Meyer.

"That's all the same to me," I said, shrugging my shoulders. "It is not midnight yet, and I am expecting my own misfortune."

Charles Haas had opened the drawing-room window to see where the shouts were coming from. He stepped out on to the balcony, and then came quickly in again.

"The fire is here!" he exclaimed. "Look!"

I rushed to the window, and saw the flames coming from the two windows of my bedroom. I ran back through the drawing-room in to the corridor, and then to the room where my child was sleeping with his governess and his nurse. They were all fast asleep. Arthur Meyer opened the hall door, the bell of which was being rung violently. I roused the two women quickly, wrapped the sleeping child in his blankets, and rushed to the door with my precious burden. I then ran downstairs, and, crossing the street, took him to Guadacelli's chocolate shop opposite, just at the corner of the Rue Caumartin.

The kind man took my little slumberer in and let him lie on a couch, where the child continued his sleep without any break. I left him in charge of his governess and his nurse, and went quickly back to the flaming house. The firemen, who had been sent for, had not yet arrived, and at all costs I was determined to rescue my poor grandmother. It was impossible to go back up the principal staircase, as it was filled with smoke.

Charles Haas, bareheaded and in evening dress, a flower in his button-hole, started with me up the narrow back staircase. We were soon on the first floor, but when once there my knees shook; it seemed as thought my heart had stopped, and I was seized with despair. The kitchen door, at the top of the first flight of stairs, was locked with a triple turn of the key. My amiable companion was tall, slight, and elegant, but not strong. I besought him to go down and fetch a hammer, a hatchet, or something, but just at that moment a new-comer wrenched the door open by a violent plunge with his shoulder against it. This new arrival was no other than M. Sohège, a friend of mine. He was a most charming and excellent man, a broad-shouldered Alsatian, well known in Paris, very lively and kind, and always ready to do any one a service. I took my friends to my grandmother's room. She was sitting up in bed, out of breath with calling Catherine, the servant who waited upon her. This maid was about twenty-five years of age, a big, strapping girl from Burgundy, and she was now sleeping peacefully, in spite of the uproar in the street, the noise of the fire-engines, which had arrived at last, and the wild shrieks of the occupants of the house. Sohège shook the maid, whilst I explained to my grandmother the reason of the tumult and why we were in her room.

"Very good," she said; and then she added calmly, " Will you give me the box, Sarah, that you will find at the bottom of the wardrobe ? The key of it is here."

" But, grandmother," I exclaimed, " the smoke is beginning to come in here. We have not any time to lose."

" Well, do as you like. I shall not leave without my box ! "

With the help of Charles Haas and of Arthur Meyer we put my grandmother on Sohège's back in spite of herself. He was of medium height, and she was extremely tall, so that her long legs touched the ground, and I was afraid she might get them

injured.　Sohège therefore took her in his arms, and Charles
Haas carried her legs.　We then set off, but the smoke stifled
us, and after descending about ten stairs I fell down in a faint.

When I came to myself I was in my mother's bed.　My little
boy was asleep in my sister's room, and my grandmother was
installed in a large armchair.　She sat bolt upright, frowning,
and with an angry expression on her lips.　She did not trouble
about anything but her box, until at last my mother was angry,
and reproached her in Dutch with only caring for herself.　She
answered excitedly, and her neck craned forward as though to
help her head to peer through the perpetual darkness which
surrounded her.　Her thin body, wrapped in an Indian shawl
of many colours, the hissing of her strident words, which flowed
freely, all contributed to make her resemble a serpent in some
terrible nightmare.　My mother did not like this woman, who
had married my grandfather when he had six big children, the
eldest of whom was sixteen and the youngest, my uncle, five
years.　This second wife had never had any children of her own,
and had been indifferent, even harsh, towards those of her
husband ; and consequently she was not liked in the family.　I
had taken charge of her because small-pox had broken out in
the family with whom she had been boarding.　She had then
wished to stay with me, and I had not had courage enough to
oppose her.

On the occasion of the fire, though, I considered she behaved
so badly that a strong dislike to her came over me, and I
resolved not to keep her with me.　News of the fire was
brought to us.　It continued to rage, and burnt everything in
my flat, absolutely everything, even to the very last book in my
library.　My greatest sorrow was that I had lost a magnificent
portrait of my mother by Bassompierre Severin, a pastelist very
much *à la mode* under the Empire ; an oil portrait of my
father, and a very pretty pastel of my sister Jeanne.　I had
not much jewellery, and all that was found of the bracelet given
to me by the Emperor was a huge shapeless mass, which I still
have.　I had a very pretty diadem, set with diamonds and
pearls, given to me by Kalil Bey after a performance at his
house.　The ashes of this had to be sifted in order to find the
stones.　The diamonds were there, but the pearls had melted.

I was absolutely ruined, for the money that my father and his

mother had left me I had spent in furniture, curiosities, and a
hundred other useless things, which were the delight of my
life. I had, too, and I own it was absurd, a tortoise named
Chrysagère. Its back was covered with a shell of gold set with
very small blue, pink, and yellow topazes. Oh, how beautiful
it was, and how droll! It used to wander round my flat,
accompanied by a smaller tortoise named Zerbinette, which was
its servant, and I used to amuse myself for hours watching
Chrysagère, flashing with a hundred lights under the rays of the
sun or the moon. Both my tortoises died in this fire.

Duquesnel, who was very kind to me at that time, came to see
me a few weeks later, for he had just received a summons from
La Foncière, the fire insurance company, whose papers I
had refused to sign the day before the catastrophe. The
company claimed a heavy sum of money from me for damages
done to the house itself. The second storey was almost entirely
destroyed, and for many months the whole building had to
be propped up. I did not possess the 40,000 francs claimed.
Duquesnel offered to give a benefit performance for me, which
would, he said, free me from all difficulties. De Chilly was
very willing to agree to anything that would be of ervice to me.
The benefit was a wonderful success, thanks to the presence of
the adorable Adelina Patti. The young singer, who was then
the Marquise de Caux, had never before sung at a benefit
performance, and it was Arthur Meyer who brought me the
news that " La Patti " was going to sing for me. Her husband
came during the afternoon to tell me how glad she was of this
opportunity of proving to me her sympathy. As soon as the
" fairy bird " was announced, every seat in the house was promptly
taken at prices which were higher than those originally fixed.
She had no reason to regret her friendly action, for never was
any triumph more complete. The students greeted her with
three cheers as she came on the stage. She was a little surprised
at this noise of bravos in rhythm. I can see her now coming
forward, her two little feet encased in pink satin. She was like a
bird hesitating as to whether it would fly or remain on the
ground. She looked so pretty, so smiling, and when she trilled
out the gem-like notes of her wonderful voice the whole house
was delirious with excitement.

Every one sprang up, and the students stood on their seats,

K

waved their hats and handkerchiefs, nodded their young heads in their feverish enthusiasm for art, and " encored " with intonations of the most touching supplication.

The divine singer then began again, and three times over she had to sing the Cavatina from *Il Barbière de Seville*, " *Una voce poco fa.*"

I thanked her affectionately afterwards, and she left the theatre escorted by the students, who followed her carriage for a long way, shouting over and over again, " Long live Adelina Patti ! " Thanks to that evening's performance I was able to pay the insurance company. I was ruined all the same, or very nearly so.

I stayed a few days with my mother, but we were so cramped for room there that I took a furnished flat in the Rue de l'Arcade. It was a dismal house, and the flat was dark. I was wondering how I should get out of my difficulties, when one morning M. C——, my father's notary, was announced. This was the man I disliked so much, but I gave orders that he should be shown in. I was surprised that I had not seen him for so long a time. He told me that he had just returned from Hamburg, that he had seen in the newspaper an account of my misfortune, and had now come to put himself at my service. In spite of my distrust, I was touched by this, and I related to him the whole drama of my fire. I did not know how it had started, but I vaguely suspected my maid Josephine of having placed my lighted candle on the little table to the left of the head of my bed. I had frequently warned her not to do this, but it was on this little piece of furniture that she always placed my waterbottle and glass, and a dessert dish with a couple of raw apples, for I adore eating apples when I wake in the night. On opening the door there was always a terrible draught, as the windows were left open until I went to bed. On closing the door after her the lace bed-curtains had probably caught fire. I could not explain the catastrophe in any other way. I had several times seen the young servant do this stupid thing, and I supposed that on the night in question she had been in a hurry to go to bed on account of her bad headache. As a rule, when I was going to undress myself she prepared everything, and then came in and told me, but this time she had not done so. Usually, too, I just went into the room myself to see that everything was right, and several times I had been obliged to move the candle. That day, however, was destined to bring me misfortune of some kind, though it was not a very great one.

" But," said the notary, " you were not insured, then ? "

" No ; I was to sign my policy the day after the event."

" Ah ! " exclaimed the man of law, " and to think that I have been told you set the flat on fire yourself in order to receive a large sum of money ! "

I shrugged my shoulders, for I had seen insinuations to this effect in a newspaper. I was very young at this time, but I already had a certain disdain for tittle-tattle.

" Oh well, I must arrange matters for you if things are like this," said Maître C——. " You are really better off than you imagine as regards the money on your father's side," he continued. " As your grandmother leaves you an annuity, you can get a good amount for this by agreeing to insure your life for 250,000 francs for forty years, for the benefit of the purchaser."

I agreed to everything, and was only too delighted at such a windfall. This man promised to send me two days after his return 120,000 francs, and he kept his word My reason for giving the details of this little episode, which after all belongs to my life, is to show how differently things turn out from what seems likely according to logic or according to our own expectations. It is quite certain that the accident which had just then happened to me scattered to the winds the hopes and plans of my life. I had arranged for myself a luxurious home with the money that my father and mother had left me. I had kept by me and invested a sufficient amount of money so as to be sure to complete my monthly salary for the next two years : I reckoned that at the end of the two years I should be in a position to demand a very high salary. And all these arrangements had been upset by the carelessness of a domestic. I had rich relatives and very rich friends, but not one amongst them stretched out a hand to help me out of the ditch into which I had fallen. My rich relatives had not forgiven me for going on to the stage. And yet Heaven knows what tears it had cost me to take up this career that had been forced upon me. My Uncle Faure came to see me at my mother's house, but my aunt would not listen to a word about me. I used to see my cousin secretly, and sometimes his pretty sister. My rich friends considered that I was wildly extravagant, and could not understand why I did not place the money I had inherited in good, sound investments.

I received a great deal of verse on the subject of my fire. Most of it was anonymous. I have kept it all, however, and I quote the following poem, which is rather nice:

Passant, te voilà sans abri :
　　La flamme a ravagé ton gîte.
Hier plus léger qu'un colibri ;
　　Ton esprit aujourd'hui s'agite,
S'exhalant en gémissements
　　Sur tout ce que le feu dévore.
Tu pleures tes beaux diamants ? . . .
　　Non, tes grands yeux les ont encore !

Ne regrette pas ces colliers
　　Qu'ont à leur cou les riches dames !
Tu trouveras dans les halliers,
　　Des tissus verts, aux fines trames !
Ta perle ? . . Mais, c'est le jais noir
　　Qui sur l'envers du fossé pousse !
Et le cadre de ton miroir
　　Est une bordure de mousse !

Tes bracelets ? . . Mais, tes bras nus,
　　Tu paraîtras cent fois plus belle !
Sur les bras jolis de Vénus,
　　Aucun cercle d'or n'étincelle !
Garde ton charme si puissant !
　　Ton parfum de plante sauvage !
Laisse les bijoux, O Passant,
　　A celles que le temps ravage !

Avec ta guitare à ton cou,
　　Va, par la France et par l'Espagne !
Suis ton chemin ; je ne sais où. . . .
　　Par la plaine et par la montagne !
Passe, comme la plume au vent !
　　Comme le son de ta mandore !
Comme un flot qui baise en rêvant,
　　Les flancs d'une barque sonore !

The proprietor of one of the hotels now very much in

vogue sent me the following letter, which I quote word for
word :

"MADAME,—If you would consent to dine every evening for a
month in our large dining-room, I would place at your service
a suite of rooms on the first floor, consisting of two bedrooms,
a large drawing-room, a small boudoir, and a bath-room. It is
of course understood that this suite of rooms would be yours
free of charge if you would consent to do as I ask.—Yours, etc.

"(P.S.) You would only have to pay for the fresh supplies
of plants for your drawing-room."

This was the extent of the man's coarseness. I asked one of
my friends to go and give the low fellow his answer.

I was in despair, though, for I felt that I could not live
without comfort and luxury.

I soon made up my mind as to what I must do, but not
without sorrow. I had been offered a magnificent engagement
in Russia, and I should have to accept it. Madame Guérard
was my sole confidant, and I did not mention my plan to
any one else. The idea of Russia terrified her, for at that
time my chest was very delicate, and cold was my most cruel
enemy. It was just as I had made up my mind to this that the
lawyer arrived. His avaricious and crafty mind had schemed
out the clever and, for him, profitable combination which was
to change my whole life once more.

I took a pretty flat on the first floor of a house in the Rue de
Rome. It was very sunny, and that delighted me more than
anything else. There were two drawing-rooms and a large
dining-room. I arranged for my grandmother to live at a
home kept by lay sisters and nuns. She was a Jewess, and carried
out very strictly all the laws laid down by her religion. The
house was very comfortable, and my grandmother took her own
maid with her, the young girl from Burgundy, to whom she
was accustomed.

When I went to see her she told me that she was much better
off there than with me. "When I was with you," she said,
"I found your boy too noisy." I very rarely went to visit her
there, for after seeing my mother turn pale at her unkind
words I never cared any more for her. She was happy, and
that was the essential thing.

I now played successfully in *Le Bâtard*, in which I had great success, in *L'Affranchi*, in *L'Autre* by George Sand, and in *Jean-Marie*, a little masterpiece by André Theuriet, which had the most brilliant success.   Porel played the part of Jean-Marie. He was at that time slender, and full of hope.   Since then his slenderness has developed into plumpness and his hope into certitude.

XV

THE FRANCO-PRUSSIAN WAR

EVIL days then came upon us. Paris began to get feverish and excited. The streets were black with groups of people, discussing and gesticulating. And all this noise was only the echo of far-distant groups gathered together in German streets. These other groups were yelling, gesticulating, and discussing, but—they knew, whilst we did not know!

I could not keep calm, but was extremely excited, until finally I was ill. War was declared, and I hate war! It exasperates me and makes me shudder from head to foot. At times I used to spring up terrified, upset by the distant cries of human voices.

Oh, war! What infamy, shame, and sorrow! War! What theft and crime, abetted, forgiven, and glorified!

Recently, I visited a huge steel works. I will not say in what country, for all countries have been hospitable to me, and I am neither a spy nor a traitress. I only set forth things as I see them. Well, I visited one of these frightful manufactories, in which the most deadly weapons are made. The owner of it all, a multi-millionaire, was introduced to me. He was pleasant, but no good at conversation, and he had a dreamy, dissatisfied look. My cicerone informed me that this man had just lost a huge sum of money, nearly sixty million francs.

"Good Heavens!" I exclaimed; "how has he lost it?"

"Oh well, he has not exactly lost the money, but has just missed making the sum, so it amounts to the same thing."

I looked perplexed, and he added, "Yes; you remember that there was a great deal of talk about war between France and Germany with regard to the Morocco affair?"

"Yes."

"Well, this prince of the steel trade expected to sell cannons for it, and for a month his men were very busy in the factory, working day and night. He gave enormous bribes to influential members of the Government, and paid some of the papers in France and Germany to stir up the people. Everything has fallen through, thanks to the intervention of men who are wise and humanitarian. The consequence is that this millionaire is in despair. He has lost sixty or perhaps a hundred million francs."

I looked at the wretched man with contempt, and I wished heartily that he could be suffocated with his millions, as remorse was no doubt utterly unknown to him.

And how many others merit our contempt just as this man does! Nearly all those who are known as "suppliers to the army," in every country in the world, are the most desperate propagators of war.

Let every man be a soldier in the time of peril. Yes, a thousand times over, yes! Let every man be armed for the defence of his country, and let him kill in order to defend his family and himself. That is only reasonable. But that there should be, in our times, young men whose sole dream is to kill in order to make a position for themselves, that is inconceivable!

It is indisputable that we must guard our frontiers and our colonies, but since all men are soldiers, why not take these guards and defenders from among "all men"? We should only have schools for officers then, and we should have no more of those horrible barracks which offend the eye. And when sovereigns visit each other and are invited to a review, would they not be much more edified as to the value of a nation if it could show a thousandth part of its effective force chosen haphazard among its soldiers, rather than the elegant evolutions of an army prepared for parade? What magnificent reviews I have seen in all the different countries I have visited! But I know from history that such and such an army as was prancing about there so finely before us had taken flight, without any great reason, before the enemy.

On July 19 war was seriously declared, and Paris then became the theatre of the most touching and burlesque scenes. Excitable and delicate as I was, I could not bear the sight of all these young men gone wild, who were yelling the "Marseillaise" and rushing along the streets in close file, shouting over and over again, "To Berlin!   To Berlin!"

My heart used to beat wildly, for I too thought that they were going to Berlin.   I understood the fury they felt, for these people had provoked us without plausible reasons, but at the same time it seemed to me that they were getting ready for this great deed without sufficient respect and dignity.   My own impotence made me feel rebellious, and when I saw all the mothers, with pale faces and eyes swollen with crying, holding their boys in their arms and kissing them in despair, the most frightful anguish seemed to choke me.   I cried, too, almost unceasingly, and I was wearing myself away with anxiety, but I did not foresee the horrible catastrophe that was to take place.

The doctors decided that I must go to Eaux-Bonnes.   I did not want to leave Paris, for I had caught the general fever of excitement.   My weakness increased, though, day by day, and on July 27 I was taken away in spite of myself.   Madame Guérard, my man-servant, and my maid accompanied me, and I also took my child with me.

In all the railway stations there were posters everywhere, announcing that the Emperor Napoleon had gone to Metz to take command of the army.

At Eaux-Bonnes I was compelled to remain in bed.   My condition was considered very serious by Dr. Leudet, who told me afterwards that he certainly thought I was going to die.   I vomited blood, and had to have a piece of ice in my mouth all the time.   At the end of about twelve days, however, I began to get up, and after this I soon recovered my strength and my calmness, and went for long rides on horseback.

The war news led us to hope for victory.   There was great joy and a certain emotion felt by every one on hearing that the young Prince Imperial had received his baptism of fire at Saar-bruck, in the engagement commanded by General Frossard.

Life seemed to me beautiful again, for I had great confidence in the issue of the war.   I pitied the Germans for having embarked on such an adventure.   But, alas! the fine, glorious progress which my brain had been so active in imagining was cut short by the atrocious news from Saint-Privat.   The political news was posted up every day in the little garden of the Casino at Eaux-Bonnes.   The public went there to get information.

Detesting, as I did, tranquillity, I used to send my man-servant to copy the telegrams. Oh, how grievous was that terrible telegram from Saint-Privat, informing us laconically of the frightful butchery; of the heroic defence of Marshal Canrobert; and of Bazaine's first treachery in not going to the rescue of his comrade.

I knew Canrobert, and was very fond of him. Later on he became one of my faithful friends, and I shall always remember the exquisite hours spent in listening to his accounts of the bravery of others—never of his own. And what an abundance of anecdotes, what wit, what charm!

This news of the battle of Saint-Privat caused my feverishness to return. My sleep was full of nightmares, and I had a relapse. The news was worse every day. After Saint-Privat came Gravelotte, where 36,000 men, French and German, were cut down in a few hours. Then came the sublime but powerless efforts of MacMahon, who was driven back as far as Sedan; and finally Sedan.

Sedan! Ah, the horrible awakening! The month of August had finished the night before, amidst a tumult of weapons and dying groans. But the groans of the dying men were mingled still with hopeful cries. But the month of September was cursed from its very birth. Its first war-cry was stifled back by the brutal and cowardly hand of Destiny.

A hundred thousand men! A hundred thousand Frenchmen compelled to capitulate, and the Emperor of France forced to hand his sword over to the King of Prussia!

Ah! that cry of grief, that cry of rage, uttered by the whole nation. It can never be forgotten!

On September 1, towards ten o'clock, Claude, my man-servant, knocked at my door. I was not asleep, and he gave me a copy of the first telegrams:

"Battle of Sedan commenced. MacMahon wounded," &c. &c.

"Ah! go back again," I said, "and as soon as a fresh telegram comes, bring me the news. I feel that something unheard of, something great and quite different, is going to happen. We have suffered so terribly this last month, that there can only be something good now, something fine, for God's scales mete out joy and suffering equally. Go at once, Claude," I added, and then, full of confidence, I soon fell asleep again, and was so tired that I slept until one o'clock. When I awoke, my maid Félicie, the most delightful girl imaginable, was seated near my bed. Her pretty face and her large dark eyes were so mournful that my heart stopped beating. I gazed at her anxiously, and she put into my hands the copy of the last telegram :

"The Emperor Napoleon has just handed over his sword. . ."

Blood rushed to my head, and my lungs were too weak to control its flow. I lay back on my pillow, and the blood escaped through my lips with the groans of my whole being.

For three days I was between life and death. Dr. Leudet sent for one of my father's friends, a shipowner named M. Maunoir. He came at once, bringing with him his young wife. She too was very ill, worse in reality than I was, in spite of her fresh look, for she died six months later. Thanks to their care and to the energetic treatment of Dr. Leudet, I came through alive from this attack.

I decided to return at once to Paris, as the siege was about to be proclaimed, and I did not want my mother and my sisters to remain in the capital. Independently of this, every one at Eaux-Bonnes was seized with a desire to get away, invalids and tourists alike. A post-chaise was found, the owner of which agreed, for an exorbitant price, to drive me to the nearest station without delay. When once in it, we were more or less comfortably seated as far as Bordeaux, but it was impossible to find five seats in the express from there. My man-servant was allowed to travel with the engine-driver. I do not know where Madame Guérard and my maid found room, but in the compartment I entered, with my little boy, there were already nine persons. An ugly old man tried to push my child out when I had put him in, but I pushed him back again energetically in my turn.

"No human force will make us get out of this carriage," I said. "Do you hear that, you ugly old man? We are here, and we shall stay."

A stout lady, who took up more room herself than three ordinary persons, exclaimed :

"Well! that is lively, for we are suffocated already. It's shameful to let eleven persons get into a compartment where there are only seats for eight!"

"Will you get out, then?" I retorted, turning to her quickly, "for without you there would only be seven of us."

The stifled laughter of the other travellers showed me that I had won over my audience. Three young men offered me their places, but I refused, declaring that I was going to stand. The three young men had risen, and they declared that they would also stand. The stout lady called a railway official. "Come here, please!" she began.

The official stopped an instant at the door.

"It is perfectly shameful," she went on. "There are eleven in this compartment, and it is impossible to move."

"Don't you believe it," exclaimed one of the young men. "Just look for yourself. We are standing up, and there are three seats empty. Send some more people in here."

The official went away laughing and muttering something about the woman who had complained. She turned to the young man and began to talk abusively to him. He bowed very respectfully in reply, and said :

"Madame, if you will calm down you shall be satisfied. We will seat seven on the other side, including the child, and then you will only be four on your side."

The ugly old man was short and slight. He looked sideways at the stout lady and murmured, "Four! Four!" His look and tone showed that he considered the stout lady took up more than one seat. This look and tone were not lost on the young man, and before the ugly old man had comprehended he said to him, "Will you come over here and have this corner? All the thin people will be together then," he added, inviting a placid, calm-looking young Englishman of eighteen to twenty years of age to take the old man's seat. The Englishman had the torso of a prize-fighter, with a face like that of a fair-haired baby. A very young woman, opposite the stout one, laughed till the tears came. All six of us then found room on the thin people's side of the carriage. We were a little crushed, but had been considerably enlivened by this little entertainment, and we certainly needed something to enliven us. The young man who had taken the matter in hand in such a witty way was tall and nice-looking. He had blue eyes, and his hair was almost white, and this gave to his face a most attractive freshness and youthfulness. My boy was on his knee during the night. With the exception of the child, the stout lady, and the young Englishman, no one went to sleep. The heat was overpowering, and the war was of course discussed. After some hesitation, one of the young men told me that I resembled Mlle. Sarah Bernhardt. I answered that there was every reason why I should resemble her. The young men then introduced themselves. The one who had recognised me was Albert Delpit, the second was a Dutchman, Baron van Zelern or von Zerlen, I do not remember exactly which, and the young man with white hair was Félix Faure. He told me that he was from Hâvre, and that he knew my grandmother very well. I kept up a certain friendship with these three men afterwards, but later on Albert Delpit became my enemy. All three are now dead—Albert Delpit died a disappointed man, for he had tried everything and succeeded in nothing, the Dutch baron was killed in a railway accident, and Félix Faure was President of the French Republic.

The young woman, on hearing my name, introduced herself in her turn.

"I think we are slightly related," she said. "I am Madame Laroque."

"Of Bordeaux?" I asked.

"Yes."

My mother's brother had married a Mlle. Laroque of Bordeaux, so that we were able to talk of our family. Altogether the journey did not seem very long, in spite of the heat, the overcrowding, and our thirst.

The arrival in Paris was more gloomy. We shook hands warmly with each other. The stout lady's husband was awaiting her; he handed her, in silence, a telegram. The unfortunate woman read it, and then, uttering a cry, burst into sobs and fell into his arms. I gazed at her, wondering what sorrow had come upon her. Poor woman, I could no longer see anything ridiculous about her! I felt a pang of remorse at the thought that we had been laughing at her so much, when misfortune had already singled her out.

On reaching home I sent word to my mother that I should be with her some time during the day. She came at once, as she wanted to know how my health was. We then arranged about the departure of the whole family, with the exception of myself, as I wanted to stay in Paris during the siege. My mother, my little boy and his nurse, my sisters, my Aunt Annette, who kept house for me, and my mother's maid were all ready to start two days later. I had taken rooms at Frascati's, at Hâvre, for the whole tribe. But the desire to leave Paris was one thing, and the possibility of doing so another. The stations were invaded by families like mine, who thought it more prudent to emigrate. I sent my man-servant to engage a compartment, and he came back three hours later with his clothes torn, after receiving no end of kicks and blows.

"Madame cannot go into that crowd," he assured me; "it is quite impossible. I should not be able to protect her. Besides, Madame will not be alone; there is Madame's mother, the other ladies, and the children. It is really quite impossible."

I sent at once for three of my friends, explained my difficulty, and asked them to accompany me. I told my steward to be ready, as well as my other man-servant and my mother's footman. He in his turn invited his younger brother, who was a priest, and who was very willing to go with us. We all set off in a railway omnibus. There were seventeen of us in all, but only nine who were really travelling. Our eight protectors were none too many, for those who were taking tickets were not human beings, but wild beasts haunted by fear and spurred on by a desire to escape. These brutes saw nothing but the little ticket office, the door leading to the train, and then the train which would ensure their escape. The presence of the young priest was a great help to us, for his religious character made people refrain sometimes from blows.

When once all my people were installed in the compartment which had been reserved for them, they waved their farewells, threw kisses, and the train started. A shudder of terror ran through me, for I suddenly felt so absolutely alone. It was the first time I had been separated from the little child who was dearer to me than the whole world.

Two arms were then thrown affectionately round me, and a voice murmured, "My dear Sarah, why did you not go, too? You are so delicate. Will you be able to bear the solitude without the dear child?"

It was Madame Guérard, who had arrived too late to kiss the boy, but was there now to comfort the mother. I gave way to my despair, regretting that I had let him go away. And yet, as I said to myself, there might be fighting in Paris! The idea never for an instant occurred to me that I might have gone away with him. I thought that I might be of some use in Paris. Of some use, but in what way? This I did not know. The idea seemed stupid, but nevertheless that was my idea. It seemed to me that every one who was fit ought to remain in Paris. In spite of my weakness, I felt that I was fit, and with reason, as I proved later on. I therefore remained, not knowing at all what I was going to do.

For some days I was perfectly dazed, missing the life around me, and missing the affection.

XVI

SARAH BERNHARDT'S AMBULANCE AT THE
ODÉON THEATRE

THE defence, however, was being organised, and I decided to
use my strength and intelligence in tending the wounded. The
question was, where could we instal an ambulance ?

The Odéon Theatre had closed its doors, but I moved heaven
and earth to get permission to organise an ambulance in that
theatre, and, thanks to Emile de Girardin and Duquesnel, my
wish was gratified. I went to the War Office and made my
declaration and my request, and my offers were accepted for a
military ambulance. The next difficulty was that I wanted
food. I wrote a line to the Prefect of Police. A military
courier arrived very soon, with a note from the Prefect containing
the following lines :

" MADAME,—If you could possibly come at once, I would wait
for you until six o'clock. If not I will receive you to-morrow
morning at eight. Excuse the earliness of the hour, but I have
to be at the Chamber at nine in the morning, and, as your note
seems to be urgent, I am anxious to do all I can to be of service
to you.

" COMTE DE KERATRY."

I remembered a Comte de Kératry who had been introduced
to me at my aunt's house, the evening I had recited poetry
accompanied by Rossini, but he was a young lieutenant, good-
looking, witty, and lively. He had introduced me to his
mother. I had recited poetry at her *soirées*. The young
lieutenant had gone to Mexico, and for some time we had kept
up a correspondence, but this had gradually ceased, and we had
not met again. I asked Madame Guérard whether she thought

that the Prefect were a near relative of my young friend's. " It may be so," she replied, and we discussed this in the carriage which was taking us at once to the Tuileries Palace, where the Prefect had his offices. My heart was very heavy when we came to the stone steps. Only a few months previously, one April morning, I had been there with Madame Guérard. Then, as now, a footman had come forward to open the door of my carriage, but the April sunshine had then lighted up the steps, caught the shining lamps of the State carriages, and sent its rays in all directions. There had been a busy, joyful coming and going of the officers then, and elegant salutes had been exchanged. On this occasion the misty, crafty-looking November sun fell heavily on all it touched. Black, dirty-looking cabs drove up one after the other, knocking against the iron gate, grazing the steps, advancing or moving back, according to the coarse shouts of their drivers. Instead of the elegant salutations I heard now such phrases as : " Well, how are you, old chap ? " " Oh, *la gueule de bois* ! " " Well, any news ? " " Yes, it's the very deuce with us ! " &c. &c.

The Palace was no longer the same.

The very atmosphere had changed. The faint perfume which elegant women leave in the air as they pass was no longer there. A vague odour of tobacco, of greasy clothes, of dirty hair, made the atmosphere seem heavy. Ah, the beautiful French Empress ! I could see her again in her blue dress embroidered with silver, calling to her aid Cinderella's good fairy to help her on again with her little slipper. The delightful young Prince Imperial, too ! I could see him helping me to arrange the pots of verbena and marguerites, and holding in his arms, which were not strong enough for it, a huge pot of rhododendrons, behind which his handsome face completely disappeared. Then, too, I could see the Emperor Napoleon III. with his half-closed eyes, clapping his hands at the rehearsal of the curtseys intended for him.

And the fair Empress, dressed in strange clothes, had rushed away in the carriage of her American dentist, for it was not even a Frenchman, but a foreigner, who had had the courage to protect the unfortunate woman. And the gentle Utopian Emperor had tried in vain to be killed on the battle-field. Two horses had been killed under him, and he had not received so much as a scratch. And after this he had given up his sword. And we

L

at home had all wept with anger, shame, and grief at this giving up of the sword. And yet what courage it must have required for so brave a man to carry out such an act. He had wanted to save a hundred thousand men, to spare a hundred thousand lives, and to reassure a hundred thousand mothers. Our poor, beloved Emperor! History will some day do him justice, for he was good, humane, and confiding. Alas, alas! he was too confiding!

I stopped a minute before entering the Prefect's suite of rooms. I was obliged to wipe my eyes, and in order to change the current of my thoughts I said to *mon petit Dame*.

"Tell me, should you think me pretty if you saw me now for the first time?"

"Oh yes!" she replied warmly.

"So much the better," I said, "for I want this old Prefect to think me pretty. There are so many things I must ask him for!"

On entering his room, my surprise was great when I recognised in him the lieutenant I knew. He had become captain, and then Prefect of Police. When my name was announced by the usher, he sprang up from his chair and came forward with his face beaming and both hands stretched out.

"Ah, you had forgotten me!" he said, and then he turned to greet Madame Guérard in a friendly way.

"But I never thought I was coming to see you!" I replied; "and I am delighted," I continued, "for you will let me have everything I ask for."

"Only that!" he remarked with a burst of laughter. "Well, will you give your orders, Madame?" he continued.

"Yes. I want bread, milk, meat, vegetables, sugar, wine, brandy, potatoes, eggs, coffee," I said straight away.

"Oh, let me get my breath!" exclaimed the Count-Prefect. "You speak so quickly that I am gasping."

I was quiet for a moment, and then I continued:

"I have started an ambulance at the Odéon, but as it is a military ambulance, the municipal authorities refuse me food. I have five wounded men already, and I can manage for them, but other wounded men are being sent to me, and I shall have to give them food."

"You shall be supplied above and beyond all your wishes,"

said the Prefect. "There is food in the Palace which was being stored by the unfortunate Empress. She had prepared enough for months and months. I will have all you want sent to you, except meat, bread, and milk, and as regards these I will give orders that your ambulance shall be included in the municipal service, although it is a military one. Then I will give you an order for salt and other things, which you will be able to get from the Opéra."

"From the Opéra?" I repeated, looking at him incredulously. "But it is only being built, and there is nothing but scaffolding there yet."

"Yes; but you must go through the little doorway under the scaffolding opposite the Rue Scribe; you then go up the little spiral staircase leading to the provision office, and there you will be supplied with what you want."

"There is still something else I want to ask," I said.

"Go on; I am quite resigned, and ready for your orders," he replied.

"Well, I am very uneasy," I said, "for they have put a stock of powder in the cellars under the Odéon. If Paris were to be bombarded and a shell should fall on the building, we should all be blown up, and that is not the aim and object of an ambulance."

"You are quite right," said the kind man, "and nothing could be more stupid than to store powder there. I shall have more difficulty about that, though," he continued, "for I shall have to deal with a crowd of stubborn *bourgeois* who want to organise the defence in their own way. You must try to get a petition for me, signed by the most influential householders and tradespeople in the neighbourhood. Now are you satisfied?" he asked.

"Yes," I replied, shaking both his hands cordially. "You have been most kind and charming. Thank you very much."

I then moved towards the door, but I stood still again suddenly, as though hypnotised by an overcoat hanging over a chair. Madame Guérard saw what had attracted my attention, and she pulled my sleeve gently.

"My dear Sarah," she whispered, "do not do that."

I looked beseechingly at the young Prefect, but he did not understand.

"What can I do now to oblige you, beautiful Madonna?" he asked.

I pointed to the coat and tried to look as charming as possible.

"I am very sorry," he said, bewildered, "but I do not understand at all."

I was still pointing to the coat.

"Give it me, will you?" I said.

"My overcoat?"

"Yes."

"What do you want it for?"

"For my wounded men when they are convalescent."

He sank down on a chair in a fit of laughter. I was rather vexed at this uncontrollable outburst, and I continued my explanation.

"There is nothing so funny about it," I said. "I have a poor fellow, for instance, two of whose fingers have been taken off. He does not need to stay in bed for that, naturally, and his soldier's cape is not warm enough. It is very difficult to warm the big *foyer* of the Odéon sufficiently, and those who are well enough have to be there. The man I tell you about is warm enough at present, because I took Henri Fould's overcoat when he came to see me the other day. My poor soldier is huge, and as Henri Fould is a giant I might never have had such an opportunity again. I shall want a great many overcoats, though, and this looks like a very warm one."

I stroked the furry lining of the coveted garment, and the young Prefect, still choking with laughter, began to empty the pockets of his overcoat. He pulled out a magnificent white silk muffler from the largest pocket.

"Will you allow me to keep my muffler?" he asked.

I put on a resigned expression and nodded my consent.

Our host then rang, and when the usher appeared he handed him the overcoat, and said in a solemn voice, in spite of the laughter in his eyes:

"Will you carry this to the carriage for these ladies?"

I thanked him again, and went away feeling very happy.

Twelve days later I returned, taking with me a letter covered with the signatures of the householders and tradesmen residing near the Odéon.

On entering the Prefect's room I was petrified to see him, instead of advancing to meet me, rush towards a cupboard, open the door, and fling something hastily into it. After this he leaned against the door as though to prevent my opening it.

" Excuse me," he said, in a witty, mocking tone, " but I caught a violent cold after your first visit. I have just put my overcoat —oh, only an ugly old overcoat, not a warm one," he added quickly, " but still an overcoat—inside there, and there it now is, and I will take the key out of the lock."

He put the key carefully into his pocket, and then came forward and offered me a chair. But our conversation soon took a more serious turn, for the news was very bad. For the last twelve days the ambulances had been crowded with wounded men. Everything was in a bad way, home politics as well as foreign politics. The Germans were advancing on Paris. The army of the Loire was being formed. Gambetta, Chanzy, Bourbaki, and Trochu were organising a desperate defence. We talked for some time about all these sad things, and I told him about the painful impression I had had on my last visit to the Tuileries, of my remembrance of every one, so brilliant, so considerate, and so happy formerly, and so deeply to be pitied at present. We were silent for a moment, and then I shook hands with him, told him I had received all he had sent, and returned to my ambulance.

The Prefect had sent me ten barrels of wine and two of brandy; 30,000 eggs, all packed in boxes with lime and bran; a hundred bags of coffee and boxes of tea, forty boxes of Albert biscuits, a thousand tins of preserves, and a quantity of other things.

M. Menier, the great chocolate manufacturer, had sent me five hundred pounds of chocolate. One of my friends, a flour dealer, had made me a present of twenty sacks of flour, ten of which were maize flour. This flour-dealer was the one who had asked me to be his wife when I was at the Conservatoire. Félix Potin, my neighbour when I was living at 11 Boulevard Malesherbes, had responded to my appeal by sending two barrels of raisins, a hundred boxes of sardines, three sacks of rice, two sacks of lentils, and twenty sugar-loaves. From M. de Rothschild I had received two barrels of brandy and a hundred bottles of his own wine for the convalescents. I also received ?

very unexpected present. Léonie Dubourg, an old school-fellow of mine at the Grand-Champs convent, sent me fifty tin boxes each containing four pounds of salt butter. She had married a very wealthy gentleman farmer, who cultivated his own farms, which it seems were very numerous. I was very much touched at her remembering me, for I had never seen her since the old days at the convent. I had also asked for all the overcoats and slippers of my various friends, and I had bought up a job lot of two hundred flannel vests. My Aunt Betsy, my blind grandmother's sister, who is still living in Holland, and is now ninety-three years of age, managed to get for me, through the charming Ambassador for the Netherlands, three hundred night-shirts of magnificent Dutch linen, and a hundred pairs of sheets. I received lint and bandages from every corner of Paris, but it was more particularly from the Palais de l'Industrie that I used to get my provisions of lint and of linen for binding wounds. There was an adorable woman there, named Mlle. Hocquigny, who was at the head of all the ambulances. All that she did was done with a cheerful gracefulness, and all that she was obliged to refuse she refused sorrowfully, but still in a gracious manner. She was at that time over thirty years of age, and although unmarried she looked more like a very young married woman. She had large, blue, dreamy eyes, and a laughing mouth, a deliciously oval face, little dimples, and, crowning all this grace, this dreamy expression, and this coquettish, inviting mouth, a wide forehead like that of the Virgins painted by the early painters, rather prominent, encircled by hair worn in smooth, wide, flat bandeaux, separated by a faultless parting. The forehead seemed like the protecting rampart of this delicious face. Mlle. Hocquigny was adored and made much of by every one, but she remained invulnerable to all homage. She was happy in being beloved, but she would not allow any one to express affection for her.

At the Palais de l'Industrie a remarkable number of celebrated doctors and surgeons were on duty, and they, as well as the con-valescents, were all more or less in love with Mlle. Hocquigny. As she and I were great friends, she confided to me her obser-vations and her sorrowful disdain. Thanks to her, I was never short of linen nor of lint. I had organised my ambulance with a very small staff. My cook was installed in the public *foyer*.

I had bought her an immense cooking range, so that she could make soups and herb-tea for fifty men. Her husband was chief attendant. I had given him two assistants, and Madame Guérard, Madame Lambquin, and I were the nurses. Two of us sat up at night, so that we each went to bed one night in three. I preferred this to taking on some woman whom I did not know. Madame Lambquin belonged to the Odéon, where she used to take the part of the duennas. She was plain and had a common face, but she was very talented. She talked loud and was very plain-spoken. She called a spade a spade, and liked frankness and no under meaning to things. At times she was a trifle embarrassing with the crudeness of her words and her remarks, but she was kind, active, alert, and devoted. My various friends who were on service at the fortifications came to me in their free time to do my secretarial work. I had to keep a book, which was shown every day to a sergeant who came from the Val-de-Grâce military hospital, giving all details as to how many men came into our ambulance, how many died, and how many recovered and left. Paris was in a state of siege; no one could go far outside the walls, and no news from outside could be received. The Germans were not, however, round the gates of the city. Baron Larrey came now and then to see me, and I had as head surgeon Dr. Duchesne, who gave up his whole time, night and day, to the care of my poor men during the five months that this truly frightful nightmare lasted.

I cannot recall those terrible days without the deepest emotion. It was no longer the country in danger that kept my nerves strung up, but the sufferings of all her children. There were all those who were away fighting, those who were brought in to us wounded or dying; the noble women of the people, who stood for hours and hours in the *queue* to get the necessary dole of bread, meat, and milk for their poor little ones at home. Ah, those poor women! I could see them from the theatre windows, pressing up close to each other, blue with cold, and stamping their feet on the ground to keep them from freezing—for that winter was the most cruel one we had had for twenty years. Frequently one of these poor, silent heroines was brought in to me, either in a swoon from fatigue or struck down suddenly with congestion caused by cold. On December 20 three of these unfortunate women were brought into the ambulance. One of them had her feet frozen, and she lost the big toe of her right foot. The second was an enormously stout woman, who was suckling her child, and her poor breasts were harder than wood. She simply howled with pain. The youngest of the three was a girl of sixteen to eighteen years of age. She died of cold, on the trestle on which I had had her placed to send her home. On December 24, there were fifteen degrees of cold. I often sent Guillaume, our attendant, out with a little brandy to warm the poor women. Oh! the suffering they must have endured— those heart-broken mothers, those sisters and *fiancées*—in their terrible dread. How excusable their rebellion seems during the Commune, and even their bloodthirsty madness!

My ambulance was full. I had sixty beds, and was obliged to improvise ten more. The soldiers were installed in the green-room and in the general *foyer*, and the officers in a room which had been formerly the refreshment-room of the theatre.

One day a young Breton, named Marie Le Gallec, was brought in. He had been struck by a bullet in the chest and another in the wrist. Dr. Duchesne bound up his chest firmly, and attended to his wrist. He then said to me very simply:

" Let him have anything he likes—he is dying."

I bent over his bed, and said to him :

" Tell me what would give you pleasure, Marie Le Gallec."

" Soup," he answered promptly, in the most comic way.

Madame Guérard hurried away to the kitchen, and soon returned with a bowl of broth and pieces of toast. I placed the bowl on the little four-legged wooden shelf, which was so convenient for the meals of our poor sufferers. The wounded man looked up at me and said, " Barra." I did not understand, and he repeated, " Barra." His poor chest caused him to hiss out the word, and he made the greatest efforts to repeat his emphatic request.

I sent immediately to the Marine Office, thinking that there would surely be some Breton seamen there, and I explained my difficulty and my ignorance of the Breton dialect.

I was informed that the word " barra " meant bread. I hurried at once to Le Gallec with a large piece of bread. His face lighted up, and taking it from me with his sound hand, he broke it up with his teeth and let the pieces fall in the bowl. He then plunged his spoon into the middle of the broth, and filled it up with bread until the spoon could stand upright in it. When it stood up without shaking about, the young soldier smiled. He was just preparing to eat this horrible concoction when the young priest from St. Sulpice who had my ambulance in charge arrived. I had sent for him on hearing the doctor's sad verdict. He laid his hand gently on the young man's shoulder, thus stopping the movement of his arm. The poor fellow looked up at the priest, who showed him the holy cup.

"Oh," he said simply, and then, placing his coarse handkerchief over the steaming soup, he put his hands together.

We had arranged the two screens which we used for isolating the dead or dying around his bed. He was left alone with the priest whilst I went on my rounds to calm those who were chaffing, or help the believers raise themselves for prayer. The young priest soon pushed aside the partition, and I then saw Marie Le Gallec, with a beaming face, eating his abominable bread sop. He soon fell asleep but awoke before long and asked for something to drink, and then died in a slight fit of choking. Fortunately I did not lose many men out of the three hundred who came into my ambulance, for the death of the unfortunate ones completely upset me.

I was very young at that time, only twenty-four years of age, but I could nevertheless see the cowardice of some of the men and the heroism of many of the others. A young Savoyard, eighteen years old, had had his forefinger shot off. Baron Larrey was quite sure that he had done it himself with his own gun, but I could not believe that. I noticed, though, that, in spite of our nursing and care, the wound did not heal. I bound it up in a different way, and the following day I saw that the bandage had been altered. I mentioned this to Madame Lambquin, who was sitting up that night with Madame Guérard.

"Good; I will keep my eye on him. You go to sleep, my child, and rely on me."

The next day when I arrived she told me that she had caught the young man scraping the wound on his finger with his knife. I called him, and told him that I should have to report this to the Val-de-Grâce Hospital.

He began to weep, and vowed to me that he would never do it again, and five days later he was well. I signed the paper authorising him to leave the ambulance, and he was sent to the army of the defence. I often wondered what became of him. Another of our patients bewildered us too. Each time that his wound seemed to be just on the point of healing up, he had a violent attack of dysentery, which prevented him getting well. This seemed suspicious to Dr. Duchesne, and he asked me to watch the man. At the end of a considerable time we were convinced that our wounded man had thought out the most comical scheme.

He slept next the wall, and therefore had no neighbour on the one side. During the night he managed to file the brass of his bedstead. He put the filings in a little pot which had been used for ointment of some kind. A few drops of water and some salt mixed with this powdered brass formed a poison which might have cost its inventor his life. I was furious at this stratagem. I wrote to the Val-de-Grâce, and an ambulance conveyance was sent to take this unpatriotic Frenchman away.

But side by side with these despicable men what heroism we saw! A young captain was brought in one day. He was a tall fellow, a regular Hercules, with a superb head and a frank expression. On my book he was inscribed as Captain Menesson. He had been struck by a bullet at the top of the arm, just at the shoulder. With a nurse's assistance I was trying as gently as possible to take off his cloak, when three bullets fell from the hood which he had pulled over his head, and I counted sixteen bullet holes in the cloak. The young officer had stood upright for three hours, serving as a target himself, whilst covering the retreat of his men as they fired all the time on the enemy. This had taken place among the Champigny vines. He had been brought in unconscious, in an ambulance conveyance. He had lost a great deal of blood, and was half dead with fatigue and weakness. He was very gentle and charming, and thought himself sufficiently well two days later to return to the fight. The doctor, however, would not allow this, and his sister, who was a nun, besought him to wait until he was something like well again.

" Oh, not quite well," she said, smiling, " but just well enough to have strength to fight."

Soon after he came into the ambulance the Cross of the Legion of Honour was brought to him, and this was a moment of intense emotion for every one. The unfortunate wounded men who could not move turned their suffering faces towards him, and, with their eyes shining through a mist of tears, gave him a fraternal look. The stronger amongst them held out their hands to the young giant.

It was Christmas-eve, and I had decorated the ambulance with festoons of green leaves. I had made pretty little chapels in front of the Virgin Mary, and the young priest from St. Sulpice came to take part in our poor but poetical Christmas service. He repeated some beautiful prayers, and the wounded men, many of whom were from Brittany, sang some sad solemn songs full of charm.

Porel, the present manager of the Vaudeville Theatre, had been wounded on the Avron Plateau. He was then convalescent and was one of my patients, together with two officers now ready to leave the ambulance. That Christmas supper is one of my most charming and at the same time most melancholy memories. It was served in the small room which we had made into a bed-room. Our three beds were covered with draperies and skins which I had had brought from home, and we used them as seats. Mlle. Hocquigny had sent me five metres of *boudin blanc* ("white-pudding"), the famous Christmas dish, and all my poor soldiers who were well enough were delighted with this delicacy. One of my friends had had twenty large *brioche* cakes made for me, and I had ordered some large bowls of punch, the coloured flames from which amused the grown-up sick children immensely. The young priest from St. Sulpice accepted a piece of *brioche*, and after taking a little white wine left us. Ah, how charming and good he was, that poor young priest! And how well he managed to make Fortin, the insupportable wounded fellow, cease talking. Gradually the latter began to get humanised, until finally he began to think the priest was a good sort of fellow. Poor young priest! He was shot by the Communists. I cried for days and days over the murder of this young St. Sulpice priest.

XVII

PARIS BOMBARDED

THE month of January arrived. The army of the enemy held Paris day by day in a still closer grip. Food was getting scarce. Bitter cold enveloped the city, and poor soldiers who fell, sometimes only slightly wounded, passed away gently in a sleep that was eternal, their brain numbed and their body half frozen.

No more news could be received from outside, but thanks to the United States Minister, who had resolved to remain in Paris, a letter arrived from time to time. It was in this way that I received a thin slip of paper, as soft as a primrose petal, bringing me the following message : " Every one well. Courage. A thousand kisses.—Your mother." This impalpable missive dated from seventeen days previously.

And so my mother, my sisters, and my little boy were at The Hague all this time, and my mind, which had been continually travelling in their direction, had been wandering along the wrong route, towards Hâvre, where I thought they were settled down quietly at the house of a cousin of my father's mother.

Where were they, and with whom ?

I had two aunts at The Hague, but the question was, were they there ? I no longer knew what to think, and from that moment I never ceased suffering the most anxious and torturing mental distress.

I was doing all in my power just then to procure some wood for fires. Comte de Kératry had sent me a large provision before his departure to the provinces in a balloon on October 9. My stock was growing very short, and I would not allow what we had in the cellars to be touched, so that in case of an emergency we should not be absolutely without any. I had all the little footstools belonging to the theatre used for firewood, all the wooden cases in which the properties were kept, a good number of old Roman benches, arm-chairs and curule chairs, that were stowed away under the theatre, and indeed everything which came to hand. Finally, taking pity on my despair, pretty Mlle. Hocquigny sent me ten thousand kilograms of wood, and then I took courage again.

I had been told about some new system of keeping meat, by which the meat lost neither its juice nor its nutritive quality. I sent Madame Guérard to the *Mairie* in the neighbourhood of the Odéon, where such provisions were distributed, but some brute answered her that when I had removed all the religious images from my ambulance I should receive the necessary food. M. Herisson, the mayor, with some functionary holding an influential post, had been to inspect my ambulance. The important personage had requested me to have the beautiful white Virgins which were on the mantelpieces and tables taken away, as well as the Divine Crucified— one hanging on the wall of each room in which there were any of the wounded. I refused in a somewhat insolent and very decided way to act in accordance with the wish of my visitor, whereupon the famous Republican turned his back on me and gave orders that I should be refused everything at the *Mairie*. I was very determined, however, and I moved heaven and earth until I succeeded in getting inscribed on the lists for distribution of food, in spite of the orders of the chief. It is only fair to say that the mayor was a charming man. Madame Guérard returned, after her third visit, with a child pushing a hand-barrow containing ten enormous bottles of the miraculous meat. I received the precious consignment with infinite joy, for my men had been almost without meat for the last three days, and the beloved *pot-au-feu* was an almost necessary resource for the poor wounded fellows. On all the bottles were directions as to opening them : " Let the meat soak so many hours," &c. &c.

Madame Lambquin, Madame Guérard, and I, together with all the staff of the infirmary, were soon grouped anxiously and inquisitively around these glass receptacles.

I told the head attendant to open the largest of the bottles, in which through the thick glass we could see an enormous piece of beef surrounded by thick, muddled-looking water. The string fastened round the rough paper which hid the cork was cut, and then, just as the man was about to put the corkscrew in, a deafening explosion was heard and a rank odour filled the room. Every one rushed away terrified. I called them all back, scared and disgusted as they were, and showed them the following words on the directions : " Do not be alarmed at the bad odour on opening the bottle." Courageously and with resignation we resumed our work, though we felt sick all the time from the abominable exhalation. I took the beef out and placed it on a dish that had been brought for the purpose. Five minutes later this meat turned blue and then black, and the stench from it was so unbearable that I decided to throw it away. Madame Lambquin was wiser, though, and more reasonable.

" No, oh no, my dear girl," she said ; " in these times it will not do to throw meat away, even though it may be rotten. Let us put it in the glass bottle again and send it back to the *Mairie*."

I followed her wise advice, and it was a very good thing I did, for another ambulance, installed at Boulevard Medicis, on opening these bottles of meat had been as horrified as we were, and had thrown the contents into the street. A few minutes after the crowd had gathered round in a mob, and, refusing to listen to anything, had yelled out insults addressed to " the aristocrats," " the clericals," and " the traitors," who were throwing good meat, intended for the sick, into the street, so that the dogs were enjoying it, while the people were starving with hunger, &c. &c.

It was with the greatest difficulty that the wretched, mad people had been prevented from invading the ambulance, and when one of the unfortunate nurses had gone out, later on, she had been mobbed and beaten until she was left half dead from fright and blows. She did not want to be carried back to her own ambulance, and the druggist begged me to take her in. I kept her for a few days, in one of the upper tier boxes of the theatre, and when she was better she asked if she might stay with me as a nurse. I granted her wish, and kept her with me afterwards as a maid.

She was a fair-haired girl, gentle and timid, and was pre-destined for misfortune. She was found dead in the Père Lachaise cemetery after the skirmish between the Communists and the Versailles troop. A stray bullet struck her in the back of the neck as she was praying at the grave of her little sister, who had died two days before from small-pox. I had taken her with me to St. Germain, where I had gone to stay during the horrors of the Commune. Poor girl! I had allowed her to go to Paris very much against my own will.

As we could not count on this preserved meat for our food, I made a contract with a knacker, who agreed to supply me, at rather a high price, with horse flesh, and until the end this was the only meat we had to eat. Well prepared and well seasoned, it was very good.

Hope had now fled from all hearts, and we were living in the expectation of we knew not what. An atmosphere of misfortune seemed to hang like lead over us, and it was a sort of relief when the bombardment commenced on December 27. At last we felt that something new was happening! It was an era of fresh suffering. There was some stir, at any rate. For the last fortnight the fact of not knowing anything had been killing us.

On January 1, 1871, we lifted our glasses to the health of the absent ones, to the repose of the dead, and the toast choked us with such a lump in our throats.

Every night we used to hear the dismal cry of " Ambulance ! Ambulance ! " underneath the windows of the Odéon. We went down to meet the pitiful procession, and one, two, or sometimes three conveyances would be there, full of our poor, wounded soldiers. There would be ten or twelve rows of them, lying or sitting up on the straw. I said that I had room for one or two, and, lifting the lantern, I looked into the conveyance, and the faces would then turn slowly towards the lamp. Some of the men would close their eyes, as they were too weak to bear even that feeble light. With the help of the sergeant who accompanied the conveyance and our attendant, one of the unfortunates would with difficulty be lifted into the narrow litter on which he was to be carried up to the ambulance.

Oh, what sorrowful anguish it was for me when, on lifting the patient's head, I discovered that it was getting heavy, oh, so heavy ! And when bending over that inert face I felt that there was no longer any breath ! The sergeant would then give the order to take him back, and the poor dead man was put in his place and another wounded man was lifted out.

The other dying men would then move back a little, in order not to profane the dead.

Ah, what grief it was when the sergeant said : "Do try to take one or two more in ! It is a pity to drag these poor chaps about from one ambulance to another. The Val-de-Grâce is full."

"Very well, I will take two more," I would say, and then I wondered where we should put them. We had to give up our own beds, and in this way the poor fellows were saved. Ever since January 1 we had all three been sleeping every night at the ambulance. We had some loose dressing-gowns of thick grey flannel, not unlike the soldiers' cloaks. The first of us who heard a cry or a groan sprang out of bed, and if necessary called the other two.

On January 10, Madame Guérard and I were sitting up at night, on one of the lounges in the green-room, awaiting the dismal cry of " Ambulance ! " There had been a fierce affray at Clamart, and we knew there would be many wounded. I was telling her of my fear that the bombs which had already reached the Museum, the Sorbonne, the Salpétrière, the Val-de-Grâce, &c., would fall on the Odéon.

"Oh, but, my dear Sarah," said the sweet woman, "the ambulance flag is waving so high above it that there could be no mistake. If it were struck it would be purposely, and that would be abominable."

"But, Guérard," I replied, "why should you expect these execrable enemies of ours to be better than we are ourselves ? Did we not behave like savages at Berlin in 1806 ? "

"But at Paris there are such admirable public monuments," she urged.

"Well, and was not Moscow full of masterpieces ? The Kremlin is one of the finest buildings in the world. That did not prevent us giving that admirable city up to pillage. Oh no, my poor *petit Dame*, do not deceive yourself. Armies may be Russian, German, French, or Spanish, but they *are* armies—that is, they are beings which form an impersonal 'whole,' a 'whole' that is ferocious and irresponsible. The Germans will bombard the whole of Paris if the possibility of doing so should be offered them. You must make up your mind to that, my dear Guérard—— "

I had not finished my sentence when a terrible detonation roused the whole neighbourhood from its slumbers. Madame Guérard and I had been seated opposite each other. We found ourselves standing up close together in the middle of the room, terrified. My poor cook, her face quite white, came to me for safety. The detonations continued rather frequently. The bombarding had commenced from our side that night. I went round to the wounded men, but they did not seem to be much disturbed. Only one, a boy of fifteen, whom we had surnamed " pink baby," was sitting up in bed. When I went to him to soothe him he showed me his little medal of the Holy Virgin.

" It is thanks to her that I was not killed," he said. " If they would put the Holy Virgin on the ramparts of Paris the bombs would not come."

He lay down again then, holding his little medal in his hand, and the bombarding continued until six in the morning. "Ambulance ! Ambulance ! " we then heard, and Madame Guérard and I went down. " Here," said the sergeant, " take this man. He is losing all his blood, and if I take him any farther he will not arrive living." The wounded man was put on the litter, but as he was German, I asked the sub-officer to take all his papers and hand them in at the Ministry. We gave the man the place of one of the convalescents, whom I installed elsewhere. I asked him his name, and he told me that it was Frantz Mayer, and that he was a soldier of the Silesian Landwehr. He then fainted from weakness caused by loss of blood. But he soon came to himself again with our care, and I then asked him whether he wanted anything, but he did not answer a word. I supposed that he did not speak French, and, as there was no one at the ambulance who spoke German, I waited until the next day to send for some one who knew his language. I must own that the poor man was not welcomed by his dormitory companions. A soldier named Fortin, who was twenty-three years of age and a veritable child of Paris, a comical fellow, mischievous, droll, and good-natured, never ceased railing against the young German, who on his side never flinched. I went several times to Fortin and begged him to be quiet, but it was all in vain. Every fresh outbreak of his was greeted with wild laughter, and his success put him into the gayest of humours, so that he continued, getting more and more excited. The others were prevented from sleep-

M

ing, and he moved about wildly in his bed, bursting out into abusive language when too abrupt a movement intensified his suffering. The unfortunate fellow had had his sciatic nerve torn by a bullet, and he had to endure the most atrocious pain.

After my third fruitless appeal for silence I ordered the two men attendants to carry him into a room where he would be alone. He sent for me, and when I went to him promised to behave well all night long. I therefore countermanded the order I had given, and he kept his word. The following day I had Frantz Mayer carried into a room where there was a young Breton who had had his skull fractured by the bursting of a shell, and therefore needed the utmost tranquillity.

One of my friends, who spoke German very well, came to see whether the Silesian wanted anything. The wounded man's face lighted up on hearing his own language, and then, turning to me, he said :

" I understand French quite well, Madame, and if I listened calmly to the horrors poured forth by your French soldier it was because I know that you cannot hold out two days longer, and I can understand his exasperation."

" And why do you think that we cannot hold out ? "

" Because I know that you are reduced to eating rats."

Dr. Duchesne had just arrived, and he was dressing the horrible wound which the patient had in his thigh.

" Well," he said, " my friend, as soon as your fever has decreased you shall eat an excellent wing of chicken." The German shrugged his shoulders, and the doctor continued, " Meanwhile drink this, and tell me what you think of it."

Dr. Duchesne gave him a glass of water, with a little of the excellent cognac which the Prefect had sent me. That was the only *tisane* that my soldiers took. The Silesian said no more, but he put on the reserved, circumspect manner of people who know and will not speak.

The bombardment continued, and the ambulance flag certainly served as a target for our enemies, for they fired with surprising exactitude, and altered their firing directly a bomb fell any distance from the neighbourhood of the Luxembourg. Thanks to this, we had more than twelve bombs one night. These dismal shells, when they burst in the air, were like the fireworks at a *fête*. The shining splinters then fell down, black and deadly.

Georges Boyer, who at that time was a young journalist, came
to call on me at the ambulance, and I told him about the
terrifying splendours of the night.

" Oh, how much I should like to see all that ! " he said.

" Come this evening, towards nine or ten o'clock, and you will
see," I replied.

We spent several hours at the little round window of my
dressing-room, which looked out towards Chatillon. It was from
there that the Germans fired the most.

We listened, in the silence of the night, to the muffled sounds
coming from yonder ; there would be a light, a formidable noise
in the distance, and the bomb arrived, falling in front of us or
behind, bursting either in the air or on reaching its goal. Once
we had only just time to draw back quickly, and even then the
disturbance in the atmosphere affected us so violently that for a
second we were under the impression that we had been struck.

The shell had fallen just underneath my dressing-room,
grazing the cornice, which it dragged down in its fall to the
ground, where it burst feebly. But what was our amazement to
see a little crowd of children swoop down on the burning pieces,
just like a lot of sparrows on fresh manure when the carriage
has passed ! The little vagabonds were quarrelling over the
débris of these engines of warfare. I wondered what they could
possibly do with them.

" Oh, there is not much mystery about it," said Boyer ; " these
little starving urchins will sell them."

This proved to be true. One of the men attendants, whom I
sent to find out, brought back with him a child of about ten
years old.

" What are you going to do with that, my little man ? " I
asked him, picking up the piece of shell, which was warm and
still dangerous, on the edge where it had burst.

" I am going to sell it," he replied.

" What for ? "

" To buy my turn in the *queue* when the meat is being
distributed."

" But you risk your life, my poor child. Sometimes the shells
come quickly, one after the other. Where were you when this
one fell ? "

" Lying down on the stone of the wall that supports the iron railings." He pointed across to the Luxembourg Gardens, opposite the stage entrance to the Odéon.

We bought up all the *débris* that the child had, without attempting to give him advice which might have sounded wise. What was the use of preaching wisdom to this poor little creature, who heard of nothing but massacres, fire, revenge, retaliation, and all the rest of it, for the sake of honour, for the sake of religion, for the sake of right? Besides, how was it possible to keep out of the way? All the people living in the Faubourg St. Germain were liable to be blown to pieces, as the enemy very luckily could only bombard Paris on that side, and not at every point. No; we were certainly in the most dangerous neighbourhood.

One day Baron Larrey came to see Frantz Mayer, who was very ill. He wrote a prescription which a young errand boy was told to wait for and bring back very, very quickly. As the boy was rather given to loitering, I went to the window. His name was Victor, but we called him "Toto." The druggist lived at the corner of the Place Medicis. It was then six o'clock in the evening. Toto looked up, and on seeing me he began to laugh and jump as he hurried to the druggist's. He had only five or six more yards to go, and as he turned round to look up at my window I clapped my hands and called out, "Good! Be quick back!" Alas! Before the poor boy could open his mouth to reply he was cut in two by a shell which had just fallen. It did not burst, but bounced a yard high, and then struck poor Toto right in the middle of the chest. I uttered such a shriek that every one came rushing to me. I could not speak, but pushed every one aside and rushed downstairs, beckoning for some one to come with me. "A litter"—"the boy"—"the druggist"—I managed to articulate. Ah, what a horror, what an awful horror! When we reached the poor child his intestines were all over the ground, his chest and his poor little red chubby face had the flesh entirely taken off. He had neither eyes, nose, nor mouth; nothing, nothing but some hair at the end of a shapeless, bleeding mass, a yard away from his head. It was as though a tiger had torn open the body with its claws and emptied it with fury and a refinement of cruelty, leaving nothing but the poor little skeleton.

Baron Larrey, who was the best of men, turned slightly

pale at this sight. He saw plenty such, certainly, but this poor little fellow was a quite useless holocaust. Ah, the injustice, the infamy of war! Will the much dreamed of time never come when wars are no longer possible ; when the monarch who wants war will be dethroned and imprisoned as a malefactor? Will the time never come when there will be a cosmopolitan council, where a wise man of every country will represent his nation, and where the rights of humanity will be discussed and respected? So many men think as I do, so many women talk as I do, and yet nothing is done. The pusillanimity of an Oriental, the ill-humour of a sovereign, may still bring thousands of men face to face. And there will still be men who are so learned, chemists who spend their time in dreaming about, and inventing a powder to blow everything up, bombs that will wound twenty or thirty men, guns repeating their deadly task until the bullets fall, spent themselves, after having torn open ten or twelve human breasts.

A man whom I liked very much was busy experimenting how to steer balloons. To achieve that means a realisation of my dream, namely, to fly in the air, to approach the sky, and have under one's feet the moist, down-like clouds. Ah, how interested I was in my friend's researches! One day, though, he came to me very much excited with a new discovery.

" I have discovered something about which I am wild with delight!" he said. He then began to explain to me that his balloon would be able to carry inflammable matter without the least danger, thanks to this and thanks to that.

" But what for ? " I asked, bewildered by his explanations and half crazy with so many technical words.

" What for ? " he repeated; " why, for war!" he replied. "We shall be able to fire and to throw terrible bombs to a distance of a thousand, twelve hundred, and even fifteen hundred yards, and it would be impossible for us to be harmed at such a distance. My balloons, thanks to a substance which is my invention, with which the covering would be coated, would have nothing to fear from fire nor yet from gas."

" I do not want to know anything more about you or your invention," I said, interrupting him brusquely. " I thought you were a humane savant, and you are a wild beast. Your researches were in connection with the most beautiful manifestation of human genius, with those evolutions in the sky which I loved so dearly. You want now to transform these into cowardly attacks turned against the earth. You horrify me! Do go!"

With this I left my friend to himself and his cruel invention, ashamed for a moment. His efforts have not succeeded, though, according to his wishes.

The remains of the poor lad were put into a small coffin, and Madame Guérard and I followed the pauper's hearse to the grave. The morning was so cold that the driver had to stop and take a glass of hot wine, as otherwise he might have died of congestion. We were alone in the carriage, for the boy had been brought up by his grandmother, who could not walk at all, and who knitted vests and stockings. It was through going to order some vests and socks for my men that I had made the acquaintance of Mère Tricottin, as she was called. At her request I had engaged her grandson, Victor Durieux, as an errand boy, and the poor old woman had been so grateful that I dared not go now to tell her of his death.

Madame Guérard went for me to the Rue de Vaugirard, where the old woman lived. As soon as she arrived the poor grandmother could see by her sad face that something had happened.

"*Bon Dieu*, my dear Madame, is the poor little thin lady dead?" This referred to me. Madame Guérard then told her, as gently as possible, the sad news. The old woman took off her spectacles, looked at her visitor, wiped them, and put them on her nose again. She then began to grumble violently about her son, the father of the dead boy. He had taken up with some low girl, by whom he had had this child, and she had always foreseen that misfortune would come upon them through it.

She continued in this strain, not sorrowing for the poor boy, but abusing her son, who was a soldier in the Army of the Loire.

Although the grandmother seemed to feel so little grief, I went to see her after the funeral.

"It is all over, Madame Durieux," I said. "But I have ecured the grave for a period of five years for the poor boy."

She turned towards me, quite comic in her vexation.

"What madness!" she exclaimed. "Now that he's with the *bon Dieu* he won't want for anything. It would have been better to have taken a bit of land that would have brought something in. Dead folks don't make vegetables grow."

This outburst was so terribly logical that, in spite of the odious brutality of it, I yielded to Mère Tricottin's desire, and gave her the same present I had given to the boy. They should each have their bit of land. The child, who had had a right to a longer life, should sleep his eternal sleep in his, whilst the old woman could wrest from hers the remainder of her life, for which death was lying in wait.

I returned to the ambulance, sad and unnerved. A joyful surprise was awaiting me. A friend of mine was there, holding in his hand a very small piece of tissue paper, on which were the following two lines in my mother's handwriting: ". We are all very well, and at Homburg." I was furious on reading this. At Homburg? All my family at Homburg, settling down tranquilly in the enemy's country. I racked my brains to think by what extraordinary combination my mother had gone to Homburg. I knew that my pretty Aunt Rosine had a lady friend there, with whom she stayed every year, for she always spent two months at Homburg, two at Baden-Baden, and one month at Spa, as she was the greatest gambler that the *bon Dieu* ever created. Anyhow, those who were so dear to me were all well, and that was the important point. But I was nevertheless annoyed with my mother for going to Homburg.

I heartily thanked the friend who had brought me the little slip of paper. It was sent to me by the American Minister, who had put himself to no end of trouble in order to give help and consolation to the Parisians. I then gave him a few lines for my mother, in case he might be able to send them to her.

The bombardment of Paris continued. One night the brothers from the Ecole Chrétienne came to ask us for conveyances and help, in order to collect the dead on the Châtillon Plateau. I let them have my two conveyances, and I went with them to the battle-field. Ah, what a terrible memory! It was like a scene from Dante! It was an icy-cold night, and we could scarcely move along. Finally, by the light of torches and lanterns, we saw that we had arrived. I got out of the vehicle with the infirmary attendant and his assistant. We had to move slowly, as at every step we trod upon the dying or the dead. We passed along murmuring, "Ambulance! Ambulance!"

When we heard a groan we turned our steps in the direction whence it came. Ah, the first man that I found in this way! He was half lying down, his body supported by a heap of dead. I raised my lantern to look at his face, and found that his ear and part of his jaw had been blown off. Great clots of blood, coagulated by the cold, hung from his lower jaw. There was a wild look in his eyes. I took a wisp of straw, dipped it in my flask, drew up a few drops of brandy, and blew them into the poor fellow's mouth between his teeth. I repeated this three or four times. A little life then came back to him, and we took him away in one of the vehicles. The same thing was done for the others. Some of them could drink from the flask, which made our work shorter. One of these unfortunate men was frightful to look at. A shell had taken all the clothes from the upper part of his body, with the exception of two ragged sleeves, which hung from the arms at the shoulders. There was no trace of a wound, but his poor body was marked all over with great black patches, and the blood was oozing slowly from the corners of his mouth. I went nearer to him, for it seemed to me that he was breathing. I had a few drops of the vivifying cordial given to him, and he then half opened his eyes and said, " Thank you." He was lifted into the conveyance, but the poor fellow died from an attack of hæmorrhage, covering all the other wounded men with a stream of dark blood.

Daylight gradually began to appear, a misty, dull dawn. The lanterns had burnt out, but we could now distinguish each other. There were about a hundred persons there : sisters of charity, military and civil male hospital attendants, the brothers from the Ecole Chrétienne, other priests, and a few ladies who, like myself, had given themselves up heart and soul to the service of the wounded.

The sight was still more dismal by daylight, for all that the night had hidden in the shadows appeared then in the tardy, wan light of that January morning.

There were so many wounded that it was impossible to transport them all, and I sobbed at the thought of my helplessness. Other vehicles kept arriving, but there were so many wounded, so very many. A number of those who had only slight wounds had died of cold.

On returning to the ambulance I met one of my friends at

Lying in her famous coffin, a favourite pose.

Painting of Sarah Bernhardt at home by Walter Spindler.

the door. He was a naval officer, and he had brought me a sailor who had been wounded at the fort of Ivry. He had been shot below the right eye. He was entered as Désiré Bloas, boatswain's mate, age 27. He was a magnificent fellow, very frank looking, and a man of few words. As soon as he was in bed, Dr. Duchesne sent for a barber to shave him, as his bushy whiskers had been ravaged by a bullet that had lodged itself in the salivary gland, carrying with it hair and flesh into the wound. The surgeon took up his pincers to extract the pieces of flesh which had stopped up the opening of the wound. He then had to take some very fine pincers to extract the hairs which had been forced in. When the barber laid his razor very gently near the wound, the unfortunate man turned livid and an oath escaped his lips. He immediately glanced at me and muttered, " Pardon, Mademoiselle." I was very young, but I appeared much younger than my age ; I looked like a very young girl, in fact. I was holding the poor fellow's hand in mine and trying to comfort him with the hundreds of consoling words that spring from a woman's heart to her lips when she has to soothe moral or physical suffering.

" Ah, Mademoiselle," said poor Bloas, when the wound was finally dressed, "you gave me courage."

When he was more at his ease I asked him if he would like something to eat.

" Yes," he replied.

" Well, my boy, would you like cheese, soup, or sweets ? " asked Madame Lambquin.

" Sweets," replied the powerful-looking fellow, smiling.

Désiré Bloas often talked to me about his mother, who lived near Brest. He had a veritable adoration for this mother, but he seemed to have a terrible grudge against his father, for one day, when I asked him whether his father was still living, he looked up with his fearless eyes and appeared to fix them on a being only visible to himself, as though challenging him, with an expression of the most pitiful contempt. Alas ! the brave fellow was destined to a cruel end, but I will return to that later.

The sufferings endured through the siege began to have their effect on the *morale* of the Parisians. Bread had just been rationed out : there were to be 300 grammes for adults and

150 grammes for children.   A silent fury took possession of the
people at this news.   Women were the most courageous, the
men were excited.   Quarrels grew bitter, for some wanted war
to the very death, and others wanted peace.

One day when I entered Frantz Mayer's room to take him his
meal, he went into the most ridiculous rage.   He threw his piece
of chicken down on the ground, and declared that he would not
eat anything, nothing more at all, for they had deceived him by
telling him that the Parisians had not enough food to last two
days before surrendering, and he had been in the ambulance
seventeen days now, and was having chicken.   What the poor
fellow did not know was that I had bought about forty chickens
and six geese at the beginning of the siege, and I was feeding
them up in my dressing-room in the Rue de Rome.   Oh, my
dressing-room was very pretty just then ; but I let Frantz believe
that all Paris was full of chickens, ducks, geese, and other
domestic bipeds.

The bombardment continued, and one night I had to have all
my patients transported to the Odéon cellars, for when Madame
Guérard was helping one of the sick men to get back into bed, a
shell fell on the bed itself, between her and the officer.   It makes
me shudder even now to think that three minutes sooner the
unfortunate man would have been killed as he lay in bed, although
the shell did not burst.

We could not stay long in the cellars.   The water was getting
deeper in them, and rats tormented us.   I therefore decided that
the ambulance must be moved, and I had the worst of the
patients conveyed to the Val-de-Grâce Hospital.   I kept about
twenty men who were on the road to convalescence.   I rented an
immense empty flat for them at 58 Rue Taitbout, and it was
there that we awaited the armistice.

I was half dead with anxiety, as I had had no news from my
own family for a long time.   I could not sleep, and had become
the very shadow of my former self.

Jules Favre was entrusted with the negotiations with Bismarck.
Oh, those two days of preliminaries !   They were the most un-
nerving days of any for the besieged.   False reports were spread.
We were told of the maddest and most exorbitant demands on
the part of the Germans, who certainly were not tender to the
vanquished.

There was a moment of stupor when we heard that we had to pay two hundred million francs in cash immediately, for our finances were in such a pitiful state that we shuddered at the idea that we might not be able to make up the sum of two hundred millions.

Baron Alphonse de Rothschild, who was shut up in Paris with his wife and brothers, gave his signature for the two hundred millions. This fine deed was soon forgotten, and there are even people who gainsay it.

Ah, the ingratitude of the masses is a disgrace to civilised humanity! "Ingratitude is the evil peculiar to the white races," said a Red-skin, and he was right.

When we heard in Paris that the armistice was signed for twenty days, a frightful sadness took possession of us all, even of those who most ardently wished for peace.

Every Parisian felt on his cheek the hand of the conqueror. It was the brand of shame, the blow given by the abominable treaty of peace.

Oh, that 31st of January 1871! I remember so well that I was anæmic from privation, undermined by grief, tortured with anxiety about my family, and I went out with Madame Guérard and two friends towards the Parc Monceau. Suddenly one of my friends, M. de Plancy, turned as pale as death. I looked to see what was the matter, and noticed a soldier passing by. He had no weapons. Two others passed, and they also had no weapons. And they were so pale too, these poor disarmed soldiers, these humble heroes; there was such evident grief and hopelessness in their very gait; and their eyes, as they looked at us women, seemed to say, "It is not our fault!" It was all so pitiful, so touching. I burst out sobbing, and went back home at once, for I did not want to meet any more disarmed French soldiers.

I decided to set off now as quickly as possible in search of my family. I asked Paul de Rémusat to get me an audience with M. Thiers, in order to obtain from him a passport for leaving Paris. But I could not go alone. I felt that the journey I was about to undertake was a very dangerous one. M. Thiers and Paul de Rémusat had warned me of this. I could see, therefore, that I should be constantly in the society of my travelling companion, and on this account I decided not to take a servant with me, but a friend.   I very naturally went at once to Madame Guérard.   Her husband, gentle though he was, refused absolutely to let her go with me, as he considered this expedition mad and dangerous.   Mad it certainly was, and dangerous too.

I did not insist, but I sent for my son's governess, Mlle. Soubise.   I asked her whether she would go with me, and did not attempt to conceal from her any of the dangers of the journey. She jumped with joy, and said she would be ready within twelve hours.   This girl is at present the wife of Commandant Monfils Chesneau.   And how strange life is, for she is now teaching the two daughters of my son, her former pupil.

Mlle. Soubise was then very young, and in appearance like a Creole.   She had very beautiful dark eyes, with a gentle, timid expression, and the voice of a child.   Her head, however, was full of adventure, romance, and day-dreams.   In appearance we might both have been taken for quite young girls, for, although I was older than she was, my slenderness and my face made me look younger.   It would have been absurd to try to take a trunk with us, so I took a bag for us both.   We only had a change of linen and some stockings.   I had my revolver, and I offered one to Mlle. Soubise, but she refused it with horror, and showed me an enormous pair of scissors in an enormous case.

" But what are you going to do with them ? " I asked.

" I shall kill myself if we are attacked," she replied

I was surprised at the difference in our characters.   I was taking a revolver, determined to protect myself by killing others ; she was determined to protect herself by killing herself.

XVIII

A BOLD JOURNEY THROUGH THE GERMAN LINES

On February 4 we started on this journey, which was to have lasted three days, and lasted eleven. At the first gate at which I presented myself for leaving Paris I was sent back in the most brutal fashion. Permissions to go outside the city had to be submitted for signature at the German outposts. I went to another gate, but it was only at the postern gate of Poissonniers that I could get my passport signed.

We were taken into a little shed which had been transformed into an office. A Prussian general was seated there. He looked me up and down, and then said .

" Are you Sarah Bernhardt ? "

" Yes," I answered.

" And this young lady is with you ? "

" Yes."

" And you think you are going to cross easily ? "

" I hope so."

" Well then, you are mistaken, and you would do better to stay inside Paris."

" No ; I want to leave. I'll see myself what will happen, but I want to leave."

He shrugged his shoulders, called an officer, said something I did not understand in German, and then went out, leaving us alone without our passports.

We had been there about a quarter of an hour when I suddenly heard a voice I knew. It was that of one of my friends, René Griffon, who had heard of my departure, and had come after me to try to dissuade me. The trouble he had taken was all in vain, though, as I was determined to leave. The general returned soon after, and Griffon was anxious to know what might happen to us.

"Everything!" returned the officer. "And worse than everything!"

Griffon spoke German, and had a short colloquy with the officer about us. This rather annoyed me, for, as I did not understand, I imagined that he was urging the general to prevent us from starting. I nevertheless resisted all persuasions, supplications, and even threats. A few minutes later a well-appointed vehicle drew up at the door of the shed.

"There you are!" said the German officer roughly. "I am sending you to Gonesse, where you will find the provision train which starts in an hour. I am recommending you to the care of the station-master, the Commandant X. After that may God take care of you!"

I stepped into the general's carriage, and said farewell to my friend, who was in despair. We arrived at Gonesse, and got out at the station, where we saw a little group of people talking in low voices. The coachman made me a military salute, refused what I wished to give him, and drove away at full speed. I advanced towards the group, wondering to whom I ought to speak, when a friendly voice exclaimed, "What, you here! Where have you come from? Where are you going?" It was Villaret, the tenor in vogue at the Opéra. He was going to his young wife, I believe, of whom he had had no news for five months. He introduced one of his friends, who was travelling with him, and whose name I do not remember; General Pelissier's son, and a very old man, so pale, and so sad-looking and woebegone, that I felt quite sorry for him. He was a M. Gerson, and was going to Belgium to take his grandson to his godmother's. His two sons had been killed during this pitiful war. One of the sons was married, and his wife had died of sorrow and despair. He was taking the orphan boy to his godmother, and he hoped to die himself as soon as possible afterwards.

Ah, the poor fellow, he was only fifty-nine then, and he was so cruelly ravaged by his grief that I took him for seventy.

Besides these five persons, there was an unbearable chatterer named Théodore Joussian, a wine dealer. Oh, he did not require any introduction.

"How do you do, Madame?" he began. "How fortunate

that you are going to travel with us. Ah, the journey will be a difficult one. Where are you going? Two women alone! It is not at all prudent, especially as all the routes are crowded with German and French sharpshooters, marauders, and thieves. Oh, haven't I demolished some of those German sharpshooters! Sh—— We must speak quietly, though; these sly fellows are very quick of hearing!" He then pointed to the German officers who were walking up and down. "Ah, the rascals!" he went on. "If I had my uniform and my gun they would not walk so boldly in front of Théodore Joussian. I have no fewer than six helmets at home . . ."

The man got on my nerves, and I turned my back on him and looked to see which of the men before me could be the station-master.

A tall young German, with his arm in a sling, came towards me with an open letter. It was the one which the general's coachman had handed to him, recommending me to his care. He held out his sound arm to me, but I refused it. He bowed and led the way, and I followed him, accompanied by Mlle. Soubise.

On arriving in his office he gave us seats at a little table, upon which knives and forks were placed for two persons. It was then three o'clock in the afternoon, and we had had nothing, not even a drop of water, since the evening before. I was very much touched by this thoughtfulness, and we did honour to the very simple but refreshing meal offered us by the young officer.

Whilst we lunched I looked at him when he was not noticing me. He was very young, and his face bore traces of recent suffering. I felt a compassionate tenderness for this unfortunate man, who was crippled for life, and my hatred for war increased still more.

He suddenly said to me, in rather bad French, "I think I can give you news of one of your friends."

"What is his name?" I asked.

"Emmanuel Bocher."

"Oh yes, he is certainly a great friend of mine. How is he?"

"He is still a prisoner, but he is very well."

"But I thought he had been released," I said.

"Some of those who were taken with him were released, on

giving their word never to take up arms against us again, but he refused to give his word."

"Oh, the brave soldier!" I exclaimed, in spite of myself.

The young German looked at me with his clear sad eyes.

"Yes," he said simply, "the brave soldier!"

When we had finished our luncheon I rose to return to the other travellers.

"The compartment reserved for you will not be here for two hours," said the young officer. "If you would like to rest, ladies, I will come for you at the right time." He went away, and before long I was sound asleep. I was nearly dead with fatigue.

Mlle. Soubise touched me on the shoulder to rouse me. The train was ready to start, and the young officer walked with me to it. I was a little amazed when I saw the carriage in which I was to travel. It had no roof, and was filled with coal. The officer had several empty sacks put in, one on the top of the other, to make our seats less hard. He sent for his officer's cloak, begging me to take it with us and send it him back, but I refused this odious disguise most energetically. It was a deadly cold day, but I preferred dying of cold to muffling up in a cloak belonging to the enemy.

The whistle was blown, the wounded officer saluted, and the train started. There were Prussian soldiers in the carriages. The subordinates, the employés, and the soldiers were just as brutish and rude as the German officers were polite and courteous.

The train stopped without any plausible reason, it started again to stop again, and it then stood still for an hour on this icy-cold night. On arriving at Creil, the stoker, the engine-driver, the soldiers, and every one else got out. I watched all these men, whistling, bawling to each other, spitting, and bursting into laughter as they pointed to us. Were they not the conquerors and we the conquered?

At Creil we stayed more than two hours. We could hear the distant sound of foreign music and the hurrahs of Germans who were making merry. All this hubbub came from a white house about five hundred yards away. We could distinguish the outlines of human beings locked in each other's arms, waltzing and turning round and round in a giddy revel.

It began to get on my nerves, for it seemed likely to continue until daylight.

I got out with Villaret, intending at any rate to stretch my limbs. We went towards the white house, and then, as I did not want to tell him my plan, I asked him to wait there for me.

Very fortunately, though, for me, I had not time to cross the threshold of this vile lodging-house, for an officer, smoking a cigarette, was just coming out of a small door. He spoke to me in German.

" I am French," I replied, and he then came up to me, speaking my language, for they could all talk French.

He asked me what I was doing there. My nerves were over-strung. I told him feverishly of our lamentable Odyssey since our departure from Gonesse, and finally of our waiting two hours in an icy-cold carriage while the stokers, engine-drivers, and conductors were all dancing in this house.

" But I had no idea that there were passengers in those carriages, and it was I who gave permission to these men to dance and drink. The guard of the train told me that he was taking cattle and goods, and that he did not need to arrive before eight in the morning, and I believed him——"

" Well, Monsieur," I said, " the only cattle in the train are the eight French passengers, and I should be very much obliged if you would give orders that the journey should be continued."

" Make your mind easy about that, Madame," he replied. " Will you come in and rest? I am here just now on a round of inspection, and am staying for a few days in this inn. You shall have a cup of tea, and that will refresh you."

I told him that I had a friend waiting for me in the road and a lady in the railway carriage.

" But that makes no difference," he said. " Let us go and fetch them."

A few minutes later we found poor Villaret seated on a mile-stone. His head was on his knees, and he was asleep. I asked him to fetch Mlle. Soubise.

" And if your other travelling companions will come and take a cup of tea they will be welcome," said the officer. I went back with him, and we entered by the little door through which I had seen him come out. It was a fairly large room which we entered, on a level with the meadow; there were some mats on the floor, a very low bed, and an enormous table, on which were two large maps of France. One of these was studded over with pins and small flags. There was also a portrait of the Emperor William, mounted and fastened up with four pins. All this belonged to the officer.

On the chimney-piece, under an enormous glass shade, were a bride's wreath, a military medal, and a plait of white hair. On each side of the glass shade was a china vase containing a branch of box. All this, together with the table and the bed, belonged to the landlady, who had given up her room to the officer.

There were five cane chairs round the table, a velvet arm-chair, and a wooden bench covered with books against the wall. A sword and belt were lying on the table, and two horse-pistols.

I was philosophising to myself on all these heterogeneous objects, when the others arrived : Mlle. Soubise, Villaret, young Gerson, and that unbearable Théodore Joussian. (I hope he will forgive me if he is living now, poor man, but the thought of him still irritates me.)

The officer had some boiling hot tea made for us, and it was a veritable treat, as we were exhausted with hunger and cold.

When the door was opened for the tea to be brought in Théodore Joussian caught a glimpse of the throng of girls, soldiers, and other people.

"Ah, my friends," he exclaimed, with a burst of laughter, "we are at His Majesty William's ; there is a reception on, and it's *chic*—I can tell you that!" With this he smacked his tongue twice. Villaret reminded him that we were the guests of a German, and that it was preferable to be quiet.

"That's enough, that's enough!" he replied, lighting a cigarette.

A frightful uproar of oaths and shouts now took the place of the deafening sound of the orchestra, and the incorrigible Southerner half opened the door.

I could see the officer giving orders to two sub-officers, who in their turn separated the groups, seizing the stoker, the engine-driver, and the other men belonging to the train, so

roughly that I was sorry for them. They were kicked in the
back, they received blows with the flat of the sword on the
shoulder; a blow with the butt end of a gun knocked the
guard of the train down. He was the ugliest brute, though,
that I have ever seen. All these people were sobered in a few
seconds, and went back towards our carriage with a hang-dog
look and a threatening mien.

We followed them, but I did not feel any too satisfied as to
what might happen to us on the way with this queer lot. The
officer evidently had a similar idea, for he ordered one of the
sub-officers to accompany us as far as Amiens. This sub-officer
got into our carriage, and we set off again. We arrived at
Amiens at six in the morning. Daylight had not yet succeeded
in piercing through the night-clouds. Light rain was falling,
which was hardened by the cold. There was not a carriage to be
had, not even a porter. I wanted to go to the Hôtel du
Cheval-Blanc, but a man who happened to be there said to me:
" It's no use, my little lady; there's no room there, even for a
lath like you. Go to the house over there with a balcony;
they can put some people up."

With these words he turned his back on me. Villaret had
gone off without saying a word. M. Gerson and his
grandson had disappeared silently in a covered country cart
hermetically closed. A stout, ruddy, thick-set matronly woman
was waiting for them, but the coachman looked as though he
were in the service of well-to-do people. General Pelissier's
son, who had not uttered a word since we had left Gonesse,
had disappeared like a ball from the hands of a conjurer.

Théodore Joussian politely offered to accompany us, and
I was so weary that I accepted his offer. He picked up our
bag and began to walk at full speed, so that we had difficulty
in keeping up with him. He was so breathless with the walk
that he could not talk, which was a great relief to me.

Finally we arrived at the house and entered, but my horror
was great on seeing that the hall of the hotel had been transformed into a dormitory. We could scarcely walk between the
mattresses laid down on the ground, and the grumbling of the
people was by no means promising.

When once we were in the office a young girl in mourning
told us that there was not a room vacant. I sank down on a

chair, and Mlle. Soubise leaned against the wall with her arms hanging down, looking most dejected.

The odious Joussian then yelled out that they could not let two women as young as we were be out in the street all night. He went to the proprietress of the hotel and said something quietly about me. I do not know what it was, but I heard my name distinctly. The young woman in mourning then looked up with moist eyes.

" My brother was a poet," she said. " He wrote a very pretty sonnet about you after seeing you play in *Le Passant* more than ten times. He took me, too, to see you, and I enjoyed myself so much that night. It is all over, though." She lifted her hands towards her head and sobbed, trying to stifle back her cries. " It's all over ! " she repeated. " He is dead ! They have killed him ! It is all over ! All over ! "

I got up, moved to the depth of my being by this terrible grief. I put my arms round her and kissed her, crying myself, and whispering to her words of comfort and hope.

Calmed by my words and touched by my sisterliness, she wiped her eyes, and taking my hand, led me gently away. Soubise followed. I signed to Joussian in an authoritative way to stay where he was, and we went up the two flights of stairs of the hotel in silence. At the end of a narrow corridor she opened a door. We found ourselves in rather a big room, reeking with the smell of tobacco. A small night-lamp, placed on a little table by the bed, was the only light in this large room. The wheezing respiration of a human breast disturbed the silence. I looked towards the bed, and by the faint light from the little lamp I saw a man half seated, propped up by a heap of pillows. The man was aged-looking rather than really old. His beard and hair were white, and his face bore traces of suffering. Two large furrows were formed from the eyes to the corners of the mouth. What tears must have rolled down that poor emaciated face !

The girl went quietly towards the bed, signed to us to come inside the room, and then shut the door. We walked across on tiptoes to the far end of the room, our arms stretched out to maintain our equilibrium. I sat down with precaution on a large Empire couch, and Soubise took a seat beside me. The man in bed half opened his eyes.

" What is it, my child ? " he asked.

" Nothing, father ; nothing serious," she replied. " I wanted to tell you, so that you should not be surprised when you woke up. I have just given hospitality in our room to two ladies who are here."

He turned his head in an annoyed way, and tried to look at us at the end of the room.

" The lady with fair hair," continued the girl, " is Sarah Bernhardt, whom Lucien liked so much, you remember ? "

The man sat up, and shading his eyes with his hand peered at us. I went near to him. He gazed at me silently, and then made a gesture with his hand. His daughter understood the gesture, and brought him an envelope from a small bureau. The unhappy father's hands trembled as he took it. He drew out slowly three sheets of paper and a photograph. He fixed his gaze on me and then on the portrait.

" Yes, yes ; it certainly is you, it certainly is you," he murmured.

I recognised my photograph, taken in *Le Passant*, smelling a rose.

" You see," said the poor man, his eyes veiled by tears, " you were this child's idol. These are the lines he wrote about you."

He then read me, in his quavering voice, with a slight Picardian accent, a very pretty sonnet, which he refused to give me. He then unfolded a second paper, on which some verses to Sarah Bernhardt were scrawled. The third paper was a sort of triumphant chant, celebrating all our victories over the enemy.

" The poor fellow still hoped, until he was killed," said the father. " He has only been dead five weeks. He had three shots in his head. The first shattered his jaw, but he did not fall. He continued firing on the scoundrels like a man possessed. The second took his ear off, and the third struck him in his right eye. He fell then, never to rise again. His comrade told us all this. He was twenty-two years old. And now—it's all over ! "

The unhappy man's head fell back on the heap of pillows. His two inert hands had let the papers fall, and great tears rolled down his pale cheeks, in the furrows formed by grief. A stifled groan burst from his lips. The girl had fallen on her knees, and buried her head in the bed-clothes, to deaden the

sound of her sobs.   Soubise and I were completely upset.   Ah!
those stifled sobs, those deadened groans seemed to buzz in my
ears, and I felt everything giving way under me.   I stretched my
hands out into space and closed my eyes.

Soon there was a distant rumbling noise, which increased and
came nearer; then yells of pain, bones knocking against each
other, the dull sound of horses' feet dashing out human brains;
armed men passed by like a destructive whirlwind, shouting,
" *Vive la guerre !* " And women on their knees, with outstretched
arms, crying out, " War is infamous !   In the name of our
wombs which bore you, of our breasts which suckled you, in the
name of our pain in childbirth, in the name of our anguish over
your cradles, let this cease ! "

But the savage whirlwind passed by, riding over the women.
I stretched my arms out in a supreme effort which woke me suddenly.   I was lying in the girl's bed.   Mlle. Soubise, who was
near me, was holding my hand.   A man whom I did not know,
but whom some one called doctor, laid me gently down again on
the bed.   I had some difficulty in collecting my thoughts.

" How long have I been here ? " I asked.

" Since last night," replied the gentle voice of Soubise.   " You
fainted, and the doctor told us that you had an attack of fever.
Oh, I have been very frightened ! "

I turned my face to the doctor.

" Yes, dear lady," he said.   " You must be very prudent now
for the next forty-eight hours, and then you may set out again.
But you have had a great many shocks for one with such delicate
health.   You must take care."

I took the draught that he was holding out to me, apologised
to the owner of the house, who had just come in, and then
turned round with my face to the wall.   I needed rest so very,
very much.

Two days later I left our sad but kindly hosts.   My
travelling companions had all disappeared.   When I went downstairs I kept meeting Prussians, for the unfortunate proprietor
had been invaded compulsorily by the German army.   He looked
at each soldier and at every officer, trying to find out whether he
were not in presence of the one who had killed his poor boy.
He did not tell me this, but it was my idea.   It seemed to me
that such was his thought and such the meaning of his gaze.

In the vehicle in which I drove to the station the kind man had put a basket of food. He also gave me a copy of the sonnet and a tracing of his son's photograph.

I left the desolate couple with the deepest emotion, and I kissed the girl on taking our departure. Soubise and I did not exchange a word on our journey to the railway station, but we were both preoccupied with the same distressing thoughts.

At the station we found that the Germans were masters there too. I asked for a first-class compartment to ourselves, or for a *coupé*, whatever they liked, provided we were alone.

I could not make myself understood.

I saw a man, oiling the wheels of the carriages, who looked to me like a Frenchman. I was not mistaken. He was an old man who had been kept on, partly out of charity and partly because he knew every nook and corner, and, being Alsatian, spoke German. This good man took me to the booking office, and explained my wish to have a first-class compartment to myself. The man who had charge of the ticket office burst out laughing. There was neither first nor second class, he said. It was a German train, and I should have to travel like every one else. The wheel-oiler turned purple with rage, which he quickly suppressed. (He had to keep his place. His consumptive wife was nursing their son, who had just been sent home from the hospital with his leg cut off and the wound not yet healed up. There were so many in the hospital.) All this he told me as he took me to the station-master. The latter spoke French very well, but he was not at all like the other German officers I had met.

He scarcely saluted me, and when I expressed my desire he replied curtly :

" It is impossible. Two places shall be reserved for you in the officers' carriage."

" But that is what I want to avoid," I exclaimed. " I do not want to travel with German officers."

" Well then, you shall be put with German soldiers," he growled angrily, and, putting on his hat, he went out slamming the door. I remained there, amazed and confused by the insolence of this ignoble brute. I turned so pale, it appears, and the blue of my eyes became so clear, that Soubise, who was acquainted with my fits of anger, was very much alarmed.

" Do be calm, Madame, I implore ! " she said. " We are two women alone in the midst of hostile people. If they liked to harm us they could, and we must accomplish the aim and object of our journey; we must see little Maurice again."

She was very clever, this charming Mlle. Soubise, and her little speech had the desired effect. To see the child again was my aim and object. I calmed down, and vowed that I would not allow myself to get angry during this journey, which promised to be fertile in incidents, and I almost kept my word. I left the station-master's office, and found the poor Alsatian waiting at the door. I gave him a couple of louis, which he hid away quickly, and then shook my hand as though he would shake it off. " You ought not to have that so visible, Madame," he said, pointing to the little bag I had hanging at my side ; " it is very dangerous."

I thanked him, but did not pay any attention to his advice. As the train was about to start we entered the only first-class compartment there was ; in it were two young German officers. They saluted, and I took this as a good omen. The train whistled, and I thought what good luck we had, as no one else would get in ! Well, the wheels had not turned round ten times when the door opened violently and five German officers leaped into our carriage.

We were nine then, and what torture it was! The station-master waved a farewell to one of the officers, and both of them burst out laughing as they looked at us. I glanced at the station-master's friend. He was a surgeon-major, and was wearing the ambulance badge on his sleeve. His wide face was congested, and a ring of sandy bushy beard surrounded the lower part of it. Two little bright, light-coloured eyes in perpetual movement lit up this ruddy face and gave him a sly look. He was broad-shouldered and thick-set, and gave one the idea of having strength without nerves. The horrid man was still laughing when the station and its master were far away from us, but what the other one had said was evidently very droll.

I was in a corner seat, with Soubise opposite me. A young German officer sat beside me, and the other young officer was next to my friend. They were both very gentle and polite, and one of them was quite delightful in his youthful charm.

The surgeon-major took off his helmet. He was very bald,

and had a very small, stubborn-looking forehead. He began to talk in a loud voice to the other officers.

Our two young bodyguards took very little part in the conversation. Among the others was a tall, affected young man, whom they addressed as baron. He was slender, very elegant, and very strong. When he saw that we did not understand German he spoke to us in English. But Soubise was too timid to answer, and I speak English very badly. He therefore resigned himself regretfully to talking French.

He was agreeable, too agreeable; he certainly had not bad manners, but he was deficient in tact. I made him understand this by turning my face towards the scenery we were passing.

We were very much absorbed in our thoughts, and had been travelling for a long time, when I suddenly felt suffocated by smoke which was filling the carriage. I looked round, and saw that the surgeon-major had lighted his pipe, and, with his eyes half closed, was sending up puffs of smoke to the ceiling.

My eyes were smarting, and I was choking with indignation, so much so that I was seized with a fit of coughing, which I exaggerated in order to attract the attention of the impolite man. The baron, however, slapped him on the knee and endeavoured to make him comprehend that the smoke inconvenienced me. He answered by an insult which I did not understand, shrugged his shoulders, and continued to smoke. Exasperated by this, I lowered the window on my side. The intense cold made itself felt in the carriage, but I preferred that to the nauseous smoke of the pipe. Suddenly the surgeon-major got up, putting his hand to his ear, which I then saw was filled with cotton-wool. He swore like an ox-driver, and, pushing past every one and stepping on my feet and on Soubise's, he shut the window violently, cursing and swearing all the time quite uselessly, for I did not understand him. He went back to his seat, continued his pipe, and sent out enormous clouds of smoke in the most insolent way. The baron and the two young Germans who had been the first in the carriage appeared to ask him something and then to remonstrate with him, but he evidently told them to mind their own business and began to abuse them. Very much calmer myself on seeing the increasing anger of the disagreeable man, and very much amused by his ear-ache, I again opened the window. He got up again, furious, showed me his ear and his swollen cheek, and I caught the word " periostitis " in the explanation he gave me on shutting the window again and threatening me. I then made him understand that I had a weak chest, and that the smoke made me cough.

The baron acted as my interpreter, and explained this to him ; but it was easy to see that he did not care a bit about that, and he once more took up his favourite attitude and his pipe. I left him in peace for five minutes, during which time he was able to imagine himself triumphant, and then with a sudden jerk of my elbow I broke the pane of glass. Stupefaction was depicted on the major's face, and he became livid. He got straight up, but the two young men rose at the same time, whilst the baron burst out laughing in the most brutal manner.

The surgeon moved a step in our direction, but he found a rampart before him ; another officer had joined the two young men, and he was a strong, hardy-looking fellow, just cut out for an obstacle. I do not know what he said to the surgeon-major, but it was something clear and decisive. The latter, not knowing how to expend his anger, turned on the baron, who was still laughing, and abused him so violently that the latter calmed down suddenly and answered in such a way that I quite understood the two men were calling each other out. That affected me but little, anyhow. They might very well kill each other, these two men, for they were equally ill-mannered.

The carriage was now quiet and icy-cold, for the wind blew in wildly through the broken pane. The sun had set. The sky was getting cloudy. It was about half-past five, and we were approaching Tergnier. The major had changed seats with his friend, in order to shelter his ear as much as possible. He kept moaning like a half-dead cow.

Suddenly the repeated whistling of a distant locomotive made us listen attentively. We then heard two, three, and four crackers bursting under our wheels. We could perfectly well feel the efforts the engine-driver was making to slacken speed, but before he could succeed we were thrown against each other by a frightful shock. There were cracks and creaks, the hiccoughs of the locomotive spitting out its smoke in irregular fits, desperate cries, shouts, oaths, sudden downfalls, a lull, then a thick smoke, broken by the flames of a fire. Our carriage was standing up,

like a horse kicking up its hind legs. It was impossible to
get our balance again.

Who was wounded and who was not wounded? We were
nine in the compartment. For my part, I fancied that all my
bones were broken. I moved one leg and then I tried the other.
Then, delighted at finding them unbroken, I tried my arms in
the same way. I had nothing broken, and neither had Soubise.
She had bitten her tongue, and it was bleeding, and this had
frightened me. She did not seem to understand anything. The
tremendous shaking had made her dizzy, and she lost her memory
for some days. I had a rather deep scratch between my eyes. I
had not had time to stretch out my arms, and my forehead had
knocked against the hilt of the sword which the officer seated
by Soubise had been holding upright.

Assistance arrived from all sides.

For some time the door of our compartment could not be
opened.

Darkness had come on when it finally yielded, and a lantern
shone feebly on our poor broken-up carriage.

I looked round for our one bag, but on finding it I let it go
immediately, for my hand was red with blood. Whose blood
was it?

Three men did not move, and one of them was the major. His
face looked to me livid. I closed my eyes, in order not to know,
and I let the man who had come to our aid pull me out of the
compartment. One of the young officers got out after me. He
took Soubise, who was almost in a fainting condition, from his
friend. The imbecile baron then got out; his shoulder was out
of joint. A doctor came forward among the rescuers. The
baron held his arm out to him, telling him at the same time to
pull it, which he did at once. The French doctor took off the
officer's cloak, told two of the railway-men to hold him, and
then, pushing against him himself, pulled at the poor arm. The
baron was very pale, and gave a low whistle. When the arm
was back in its place, the doctor shook the baron's other hand.
"Cristi!" he said, "I must have hurt you very much. You
are most courageous." The German saluted, and I helped him
on again with his cloak.

The doctor was then fetched away, and I saw that he was
taken back to our compartment. I shuddered in spite of myself.

We were now able to find out what had been the cause of our accident. A locomotive attached to two vans of coal had been shunting on to a side line in order to let us pass, when one of the vans got off the rails, and the locomotive tired its lungs with whistling the alarm, whilst men ran to meet us, scattering crackers. Everything had been in vain, and we had run against the overturned van.

What were we to do? The roads, softened by the recent wet weather, were all broken up by the cannons. We were about four miles from Tergnier, and a thin penetrating rain was making our clothes stick to our bodies.

There were four carriages, but they were for the wounded. Other carriages would come, but there were the dead to be carried away. An improvised litter was just being borne along by two workmen. The major was lying on it, so livid that I clenched my hands until my nails entered the flesh. One of the officers wanted to question the doctor who was following. "Oh no!" I exclaimed. "Please, please do not. I do not want to know. The poor fellow!"

I stopped my ears, as though some one was about to shout out something horrible to me, and I never knew his fate.

We were obliged to resign ourselves to setting out on foot. We went about two kilometres as bravely as possible, and then I stopped, quite exhausted. The mud which clung to our shoes made these very heavy. The effort we had to make at every step to get our feet out of the mire tired us out. I sat down on a milestone, and declared that I would not go any farther.

My sweet companion wept: the two young German officers who had acted as bodyguards made a seat for me by crossing their hands, and so we went nearly another mile. My companion could not walk any farther. I offered her my place, but she refused it.

"Well then, let us wait here!" I said, and, quite at the end of our strength, we rested against a little broken tree.

It was now night, and such a cold night!

Soubise and I huddled close together, trying to keep each other warm. I began to fall asleep, seeing before my eyes the wounded men of Châtillon, who had died seated against the little shrubs. I did not want to move again, and the torpor seemed to me thoroughly delicious.

A cart passed by, however, on its way to Tergnier. One of the young men hailed it, and when a price was agreed upon I felt myself picked up from the ground, lifted into the vehicle, and carried along by the jerky, rolling movement of two loose wheels, which climbed the hills, sank into the mire, and jumped over the heaps of stones, whilst the driver whipped up his beasts and urged them on with his voice. He had a " don't care, let what will happen " way of driving, which was characteristic of those days.

I was aware of all this in my semi-sleep, for I was not really asleep, but I did not want to answer any questions. I gave myself up to this prostration of my whole being with a certain amount of enjoyment.

A rough jerk, however, indicated that we had arrived at Tergnier. The cart had drawn up at the hotel, and we had to get out. I pretended to be still sleeping heavily. But it was no use, for I had to wake up. The two young men helped me up to my room.

I asked Soubise to arrange about the payment of the cart before the departure of our excellent young companions, who were sorry to leave us. I signed for each of them a voucher, on a sheet of the hotel paper, for a photograph. Only one of them ever claimed it. This was six years later, and I sent it to him.

The Tergnier hotel could only give us one room. I let Soubise go to bed, and I slept in an arm-chair, dressed as I was.

The following morning I asked about a train for Cateau, but was told that there was no train.

We had to work marvels to procure a vehicle, but finally Dr. Meunier, or Mesnier, agreed to lend us a two-wheeled conveyance. That was something, but there was no horse. The poor doctor's horse had been requisitioned by the enemy. A wheelwright for an exorbitant price let me have a colt that had never been in the shafts, and which went wild when the harness was put on. The poor little beast calmed down after being well lashed, but his wildness then changed into stubbornness. He stood still on his four legs, which were trembling furiously, and refused to move. With his neck stretched towards the ground, his eye fixed, and his nostrils dilating, he would not budge any more than a stake in the earth. Two men then held the light

carriage back ; the halter was taken off the colt's neck ; he shook
his head for an instant, and, thinking himself free and without
any impediments, began to advance. The men were scarcely holding the vehicle. He gave two little kicks, and then began to
trot. Oh, it was only a very short trot. A boy then stopped
him, some carrots were given to him, his mane was stroked, and
the halter was put on again. He stopped suddenly, but the boy,
jumping into the gig and holding the reins lightly, spoke to
him and encouraged him to move on. The colt, not feeling any
resistance, began to trot along for about a quarter of an hour,
and then came back to us at the door of the hotel.

I had to leave a deposit of four hundred francs with the
notary of the place, in case the colt should die.

Ah, what a journey that was with the boy, Soubise, and me
sitting close together in that little gig, the wheels of which
creaked at every jolt! The unhappy colt was steaming like
a *pot-au-feu* when the lid is raised. We started at eleven in
the morning, and when we had to stop, because the poor beast
could not go any farther, it was five in the afternoon, and we
had not gone five miles. Oh, that poor colt, he was certainly
to be pitied! We were not very heavy, all three of us together,
but we were too much for him. We were just a few yards away
from a sordid-looking house. I knocked, and an old woman,
enormous in size, opened the door.

" What do you want ? " she asked.

" Hospitality for an hour and shelter for our horse."

She looked out on to the road and saw our turn-out.

" Hey, father ! " she called out in a husky voice, " come and
look here ! "

A stout man, quite as stout as she was, but older, came hob-
bling heavily along. She pointed to the gig, so oddly equipped,
and he burst out laughing and said to me in an insolent way :

" Well, what do you want ? "

I repeated my phrase : " Hospitality for an hour," &c. &c.

" Perhaps we can do it, but it'll want paying for."

I showed him twenty francs. The old woman gave him
a nudge.

" Oh, but in these times, you know, it's well worth forty
francs."

" Very good," I said, " agreed ; forty francs."

He then let me go inside the house with Mlle. Soubise, and sent his son towards the boy, who was coming along holding the colt by his mane. He had taken off the halter very considerately and thrown my rug over its steaming sides. On reaching the house the poor beast was quickly unharnessed and taken into a little enclosure, at the far end of which a few badly-joined planks served as a stable for an old mule, which was aroused by the fat woman with kicks and turned out into the enclosure. The colt took its place, and when I asked for some oats for it she replied :

" Perhaps we could get it some, but that isn't included in the forty francs."

" Very well," I said, and I gave our boy five francs to fetch the oats, but the old shrew took the money from him and handed it to her lad, saying :

" You go ; you know where to find them, and come back quick."

Our boy remained with the colt, drying it and rubbing it down as well as he could. I went back to the house, where I found my charming Soubise with her sleeves turned up and her delicate hands washing two glasses and two plates for us. I asked if it would be possible to have some eggs.

" Yes, but——"

I interrupted our monstrous hostess.

" Don't tire yourself, Madame, I beg," I said. " It is understood that the forty francs are your tip, and that I am to pay for everything else."

She was confused for a moment, shaking her head and trying to find words, but I asked her to give me the eggs. She brought me five eggs, and I began to make an omelette, as my culinary glory is an omelette.

The water was nauseous, so we drank cider. I sent for the boy and made them serve him something to eat in our presence, for I was afraid that the ogress would give him too economical a meal.

When I paid the fabulous bill of seventy-five francs, inclusive of course of the forty francs, the matron put on her spectacles, and taking one of the gold pieces, looked at it on one side, then on the other, made it ring on a plate and then on the ground. She did this with each of the three gold pieces. I could not help laughing.

"Oh, there's nothing to laugh at," she grunted. "For the last six months we've had nothing but thieves here."

"And you know something about theft!" I said.

She looked at me, trying to make out what I meant, but the laughing expression in my eyes took away her suspicions. This was very fortunate, as they were people capable of doing us harm. I had taken the precaution, when sitting down to table, of putting my revolver near me.

"You know how to fire that?" asked the lame man.

"Oh yes, I shoot very well," I answered, though it was not true.

Our steed was then put in again in a few seconds, and we proceeded on our way. The colt appeared to be quite joyful. He stamped, kicked a little, and began to go at a pretty steady pace.

Our disagreeable hosts had indicated the way to St. Quentin, and we set off, after our poor colt had made various attempts at standing still. I was dead tired and fell asleep, but after about an hour the vehicle stopped abruptly and the wretched beast began to snort and put his back up, supporting himself on his four stiff, trembling legs.

It had been a gloomy day, and a lowering sky full of tears seemed to be falling slowly over the earth. We had stopped in the middle of a field which had been ploughed up all over by the heavy wheels of cannons. The rest of the ground had been trampled by horses' feet and the cold had hardened the little ridges of earth, leaving icicles here and there, which glittered dismally in the thick atmosphere.

We got down from the vehicle, to try to discover what was making our little animal tremble in this way. I gave a cry of horror, for, only about five yards away, some dogs were pulling wildly at a dead body, half of which was still underground. It was a soldier, and fortunately one of the enemy. I took the whip from our young driver and lashed the horrid animals as hard as I could. They moved away for a second, showing their teeth, and then returned to their voracious and abominable work, growling sullenly at us.

Our boy got down and led the snorting pony by the bridle. We went on with some difficulty, trying to find the road in these devastated plains.

Darkness came over us, and it was icy cold.

The moon feebly pushed aside her veils and shone over the landscape with a wan, sad light. I was half dead with fright. It seemed to me that the silence was broken by cries from underground, and every little mound of earth appeared to me to be a head.

Mlle. Soubise was crying, with her face hidden in her hands. After going along for half an hour, we saw in the distance a little group of people coming along carrying lanterns. I went towards them, as I wanted to find out which way to go. I was embarrassed on getting nearer to them, for I could hear sobs. I saw a poor woman, who was very corpulent, being helped along by a young priest. The whole of her body was shaken by her fits of grief. She was followed by two sub-officers and by three other persons. I let her pass by, and then questioned those who were following her. I was told that she was looking for the bodies of her husband and son, who had both been killed a few days before on the St. Quentin plains. She came each day at dusk, in order to avoid general curiosity, but she had not yet met with any success. It was hoped that she would find them this time, as one of these sub-officers, who had just left the hospital, was taking her to the spot where he had seen the poor woman's husband fall, mortally wounded. He had fallen there himself, and had been picked up by the ambulance people.

I thanked these persons, who showed me the sad road we must take, the best one there was, through the cemetery, which was still warm under the ice.

We could now distinguish groups of people searching about, and it was all so horrible that it made me want to scream out.

Suddenly the boy who was driving us pulled my coat-sleeve.

" Oh, Madame," he said, " look at that scoundrel stealing."

I looked, and saw a man lying down full length, with a large bag near him. He had a dark lantern, which he held towards the ground. He then got up, looked round him, for his outline could be seen distinctly on the horizon, and began his work again.

When he caught sight of us he put out his lamp and crouched down on the ground. We walked on in silence straight towards him. I took the colt by the bridle, on the other side, and the

o

boy no doubt understood what I intended to do, for he let me lead the way. I walked straight towards the man, pretending not to know he was there. The colt backed, but we pulled hard and made it advance. We were so near to the man that I shuddered at the thought that the wretch would perhaps allow himself to be trampled over by the animal and the light vehicle rather than reveal his presence. Fortunately, I was mistaken. A stifled voice murmured, "Take care there! I am wounded. You will run over me." I took the gig lantern down. We had covered it with a jacket, as the moon lighted us better, and I now turned it on the face of this wretch. I was stupefied to see a man of from sixty-five to seventy years of age, with a hollow-looking face, framed with long, dirty white whiskers. He had a muffler round his neck, and was wearing a peasant's cloak of a dark colour. Around him, shown up by the moon, were sword belts, brass buttons, sword hilts, and other objects that the infamous old fellow had torn from the poor dead.

"You are not wounded. You are a thief and a violator of tombs! I shall call out and you will be killed. Do you hear that, you miserable wretch?" I exclaimed, and I went so near to him that I could feel his breath sully mine. He crouched down on his knees and, clasping his criminal hands, implored me in a trembling, tearful voice.

"Leave your bag there, then," I said, "and all those things. Empty your pockets; leave everything and go. Run, for as soon as you are out of sight I shall call one of those soldiers who are making searches, and give them your plunder. I know I am doing wrong, though, in letting you go free."

He emptied his pockets, groaning all the time, and was just going away when the lad whispered, "He's hiding some boots under his cloak." I was furious with rage with this vile thief, and I pulled his big cloak off.

"Leave everything, you wretched man," I exclaimed, "or I will call the soldiers."

Six pairs of boots, taken from the corpses, fell noisily on to the hard ground. The man stooped down for his revolver, which he had taken out of his pocket at the same time as the stolen objects.

"Will you leave that, and get away quickly?" I said. "My patience is at an end."

" But if I am caught I shan't be able to defend myself," he exclaimed, in a fit of desperate rage.

" It will be because God willed it so," I answered. " Go at once, or I will call." The man then made off, abusing me as he went.

Our little driver then fetched a soldier, to whom I related the adventure, showing him the objects.

" Which way did the rascal go ? " asked a sergeant who had come with the soldier.

" I can't say," I replied.

" Oh well, I don't care to run after him," he said ; " there are enough dead men here."

We continued our way until we came to a place where several roads met, and it was then possible for us to take a route a little more suitable for vehicles.

After going through Busigny and a wood, where there were bogs in which we only just escaped being swallowed up, our painful journey came to an end, and we arrived at Cateau in the night, half dead with fatigue, fright, and despair.

I was obliged to take a day's rest there, for I was prostrate with feverishness. We had two little rooms, roughly white-washed but quite clean. The floor was of red, shiny bricks, and there was a polished wood bed and white curtains.

I sent for a doctor for my charming little Soubise, who, it seemed to me, was worse than I was. He thought we were both in a very bad state, though. A nervous feverishness had taken all the use out of my limbs and made my head burn. She could not keep still, but kept seeing spectres and fires, hearing shouts and turning round quickly, imagining that some one had touched her on the shoulder. The good man gave us a soothing draught to overcome our fatigue, and the next day a very hot bath brought back the suppleness to our limbs. It was then six days since we had left Paris, and it would take about twenty more hours to reach Homburg, for in those days trains went much less quickly than at present. I took a train for Brussels, where I was counting on buying a trunk and a few necessary things.

From Cateau to Brussels there was no hindrance to our journey, and we were able to take the train again the same evening.

I had replenished our wardrobe, which certainly needed it,

and we continued our journey without much difficulty as far as
Cologne.   But on arriving in that city we had a cruel disappointment.   The train had only just entered the station,
when a railway official, passing quickly in front of the carriages,
shouted something in German which I did not catch.   Every
one seemed to be in a hurry, and men and women pushed each
other without any courtesy.

I addressed another official and showed him our tickets.   He
took up my bag, very obligingly, and hurried after the crowd.
We followed, but I did not understand the excitement until the
man flung my bag into a compartment and signed to me to get
in as quickly as possible.

Soubise was already on the step when she was pushed aside
violently by a railway porter, who slammed the door, and before
I was fully aware of what had happened the train had disappeared.   My bag had gone, and our trunk also.   The trunk
had been placed in a luggage van that had been unhooked from
the train which had just arrived, and immediately fastened on
to the express now departing.   I began to cry with rage.   An
official took pity on us and led us to the station-master.   He
was a very superior sort of man, who spoke French fairly well.
I sank down in his great leather arm-chair and told him my
misadventure, sobbing nervously.   He looked kind and sympathetic.   He immediately telegraphed for my bag and trunk to
be given into the care of the station-master at the first station.

" You will have them again to-morrow, towards mid-day," he
said.

"Then I cannot start this evening ? " I asked.

" Oh no, that is impossible," he replied.   " There is no train,
for the express that will take you to Homburg does not start
before to-morrow morning."

" Oh God, God ! " I exclaimed, and I was seized with veritable
despair, which soon affected Mlle. Soubise too.

The poor station-master was rather embarrassed, and tried to
soothe me.

" Do you know any one here ? " he asked.

" No, no one.   I do not know any one in Cologne."

" Well then, I will have you driven to the Hôtel du Nord.
My sister-in-law has been there for two days, and she will look
after you."

Half an hour later his carriage arrived, and he took us to the Hôtel du Nord, after driving a long way round to show us the city. But at that epoch I did not admire anything belonging to the Germans.

On arriving at the Hôtel du Nord, he introduced us to his sister-in-law, a fair-haired young woman, pretty, but too tall and too big for my taste. I must say, though, that she was very sweet and affable. She engaged two bedrooms for us near her own rooms. She had a flat on the ground floor, and she invited us to dinner, which was served in her drawing-room. Her brother-in-law joined us in the evening. The charming woman was very musical. She played to us from Berlioz, Gounod, and even Auber. I thoroughly appreciated the delicacy of this woman in only letting us hear French composers. I asked her to play us something from Mozart and Wagner. At that name she turned to me and exclaimed, " Do you like Wagner ? "

" I like his music," I replied, " but I detest the man."

Mlle. Soubise whispered to me, " Ask her to play Liszt."

She overheard, and complied with infinite graciousness. I must admit that I spent a delightful evening there.

At ten o'clock the station-master (whose name I have very stupidly forgotten, and I cannot find it in any of my notes) told me that he would call for us at eight the following morning, and he then took leave of us. I fell asleep, lulled by Mozart, Gounod, &c.

At eight o'clock the next morning a servant came to tell me that the carriage was waiting for us. There was a gentle knock at my door, and our beautiful hostess of the previous evening said sweetly, " Come, you must start ! " I was really very much touched by the delicacy of the pretty German woman.

It was such a fine day that I asked her if we should have time to walk there, and on her reply in the affirmative we all three started for the station, which is not far from the hotel. A special compartment had been reserved for us, and we installed ourselves in it as comfortably as possible. The brother and sister shook hands with us, and wished us a pleasant journey.

When the train had started I discovered in one of the corners a bouquet of forget-me-nots with the sister's card and a box of chocolates from the station-master.

I was at last about to arrive at my goal, and was in a state of wild excitement at the idea of seeing once more all my beloved ones.   I should have liked to have gone to sleep.   My eyes, which had grown larger with anxiety, travelled through space more rapidly than the train went.   I fumed each time it stopped, and envied the birds I saw flying along.   I laughed with delight as I thought of the surprised faces of those I was going to see again, and then I began to tremble with anxiety.   What had happened to them, and should I find them all?   I should if— ah, those " ifs," those " becauses," and those " buts "!   My mind became full of them, they bristled with illnesses and accidents, and I began to weep.   My poor little travelling companion began to weep too.

Finally we came within sight of Homburg.   Twenty more minutes of this turning of wheels and we should enter the station. But just as though all the sprites and devils from the infernal regions had concerted to torture my patience, we stopped short. All heads were out of the windows.   " What is it? "   " What's the matter? "   " Why are we not going on? "   There was a train in front of us at a standstill, with a broken brake, and the line had to be cleared.   I fell back on my seat, clenching my teeth and hands, and looking up in the air to distinguish the evil spirits which were so bent on tormenting me, and then I resolutely closed my eyes.   I muttered some invectives against the invisible sprites, and declared that, as I would not suffer any more, I was now going to sleep.   I then fell fast asleep, for the power of sleeping when I wish is a precious gift which God has bestowed on me.   In the most frightful circumstances and the most cruel moments of life, when I have felt that my reason was giving way under shocks that have been too great or too painful, my will has laid hold of my reason, just as one holds a bad-tempered little dog that wants to bite, and, subjugating it, my will has said to my reason : " Enough.   You can take up again to-morrow your suffering and your plans, your anxiety, your sorrow and your anguish.   You have had enough for to-day. You would give way altogether under the weight of so many troubles, and you would drag me along with you.   I will not have it !   We will forget everything for so many hours and go to sleep together! "   And I have gone to sleep.   This, I swear to.

Mlle. Soubise roused me as soon as the train entered the

station. I was refreshed and calmer. A minute later we were in a carriage and had given the address, 7 Ober Strasse.

We were soon there, and I found all my adored ones, big and little, and they were all very well. Oh, what happiness it was! The blood pulsed in all my arteries. I had suffered so much that I burst out into delicious laughter and sobs.

Who can ever describe the infinite pleasure of tears of joy! During the next two days the maddest things occurred, which I will not relate, so incredible would they sound. Among others, fire broke out in the house; we had to escape in our night clothes and camp out for six hours in five feet of snow, &c. &c.

XIX

MY RETURN TO PARIS—THE COMMUNE—AT
ST. GERMAIN-EN-LAYE

EVERYBODY being safe and sound, we set out for Paris, but on arriving at St. Denis we found there were no more trains. It was four o'clock in the morning. The Germans were masters of all the suburbs of Paris, and trains only ran for their service. After an hour spent in running about, in discussions and rebuffs, I met with an officer of higher rank, who was better educated and more agreeable. He had a locomotive prepared to take me to the Gare du Hâvre (Gare St. Lazare).

The journey was very amusing. My mother, my aunt, my sister Régina, Mlle. Soubise, the two maids, the children, and I all squeezed into a little square space, in which there was a very small, narrow bench, which I think was the place for the signal-man in those days. The engine went very slowly, as the rails were frequently obstructed by carts or railway carriages.

We left at five in the morning and arrived at seven. At a place which I cannot locate our German conductors were exchanged for French conductors. I questioned them, and learnt that revolutionary troubles were beginning in Paris.

The stoker with whom I was talking was a very intelligent and very advanced individual.

" You would do better to go somewhere else, and not to Paris," he said, " for before long they will come to blows there."

We had arrived. But as no train was expected in at that hour, it was impossible to find a carriage. I got down with my tribe from the locomotive, to the great amazement of the station officials.

I was no longer very rich, but I offered twenty francs to one

As Doña Sol in Victor Hugo's *Hernani*, first performed in 1877.

At her easel (1878–79).

of the men if he would see to our six bags. We were to send for my trunk and those belonging to my family later on.

There was not a single carriage outside the station. The children were very tired, but what was to be done? I was then living at No. 4 Rue de Rome, and this was not far away, but my mother scarcely ever walked, for she was delicate and had a weak heart. The children, too, were very, very tired. Their eyes were puffed up and scarcely open, and their little limbs were benumbed by the cold and immobility. I began to get desperate, but a milk cart was just passing by, and I sent a porter to hail it. I offered twenty francs if the man would drive my mother and the two children to 4 Rue de Rome.

"And you too, if you like, young lady," said the milkman. "You are thinner than a grasshopper, and you won't make it any heavier."

I did not want inviting twice; although rather annoyed by the man's speech.

When once my mother was installed, in spite of her hesitation, by the side of the milkman, and the children and I were in amongst the full and empty milk-pails, I said to our driver, "Would you mind coming back to fetch the others?" I pointed to the remaining group, and added, "You shall have twenty francs more."

"Right you are!" said the worthy fellow. "A good day's work! Don't you tire your legs, you others. I'll be back for you directly!"

He then whipped up his horse and we started at a wild rate. The children rolled about and I held on. My mother set her teeth and did not utter a word, but from under her long lashes she glanced at me with a displeased look.

On arriving at my door the milkman drew up his horse so sharply that I thought my mother would have fallen out on to the animal's back. We had arrived, though, and we got out. The cart started off again at full speed. My mother would not speak to me for about an hour. Poor, pretty mother, it was not my fault.

I had gone away from Paris eleven days before, and had then left a sad city. The sadness had been painful, the result of a great and unexpected misfortune. No one had dared to look up, fearing to be blown upon by the same wind which was blowing the German flag floating yonder towards the Arc de Triomphe.

I now found Paris effervescent and grumbling. The walls were placarded with multi-coloured posters; and all these posters contained the wildest harangues. Fine noble ideas were side by side with absurd threats. Workmen on their way to their daily toil stopped in front of these bills. One would read aloud, and the gathering crowd would begin to read over again.

And all these human beings, who had just been suffering so much through this abominable war, now echoed these appeals for vengeance. They were very much to be excused.

This war, alas! had hollowed out under their very feet a gulf of ruin and of mourning. Poverty had brought the women to rags, the privations of the siege had lowered the vitality of the children, and the shame of the defeat had discouraged the men.

Well, these appeals to rebellion, these anarchist shouts, these yells from the crowd, shrieking: "Down with thrones! Down with the Republic! Down with the rich! Down with the priests! Down with the Jews! Down with the army! Down with the masters! Down with those who work! Down with everything!"—all these cries roused the benumbed hearers. The Germans, who fomented all these riots, rendered us a real service without intending it. Those who had given themselves up to resignation were stirred out of their torpor. Others, who demanded revenge, found an aliment for their inactive forces. None of them agreed. There were ten or twenty different parties, devouring each other and threatening each other. It was terrible.

But it was the awakening. It was life after death. I had among my friends about ten of the leaders of different opinions, and all of them interested me, the maddest and the wisest of them.

I often saw Gambetta at Girardin's, and it was a joy to me to listen to this admirable man. What he said was so wise, so well-balanced, and so captivating.

This man, with his heavy stomach, his short arms, and huge head, had a halo of beauty round him when he spoke.

Gambetta was never common, never ordinary. He took snuff, and the gesture of his hand when he brushed away the stray grains was full of grace. He smoked huge cigars, but could smoke them without inconveniencing any one. When he was tired of politics and talked literature it was a real charm, for he knew everything and quoted poetry admirably. One evening, after a dinner at Girardin's, we played together the whole scene of the first act of *Hernani* with Dona Sol. And if he was not as handsome as Mounet-Sully, he was just as admirable in it.

On another occasion he recited the whole of " Ruth and Boaz," commencing with the last verse.

But I preferred his political discussions, especially when he criticised the speech of some one who was of the opposite opinion to himself. The eminent qualities of this politician's talent were logic and weight, and his seductive force was his chauvinism. The early death of so great a thinker is a disconcerting challenge flung at human pride.

I sometimes saw Rochefort, whose wit delighted me. I was not at ease with him, though, for he was the cause of the fall of the Empire, and, although I am very republican, I liked the Emperor Napoleon III. He had been too trustful, but very unfortunate, and it seemed to me that Rochefort insulted him too much after his misfortune.

I also frequently saw Paul de Rémusat, the favourite of Thiers. He had great refinement of mind, broad ideas, and fascinating manners. Some people accused him of Orleanism. He was a Republican, and a much more advanced Republican than Thiers. One must have known him very little to believe him to be anything else but what he said he was. Paul de Rémusat had a horror of untruth. He was sensitive, and had a very straightforward, strong character. He took no active part in politics, except in private circles, and his advice always prevailed, even in the Chamber and in the Senate. He would never speak except when in committee. The Ministry of Fine Arts was offered to him a hundred times, but he refused it a hundred times. Finally, after my repeated entreaties, he almost allowed himself to be appointed Minister of Fine Arts, but at the last moment he declined, and wrote me a delightful letter, from which I quote a few passages. As the letter was not written for publication, I do not consider that I have a right to give the whole of it, but there seems to be no harm in publishing these few lines :

" Allow me, my charming friend, to remain in the shade. I can see better there than in the dazzling brilliancy of honours. You are grateful to me sometimes for being attentive to the miseries you point out to me. Let me keep my independence. It is more agreeable to me to have the right to relieve every one than to be obliged to relieve no matter whom. . . . In matters of art I have made for myself an ideal of beauty, which would naturally seem too partial. . . ."

It is a great pity that the scruples of this delicate-minded man did not allow him to accept this office. The reforms that he pointed out to me were, and still are, very necessary ones. However, that cannot be helped.

I also knew and frequently saw a mad sort of fellow, full of dreams and Utopian follies. His name was Flourens, and he was tall and nice-looking. He wanted every one to be happy and every one to have money, and he shot down the soldiers without reflecting that he was commencing by making one or more of them unhappy. Reasoning with him was impossible, but he was charming and brave. I saw him two days before his death. He came to see me with a very young girl who wanted to devote herself to dramatic art. I promised him to help her. Two days later the poor child came to tell me of the heroic death of Flourens. He had refused to surrender, and, stretching out his arms, had shouted to the hesitating soldiers, " Shoot, shoot! I should not have spared you! " And their bullets had killed him.

Another man, not so interesting, whom I looked upon as a dangerous madman, was a certain Raoul Rigault. For a short time he was Prefect of Police. He was very young and very daring, wildly ambitious, determined to do anything to succeed, and it seemed to him more easy to do harm than good. That man was a real danger. He belonged to a group of students who used to send me verses every day. I came across them everywhere, enthusiastic and mad. They had been nicknamed in Paris the *Saradoteurs* (Sara-dotards). One day he brought me a little one-act play. The piece was so stupid and the verses were so insipid that I sent it him back with a few words, which he no doubt considered unkind, for he bore me malice for them, and attempted to avenge himself in the following way. He called on me one day, and Madame Guérard was there when he was shown in.

" Do you know that I am all-powerful at present ? " he said.

" In these days there is nothing surprising in that," I replied.

" I have come to see you, either to make peace or declare war," he continued.

This way of talking did not suit me, and I sprang up. " As I can foresee that your conditions of peace would not suit me, *cher Monsieur*, I will not give you time to declare war. You are one of the men one would prefer, no matter how spiteful they might be, as enemies rather than friends." With these words I rang for my footman to show the Prefect of Police to the door. Madame Guérard was in despair. " That man will do us some harm, my dear Sarah, I assure you," she said.

She was not mistaken in her presentiment, except that she was thinking of me and not of herself, for his first vengeance was taken on her, by sending away one of her relatives, who was a police commissioner, to an inferior and dangerous post. He then began to invent a hundred miseries for me. One day I received an order to go at once to the Prefecture of Police on urgent business. I took no notice. The following day a mounted courier brought me a note from Sire Raoul Rigault, threatening to send a prison van for me. I took no notice whatever of the threats of this wretch, who was shot shortly after and died without showing any courage.

Life, however, was no longer possible in Paris, and I decided to go to St. Germain-en-Laye. I asked my mother to go with me, but she went to Switzerland with my youngest sister.

The departure from Paris was not as easy as I had hoped. Communists with gun on shoulder stopped the trains and searched in all our bags and pockets, and even under the cushions of the railway carriages. They were afraid that the passengers were taking newspapers to Versailles. This was monstrously stupid.

The installation at St. Germain was not an easy thing either. Nearly all Paris had taken refuge in this little place, which is as pretty as it is dull. From the height of the terrace, where the crowd remained morning and night, we could see the alarming progress of the Commune.

On all sides of Paris the flames rose, proud and destructive.

The wind often brought us burnt papers, which we took to the Council House. The Seine brought quantities along with it, and the boatmen collected these in sacks. Some days—and these were the most distressing of all—an opaque veil of smoke enveloped Paris. There was no breeze to allow the flames to pierce through.

The city then burnt stealthily, without our anxious eyes being able to discover the fresh buildings that these furious madmen had set alight.

I went for a ride every day in the forest. Sometimes I would go as far as Versailles, but this was not without danger. We often came across poor starving wretches in the forest, whom we joyfully helped, but often, too, there were prisoners who had escaped from Poissy, or Communist sharpshooters trying to shoot a Versailles soldier.

One day, on the way back from Triel, where Captain O'Connor and I had been for a gallop over the hills, we entered the forest rather late in the evening, as it was a shorter way. A shot was fired from a neighbouring thicket, which made my horse bound so suddenly towards the left that I was thrown. Fortunately my horse was quiet. O'Connor hurried to me, but I was already up and ready to mount again. "Just a second," he said; "I want to search that thicket." A short gallop soon brought him to the spot, and I then heard a shot, some branches breaking under flying feet, then another shot not at all like the two former ones, and my friend appeared again with a pistol in his hand.

" You have not been hit ? " I asked.

" Yes, the first shot just touched my leg, but the fellow aimed too low. The second he fired haphazard. I fancy, though, that he has a bullet from my revolver in his body."

" But I heard some one running away," I said.

"Oh," replied the elegant captain, chuckling, "he will not go far."

" Poor wretch ! " I murmured.

"Oh no," exclaimed O'Connor, "do not pity them, I beg. They kill numbers of our men every day; only yesterday five soldiers from my regiment were found on the Versailles road, not only killed, but mutilated," and gnashing his teeth, he finished his sentence with an oath.

I turned towards him rather surprised, but he took no notice.

We continued our way, riding as quickly as the obstacles in the forest would allow us. Suddenly, our horses stopped short, snorting and sniffing. O'Connor took his revolver in his hand, got off, and led his horse. A few yards from us there was a man lying on the ground.

" That must be the wretch who shot at me," said my companion, and bending down over the man he spoke to him. A moan was the only reply. O'Connor had not seen his man, so that he could not have recognised him. He lighted a match, and we saw that this one had no gun. I had dismounted, and was trying to raise the unfortunate man's head, but I withdrew my hand, covered with blood. He had opened his eyes, and fixed them on O'Connor.

" Ah, it's you, Versailles dog!" he said. " It was you who shot me! I missed you, but——" He tried to pull out the revolver from his belt, but the effort was too great, and his hand fell down inert. O'Connor on his side had cocked his revolver, but I placed myself in front of the man, and besought him to leave the poor fellow in peace. I could scarcely recognise my friend, for this handsome, fair-haired man, so polite, rather a snob, but very charming, seemed to have turned into a brute. Leaning towards the unfortunate man, his under-jaw protruded, he was muttering under his teeth some inarticulate words; his clenched hand seemed to be grasping his anger, just as one does an anonymous letter before flinging it away in disgust.

" O'Connor, let this man alone, please! " I said.

He was as gallant a man as he was a good soldier. He gave way, and seemed to become aware of the situation again. " Good! " he said, helping me to mount once more. " When I have taken you back to your hotel, I will come back with some men to pick up this wretch."

Half an hour later we were back home, without having exchanged another word during our ride.

I kept up my friendship with O'Connor, but I could never see him again without thinking of that scene. Suddenly, when he was talking to me, the brute-like mask under which I had seen him for a second would fix itself again over his laughing face. Quite recently, in March 1905, General O'Connor, who was commanding in Algeria, came to see me one evening in my

dressing-room at the theatre.   He told me about his difficulties
with some of the great Arab chiefs.

"I fancy," he said, laughing, "that we shall have a brush
together."

Again I saw the captain's mask on the general's face.

I never saw him again, for he died six months afterwards.

We were at last able to go back to Paris.   The abominable
and shameful peace had been signed, the wretched Commune
crushed.   Everything was supposed to be in order again.   But
what blood and ashes!   What women in mourning!   What
ruins!

In Paris, we inhaled the bitter odour of smoke.   All that
I touched at home left on my fingers a somewhat greasy
and almost imperceptible colour.   A general uneasiness beset
France, and more especially Paris.   The theatres, however,
opened their doors once more, and that was a general relief.

One morning I received from the Odéon a notice of rehearsal.
I shook out my hair, stamped my feet, and sniffed the air like a
young horse snorting.

The race-ground was to be opened for us again.   We should
be able to gallop afresh through our dreams.   The lists were
ready.   The contest was beginning.   Life was commencing again.
It is truly strange that man's mind should have made of life a
perpetual strife.   When there is no longer war there is battle,
for there are a hundred thousand of us aiming for the same
object. God has created the earth and man for each other.   The
earth is vast.   What ground there is uncultivated!   Miles upon
miles, acres upon acres of new land waiting for arms that will
take from its bosom the treasures of inexhaustible Nature.   And
we remain grouped round each other, crowds of famishing people
watching other groups, which are also lying in wait.

The Odéon opened its doors to the public with a repertory
programme.   Some new pieces were given us to study.   One of
these met with tremendous success.   It was André Theuriet's
Jean-Marie, and was produced in October 1871.   This one-
act play is a veritable masterpiece, and it took its author
straight to the Academy.   Porel, who played the part of Jean-
Marie, met with an enormous success.   He was at that time
slender, nimble, and full of youthful ardour.   He needed a little
more poetry, but the joyous laughter of his thirty-two teeth

made up in ardour for what was wanting in poetic desire. It was very good, anyhow.

My *rôle* of the young Breton girl, submissive to the elderly husband forced upon her, and living eternally with the memory of the *fiancé* who was absent, and perhaps dead, was pretty, poetical, and touching by reason of the final sacrifice. There was even a certain grandeur in the concluding part of the piece. It had, I must repeat, an immense success, and increased my growing reputation.

I was, however, awaiting the event which was to consecrate me a star. I did not quite know what I was expecting, but I knew that my Messiah had to come. And it was the greatest poet of the last century who was to place on my head the crown of the elect.

XX

At the end of that year 1871, we were told, in rather a mysterious and solemn way, that we were going to play a piece of Victor Hugo's. My mind at that time of my life was still closed to great ideas. I was living in rather a *bourgeois* atmosphere, what with my somewhat cosmopolitan family, their rather snobbish acquaintances and friends, and the acquaintances and friends I had chosen in my independent life as an artiste.

I had heard Victor Hugo spoken of ever since my childhood as a rebel and a renegade, and his works, which I had read with passion, did not prevent my judging him with very great severity. And I blush to-day with anger and shame when I think of all my absurd prejudices, fomented by the imbecile or insincere little court which flattered me. I had a great desire, nevertheless, to play in *Ruy Blas*. The *rôle* of the Queen seemed so charming to me.

I mentioned my wish to Duquesnel, who said he had already thought of it. Jane Essler, an artiste then in vogue, but a trifle vulgar, had great chances, though, against me. She was on very amicable terms with Paul Meurice, Victor Hugo's intimate friend and adviser. One of my friends brought Auguste Vacquerie to my house. He was another friend, and even a relative, of the "illustrious master."

Auguste Vacquerie promised to speak to Victor Hugo, and two days later he came again, assuring me that I had every chance in my favour. Paul Meurice himself, a very straight-forward man, a delightful soul, had proposed me to the author. And Geffroy, the admirable artiste who had retired from the Comédie Française, and was now asked to play *Don Salluste*, had said, it appears, that he could only see one little Queen of Spain worthy to wear the crown, and I was that one. I did not know Geffroy; I did not know Paul Meurice; and was rather astonished that they should know me.

The play was to be read to the artistes at Victor Hugo's, December 6, 1871, at two o'clock. I was very much spoilt, and very much praised and flattered, so that I felt hurt at the unceremoniousness of a man who did not condescend to disturb himself, but asked women to go to his house when there was neutral ground, the theatre, for the reading of plays. I mentioned this unheard-of incident at five o'clock to my little court, and men and women alike exclaimed: "What! That man who was only the other day an outlaw! That man who has only just been pardoned! That nobody!—dares to ask the little Idol, the Queen of *Hearts*, the Fairy of Fairies, to put herself to inconvenience!"

All my little sanctuary was in a tumult; men and women alike could not keep still.

"She must not go," they said. "Write him this"—"Write him that." And they were composing impertinent, disdainful letters when Marshal Canrobert was announced. He belonged at that time to my little five o'clock court, and he was soon posted on what had taken place by my turbulent visitors. He was furiously angry at the imbecilities uttered against the great poet.

"You must not go to Victor Hugo's," he said to me, "for it seems to me that he has no reason to deviate from the regular custom. But say that you are suddenly unwell; follow my advice and show the respect for him that we owe to genius."

I followed my great friend's counsel, and sent the following letter to the poet:

" MONSIEUR,—The Queen has taken a chill, and her Camerara Mayor forbids her to go out. You know better than any one else the etiquette of the Spanish Court. Pity your Queen, Monsieur."

I sent the letter, and the following was the poet's reply:

"I am your valet, Madame.

" VICTOR HUGO."

The next day the play was read on the stage to the artistes.

I believe that the reading did not take place, or at least not entirely, at the Master's house.

I then made the acquaintance of the monster. Ah, what a grudge I had for a long time against all those silly people who had prejudiced me !

The monster was charming—so witty and refined, and so gallant, with a gallantry that was a homage and not an insult. He was so good, too, to the humble, and always so gay. He was not, certainly, the ideal of elegance, but there was a moderation in his gestures, a gentleness in his way of speaking, which savoured of the old French peer. He was quick at repartee, and his observations were gentle but pertinent. He recited poetry badly, but adored hearing it well recited. He often made sketches during the rehearsals.

He frequently spoke in verse when he wished to reprimand an artiste. One day during a rehearsal he was trying to convince poor Talien about his bad elocution. I was bored by the length of the colloquy, and sat down on the table swinging my legs. He understood my impatience, and getting up from the middle of the orchestra stalls, he exclaimed,

> " *Une Reine d'Espagne honnête et respectable*
> *Ne devrait point ainsi s'asseoir sur une table.*"

I sprang up from the table slightly embarrassed, and wanted to answer him in rather a piquant or witty way—but I could not find anything to say, and remained there confused and in a bad temper.

One day, when the rehearsal was over an hour earlier than usual, I was waiting, my forehead pressed against the window-pane, for the arrival of Madame Guérard, who was coming to fetch me. I was gazing idly at the footpath opposite, which is bounded by the Luxembourg railings. Victor Hugo had just crossed the road, and was about to walk on. An old woman attracted his attention. She had just put a heavy bundle of linen down on the ground, and was wiping her forehead, on which were great beads of perspiration. In spite of the cold, her toothless mouth was half open, as she was panting, and her eyes had an expression of distressing anxiety as she looked at the wide road she had to cross, with carriages and omnibuses passing each other. Victor Hugo approached her, and after a short conversation he drew a piece of money from his pocket, handed it to the old woman; then, taking off his hat, he confided it to her, and with a quick movement and a laughing face lifted the bundle on to his shoulder and crossed the road, followed by the bewildered woman. I rushed downstairs to embrace him for it, but by the time I had reached the passage I jostled against de Chilly, who wanted to stop me, and when I descended the staircase Victor Hugo had disappeared. I could only see the old woman's back, but it seemed to me that she hobbled along now more briskly.

The next day I told the poet that I had witnessed his delicate good deed.

" Oh," said Paul Meurice, his eyes wet with emotion, " every day that dawns is a day of kindness for him."

I embraced Victor Hugo, and we went to the rehearsal.

Oh, those rehearsals of *Ruy Blas!* I shall never forget them, for there was such good grace and charm about everything. When Victor Hugo arrived, everything brightened up. His two satellites, Auguste Vacquerie and Paul Meurice, scarcely ever left him, and when the Master was absent they kept up the divine fire.

Geffroy, severe, sad, and distinguished, often gave me advice. During the intervals for rest I posed for him in various attitudes, for he was a painter. In the *foyer* of the Comédie Francaise there are two pictures by him, representing two generations of Sociétaires of both sexes. The pictures are not of very original composition, neither are they of beautiful colouring, but they are faithful likenesses, it appears, and rather happily grouped.

Lafontaine, who was playing Ruy Blas, often had long discussions with the Master, in which Victor Hugo never yielded. And I must confess that he was always right.

Lafontaine had conviction and self-assurance, but his elocution was very bad for poetry. He had lost his teeth, and they were replaced by a set of false ones. This gave a certain slowness to his delivery, and there was a little odd clacking sound between his real palate and his artificial rubber palate, which often distracted the ear listening attentively to catch the beauty of the poetry.

As for poor Talien, who was playing Don Guritan, he made

a hash of it every minute. His comprehension of the *rôle* was quite erroneous. Victor Hugo explained it to him clearly and intelligently. Talien was a well-intentioned comedian, a hard worker, always conscientious, but as stupid as a goose. What he did not understand at first he never understood. As long as he lived he would never understand. But, as he was straightforward and loyal, he put himself into the hands of the author, and gave himself up then in complete abnegation. "That is not as I understood it," he would say, "but I will do as you tell me."

He would then rehearse, word by word and gesture by gesture, with the inflexions and movements required. This got on my nerves in the most painful way, and was a cruel blow dealt at the solidarity of my artistic pride. I often took this poor Talien aside and tried to urge him on to rebellion, but it was all in vain.

He was tall, and his arms were too long, and his eyes tired; his nose was weary with having grown too long, and it sank over his lips in heartrending dejection. His forehead was covered with thick hair, and his chin seemed to be running away in a hurry from his ill-built face. A great kindliness was diffused all over his being, and this kindliness was his very self. Every one was therefore infinitely fond of him.

XXI

A MEMORABLE SUPPER

JANUARY 26, 1872, was an artistic *fête* for the Odéon. The *Tout-Paris* of first nights and the vibrating younger elements were to meet in the large, solemn, dusty theatre. Ah, what a splendid, stirring performance it was! What a triumph for Geffroy, pale, sinister, and severe-looking in his black costume as Don Salluste. Mélingue rather disappointed the public as Don César de Bazan, and the public was in the wrong. The *rôle* of Don César de Bazan is a treacherously good *rôle*, which always tempts artists by the brilliancy of the first act; but the fourth act, which belongs entirely to him, is distressingly heavy and useless. It might be taken out of the piece, just like a periwinkle out of its shell, and the piece would be none the less clear and complete.

This 26th of January rent asunder, though, for me the thin veil which still made my future hazy, and I felt that I was destined for celebrity. Until that day I had remained the students' little fairy. I became then the Elect of the public.

Breathless, dazed, and yet delighted by my success, I did not know to whom to reply in the ever-changing stream of male and female admirers. Then, suddenly, I saw the crowd separating and forming two lines, and I caught a glimpse of Victor Hugo and Girardin coming towards me. In a second all the stupid ideas I had had about this immense genius flashed across me. I remembered my first interview, when I had been stiff and barely polite to this kind, indulgent man. At that moment, when all my life was opening its wings, I should have liked to cry out to him my repentance and to tell him of my devout gratitude.

Before I could speak, though, he was down on his knee, and

raising my two hands to his lips, he murmured, "Thank you! Thank you!"

And so it was he who said "Thank you." He, the great Victor Hugo, whose soul was so beautiful, whose universal genius filled the world! He, whose generous hands flung pardons like gems to all his insulters. Ah, how small I felt, how ashamed, and yet how happy! He then rose, shook the hands that were held out to him, finding for every one the right word.

He was so handsome that night, with his broad forehead, which seemed to retain the light, his thick, silvery fleece of hair, and his laughing luminous eyes.

Not daring to fling myself in Victor Hugo's arms, I fell into Girardin's, the sure friend of my first steps, and I burst into tears. He took me aside in my dressing-room. "You must not let yourself be intoxicated with this great success now," he said. "There must be no more risky jumps, now that you are crowned with laurels. You will have to be more yielding, more docile, more sociable."

"I feel that I shall never be yielding nor docile, my friend," I answered looking at him, "I will try to be more sociable, but that is all I can promise. As to my crown, I assure you that in spite of my risky jumps, and I feel that I shall always be making some, the crown will not shake off."

Paul Meurice, who had come up to us, overheard this conversation, and reminded me of it on the evening of the first performance of *Angelo* at the Sarah Bernhardt Theatre, on February 7, 1905.

On returning home, I sat up a long time talking to Madame Guérard, and when she wanted to go I begged her to stay longer. I had become so rich in hopes for the future that I was afraid of thieves. *Mon petit Dame* stayed on with me, and we talked till daybreak. At seven o'clock we took a cab and I drove my dear friend home, and then continued driving for another hour. I had already achieved a fair number of successes: *Le Passant*, *Le Drame de la Rue de la Paix*, Anna Danby in *Kean*, and *Jean-Marie*, but I felt that the *Ruy Blas* success was greater than any of the others, and that this time I had become some one to be criticised, but not to be overlooked.

I often went in the morning to Victor Hugo's, and he was always very charming and kind.

When I was quite at my ease with him, I spoke to him about my first impressions, about all my stupid, nervous rebellion with regard to him, about all that I had been told and all that I had believed in my naïve ignorance about political matters.

One morning the Master took great delight in my conversation. He sent for Madame Drouet, the sweet soul, the companion of his glorious and rebellious mind. He told her, in a laughing but melancholy way, that the evil work of bad people is to sow error in every soil, whether favourable or not. That morning is engraved for ever in my mind, for the great man talked a long time. Oh, it was not for me, but for what I represented in his eyes. Was I not, as a matter of fact, the young generation, in which a *bourgeois* and clerical education had warped the intelligence by closing the mind to every generous idea, to every flight towards the new?

When I left Victor Hugo that morning I felt myself more worthy of his friendship.

I then went to Girardin's, as I wanted to talk to some one who loved the poet, but he was out.

I went next to Marshal Canrobert's, and there I had a great surprise. Just as I was getting out of the carriage, I nearly fell into the arms of the Marshal, who was coming out of his house.

" What is it? What's the matter? Is it postponed?" he asked, laughing.

I did not understand, and gazed at him rather bewildered.

"Well, have you forgotten that you invited me to luncheon?" he asked.

I was quite confused, for I had entirely forgotten it.

"Well, all the better!" I said; "I very much wanted to talk to you. Come; I am going to take you with me now."

I then related my visit to Victor Hugo, and repeated all the fine thoughts he had uttered, forgetting that I was constantly saying things that were contrary to the Marshal's ideas. This admirable man could admire, though, and if he could not change his opinions, he approved the great ideas which were to bring about great changes.

One day, when he and Busnach were both at my house, there was a political discussion which became rather violent. I was afraid for a moment that things might take a bad turn, as Busnach was the most witty and at the same time the rudest

man in France.   It is only fair to say, though, that if
Marshal Canrobert was a polite man and very well bred, he was
not at all behind William Busnach in wit.   The latter was
worked up by the chafing speeches of the Marshal.

"I challenge you, Monsieur," he exclaimed, "to write about
the odious Utopias that you have just been supporting!"

"Oh, Monsieur Busnach," replied Canrobert coldly, "we do
not use the same steel for writing history!   You use a pen, and
I a sword."

The luncheon that I had so completely forgotten was nevertheless a luncheon arranged several days previously.   On reaching
home we found there Paul de Rémusat, charming Mlle. Hocquigny,
and M. de Monbel, a young *attaché d'ambassade*.   I explained
my lateness as well as I could, and that morning finished in the
most delicious harmony of ideas.

I have never felt more than I did that day the infinite joy of
listening.

During a silence Mlle. Hocquigny turned to the Marshal and
said :

"Are you not of the opinion that our young friend should
enter the Comédie Française?"

"Ah, no, no!" I exclaimed;   "I am so happy at the Odéon.
I began at the Comédie, and the short time I remained there
I was very unhappy."

"You will be obliged to go back there, my dear friend—
obliged.   Believe me, it will be better early than late."

"Well, do not spoil to-day's pleasure for me, for I have never
been happier!"

One morning shortly after this my maid brought me a letter.
The large round stamp, on which are the words "Comédie
Française" was on the corner of the envelope.

I remembered that ten years previously, almost day for day,
our old servant Marguerite had, with my mother's permission,
handed me a letter in the same kind of envelope.

My face then had flushed with joy, but this time I felt a
faint tinge of pallor touch my cheeks.

When events occur which disturb my life, I always have a
movement of recoil.   I cling for a second to what is, and then
I fling myself headlong into what is to be.   It is like a gymnast
who clings first to his trapeze bar in order to fling himself

afterwards with full force into space. In one second what now
is becomes for me what was, and I love it with tender emotion
as something dead.   But I adore what is to be without seeking
even to know about it, for what is to be is the unknown, the
mysterious attraction.   I always fancy that it will be something
unheard of, and I shudder from head to foot in delicious
uneasiness.   I receive quantities of letters, and it seems to me
that I never receive enough.   I watch them accumulating just
as I watch the waves of the sea.   What are they going to
bring me, these mysterious envelopes, large, small, pink, blue,
yellow, white ?   What are they going to fling upon the rock,
these great wild waves, dark with seaweed ?   What sailor-boy's
corpse ?   What remains of a wreck ?   What are these little
brisk waves going to leave on the beach, these reflections of a
blue sky, little laughing waves ?   What pink " sea-star " ?
What mauve anemone ?   What pearly shell ?

So I never open my letters immediately.   I look at the
envelopes, try to recognise the handwriting and the seal ; and it
is only when I am quite certain from whom the letter comes that
I open it.   The others I leave my secretary to open or a kind
friend, Suzanne Seylor.   My friends know this so well that they
always put their initials in the corner of their envelopes.

At that time I had no secretary, but *mon petit Dame* served
me as such.

I looked at the envelope a long time, and gave it at last to
Madame Guérard.

" It is a letter from M. Perrin, director of the Comédie
Française," she said.   " He asks if you can fix a time to see him
on Tuesday or Wednesday afternoon at the Comédie Française
or at your own house."

" Thanks.   What day is it to-day ? " I asked.

" Monday," she replied.

I then installed Madame Guérard at my desk, and asked her
to reply that I would go there the following day at three
o'clock.

I was earning very little at that time at the Odéon.   I was
living on what my father had left me—that is, on the transaction
made by the Havre notary—and not much remained.   I therefore went to see Duquesnel and showed him the letter.

" Well, what are you going to do ? " he asked.

" Nothing. I have come to ask your advice."

" Oh well, I advise you to remain at the Odéon. Besides, your engagement does not terminate for another year, and I shall not allow you leave ! "

" Well, raise my salary, then," I said. " I am offered twelve thousand francs a year at the Comédie. Give me fifteen thousand here and I will stay, for I do not want to leave."

" Listen to me," said the charming manager in a friendly way. " You know that I am not free to act alone. I will do my best, I promise you." And Duquesnel certainly kept his word. " Come here to-morrow before going to the Comédie, and I will give you Chilly's reply. But take my advice, and if he obstinately refuses to increase your salary, do not leave; we shall find some way. . . . And besides—— Anyhow, I cannot say any more."

I returned the following day according to arrangement.

I found Duquesnel and Chilly in the managerial office. Chilly began at once somewhat roughly :

" And so you want to leave, Duquesnel tells me. Where are you going ? It is most stupid, for your place is here. Just consider, and think it over for yourself. At the Gymnase they only give modern pieces, dressy plays. That is not your style. At the Vaudeville it is the same. At the Gaîté you would spoil your voice. You are too distinguished for the Ambigu."

I looked at him without replying. I saw that his partner had not spoken to him about the Comédie Française. He felt awkward, and mumbled :

" Well then, you are of my opinion ? "

" No," I answered ; " you have forgotten the Comédie."

He was sitting in his big arm-chair, and he burst out laughing.

" Ah no, my dear girl," he said, " you must not tell me that. They've had enough of your queer character at the Comédie. I dined the other night with Maubant, and when some one said that you ought to be engaged at the Comédie Française he nearly choked with rage. I can assure you the great tragedian did not show much affection for you."

" Oh well, you ought to have taken my part," I exclaimed, irritated. " You know very well that I am a most serious member of your company."

" But I did take your part," he said, " and I added even that it would be a very fortunate thing for the Comédie if it could have an artiste with your will power, which perhaps might relieve the monotonous tone of the house ; and I only spoke as I thought, but the poor tragedian was beside himself. He does not consider that you have any talent.   In the first place, he maintains that you do not know how to recite verse.   He declares that you make all your *a*'s too broad.   Finally, when he had no arguments left he declared that as long as he lives you will never enter the Comédie Française."

I was silent for a moment, weighing the pros and cons of the probable result of my experiment.   Finally coming to a decision, I murmured somewhat waveringly :

" Well then, you will not give me a higher salary ? "

" No, a thousand times no ! " yelled Chilly.   " You will try to make me pay up when your engagement comes to an end, and then we shall see.   But I have your signature until then. You have mine, too, and I hold to our engagement.   The Théâtre Français is the only one that would suit you beside ours, and I am quite easy in my mind with regard to that theatre."

" You make a mistake perhaps," I answered.   He got up brusquely and came and stood opposite me, his two hands in his pockets.   He then said in an odious and familiar tone :

" Ah, that's it, is it ?   You think I am an idiot, then ? "

I got up too, and said coldly, pushing him gently back, " I think you are a triple idiot."   I then hurried away towards the staircase, and all Duquesnel's shouting was in vain.   I ran down the stairs two at a time.

On arriving under the Odéon arcade I was stopped by Paul Meurice, who was just going to invite Duquesnel and Chilly, on behalf of Victor Hugo, to a supper to celebrate the one hundredth performance of *Ruy Blas*.

" I have just come from your house," he said.   " I have left you a few lines from Victor Hugo."

" Good, good ; that's all right," I replied, getting into my carriage.   " I shall see you to-morrow then, my friend."

" Good Heavens, what a hurry you are in ! " he said.

" Yes ! " I replied, and then, leaning out of the window, I said to my coachman, " Drive to the Comédie Française."

I looked at Paul Meurice to wish him farewell. He was standing stupefied on the arcade steps.

On arriving at the Comédie I sent my card to Perrin, and five minutes later was ushered in to that icy mannikin. There were two very distinct personages in this man. The one was the man he was himself, and the other the one he had created for the requirements of his profession. Perrin himself was gallant, pleasant, witty, and slightly timid ; the mannikin was cold, and somewhat given to posing.

I was first received by Perrin the mannikin. He was standing up, his head bent, bowing to a woman, his arm outstretched to indicate the hospitable arm-chair. He waited with a certain affectation until I was seated before sitting down himself. He then picked up a paper-knife, in order to have something to do with his hands, and in a rather weak voice, the voice of the mannikin, he remarked :

"Have you thought it over, Mademoiselle ? "

" Yes, Monsieur, and here I am to give my signature."

Before he had time to give me any encouragement to dabble with the things on his desk, I drew up my chair, picked up a pen, and prepared to sign the paper. I did not take enough ink at first, and I stretched my arm out across the whole width of the writing table, and dipped my pen this time resolutely to the bottom of the ink-pot. I took too much ink, however, this time, and on the return journey a huge spot of it fell on the large sheet of white paper in front of the mannikin.

He bent his head, for he was slightly short-sighted, and looked for a moment like a bird when it discovers a hemp-seed in its grain. He then proceeded to put aside the blotted sheet.

" Wait a minute, oh, wait a minute ! " I exclaimed, seizing the inky paper. " I want to see whether I am doing right or not to sign. If that is a butterfly I am right, and if anything else, no matter what, I am wrong." I took the sheet, doubled it in the middle of the enormous blot, and pressed it firmly together. Emile Perrin thereupon began to laugh, giving up his mannikin attitude entirely. He leaned over to examine the paper with me, and we opened it very gently just as one opens one's hand after imprisoning a fly. When the paper was spread open, in the midst of its whiteness a magnificent black butterfly with outspread wings was to be seen.

" Well then," said Perrin, with nothing of the mannikin left, " we were quite right in signing."

After this we talked for some time, like two friends who meet again, for this man was charming and very fascinating, in spite of his ugliness. When I left him we were friends and delighted with each other.

I was playing in *Ruy Blas* that night at the Odéon. Towards ten o'clock Duquesnel came to my dressing-room.

" You were rather rough on that poor Chilly," he said. " And you really were not nice. You ought to have come back when I called you. Is it true, as Paul Meurice tells us, that you went straight to the Théâtre Français ? "

" Here, read for yourself," I said, handing him my engagement with the Comédie.

Duquesnel took the paper and read it.

" Will you let me show it to Chilly ? " he asked.

" Show it him, certainly," I replied.

He came nearer, and said in a grave, hurt tone :

" You ought never to have done that without telling me first. It shows a lack of confidence I do not deserve."

He was right, but the thing was done. A moment later Chilly arrived, furious, gesticulating, shouting, stammering in his anger.

" It is abominable ! " he said. " It is treason, and you had not even the right to do it. I shall make you pay damages."

As I felt in a bad humour, I turned my back on him, and apologised as feebly as possible to Duquesnel. He was hurt, and I was a little ashamed, for this man had given me nothing but proofs of kindliness, and it was he who, in spite of Chilly and many other unwilling people, had held the door open for my future.

Chilly kept his word, and brought an action against me and the Comédie. I lost, and had to pay six thousand francs damages to the managers of the Odéon.

A few weeks later Victor Hugo invited the artistes who performed in *Ruy Blas* to a big supper in honour of the one hundredth performance. This was a great delight to me, as I had never been present at a supper of this kind.

I had scarcely spoken to Chilly since our last scene. On the night in question he was placed at my right, and we had to get reconciled. I was seated to the right of Victor Hugo, and to his left was Madame Lambquin, who was playing the Camerara Mayor, and Duquesnel was next to Madame Lambquin. Opposite the illustrious poet was another poet, Théophile Gautier, with his lion's head on an elephant's body. He had a brilliant mind, and said the choicest things with a horse laugh. The flesh of his fat, flabby, wan face was pierced by two eyes veiled by heavy lids. The expression of them was charming, but far away. There was in this man an Oriental nobility choked by Western fashion and customs. I knew nearly all his poetry, and I gazed at him with affection—the fond lover of the beautiful.

It amused me to imagine him dressed in superb Oriental costumes. I could see him lying down on huge cushions, his beautiful hands playing with gems of all colours; and some of his verses came in murmurs to my lips. I was just setting off with him in a dream that was infinite, when a word from my neighbour, Victor Hugo, made me turn towards him.

What a difference! He was just himself, the great poet—the most ordinary of beings except for his luminous forehead. He was heavy-looking, although very active. His nose was common, his eyes lewd, and his mouth without any beauty; his voice alone had nobility and charm. I liked to listen to him whilst looking at Théophile Gautier.

I was a little embarrassed, though, when I looked across the table, for at the side of the poet was an odious individual, Paul de St. Victor. His cheeks looked like two bladders from which the oil they contained was oozing out. His nose was sharp and like a crow's beak, his eyes evil-looking and hard; his arms were too short, and he was too stout. He looked like a jaundice.

He had plenty of wit and talent, but he employed both in saying and writing more harm than good. I knew that this man hated me, and I promptly returned him hatred for hatred.

In answer to the toast proposed by Victor Hugo thanking every one for such zealous help on the revival of his work, each person raised his glass and looked towards the poet, but the illustrious master turned towards me and continued, " As to you, Madame——"

Just at this moment Paul de St. Victor put his glass down so violently on the table that it broke. There was an instant of stupor, and then I leaned across the table and held my glass out towards Paul de St. Victor.

"Take mine, Monsieur," I said, "and then when you drink you will know what my thoughts are in reply to yours, which you have just expressed so clearly ! "

The horrid man took my glass, but with what a look !

Victor Hugo finished his speech in the midst of applause and cheers. Duquesnel then leaned back and spoke to me quietly. He asked me to tell Chilly to reply to Victor Hugo. I did as requested. But he gazed at me with a glassy look, and in a far-away voice replied :

"Some one is holding my legs." I looked at him more attentively, whilst Duquesnel asked for silence for M. de Chilly's speech. I saw that his fingers were grasping a fork desperately ; the tips of his fingers were white, the rest of the hand was violet. I took his hand, and it was icy cold ; the other was hanging down inert under the table. There was silence, and all eyes turned towards Chilly.

"Get up," I said, seized with terror. He made a movement, and his head suddenly fell forward with his face on his plate. There was a muffled uproar, and the few women present surrounded the poor man. Stupid, commonplace, indifferent things were uttered in the same way that one mutters familiar prayers. His son was sent for, and then two of the waiters came and carried the body away, living but inert, and placed it in a small drawing-room.

Duquesnel stayed with him, begging me, however, to go back to the poet's guests. I returned to the room where the supper had taken place. Groups had been formed, and when I was seen entering I was asked if he was still as ill.

"The doctor has just arrived, and he cannot yet say," I replied.

"It is indigestion," said Lafontaine (Ruy Blas), tossing off a glass of liqueur brandy.

"It is cerebral anæmia," pronounced Talien (Don Guritan), clumsily, for he was always losing his memory.

Victor Hugo approached and said very simply :

"It is a beautiful kind of death."

He then took my arm and led me away to the other end of the room, trying to chase my thoughts away by gallant and

Q

poetical whispers. Some little time passed with this gloom weighing on us, and then Duquesnel appeared. He was pale, but appeared as if nothing serious was the matter. He was ready to answer all questions.

Oh yes; he had just been taken home. It would be nothing, it appeared. He only needed rest for a couple of days. Probably his feet had been cold during the meal.

"Yes," put in one of the *Ruy Blas* guests, "there certainly was a fine draught under the table."

"Yes," Duquesnel was just replying to some one who was worrying him, "yes; no doubt there was too much heat for his head."

"Yes," added another of the guests, "our heads were nearly on fire with that wretched gas."

I could see the moment arriving when Victor Hugo would be reproached by all of his guests for the cold, the heat, the food, and the wine of his banquet. All these imbecile remarks got on Duquesnel's nerves. He shrugged his shoulders, and drawing me away from the crowd, said :

"It's all over with him."

I had had the presentiment of this, but the certitude of it now caused me intense grief.

"I want to go," I said to Duquesnel. "Kindly tell some one to ask for my carriage."

I moved towards the small drawing-room which served as a cloak-room for our wraps, and there old Madame Lambquin knocked up against me. Slightly intoxicated by the heat and the wine, she was waltzing with Talien.

"Ah, I beg your pardon, little Madonna," she said ; "I nearly knocked you over."

I pulled her towards me, and without reflecting whispered to her, "Don't dance any more, Mamma Lambquin ; Chilly is dying." She was purple, but her face turned as white as chalk. Her teeth began to chatter, but she did not utter a word.

"Oh, my dear Lambquin," I murmured ; "I did not know I should make you so wretched."

She was not listening to me, though, any longer ; she was putting on her cloak.

"Are you leaving ?" she asked me,

"Yes," I replied.

"Will you drive me home? I will then tell you——"

She wrapped a black fichu round her head, and we both went downstairs, accompanied by Duquesnel and Paul Meurice, who saw us into the carriage.

She lived in the St. Germain quarter and I in the Rue de Rome. On the way the poor woman told me the following story.

"You know, my dear," she began, "I have a mania for somnambulists and fortune-tellers of all kinds. Well, last Friday (you see, I only consult them on a Friday) a woman who tells fortunes by cards said to me, 'You will die a week after a man who is dark and not young, and whose life is connected with yours.' Well, my dear, I thought she was just making game of me, for there is no man whose life is connected with mine, as I am a widow and have never had any *liaison*. I therefore abused her for this, as I pay her seven francs. She charges ten francs to other people, but seven francs to artistes. She was furious at my not believing her, and she seized my hands and said, 'It's no good yelling at me, for it is as I say. And if you want me to tell you the exact truth, it is a man who supports you; and, even to be more exact still, there are two men who support you, the one dark and the other fair; it's a nice thing that!' She had not finished her speech before I had given her such a slap as she had never had in her life, I can assure you. Afterwards, though, I puzzled my head to find out what the wretched woman could have meant. And all I could find was that the two men who support me, the one dark and the other fair, are our two managers, Chilly and Duquesnel. And now you tell me that Chilly——"

She stopped short, breathless with her story, and again seized with terror. "I feel stifled," she murmured, and in spite of the freezing cold we lowered both the windows. On arriving I helped her up her four flights of stairs, and after telling the *concierge* to look after her, and giving the woman a twenty-franc piece to make sure that she would do so, I went home myself, very much upset by all these incidents, as dramatic as they were unexpected, in the middle of a *fête*.

Three days later Chilly died, without ever recovering consciousness.

Twelve days later poor Lambquin died. To the priest who gave her absolution she said, "I am dying because I listened to and believed the demon."

XXII

AT THE COMÉDIE FRANÇAISE AGAIN—SCULPTURE

I LEFT the Odéon with very great regret, for I adored and still adore that theatre. It always seems as though in itself it were a little provincial town. Its hospitable arcades, under which so many poor old *savants* take fresh air and shelter themselves from the sun; the large flagstones all round, between the crevices of which microscopic yellow grass grows ; its tall pillars, blackened by time, by hands, and by the dirt from the road ; the uninterrupted noise going on all around, the departure of the omnibuses, like the departure of the old coaches, the fraternity of the people who meet there ; everything, even to the very railings of the Luxembourg, gives it a quite special aspect in the midst of Paris. Then too there is a kind of odour of the colleges there—the very walls are impregnated with youthful hopes. People are not always talking there of yesterday, as they do in the other theatres. The young artistes who come there talk of to-morrow.

In short, my mind never goes back to those few years of my life without a childish emotion, without thinking of laughter and without a dilation of the nostrils, inhaling again the odour of little ordinary bouquets, clumsily tied up, bouquets which had all the freshness of flowers that grow in the open air, flowers that were the offerings of the hearts of twenty summers, little bouquets paid for out of the purses of students.

I would not take anything away with me from the Odéon. I left the furniture of my dressing-room to a young artiste. I left my costumes, all the little toilette knick-knacks—I divided them and gave them away. I felt that my life of hopes and dreams was to cease there. I felt that the ground was now ready for the fruition of all the dreams, but that the struggle with life was about to commence, and I divined rightly.

My first experience at the Comédie Française had not been a success. I knew that I was going into the lions' den. I counted few friends in this house, except Laroche, Coquelin, and Mounet-Sully—the first two my friends of the Conservatoire and the latter of the Odéon. Among the women, Marie Lloyd and Sophie Croizette, both friends of my childhood; the disagreeable Jouassain, who was nice only to me; and the adorable Marie Brohan, whose kindness delighted the soul, whose wit charmed the mind, and whose indifference rebuffed devotion.

M. Perrin decided that I should make my *début* in *Mademoiselle de Belle-Isle*, according to Sarcey's wish.

The rehearsals began in the *foyer*, which troubled me very much. Mlle. Brohan was to play the part of the Marquise de Prie. At this time she was so fat as to be almost unsightly, while I was so thin that the composers of popular and comic verses took my meagre proportions as their theme and the cartoonists as a subject for their albums.

It was therefore impossible for the Duc de Richelieu to mistake the Marquise de Prie (Madeleine Brohan) for Mademoiselle de Belle-Isle (Sarah Bernhardt) in the irreverent nocturnal rendezvous given by the Marquise to the Duc, who thinks he embraces the chaste Mademoiselle de Belle-Isle.

At each rehearsal Bressant, who took the part of the Duc de Richelieu, would stop, saying, "No, it is too ridiculous. I must play the Duc de Richelieu with both my arms cut off!" And Madeleine left the rehearsal to go to the director's room in order to try and get rid of the *rôle*.

This was exactly what Perrin wanted; he had from the earliest moment thought of Croizette, but he wanted to have his hand forced for private and underhand reasons which he knew and which others guessed.

At last the change took place, and the serious rehearsals commenced.

Then the first performance was announced for November 6 (1872).

I have always suffered, and still suffer, terribly from stage fright, especially when I know that much is expected of me. And I knew a long time beforehand that every seat in the house had been booked ; I knew that the Press expected a great success, and that Perrin himself was reckoning on a long series of big receipts.

Alas ! all these hopes and predictions went for nothing, and my *re-début* at the Comédie Française was only moderately successful.

The following is an extract from the *Temps* of November 11, 1872. It was written by Francisque Sarcey, with whom I was not then acquainted, but who was following my career with very great interest. " It was a very brilliant assembly, as this *début* had attracted all theatre-lovers. The fact is, beside the special merit of Mlle. Sarah Bernhardt, a whole crowd of true or false stories had been circulated about her personally, and all this had excited the curiosity of the Parisian public. Her appearance was a disappointment. She had by her costume exaggerated in a most ostentatious way a slenderness which is elegant under the veils and ample drapery of the Grecian and Roman heroines, but which is objectionable in modern dress. Then, too, either powder does not suit her, or stage fright had made her terribly pale. The effect of this long white face emerging from a long black sheath was certainly unpleasant [I looked like an ant], particularly as the eyes had lost their brilliancy and all that relieved the face were the sparkling white teeth. She went through the first three acts with a convulsive tremor, and we only recognised the Sarah of *Ruy Blas* by two couplets which she gave in her enchanting voice with the most wonderful grace, but in all the more powerful passages she was a failure. I doubt whether Mlle. Sarah Bernhardt will ever, with her delicious voice, be able to render those deep thrilling notes, expressive of paroxysms of violent passion, which are capable of carrying away an audience. If only nature had endowed her with this gift she would be a perfect artiste, and there are none such on the stage. Roused by the coldness of her public, Mlle. Sarah Bernhardt was entirely herself in the fifth act. This was certainly our Sarah once more, the Sarah of *Ruy Blas*, whom we had admired so much at the Odéon. . . ."

As Sarcey said, I made a complete failure of my *début*. My excuse, though, was not the " stage fright " to which he attributed it, but the terrible anxiety I felt on seeing my mother hurriedly leave her seat in the dress circle five minutes after my appearance on the stage.

I had glanced at her on entering, and had noticed her death-like pallor. When she went out I felt that she was about to have one of those attacks which endangered her life, so that the first act seemed to me interminable. I uttered one word after another, stammering through my sentences hap-hazard, with only one idea in my head, a longing to know what had happened. Oh, the public cannot conceive of the tortures endured by the unfortunate comedians who are there before them in flesh and blood on the stage, gesticulating and uttering phrases, while their heart, all torn with anguish, is with the beloved absent one who is suffering. As a rule, one can fling away the worries and anxieties of every-day life, put off one's own personality for a few hours, take on another, and, forgetting everything else, enter as it were into another life. But that is impossible when our dear ones are suffering. Anxiety then lays hold of us, attenuating the bright side, magnifying the dark, maddening our brain, which is living two lives at once, and tormenting our heart, which is beating as though it would burst.

These were the sensations I experienced during the first act.

"Mamma! What has happened to Mamma?" were my first words on leaving the stage. No one could tell me anything.

Croizette came up to me and said, "What's the matter? I hardly recognise you as you are, and you weren't yourself at all just now in the play."

In a few words I told her what I had seen and all that I had felt. Frédéric Febvre sent at once to get news, and the doctor came hurrying to me.

"Your mother had a fainting fit, Mademoiselle," he said, "but they have just taken her home."

"It was her heart, wasn't it?" I asked, looking at him.

"Yes," he replied; "Madame's heart is in a very agitated state."

"Oh, I know how ill she is," I said, and not being able to control myself any longer, I burst into sobs. Croizette helped me back to my dressing-room. She was very kind; we had known each other from childhood, and were very fond of each other. Nothing ever estranged us, in spite of all the malicious gossip of envious people and all the little miseries due to vanity.

My dear Madame Guérard took a cab and hurried away to my mother to get news for me. I put a little more powder on, but the public, not knowing what was taking place, were annoyed with me, thinking I was guilty of some fresh caprice, and received me still more coldly than before. It was all the same to me, as I was thinking of something else. I went on saying Mlle. de Belle-Isle's words (a most stupid and tiresome *rôle*), but all the time I, Sarah, was waiting for news about my mother. I was watching for the return of *mon petit Dame*. " Open the door on the O.P. side just a little way," I had said to her, " and make a sign like this if Mamma is better, and like that if she is worse." But I had forgotten which of the signs was to stand for better, and when, at the end of the third act I saw Madame Guérard opening the door and nodding her head for " yes," I became quite idiotic.

It was in the big scene of the third act, when Mlle. de Belle-Isle reproaches the Duc de Richelieu (Bressant) with doing her such irreparable harm. The Duc replies, " Why did you not say that some one was listening, that some one was hidden ? " I exclaimed, " It's Guérard bringing me news ! " The public had not time to understand, for Bressant went on quickly, and so saved the situation.

After an unenthusiastic call I heard that my mother was better, but that she had had a very serious attack. Poor mamma, she had thought me such a fright when I made my appearance on the stage that her superb indifference had given way to grievous astonishment, and that in its turn to rage on hearing a lady seated near her say in a jeering tone, " Why, she's like a dried bone, this little Bernhardt ! "

I was greatly relieved on getting the news, and I played my last act with confidence. The great success of the evening, though, was Croizette's, who was charming as the Marquise de Prie. My success, nevertheless, was assured in the performances which followed, and it became so marked that I was accused of paying for applause. I laughed heartily at this, and never even contradicted the report, as I have a horror of useless words.

I next appeared as Junie in *Britannicus*, with Mounet-Sully, who played admirably as Nero. In this delicious *rôle* of Junie I obtained an immense and incredible success.

Then in 1873 I played Chérubin in *Le Mariage de Figaro*. Croizette played Suzanne, and it was a real treat for the public to see that delightful creature play a part so full of gaiety and charm.

Chérubin was for me the opportunity of a fresh success.

In the month of March 1873 Perrin took it into his head to stage *Dalila*, by Octave Feuillet. I was then taking the part of young girls, young princesses, or boys. My slight frame, my pale face, my delicate aspect marked me out for the time being for the *rôle* of victim. Perrin, who thought that the victims attracted pity, and that it was for this reason I pleased my audiences, cast the play most ridiculously : he gave me the *rôle* of Dalila, the swarthy, wicked, and ferocious princess, and to Sophie Croizette he gave the *rôle* of the fair young dying girl.

The piece, with this strange cast, was destined to fail. I forced my character in order to appear the haughty and voluptuous siren ; I stuffed my bodice with wadding and the hips under my skirts with horse-hair ; but I kept my small, thin, sorrowful face. Croizette was obliged to repress the advantages of her bust by bands which oppressed and suffocated her, but she kept her pretty plump face with its dimples.

I was obliged to put on a strong voice, she to soften hers. In fact, it was absurd. The piece was a *demi-succès*.

After that I created *L'Absent*, a pretty piece in verse, by Eugène Manuel ; *Chez l'Avocat*, a very amusing thing in verse, by Paul Ferrier, in which Coquelin and I quarrelled beautifully. Then, on August 22, I played with immense success the *rôle* of Andromaque. I shall never forget the first performance, in which Mounet-Sully obtained a delirious triumph. Oh, how fine he was, Mounet-Sully, in his *rôle* of Orestes ! His entrance, his fury, his madness, and the plastic beauty of this marvellous artiste— how magnificent !

After *Andromaque* I played Aricie in *Phèdre*, and in this secondary *rôle* it was I who really made the success of the evening.

I took such a position in a very short time at the Comédie that some of the artistes began to feel uneasy, and the management shared their anxiety. M. Perrin, an extremely intelligent man, whom I have always remembered with great affection, was horribly authoritative. I was also, so that there was always perpetual warfare between us. He wanted to impose his will on me, and I would not submit to it. He was always ready to laugh at my outbursts when they were against the others, but he was furious when they were directed against himself. As for me, I will own that to get Perrin in a fury was one of my delights. He stammered so when he tried to talk quickly, he who weighed every word on ordinary occasions; the expression of his eyes, which was generally wavering, grew irritated and deceitful, and his pale, distinguished-looking face became mottled with patches of wine-dreg colour.

His fury made him take his hat off and put it on again fifteen times in as many minutes, and his extremely smooth hair stood on end with this mad gallop of his head-gear. Although I had certainly arrived at the age of discretion, I delighted in my wicked mischievousness, which I always regretted after, but which I was always ready to recommence; and even now, after all the days, weeks, months, and years that I have lived since then, it still gives me infinite pleasure to play a joke on any one.

All the same, life at the Comédie began to affect my nerves.

I wanted to play Camille in *On ne badine pas avec l'amour :* the *rôle* was given to Croizette. I wanted to play Célimène : that *rôle* was Croizette's. Perrin was very partial to Croizette. He admired her, and as she was very ambitious, she was most thoughtful and docile, which charmed the authoritative old man. She always obtained everything she wanted, and as Sophie Croizette was frank and straightforward, she often said to me when I was grumbling, " Do as I do ; be more yielding. You pass your time in rebelling ; I appear to be doing everything that Perrin wants me to do, but in reality I make him do all I want him to. Try the same thing." I accordingly screwed up my courage and went up to see Perrin. He nearly always said to me when we met, " Ah, how do you do, Mademoiselle Revolt ? Are you calm to-day ? "

" Yes, very calm," I replied ; " but be amiable and grant me what I am going to ask you." I tried to be charming, and spoke in my prettiest way. He almost purred with satisfaction, and was witty (this was no effort to him, as he was naturally so), and we got on very well together for a quarter of an hour. I then made my petition :

" Let me play Camille in *On ne badine pas avec l'amour*."

" That's impossible, my dear child," he replied ; " Croizette is playing it."

" Well then, we'll both play it ; we'll take it in turns."

" But Mademoiselle Croizette wouldn't like that."

" I've spoken to her about it, and she would not mind it."

" You ought not to have spoken to her about it."

" Why not ? "

" Because the management does the casting, not the artistes."

He didn't purr any more, he only growled. As for me, I was in a fury, and a few minutes later I went out of the room, banging the door after me.

All this preyed on my mind, though, and I used to cry all night. I then decided to take a studio and devote myself to sculpture. As I was not able to use my intelligence and my energy in creating *rôles* at the theatre, as I wished, I gave myself up to another art, and began working at sculpture with frantic enthusiasm. I soon made great progress, and started on an enormous composition, *After the Storm*. I was indifferent now to the theatre. Every morning at eight my horse was brought round, and I went for a ride, and at ten I was back in my studio, 11 Boulevard de Clichy. I was very delicate, and my health suffered from the double effort I was making. I used to vomit blood in the most alarming way, and for hours together I was unconscious. I never went to the Comédie except when obliged by my duties there. My friends were seriously concerned about me, and Perrin was informed of what was going on. Finally, incited by the Press and the Department of Fine Arts, he decided to give me a *rôle* to create in Octave Feuillet's play *Le Sphinx*.

The principal part was for Croizette, but on hearing the play read I thought the part destined for me charming, and I resolved that it should also be the principal *rôle*. There would have to be two principal ones, that was all. The rehearsals went along very smoothly at the start, but it soon became evident that my *rôle* was more important than had been imagined, and friction soon began.

Croizette herself got nervous, Perrin was annoyed, and all this by-play had the effect of calming me. Octave Feuillet, a shrewd, charming man, extremely well-bred and slightly ironical, thoroughly enjoyed the skirmishes that took place. War was doomed to break out, however, and the first hostilities came from Sophie Croizette.

I always wore in my bodice three or four roses, which were apt to open under the influence of the warmth, and some of the petals naturally fell. One day Sophie Croizette slipped down full length on the stage, and as she was tall and not slim, she fell rather unbecomingly, and got up again ungracefully. The stifled laughter of some of the subordinate persons present stung her to the quick, and turning to me she said, "It's your fault; your roses fall and make every one slip down." I began to laugh.

"Three petals of my roses have fallen," I replied, "and there they all three are by the arm-chair on the prompt side, and you fell on the O.P. side. It isn't my fault, therefore; it is just your own awkwardness." The discussion continued, and was rather heated on both sides. Two clans were formed, the "Croizettists" and the "Bernhardtists." War was declared, not between Sophie and me, but between our respective admirers and detractors. The rumour of these little quarrels spread in the world outside the theatre, and the public too began to form clans. Croizette had on her side all the bankers and all the people who were suffering from repletion. I had all the artists, the students, dying folks, and the failures. When once war was declared there was no drawing back from the strife. The first, the most fierce, and the definitive battle was fought over the moon.

We had begun the full dress rehearsals. In the third act the scene was laid in a forest glade. In the middle of the stage was a huge rock upon which was Blanche (Croizette) kissing Savigny (Delaunay), who was supposed to be my husband. I (Berthe de Savigny) had to arrive by a little bridge over a stream of water. The glade was bathed in moonlight. Croizette had just played her part, and her kiss had been greeted with a burst of applause. This was rather daring in those days for the Comédie Française. (But since then what have they not given there?)

Suddenly a fresh burst of applause was heard. Amazement could be read on some faces, and Perrin stood up terrified. I was crossing over the bridge, my pale face ravaged with grief, and the *sortie de bal* which was intended to cover my shoulders was dragging along, just held by my limp fingers; my arms were hanging down as though despair had taken the use out of them. I was bathed in the white light of the moon, and the effect, it seems, was striking and deeply impressive. A nasal, aggressive voice cried out, " One moon effect is enough. Turn it off for Mademoiselle Bernhardt."

I sprang forward to the front of the stage. " Excuse me, Monsieur Perrin," I exclaimed, " you have no right to take my moon away. The manuscript reads, *Berthe advances, pale, convulsed with emotion, the rays of the moon falling on her*. . . I am pale and I am convulsed. I must have my moon."

" It is impossible," roared Perrin. " Mademoiselle Croizette's words : ' You love me, then ! ' and her kiss must have this moonlight. She is playing the Sphinx; that is the chief part in the play, and we must leave her the principal effect."

" Very well, then ; give Croizette a brilliant moon, and give me a less brilliant one. I don't mind that, but I must have my moon." All the artistes and all the *employés* of the theatre put their heads in at all the doorways and openings both on the stage and in the house itself. The " Croizettists " and the " Bernhardtists " began to comment on the discussion.

Octave Feuillet was appealed to, and he got up in his turn.

" I grant that Mademoiselle Croizette is very beautiful in her moon effect. Mademoiselle Sarah Bernhardt is ideal too, with her ray of moonlight. I want the moon therefore for both of them."

Perrin could not control his anger. There was a discussion between the author and the director, followed by others between the artistes, and between the door-keeper and the journalists who were questioning him. The rehearsal was interrupted. I declared that I would not play the part if I did not have my moon. For the next two days I received no notice of another rehearsal, but through Croizette I heard that they were trying my *rôle* of Berthe privately. They had given it to a young woman whom we had nicknamed " the Crocodile," because she followed all the rehearsals just as that animal follows boats—she was always hoping to snatch up some *rôle* that might happen to be thrown overboard. Octave Feuillet refused to accept the change of artistes, and he came himself to fetch me, accompanied by Delaunay, who had negotiated matters.

" It's all settled," he said, kissing my hands ; " there will be a moon for both of you."

The first night was a triumph both for Croizette and for me.

The party strife between the two clans waxed warmer and warmer, and this added to our success and amused us both immensely, for Croizette was always a delightful friend and a loyal comrade. She worked for her own ends, but never against any one else.

After *Le Sphinx* I played a pretty piece in one act by a young pupil of the Ecole Polytechnique, Louis Denayrouse, *La Belle Paule.* This author has now become a renowned scientific man, and has renounced poetry.

I had begged Perrin to give me a month's holiday, but he refused energetically, and compelled me to take part in the rehearsals of *Zaïre* during the trying months of June and July, and, in spite of my reluctance, announced the first performance for August 6. That year it was fearfully hot in Paris. I believe that Perrin, who could not tame me alive, had, without really any bad intention, but by pure autocracy, the desire to tame me dead. Doctor Parrot went to see him, and told him that my state of weakness was such that it would be positively dangerous for me to act during the trying heat. Perrin would hear nothing of it. Then, furious at the obstinacy of this intellectual *bourgeois*, I swore I would play on to the death.

Often, when I was a child, I wished to kill myself in order to vex others. I remember once having drunk the contents of a large ink-pot after being compelled by mamma to swallow a "panade,"[1] because she imagined that panades were good for the health. Our nurse had told her my dislike to this form of nourishment, adding that every morning I emptied the panade into the slop-pail. I had, of course, a very bad stomach-ache, and screamed out in pain. I cried to mamma, "It is you who have killed me!" and my poor mother wept. She never knew the truth, but they never again made me swallow anything against my will.

Well, after so many years I experienced the same bitter and childish sentiment. "I don't care," I said ; "I shall certainly fall senseless vomiting blood, and perhaps I shall die! And it will serve Perrin right. He will be furious!" Yes, that is what

[1] Bread stewed a long time in water and flavoured with a little butter and sugar, a kind of "sops" given to children in France.

I thought. I am at times very foolish. Why? I don't know how to explain it, but I admit it.

The 6th of August, therefore, I played, in tropical heat, the part of Zaïre. The entire audience was bathed in perspiration. I saw the spectators through a mist. The piece, badly staged as regards scenery, but very well presented as regards costume, was particularly well played by Mounet-Sully (Orosmane), Laroche (Nérestan), and myself (Zaïre), and obtained an immense success.

I was determined to faint, determined to vomit blood, determined to die, in order to enrage Perrin. I played with the utmost passion. I had sobbed, I had loved, I had suffered, and I had been stabbed by the poignard of Orosmane, uttering a true cry of suffering, for I had felt the steel penetrate my breast. Then, falling panting, dying, on the Oriental divan, I had meant to die in reality, and dared scarcely move my arms, convinced as I was that I was in my death agony, and somewhat afraid, I must admit, at having succeeded in playing such a nasty trick on Perrin. But my surprise was great when the curtain fell at the close of the piece and I got up quickly to answer to the call and bow to the audience without languor, without fainting, feeling strong enough to go through my part again if it had been necessary.

And I marked this performance with a little white stone—for that day I learned that my vital force was at the service of my intellectual force. I had desired to follow the impulse of my brain, whose conceptions seemed to me to be too forceful for my physical strength to carry out. And I found myself, after having given out all of which I was capable—and more—in perfect equilibrium.

Then I saw the possibility of the longed-for future.

I had fancied, and up to this performance of Zaïre I had always heard and read in the papers that my voice was pretty, but weak; that my gestures were gracious, but vague; that my supple movements lacked authority, and that my glance lost in heavenward contemplation could not tame the wild beasts (the audience). I thought then of all that.

I had received proof that I could rely on my physical strength, for I had commenced the performance of Zaïre in such a state of weakness that it was easy to predict that I should not finish the first act without fainting.

On the other hand, although the *rôle* was easy, it required two or three shrieks, which might have provoked the vomiting of blood that frequently troubled me at that time.

That evening, therefore, I acquired the certainty that I could count on the strength of my vocal cords, for I had uttered my shrieks with real rage and suffering, hoping to break something, in my wild desire to be revenged on Perrin.

Thus this little comedy turned to my profit. Being unable to die at will, I changed my batteries and resolved to be strong, vivacious, and active, to the great annoyance of some of my contemporaries, who had only put up with me because they thought I should soon die, but who began to hate me as soon as they acquired the conviction that I should perhaps live for a long time. I will only give one example, related by Alexandre Dumas *fils*, who was present at the death of his intimate friend Charles Narrey, and heard his dying words: "I am content to die because I shall hear no more of Sarah Bernhardt and of the grand Français" (Ferdinand de Lesseps).

But this revelation of my strength rendered more painful to me the sort of *farniente* to which Perrin condemned me.

In fact, after *Zaïre*, I remained months without doing anything of importance, playing only now and again. Discouraged and disgusted with the theatre, my passion for sculpture increased. After my morning ride and a light meal I used to rush to my studio, where I remained till the evening.

Friends came to see me, sat round me, played the piano, sang; politics were discussed—for in this modest studio I received the most illustrious men of all parties. Several ladies came to take tea, which was abominable and badly served, but I did not care about that. I was absorbed by this admirable art. I saw nothing, or, to speak more truly, I *would not* see anything.

I was making the bust of an adorable young girl, Mlle. Emmy de * * *. Her slow and measured conversation had an infinite charm. She was a foreigner, but spoke French so perfectly that I was stupefied. She smoked a cigarette all the time, and had a profound disdain for those who did not understand her.

I made the sittings last as long as possible, for I felt that this delicate mind was imbuing me with her science of seeing into the beyond, and often in the serious steps of my life I have said to myself, " What would Emmy have done ? What would she have thought ? "

I was somewhat surprised one day by the visit of Adolphe de Rothschild, who came to give me an order for his bust. I commenced the work immediately. But I had not properly considered this admirable man—he had nothing of the æsthetic, but the contrary. I tried nevertheless, and I brought all my will to bear in order to succeed in this first order, of which I was so proud. Twice I dashed the bust which I had commenced on the ground, and after a third attempt I definitely gave up, stammering idiotic excuses which apparently did not convince my model, for he never returned to me. When we met in our morning rides he saluted me with a cold and rather severe bow.

After this defeat I undertook the bust of a beautiful child, Miss Multon, a delightful little American, whom later on I came across in Denmark, married and the mother of a family, but still as pretty as ever.

My next bust was that of Mlle. Hocquigny, that admirable person who was keeper of the linen in the commissariat during the war, and who had so powerfully helped me and my wounded at that time.

Then I undertook the bust of my young sister Régina, who had, alas! a weak chest. A more perfect face was never made by the hand of God ! Two leonine eyes shaded by long, long brown lashes, a slender nose with delicate nostrils, a tiny mouth, a wilful chin, and a pearly skin crowned by meshes of sunrays, for I have never seen hair so blonde and so pale, so bright and so silky. But this admirable face was without charm ; the exprèssion was hard and the mouth without a smile. I tried my best to reproduce this beautiful face in marble, but it needed a great artist and I was only a humble amateur.

When I exhibited the bust of my little sister, it was five months after her death, which occurred after a six months' illness, full of false hopes. I had taken her to my home, No. 4 Rue de Rome, to the little *entresol* which I had inhabited since the terrible fire which had destroyed my furniture, my books, my pictures, and all my scant possessions. This flat in the Rue de Rome was very small. My bedroom was quite tiny. The big bamboo bed took up all the room. In front of

R

the window was my coffin, where I frequently installed myself to study my parts. Therefore, when I took my sister to my home I found it quite natural to sleep every night in this little bed of white satin which was to be my last couch, and to put my sister in the big bamboo bed, under the lace hangings.

She herself found it quite natural also, for I would not leave her at night, and it was impossible to put another bed in the little room. Besides, she was accustomed to my coffin.

One day my manicurist came into the room to do my hands, and my sister asked her to enter quietly, because I was still asleep. The woman turned her head, believing that I was asleep in the arm-chair, but seeing me in my coffin she rushed away shrieking wildly. From that moment all Paris knew that I slept in my coffin, and gossip with its thistle-down wings took flight in all directions.

I was so accustomed to the turpitudes which were written about me that I did not trouble about this. But at the death of my poor little sister a tragi-comic incident happened. When the undertaker's men came to the room to take away the body they found themselves confronted with two coffins, and losing his wits, the master of ceremonies sent in haste for a second hearse. I was at that moment with my mother, who had lost consciousness, and I just got back in time to prevent the black-clothed men taking away my coffin. The second hearse was sent back, but the papers got hold of this incident. I was blamed, criticised, &c.

It really was not my fault.

XXIII

A DESCENT INTO THE ENFER DU PLOGOFF—MY FIRST APPEARANCE AS PHÈDRE—THE DECORATION OF MY NEW MANSION

AFTER the death of my sister I fell seriously ill. I had tended her day and night, and this, in addition to the grief I was suffering, made me anæmic. I was ordered to the South for two months. I promised to go to Mentone, and I turned immediately towards Brittany, the country of my dreams.

I had with me my little boy, my steward and his wife. My poor Guérard, who had helped me to tend my sister, was in bed ill with phlebitis. I would much have liked to have her with me.

Oh, the lovely holiday that we had there! Thirty-five years ago Brittany was wild, inhospitable, but as beautiful—perhaps more beautiful than at present, for it was not furrowed with roads ; its green slopes were not dotted with small white villas ; its inhabitants—the men—were not dressed in the abominable modern trousers, and the women did not wear miserable little hats with feathers. No! The Bretons proudly displayed their well-shaped legs in gaiters or rough stockings, their feet shod with buckled shoes ; their long hair was brought down on the temples, hiding any awkward ears and giving to the face a nobility which the modern style does not admit of. The women, with their short skirts, which showed their slender ankles in black stockings, and with their small heads under the wings of the head-dress, resembled sea-gulls. I am not speaking, of course, of the inhabitants of Pont l'Abbé or of Bourg de Batz, who have entirely different aspects.

I visited nearly the whole of Brittany, but made my chief stay at Finistère. The Pointe du Raz enchanted me. I remained twelve days at Audierne, in the house of Father Batifoulé, who was so big and so fat that they had been obliged to cut a piece out of the table to let in his immense abdomen. I set out every morning at ten o'clock. My steward Claude himself prepared my lunch, which he packed up very carefully in three little baskets, then climbing into the comical vehicle of Father Batifoulé, my little boy driving, we set out for the Baie des Trépassés. Ah, that beautiful and mysterious shore, all bristling with rocks! The lighthouse keeper would be looking out for me, and would come to meet me. Claude gave him my provisions, with a thousand recommendations as to the manner of cooking the eggs, warming up the lentils, and toasting the bread. He carried off everything, then returned with two old sticks in which he had stuck nails to make them into picks, and we commenced the terrifying ascent of the Pointe du Raz, a kind of labyrinth full of disagreeable surprises, of crevasses across which we had to jump over the gaping and roaring abyss, of arches and tunnels through which we had to crawl on all fours, having overhead—touching us even—a rock which had fallen there in unknown ages and was only held in equilibrium by some inexplicable cause. Then all at once the path became so narrow that it was impossible to walk straight forward ; we had to turn and put our backs against the cliff and advance with both arms spread out and fingers holding on to the few asperities of the rock.

When I think of what I did in those moments, I tremble, for I have always been, and still am, subject to dizziness ; and I went over this path along a steep precipitous rock, 30 metres high, in the midst of the infernal noise of the sea, at this place eternally furious, and which raged fearfully against this indestructible cliff. And I must have taken a mad pleasure in it, for I accomplished this journey five times in eleven days.

After this challenge thrown down to reason we descended, and installed ourselves in the Baie des Trépassés. After a bath we had lunch, and I painted till sunset.

The first day there was nobody there. The second day a child came to look at us. The third day about ten children stood around asking for sous. I was foolish enough to give them some, and the following day there were twenty or thirty boys, some of them from sixteen to eighteen years old. Seeing near my easel something not particularly agreeable, I begged one of them to take it away and throw it into the sea, and for that I gave, I think, fifty centimes. When I came back the following day to finish my painting the whole population of the neighbouring village had chosen this place to relieve their corporal necessities, and as soon as I arrived the same boys, but in increased numbers, offered, if properly paid, to take away what they had put there.

I had the ugly band routed by Claude and the lighthouse keeper, and as they took to throwing stones at us, I pointed my gun at the little group. They fled howling. Only two boys, of six and ten years of age, remained there. We did not take any notice of them, and I installed myself a little farther on, sheltered by a rock which kept the wind away. The two boys followed. Claude and the keeper Lucas were on the look out to see that the band did not come back.

They were stooping down over the extreme point of the rock which was above our heads. They seemed peaceful, when suddenly my young maid jumped up: " Horrors! Madame! Horrors! They are throwing lice down on us!" And in fact the two little good-for-nothings had been for the last hour searching for all the vermin they could find on themselves, and throwing it on us.

I had the two little beggars caught, and they got a well-deserved correction.

There was a crevasse which was called the " Enfer du Plogoff." I had a wild desire to go down this crevasse, but the guardian dissuaded me, constantly giving as objections the danger of slipping, and his fear of responsibility in case of accident. I persisted nevertheless in my intention, and after a thousand promises, in addition to a certificate to testify that, notwithstanding the supplications of the guardian and the certainty of the danger that I ran, I had persisted all the same, &c., and after having made a small present of ten louis to the good fellow, I obtained facilities for descending the Enfer du Plogoff—that is to say, a wide belt to which a strong rope was fastened. I buckled this belt round my waist, which was then so slender—43 centimetres—that it was necessary to make additional holes in order to fasten it.

Then the guardian put on each of my hands a wooden shoe

the sole of which was bordered with big nails jutting out two centimetres. I stared at these wooden shoes, and asked for an explanation before putting them on.

"Well," said the guardian Lucas, "when I let you down, as you are no fatter than a herring bone, you will get shaken about in the crevasse, and will risk breaking your bones, while if you have the 'sabots' on your hands you can protect yourself against the walls by putting out your arms to the right and the left, according as you are shaken up against them. I do not say that you will not have a few bangs, but that is your own fault; you will go. Now listen, my little lady. When you are at the bottom, on the rock in the middle, mind you don't slip, for that is the most dangerous of all; if you fall in the water I will pull the rope, for sure, but I don't answer for anything. In that cursed whirlpool of water you might be caught between two stones, and it would be no use for me to pull: I should break the rope, and that would be all."

Then the man grew pale and made the sign of the cross; he leaned towards me, murmuring in a dreamy voice, "It is the shipwrecked ones who are there under the stones, down there. It is they who dance in the moonlight on the 'shore of the dead.' It is they who put the slippery sea-weed on the little rock down there, in order to make travellers slip, and then they drag them to the bottom of the sea." Then, looking me in the eyes, he said, "Will you go down all the same?"

"Yes, certainly, Père Lucas; I will go down at once."

My little boy was building forts and castles on the sand with Félicie. Only Claude was with me. He did not say a word, knowing my unbridled desire to meet danger. He looked to see if the belt was properly fastened, and asked my permission to tie the tongue of the belt to the belt itself; then he passed a strong cord several times around to strengthen the leather, and I was let down, suspended by the rope in the blackness of the crevasse. I extended my arms to the right and the left, as the guardian had told me to do, and even then I got my elbows scraped. At first I thought that the noise I heard was the reverberation of the echo of the blows of the wooden shoes against the edges of the crevasse, but suddenly a frightful din filled my ears: successive firings of cannons, strident ringings, crackings of a whip, plaintive howls, and repeated monotonous cries as of a hundred fishermen drawing up a net filled with fish, sea-weed, and pebbles. All the noises mingled under the mad violence of the wind. I became furious with myself, for I was really afraid.

The lower I went, the louder the howlings became in my ears and my brain, and my heart beat the order of retreat. The wind swept through the narrow tunnel and blew in all directions round my legs, my body, my neck. A horrible fear took possession of me.

I descended slowly, and at each little shock I felt that the four hands holding me above had come to a knot. I tried to remember the number of knots, for it seemed to me that I was making no progress.

Then I opened my mouth to call out, "Draw me up!" but the wind, which danced in mad folly around me, filled my mouth and drove back the words. I was nearly suffocated. Then I shut my eyes and ceased to struggle. I would not even put out my arms. A few instants after I pulled up my legs in unspeakable terror. The sea had just seized them in a brutal embrace which had wet me through. However, I recovered courage, for now I could see clearly. I stretched out my legs, and found myself upright on the little rock. It is true it was very slippery.

I took hold of a large ring fixed in the vault which overhung the rock, and I looked round. The long and narrow crevasse grew suddenly wider at its base, and terminated in a large grotto which looked out over the open sea; but the entrance of this grotto was protected by a quantity of both large and small rocks, which could be seen for a distance of a league in front on the surface of the water—which explains the terrible noise of the sea dashing into the labyrinth and the possibility of standing upright on a stone, as the Bretons say, with the wild dance of the waves all around.

However, I saw very plainly that a false step might be fatal in the brutal whirl of waters, which came rushing in from afar with dizzy speed and broke against the insurmountable obstacle, and in receding dashed against other waves which followed them. From this cause proceeded the perpetual fusillade of waters which rushed into the crevasse without danger of drowning me.

It now began to grow dark, and I experienced a fearful anguish in discovering on the crest of a little rock two enormous eyes, which looked fixedly at me. Then a little farther, near a tuft of seaweed, two more of these fixed eyes. I saw no body to these beings—nothing but the eyes. I thought for a minute that I was losing my senses, and I bit my tongue till the blood came ; then I pulled violently at the rope, as I had agreed to do in order to give the signal for being drawn up. I felt the trembling joy of the four hands pulling me, and my feet lost their hold as I was hauled up by my guardians. The eyes were lifted up also, uneasy at seeing me depart. And while I mounted through the air I saw nothing but eyes everywhere—eyes throwing out long feelers to reach me.

I had never seen an octopus, and I did not even know of the existence of these horrible beasts.

During the ascent, which appeared to me interminable, I imagined I saw these beasts along the walls, and my teeth were chattering when I was drawn out on to the green hillock.

I immediately told the guardian the cause of my terror, and he crossed himself, saying, " Those are the eyes of the ship-wrecked ones. No one must stay there ! "

I knew very well that they were not the eyes of shipwrecked ones, but I did not know what they were. For I thought I had seen some strange beasts that no one had ever seen before.

It was only at the hotel with Père Batifoulé that I learnt about the octopus.

Only five more days' holiday were left to me, and I passed them at the Pointe du Raz, seated in a niche of rock which has been since named " Sarah Bernhardt's Arm-chair." Many tourists have sat there since.

After my holiday I returned to Paris. But I was still very weak, and could only take up my work towards the month of November. I played all the pieces of my *répertoire*, and I was annoyed at not having any new *rôles*.

One day Perrin came to see me in my sculptor's studio. He began to talk at first about my busts ; he told me that I ought to do his medallion, and asked me incidentally if I knew the *rôle* of Phèdre. Up to that time I had only played Aricie, and the part of Phèdre seemed formidable to me. I had, however, studied it for my own pleasure.

" Yes, I know the *rôle* of Phèdre. But I think if ever I had to play it I should die of fright."

He laughed with his silly little laugh, and said to me, squeezing my hand (for he was very gallant), "Work it up. I think that you will play it."

In fact, eight days after I was called to the manager's office, and Perrin told me that he had announced *Phèdre* for December 21, the *fête* of Racine, with Mlle. Sarah Bernhardt in the part of Phèdre. I thought I should have fallen.

"Well, but what about Mademoiselle Rousseil?" I asked.

"Mademoiselle Rousseil wants the committee to promise that she shall become a Sociétaire in the month of January, and the committee, which will without doubt appoint her, refuses to make this promise, and declares that her demand is like a threat. But perhaps Mademoiselle Rousseil will change her plans, and in that case you will play Aricie and I will change the bill."

Coming out from Perrin's I ran up against M. Régnier. I told him of my conversation with the manager and of my fears.

"No, no," said the great artiste to me, "you must not be afraid! I see very well what you are going to make of this *rôle*. But all you have to do is to be careful and not force your voice. Make the *rôle* rather more sorrowful than furious—it will be better for every one, even Racine."

Then, joining my hands, I said, "Dear Monsieur Régnier, help me to work up Phèdre, and I shall not be so much afraid!"

He looked at me rather surprised, for in general I was neither docile nor apt to be guided by advice. I own that I was wrong, but I could not help it. But the responsibility which this put upon me made me timid. Régnier accepted, and made an appointment with me for the following morning at nine o'clock.

Roselia Rousseil persisted in her demand to the committee, and *Phèdre* was billed for December 21, with Mlle. Sarah Bernhardt for the first time in the *rôle* of Phèdre.

This caused quite a sensation in the artistic world and in theatrical circles. That evening over two hundred people were turned away at the box office. When I was informed of the fact I began to tremble a good deal.

Régnier comforted me as best he could, saying, "Courage! Cheer up! Are you not the spoiled darling of the public? They will take into consideration your inexperience in important leading parts," &c.

These were the last words he should have said to me. I

should have felt stronger if I had known that the public were come to oppose and not to encourage me.

I began to cry bitterly like a child. Perrin was called, and consoled me as well as he could; then he made me laugh by putting powder on my face so awkwardly that I was blinded and suffocated.

Everybody on the stage knew about it, and stood at the door of my dressing-room wishing to comfort me. Mounet-Sully, who was playing Hippolyte, told me that he had dreamed " we were playing *Phèdre*, and you were hissed ; and my dreams always go by contraries—so," he cried, " we shall have a tremendous success."

But what put me completely in a good humour was the arrival of the worthy Martel, who was playing Théramène, and who had come so quickly, believing me to be ill, that he had not had time to finish his nose. The sight of this grey face, with a wide bar of red wax commencing between the two eyebrows, coming down to half a centimetre below his nose and leaving behind it the end of the nose with two large black nostrils—this face was indescribable ! And everybody laughed irrepressibly. I knew that Martel made up his nose, for I had already seen this poor nose change shape at the second performance of *Zaïre*, under the tropical depression of the atmosphere, but I had never realised how much he lengthened it. This comical apparition restored all my gaiety, and from thenceforth I was in full possession of my faculties.

The evening was one long triumph for me. And the Press was unanimous in praise, with the exception of the article of Paul de St. Victor, who was on very good terms with a sister of Rachel, and could not get over " my impertinent presumption in daring to measure myself with the great dead artiste." These are his own words addressed to Girardin, who immediately communicated them to me. How mistaken he was, poor St. Victor ! I had never seen Rachel, but I worshipped her talent, for I had surrounded myself with her most devoted admirers, and they little thought of comparing me with their idol.

A few days after this performance of *Phèdre* the new piece of Bornier was read to us—*La Fille de Roland*. The part of Berthe was confided to me, and we immediately began the rehearsals of this fine piece, the verses of which were nevertheless a little flat, though the play rang with patriotism. There was in one act a terrible duel, not seen by the public, but related by Berthe, the daughter of Roland, while the incidents happened under the eyes of the unhappy girl, who from a window of the castle followed in anguish the fortunes of the encounter. This scene was the only important one of my much-sacrificed *rôle*.

The play was ready to be performed, when Bornier asked that his friend Emile Augier might attend the dress rehearsal. When this rehearsal was over Perrin came to me; he had an affectionate and constrained air. As to Bornier, he came straight to me in a decided and quarrelsome manner. Emile Augier followed him. "Well——" he said to me. I looked straight at him, feeling at the moment that he was my enemy. He stopped short and scratched his head, then turned towards Augier and said:

"I beg you, *cher maître*, explain to Mademoiselle yourself."

Emile Augier was a broad man, with wide shoulders and a common appearance, and was at that time rather stout. He was in very good repute at the Théâtre Français, of which he was at that epoch the successful author. He came near me.

"You managed the part at the window very well, Mademoiselle, but it is ridiculous; it is not your fault, but that of the author, who has written a most improbable scene. The public would laugh immoderately. This scene must be taken out."

I turned towards Perrin, who was listening silently. "Are you of the same opinion, sir?"

"I talked it over a short time ago with these gentlemen, but the author is master to do as he pleases with his work."

Then, addressing myself to Bornier, I said, "Well, my dear author, what have you decided?"

Little Bornier looked at big Emile Augier. There was in this beseeching and piteous glance an expression of sorrow at having to cut out a scene which he prized, and of fear at vexing an Academician just at the time when he was hoping to become a member of the Academy.

"Cut it out, cut it out—or you are done for!" brutally replied Augier, and he turned his back. Then poor Bornier, who resembled a Breton gnome, came up to me. He scratched himself desperately, for the unfortunate man suffered from a distressing skin disease. He did not speak. He looked at us searchingly. Poignant anxiety was expressed on his face. Perrin, who had come up to me, guessed the private little drama which was taking place in the heart of the mild Bornier.

"Refuse energetically," murmured Perrin to me.

I understood, and declared firmly to Bornier that if this scene were cut out I should refuse the part. Then Bornier seized both my hands, which he kissed ardently, and running up to Augier he exclaimed, with comic emphasis :

"But I cannot cut it out—I cannot cut it out! She will not play! And the day after to-morrow the play is to be performed." Then, as Emile Augier made a gesture and would have spoken: "No! No! To put back my play eight days would be to kill it! I cannot cut it out! Oh, mon Dieu!" And he cried and gesticulated with his two long arms, and he stamped with his short legs. His large hairy head went from right to left. He was at the same time funny and pitiable. Emile Augier was irritated, and turned on me like a hunted boar on a pursuing dog :

"Will you take the responsibility, Mademoiselle, of the absurd window scene on the first performance ? "

"Certainly, Monsieur ; and I even promise to make of this scene, which I find very beautiful, an enormous success ! "

He shrugged his shoulders rudely, muttering something very disagreeable between his teeth.

When I left the theatre I found poor Bornier quite transfigured. He thanked me a thousand times, for he thought very highly of this scene, and he dared not thwart Emile Augier. Both Perrin and myself had divined the legitimate emotions of this poor poet, so gentle and so well bred, but a trifle Jesuitical.

The play was an immense success. But the window scene on the first night was a veritable triumph.

It was a short time after the terrible war of 1870. The play contained frequent allusions to it, and owing to the patriotism of the public made an even greater success than it deserved as a play. I sent for Emile Augier. He came to my dressing-room with a surly air, and said to me from the door :

"So much the worse for the public! It only proves that the public is idiotic to make a success of such vileness ! " And he disappeared without having even entered my dressing-room.

His outburst made me laugh, and as the triumphant Bornier had embraced me repeatedly, I scratched myself all over.

Two months later I played *Gabrielle*, by this same Augier, and I had incessant quarrels with him. I found the verses of this play execrable. Coquelin, who took the part of my husband, made a great success. As for me, I was as mediocre as the play itself, which is saying a great deal.

I had been appointed a Sociétaire in the month of January, and since then it seemed to me that I was in prison, for I had undertaken an engagement not to leave the House of Molière for many years. This idea made me sad. It was at Perrin's instigation that I had asked to become a Sociétaire, and now I regretted it very much.

During all the latter part of the year I only played occasionally.

My time was then occupied in looking after the building of a pretty little mansion which I was having erected at the corner of the Avenue de Villiers and the Rue Fortuny. A sister of my grandmother had left me in her will a nice legacy, which I used to buy the ground. My great desire was to have a house that should be entirely my own, and I was then realising it. The son-in-law of M. Régnier, Félix Escalier, a fashionable architect, was building me a charming place. Nothing amused me more than to go with him in the morning over the unfinished house. Afterwards I mounted the movable scaffolds. Then I went on the roofs. I forgot my worries of the theatre in this new occupation. The thing I most desired just then was to become an architect. When the building was finished, the interior had to be thought of. I spent much time in helping my painter friends who were decorating the ceilings in my bedroom, in my dining-room, in my hall : Georges Clairin ; the architect Escalier, who was also a talented painter ; Duez, Picard, Butin, Jadin, and Parrot. I was deeply interested. And I recollect a joke which I played on one of my relations.

My aunt Betsy had come from Holland, her native country, in order to spend a few days in Paris. She was staying with my mother. I invited her to lunch in my new unfinished habitation. Five of my painter friends were working, some in one room, some in another, and everywhere lofty scaffoldings were erected. In order to be able to climb the ladders more easily I was wearing my sculptor's costume. My aunt, seeing me thus

arrayed, was horribly shocked, and told me so.   But I was preparing yet another surprise for her.   She thought these young
workers were ordinary house-painters, and considered I was too
familiar with them.   But she nearly fainted when midday came
and I rushed to the piano to play " The Complaint of the
Hungry Stomachs."   This wild melody had been improvised by
the group of painters, but revised and corrected by poet friends.
Here it is :

> Oh ! Peintres de la Dam' jolie,
> De vos pinceaux arrêtez la folie !
> Il faut descendr' des escabeaux,
> Vous nettoyer et vous faire très beaux !
> > Digue, dingue, donne !
> > L'heure sonne.
> > Digue, dingue, di . . .
> > C'est midi !

> Sur les grils et dans les cass'roles
> Sautent le veau, et les œufs et les soles.
> Le bon vin rouge et l'Saint-Marceaux
> Feront gaiment galoper nos pinceaux !
> > Digue, dingue, donne !
> > L'heure sonne.
> > Digue, dingue, di . . .
> > C'est midi !

> Voici vos peintres, Dam' jolie
> Qui vont pour vous débiter leur folie.
> Ils ont tous lâché l'escabeau
> Sont frais, sont fiers, sont propres et très beaux !
> > Digue, dingue, donne
> > L'heure sonne
> > Digue, dingue, di . . .
> > C'est midi.

When the song was finished I went into my bedroom and made
myself into a *belle dame* for lunch.

My aunt had followed me.   " But, my dear," said she, " you
are mad to think I am going to eat with all these workmen.
Certainly in all Paris there is no one but yourself who would do
such a thing."

" No, no, Aunt ; it is all right."

And I dragged her off, when I was dressed, to the dining-
room, which was the most habitable room of the house.   Five

young men solemnly bowed to my aunt, who did not recognise
them at first, for they had changed their working clothes and
looked like five nice young society swells. Madame Guérard
lunched with us. Suddenly in the middle of lunch my aunt
cried out, " But these are the workmen ! " The five young men
rose and bowed low. Then my poor aunt understood her mistake
and excused herself in every possible manner, so confused was
she.

XXIV

ONE day Alexandre Dumas, junior, was announced. He came to bring me the good news that he had finished his play for the Comédie Française, *L'Etrangère*, and that my *rôle*, the Duchesse de Septmonts, had come out very well. " You can," he said to me, "make a fine success out of it." I expressed my gratitude to him.

A month after this visit we were requested to attend the reading of this piece at the Comédie.

The reading was a great success, and I was delighted with my *rôle*, Catherine de Septmonts. I also liked the *rôle* of Croizette, Mrs. Clarkson.

Got gave us each copies of our parts, and thinking that he had made a mistake, I passed on to Croizette the *rôle* of l'Etrangère which he had just given me, saying to her, " Here, Got has made a mistake—here is your *rôle*."

"But he is not making any mistake. It is I who am to play the Duchesse de Septmonts."

I burst out into irrepressible laughter, which surprised everybody present, and when Perrin, annoyed, asked me at whom I was laughing like that, I exclaimed :

"At all of you—you, Dumas, Got, Croizette, and all of you who are in the plot, and who are all a little afraid of the result of your cowardice. Well, you need not alarm yourselves. I was delighted to play the Duchesse de Septmonts, but I shall be ten times more delighted to play l'Etrangère. And this time, my dear Sophie, I'll be quits with you ; no ceremony, I tell you ; for you have played me a little trick which was quite unworthy of our friendship ! "

The rehearsals were strained on all sides. Perrin, who was a warm partisan of Croizette, bewailed the want of suppleness of her talent, so much so that one day Croizette, losing all patience, burst out:

" Well, Monsieur, you should have left the *rôle* to Sarah ; she would have played it with the voice you wish in the love scenes ; I cannot do any better. You irritate me too much : I have had enough of it ! " And she ran off, sobbing, into the little *guignol*, where she had an attack of hysteria.

I followed her and consoled her as well as I could. And in the midst of her tears she kissed me, murmuring, " It is true. It is they who instigated me to play this nasty trick, and now they are annoying me." Croizette used vulgar expressions, very vulgar ones, and at times uttered many a Gallic joke.

That day we made up our quarrel entirely.

A week before the first performance I received an anonymous letter informing me that Perrin was trying his very best to get Dumas to change the name of the play. He wished—it goes without saying—to have the piece called *La Duchesse de Septmonts*.

I rushed off to the theatre to find Perrin at once.

At the entrance door I met Coquelin, who was playing the part of the Duc de Septmonts, which he did marvellously well. I showed him the letter. He shrugged his shoulders. " It is infamous ! But why do you take any notice of an anonymous letter ? It is not worthy of you ! "

We were talking at the foot of the staircase when the manager arrived.

" Here, show the letter to Perrin ! " And he took it from my hands in order to show it to him. Perrin blushed slightly.

" I know this writing," he said. " Some one from the theatre has written this letter."

I snatched it back from him. " Then it is some one who is well informed, and what he says is perhaps true. Is it not so ? Tell me. I have the right to know."

" I detest anonymous letters." And he went up the stairs, bowing slightly, but without saying anything further.

" Ah, if it is true," said Coquelin, " it is too much. Would you like me to go and see Dumas, and I will get to know at once ? "

s

"No, thank you. But you have put an idea into my head. I'll go there." And shaking hands with him, I went off to see the younger Dumas. He was just going out.

"Well, well? What is the matter? Your eyes are blazing!"

I went with him into the drawing-room and asked my question at once. He had kept his hat on, and took it off to recover his self-possession. And before he could speak a word I got furiously angry; I fell into one of those rages which I sometimes have, and which are more like attacks of madness. And in fact, all that I felt of bitterness towards this man, towards Perrin, towards all this theatrical world that should have loved me and upheld me, but which betrayed me on every occasion—all the hot anger that I had been accumulating during the rehearsals, the cries of revolt against the perpetual injustice of these two men, Perrin and Dumas—I burst out with everything in an avalanche of stinging words which were both furious and sincere. I reminded him of his promise made in former days; of his visit to my hotel in the Avenue de Villiers; of the cowardly and underhand manner in which he had sacrificed me, at Perrin's request and on the wishes of the friends of Sophie. I spoke vehemently, without allowing him to edge in a single word. And when, worn out, I was forced to stop, I murmured, out of breath with fatigue, "What—what—what have you to say for yourself?"

"My dear child," he replied, much touched, "if I had examined my own conscience I should have said to myself all that you have just said to me so eloquently! But I can truly say, in order to excuse myself a little, that I really believed that you did not care at all about the stage; that you much preferred your sculpture, your painting, and your court. We have seldom talked together, and people led me to believe all that I was perhaps too ready to believe. Your grief and anger have touched me deeply. I give you my word that the play shall keep its title of *L'Etrangère*. And now embrace me with good grace, to show that you are no longer angry with me."

I embraced him, and from that day we were good friends.

That evening I told the whole tale to Croizette, and I saw that she knew nothing about this wicked scheme. I was very

pleased to know that.   The play was very successful.   Coquelin,
Febvre, and I carried off the laurels of the day.

I had just commenced in my studio in the Avenue de Clichy
a large group, the inspiration for which I had gathered from the
sad history of an old woman whom I often saw at nightfall in
the Baie des Trépassés.

One day I went up to her, wishing to speak to her, but I was
so terrified by her aspect of madness that I rushed off at once,
and the guardian told me her history.

She was the mother of five sons, all sailors.   Two had been
killed by the Germans in 1870, and three had been drowned.
She had brought up the little son of her youngest boy, always
keeping him far from the sea and teaching him to hate the
water.   She had never left the little lad, but he became so sad
that he was really ill, and he said he was dying because he
wanted to see the sea.   " Well, make haste and get well," said
the grandmother tenderly, " and we will go to see it together."

Two days later the child was better, and the grandmother left
the valley in the company of her little grandson to go and see
the ocean, the grave of her three sons.

It was a November day ; a low sky hung over the ocean,
narrowing the horizon.   The child jumped with joy.   He ran,
gambolled, and sang for happiness when he saw all this living
water.

The grandmother sat on the sand, and hid her tearful eyes in
her two trembling hands ; then suddenly, struck by the silence,
she looked up in terror.   There in front of her she saw a boat
drifting, and in the boat her boy, her little lad of eight years
old, who was laughing right merrily, paddling as well as he could
with one oar that he could hardly hold, and crying out, " I am
going to see what there is behind the mist, and I will come
back."

He never came back.   And the following day they found the
poor old woman talking low to the waves which came and
bathed her feet.   She came every day to the water's edge,
throwing in the bread which kind folks gave her, and saying to
the waves, " You must carry that to the little lad."

This touching narrative had remained in my memory.   I can
still see the tall old woman, with her brown cape and hood.

I worked feverishly at this group.   It seemed to me now that I was destined to be a sculptor, and I began to despise the stage. I only went to the theatre when I was compelled by my duties, and I left as soon as possible.

I had made several designs, none of which pleased me. Just when I was going to throw down the last one in discouragement, the painter Georges Clairin, who came in just at that moment to see me, begged me not to do so. And my good friend Mathieu Meusnier, who was a man of talent, also added his voice against the destruction of my design.

Excited by their encouragement, I decided to hurry on with the work and to make a large group. I asked Meusnier if he knew any tall, bony old woman, and he sent me two, neither of whom suited me. Then I asked all my painter and sculptor friends, and during eight days all sorts of old and infirm women came for my inspection. I fixed at last on a charwoman who was about sixty years old. She was very tall, and had very sharp-cut features. When she came in I felt a slight sentiment of fear. The idea of remaining alone with this female *gendarme* for hours together made me feel uneasy. But when I heard her speak I was more comfortable. Her timid, gentle voice and frightened gestures, like a shy young girl, contrasted strangely with the build of the poor woman. When I showed her the design she was stupefied. " Do you want me to have my neck and shoulders bare ? I really cannot." I told her that nobody ever came in when I worked, and I asked to see her neck immediately.

Oh, that neck ! I clapped my hands with joy when I saw it. It was long, emaciated, terrible. The bones literally stood out almost bare of flesh ; the sterno-cleido-mastoid was remarkable—it was just what I wanted. I went up to her and gently bared her shoulder. What a treasure I had found ! The shoulder bone was visible under the skin, and she had two immense " salt-cellars " ! The woman was ideal for my work. She seemed destined for it. She blushed when I told her so. I asked to see her feet. She took off her thick boots and showed a dirty foot which had no character. " No," I said, "thank you. Your feet are too small ; I will take only your head and shoulders."

After having fixed the price I engaged her for three months. At the idea of earning so much money for three months the poor woman began to cry, and I felt so sorry for her that I told her she would not have to seek for work that winter, because she had already told me that she generally spent six months of the year in the country, in Sologne, near her grandchildren.

Having found the grandmother, I now needed the child.

I passed a review of a whole army of professional Italian models. There were some lovely children, real little Jupins. The mothers undressed their children in a second, and the children posed quite naturally and took attitudes which showed off their muscles and the development of the torso. I chose a fine little boy of seven years old, but who looked more like nine. I had already had in the workmen, who had followed out my design and put up the scaffolding necessary to make my work sufficiently stable and to support the weight. Enormous iron supports were fixed into the plaster by bolts and pillars of wood and iron wherever necessary. The skeleton of a large piece of sculpture looks like a giant trap put up to catch rats and mice by the thousand.

I gave myself up to this enormous work with the courage of ignorance. Nothing discouraged me.

Often I worked on till midnight, sometimes till four o'clock in the morning. And as one humble gas-burner was totally insufficient to work by, I had a crown or rather a silver circlet made, each bud of which was a candlestick, and each had its candle burning, and those of the back row were a little higher than those of the front. And with this help I was able to work almost without ceasing. I had no watch or clock in the room, as I wished to ignore time altogether, except on the days I had to perform at the theatre. Then my maid would come and call for me. How many times have I gone without lunch or dinner. Then I would perhaps faint, and so be compelled to send for something to eat to restore my strength.

I had almost finished my group, but I had done neither the feet nor the hands of the grandmother. She was holding her little dead grandson on her knees, but her arms had no hands and her legs had no feet. I looked in vain for the hands and feet of my ideal, large and bony. One day, when my friend Martel came to see me at my studio and to look at this group, which was much talked of, I had an inspiration. Martel was big, and thin enough to make Death jealous. I watched him walking round my work. He was looking at it as a *connoisseur*. But I was looking at *him*. Suddenly I said :

" My dear Martel, I beg you—I beseech you—to pose for the hands and feet of my grandmother ! "

He burst out laughing, and with perfectly good grace he took off his shoes and took the place of my model.

He came ten days in succession, and gave me three hours each day.

Thanks to him, I was able to finish my group. I had it moulded and sent to the Salon (1876), where it met with genuine success.

Is there any need to say that I was accused of having got some one else to make this group for me ? I sent a summons to one critic. He was no other than Jules Claretie, who had declared that this work, which was very interesting, could not have been done by me. Jules Claretie apologised very politely, and that was the end of it.

The Jury, after a full investigation, awarded me an " honourable mention," and I was wild with joy.

I was very much criticised, but also very much praised. Nearly all the criticisms referred to the neck of my old Breton woman, that neck on which I had worked with such eagerness.

The following is from an article by René Delorme :

" The work of Mlle. Sarah Bernhardt deserves to be studied in detail. The head of the grandmother, well worked out as to the profound wrinkles it bears, expresses that intense sorrow in which everything else counts as nothing.

" The only reproach I have to make against this artist is that she has brought too much into prominence the muscles of the neck of the old grandmother. This shows a lack of experience. She is pleased with herself for having studied anatomy so well, and is not sorry for the opportunity of showing it. It is," &c. &c.

Certainly this gentleman was right. I had studied anatomy eagerly and in a very amusing manner. I had had lessons from Doctor Parrot, who was so good to me. I had continually with me a book of anatomical designs, and when I was at home I stood before the glass and said suddenly to myself, putting my finger on some part of my body, " Now then, what is that ? " I had to answer immediately, without hesitation, and when I hesitated I compelled myself to learn by heart the muscles of the head or the arm, and did not sleep till this was done.

A month after the exhibition there was a reading of Parodi's play, *Rome Vaincue*, at the Comédie Française. I refused the *rôle* of the young vestal Opimia, which had been allotted to me, and energetically demanded that of Posthumia, an old, blind Roman woman with a superb and noble face.

No doubt there was some connection in my mind between my old Breton weeping over her grandson and the august patrician claiming forgiveness for her grand-daughter.

Perrin was at first astounded. Afterwards he acceded to my request. But his order-loving mind and his taste for symmetry made him anxious about Mounet-Sully, who was also playing in the piece. He was accustomed to seeing Mounet-Sully and me playing the two heroes, the two lovers, the two victims. How was he to arrange matters so that we should still be the two— something or other? *Eureka!* There was in the play an old idiot named Vestæpor, who was quite unnecessary for the action of the piece, but had been brought in to satisfy Perrin. "Eureka!" cried the director of the Comédie; "Mounet-Sully shall play Vestæpor!" Equilibrium was restored. The god of the *bourgeois* was content.

The piece, which was really quite mediocre, obtained a great success at the first performance (September 27, 1876), and personally I was very successful in the fourth act. The public was decidedly in my favour, in spite of everything and everybody.

XXV

"HERNANI"—A TRIP IN A BALLOON

THE performances of *Hernani* made me a still greater favourite with the public.

I had already rehearsed with Victor Hugo, and it was a real pleasure to me to see the great poet almost each day. I had never discontinued my visits, but I was never able to have any conversation with him in his own house. There were always men in red ties gesticulating, or women in tears reciting. He was very good; he used to listen with half-closed eyes, and I thought he was asleep. Then, roused by the silence, he would say a consoling word, for Victor Hugo could not promise without keeping his word. He was not like me: I promise everything with the firm intention of keeping my promises, and two hours after I have forgotten all about them. If any one reminds me of what I have promised, I tear my hair, and to make up for my forgetfulness I say anything, I buy presents—in fact, I complicate my life with useless worries. It has always been thus, and always will be so.

As was I grumbling one day to Victor Hugo that I never could have a chance of talking with him, he invited me to lunch, saying that after lunch we could talk together alone. I was delighted with this lunch, to which Paul Meurice, the poet Léon Cladel, the Communard Dupuis, a Russian lady whose name I do not remember, and Gustave Doré were also invited. In front of Victor Hugo sat Madame Drouet, the friend of his unlucky days.

But what a horrible lunch we had! It was really bad and badly served. My feet were frozen by the draughts from the three doors, which fitted badly, and one could positively *hear* the wind blowing under the table. Near me was Mr. X., a German socialist, who is to-day a very successful man. This man had such dirty hands and ate in such a way that he made me feel sick. I met him afterwards at Berlin. He is now quite clean and proper, and, I believe, an imperialist. But the uncomfortable feeling this uncongenial neighbour inspired in me, the cold draughts blowing on my feet, mortal boredom—all this reduced me to a state of positive suffering, and I lost consciousness.

When I recovered I found myself on a couch, my hand in that of Madame Drouet, and in front of me, sketching me, Gustave Doré.

" Oh, don't move," he exclaimed ; " you are so pretty like that !" These words, though they were so inappropriate, pleased me nevertheless, and I complied with the wish of the great artist, who was one of my friends.

I left the house of Victor Hugo without saying good-bye to him, a trifle ashamed of myself.

The next day he came to see me. I told him some tale to account for my illness, and I saw no more of him except at the rehearsals of *Hernani*.

The first performance of *Hernani* took place on November 21, 1877. It was a triumph alike for the author and the actors. *Hernani* had already been played ten years earlier, but Delaunay, who then took the part of Hernani, was the exact contrary of what this part should have been. He was neither epic, romantic, nor poetic. He had not the style of those grand epic poems. He was charming, graceful, and wore a perpetual smile ; of middle height, with studied movements, he was ideal in Musset, perfect in Emile Augier, charming in Molière, but execrable in Victor Hugo.

Bressant, who took the part of Charles Quint, was shockingly bad. His amiable and flabby style and his weak and wandering eyes effectively prevented all grandeur. His two enormous feet, generally half hidden under his trousers, assumed immense proportions. I could see nothing else. They were very large, flat, and slightly turned in at the toes. They were a nightmare ! But think of their possessor repeating the admirable couplet of Charles Quint to the shade of Charlemagne ! It was absurd ! The public coughed, wriggled, and showed that they found the whole thing painful and ridiculous.

In our performance it was Mounet-Sully, in all the

splendour of his talent, who played Hernani. And it was Worms, that admirable artiste, who played Charles Quint—and how well he took the part! How he rolled out the lines! What a splendid diction he had! This performance of November 21, 1877, was a triumph. I came in for a good share in the general success. I played Dona Sol. Victor Hugo sent me the following letter:

" MADAME,—You have been great and charming; you have moved me—me, the old combatant—and at one moment, while the public whom you had enchanted cheered you, I wept. This tear which you caused me to shed is yours, and I place myself at your feet.

" VICTOR HUGO."

With this letter came a small box containing a fine chain bracelet, from which hung one diamond drop. I lost this bracelet at the house of the rich nabob, Alfred Sassoon. He wauted to give me another, but I refused. He could not give me back the tear of Victor Hugo.

My success at the Comédie was assured, and the public treated me as a spoiled child. My comrades were a little jealous of me.

Perrin made trouble for me at every turn. He had a sort of friendship for me, but he would not believe that I could get on without him, and as he always refused to do as I wanted, I did not go to him for anything. I used to send a letter to the Ministry, and I always won my cause.

As I had a continual thirst for what was new, I now tried my hand at painting. I knew how to draw a little, and had a well-developed sense of colour. I first did two or three small pictures, then I undertook the portrait of my dear Guérard.

Alfred Stevens thought it was vigorously done, and Georges Clairin encouraged me to continue with painting. Then I launched out courageously, boldly. I began a picture which was nearly two metres in size, *The Young Girl and Death.*

Then came a cry of indignation against me.

Why did I want to do anything else but act, since that was my career?

Why did I always want to be before the public?

Perrin came to see me one day when I was very ill. He began

to preach. " You are killing yourself, my dear child," he said. " Why do you go in for sculpture, painting, &c ? Is it to prove that you can do it ? "

" Oh, no, no," I answered; " it is merely to create a necessity for staying here."

" I don't understand," said Perrin, listening very attentively.

" This is how it is. I have a wild desire to travel, to see something else, to breathe another air, and to see skies that are higher than ours and trees that are bigger—something different, in short. I have therefore had to create for myself some tasks which will hold me to my chains. If I did not do this, I feel that my desire to see other things in the world would win the day, and I should do something foolish."

This conversation was destined to go against me some years later, when the Comédie brought a law-suit against me.

The Exhibition of 1878 put the finishing stroke to the state of exasperation that Perrin and some of the artistes of the theatre had conceived against me. They blamed me for everything— for my painting, my sculpture, and my health. I had a terrible scene with Perrin, and it was the last one, for from that time forth we did not speak to each other again ; a formal bow was the most that we exchanged afterwards.

The climax was reached over my balloon ascension. I adored and I still adore balloons. Every day I went up in M. Giffard's captive balloon. This persistency had struck the *savant*, and he asked a mutual friend to introduce him.

" Oh, Monsieur Giffard," I said, " how I should like to go up in a balloon that is not captive ! "

" Well, Mademoiselle, you shall do so if you like," he replied very kindly.

" When ? " I asked.

" Any day you like."

I should have liked to start immediately, but, as he pointed out, he would have to fit the balloon up, and it was a great responsibility for him to undertake. We therefore fixed upon the following Tuesday, just a week from then. I asked M. Giffard to say nothing about it, for if the newspapers should get hold of this piece of news my terrified family would not allow me to go. M. Tissandier, who a little time after was doomed, poor fellow, to be killed in a balloon accident, promised to accompany me. Something happened, however, to prevent his going with me, and it was young Godard who the following week accompanied me in the " Dona Sol," a beautiful orange-coloured balloon specially prepared for my expedition. Prince Jerome Napoleon (Plon-Plon), who was with me when Giffard was introduced, insisted on going with us. But he was heavy and rather clumsy, and I did not care much about his conversation, in spite of his marvellous wit, for he was spiteful, and rather delighted when he could get a chance to attack the Emperor Napoleon III., whom I liked very much.

We started alone, Georges Clairin, Godard, and I. The rumour of our journey had spread, but too late for the Press to get hold of the news. I had been up in the air about five minutes when one of my friends, Comte de M——, met Perrin on the Saints-Pères Bridge.

" I say," he began, " look up in the sky. There is your star shooting away."

Perrin gazed up, and, pointing to the balloon which was rising, he asked, " Who is in that ? "

" Sarah Bernhardt," replied my friend. Perrin, it appears, turned purple, and, clenching his teeth, he murmured, " That's another of her freaks, but she will pay for this."

He hurried away without even saying good-bye to my young friend, who stood there stupefied at this unreasonable burst of anger.

And if he had suspected my infinite joy at thus travelling through the air, Perrin would have suffered still more.

Ah ! our departure ! It was half-past five. I shook hands with a few friends. My family, whom I had kept in the most profound ignorance, was not there. I felt my heart tighten somewhat when, after the words " Let her go ! " I found myself in about a second some fifty yards above the earth. I still heard a few cries : " Wait ! Come back ! Don't let her be killed !' And then nothing more. Nothing. There was the sky above and the earth beneath. Then suddenly I was in the clouds. I had left a misty Paris. I now breathed under a blue sky and saw a radiant sun. Around us were opaque mountains of clouds with irradiated edges. Our balloon plunged into a milky vapour quite warm from the sun. It was splendid ! It was stupefying ! Not a sound, not a breath ! But the balloon was scarcely moving at all. It was only towards six o'clock that the currents of air caught us, and we took our flight towards the east. We were at an altitude of about 1700 metres. The spectacle became fairylike. Large fleecy clouds were spread below us like a carpet. Large orange curtains fringed with violet came down from the sun to lose themselves in our cloudy carpet.

At twenty minutes to seven we were about 2500 metres above the earth, and cold and hunger commenced to make themselves felt.

The dinner was copious—we had *foie gras*, fresh bread, and oranges. The cork of our champagne bottle flew up into the clouds with a pretty, soft noise. We raised our glasses in honour of M. Giffard.

We had talked a great deal. Night began to put on her heavy dark mantle. It became very cold. We were then at 2600 metres, and I had a singing in my ears. My nose began to bleed. I felt very uncomfortable, and began to get drowsy without being able to prevent it. Georges Clairin got anxious, and young Godard cried out loudly, to wake me up, no doubt : " Come, come ! We shall have to go down. Let us throw out the guide-rope ! "

This cry woke me up. I wanted to know what a guide-rope was. I got up feeling rather stupefied, and in order to rouse me Godard put the guide-rope into my hands. It was a strong rope of about 120 metres long, to which were attached at certain distances little iron hooks. Clairin and I let out the rope, laughing, while Godard, bending over the side of the car, was looking through a field-glass.

" Stop ! " he cried suddenly. " There are a lot of trees ! "

We were over the wood of Ferrières. But just in front of us there was a little open ground suitable for our descent.

" There is no doubt about it," cried Godard ; " if we miss this plain we shall come down in the dead of night in the wood of Ferrières, and that will be very dangerous ! " Then, turning to me, " Will you," he said, " open the valve ? "

I immediately did so, and the gas came out of its prison whistling a mocking air. The valve was shut by order of the aeronaut, and we descended rapidly. Suddenly the stillness of the night was broken by the sound of a horn. I trembled. It was Louis Godard, who had pulled out of his pocket, which was a veritable storehouse, a sort of horn on which he blew with violence. A loud whistle answered our call, and 500 metres below us we saw a man who was shouting his hardest to make us hear. As we were very close to a little station, we easily guessed that this man was the station-master.

"Where are we?" cried Louis Godard through his horn.

"At—in—in—ille!" answered the station-master. It was impossible to understand.

"Where are we?" thundered Georges Clairin in his most formidable tones.

"At—in—in—ille!" shouted the station-master, with his hand curved round his mouth.

"Where are we?" cried I in my most crystalline accents.

"At—in—in—ille!" answered the station-master and his porters.

It was impossible to get to know anything. We had to lower the balloon. At first we descended rather too quickly, and the wind blew us towards the wood. We had to go up again. But ten minutes later we opened the valve again and made a fresh descent. The balloon was then to the right of the station, and far from the amiable station-master.

"Throw out the anchor!" cried young Godard in a commanding tone. And assisted by Georges Clairin, he threw out into space another rope, to the end of which was fastened a formidable anchor. The rope was 80 metres long.

Down below us a crowd of children of all ages had been running ever since we stopped above the station. When we got to about 300 metres from earth Godard called out to them, "Where are we?"

"At Vachère!"

None of us knew Vachère. But we descended nevertheless.

"Hullo! you fellows down there, take hold of the rope that's dragging," cried the aeronaut, "and mind you don't pull too hard!" Five vigorous men seized hold of the rope. We were 130 metres from the ground, and the sight was becoming interesting. Darkness began to blot out everything. I raised my head to see the sky, but I remained with my mouth open with astonishment. I saw only the lower end of our balloon, which was overhanging its base, all loose and baggy. It was very ugly.

We anchored gently, without the little dragging which I had

hoped would happen, and without the little drama which I had half expected.

It began to rain in torrents as we left the balloon.

The young owner of a neighbouring château ran up, like the peasants, to see what was going on. He offered me his umbrella.

"Oh, I am so thin I cannot get wet. I pass between the drops."

The saying was repeated and had a great success.

"What time is there a train?" asked Godard.

"Oh, you have plenty of time," answered an oily and heavy voice. "You cannot leave before ten o'clock, as the station is a long way from here, and in such weather it will take Madame two hours to walk there."

I was confounded, and looked for the young gentleman with the umbrella, which I could have used as walking-stick, as neither Clairin nor Godard had one. But just as I was accusing him of going away and leaving us, he jumped lightly out of a vehicle which I had not heard drive up.

"There!" said he. "There is a carriage for you and these gentlemen, and another for the body of the balloon."

"*Ma foi!* You have saved us," said Clairin, clasping his hand, "for it appears the roads are in a very bad state."

"Oh," said the young man, "it would be impossible for the feet of Parisians to walk even half the distance."

Then he bowed and wished us a pleasant journey.

Rather more than an hour later we arrived at the station of Emerainville. The station-master, learning who we were, received us in a very friendly manner. He made his apologies for not having heard when we called out an hour previously from our floating vehicle. We had a frugal meal of bread, cheese, and cider set before us. I have always detested cheese, and would never eat it : there is nothing poetical about it. But I was dying with hunger.

"Taste it, taste it," said Georges Clairin.

I bit a morsel off, and found it excellent.

We got back very late, in the middle of the night, and I found my household in an extreme state of anxiety. Our friends who had come to hear news of us had stayed. There was quite a crowd. I was somewhat annoyed at this, as I was half dead with fatigue.

I sent everybody away rather sharply, and went up to my room. As my maid was helping me to undress she told me that some one had come for me from the Comédie Française several times.

"Oh, mon Dieu!" I cried anxiously. "Could the piece have been changed?"

"No, I don't think so," said the maid. "But it appears that Monsieur Perrin is furious, and that they are all in a rage with you. Here is the note which was left for you."

I opened the letter. I was requested to call on the manager the following day at two o'clock.

On my arrival at Perrin's at the time appointed I was received with exaggerated politeness which had an undercurrent of severity.

Then commenced a series of recriminations about my fits of ill-temper, my caprices, my eccentricities; and he finished his speech by saying that I had incurred a fine of one thousand francs for travelling without the consent of the management.

I burst out laughing. "The case of a balloon has not been foreseen," I said; "and I vow that I will pay no fine. Outside the theatre I do as I please, and that is no business of yours, my dear Monsieur Perrin, so long as I do nothing to interfere with my theatrical work. And besides, you bore me to death—I will resign. Be happy."

I left him ashamed and anxious.

The next day I sent in my written resignation to M. Perrin, and a few hours afterwards I was sent for by M. Turquet, Minister of Fine Arts. I refused to go, and they sent a mutual friend, who stated that M. Perrin had gone a step farther than he had any right to; that the fine was annulled, and that I must cancel my resignation. So I did.

But the situation was strained. My fame had become annoying for my enemies, and a little trying, I confess, for my friends. But at that time all this stir and noise amused me vastly. I did nothing to attract attention. My somewhat fantastic tastes, my paleness and thinness, my peculiar way of dressing, my scorn of fashion, my general freedom in all respects, made me a being quite apart from all others. I did not recognise the fact.

I did not read, I never read, the newspapers. So I did not know what was said about me, either favourable or unfavourable.

Surrounded by a court of adorers of both sexes, I lived in a sunny dream.

All the royal personages and the notabilities who were the guests of France during the Exhibition of 1878 came to see me. This was a constant source of pleasure to me.

The Comédie was the first theatre to which all these illustrious visitors went, and Croizette and I played nearly every evening. While I was playing Amphytrion I fell seriously ill, and was sent to the south.

I remained there two months. I lived at Mentone, but I made Cap Martin my headquarters. I had a tent put up here on the spot that the Empress Eugénie afterwards selected for her villa. I did not want to see anybody, and I thought that by living in a tent so far from the town I should not be troubled with visitors. This was a mistake. One day when I was having lunch with my little boy I heard the bells of two horses and a carriage. The road overhung my tent, which was half hidden by the bushes. Suddenly a voice which I knew, but could not recognise, cried in the emphatic tone of a herald, " Does Sarah Bernhardt, Sociétaire of the Comédie Française, reside here ? "

We did not move. The question was asked again. Again the answer was silence. But we heard the sound of breaking branches, the bushes were pushed apart, and at two yards from the tent the unwelcome voice recommenced.

We were discovered. Somewhat annoyed, I came out. I saw before me a man with a large *tussore* cloak on, a field-glass strapped on his shoulders, a grey bowler hat, and a red, happy face, with a little pointed beard. I looked at this commonplace-looking individual with anything but favour. He lifted his hat.

" Madame Sarah Bernhardt is here ? "

" What do you want with me, sir ? "

" Here is my card, Madame."

I read, " Gambard, Nice, Villa des Palmiers." I looked at him with astonishment, and he was still more astonished to see that his name did not produce any impression on me. He had a foreign accent.

" Well, you see, Madame, I came to ask you to sell me your group, *After the Tempest.*"

I began to laugh.

T

"Ma foi, Monsieur, I am treating for that with the firm of Susse, and they offer me 6000 francs. If you will give ten you may have it."

"All right," he said. "Here are 10,000 francs. Have you pen and ink?"

"No."

"Ah," said he, "allow me!" And he produced a little case in which there were pen and ink.

I made out the receipt, and gave him an order to take the group from my studio in Paris. He went away, and I heard the bells of the horses ringing and then dying away in the distance. After this I was often invited to the house of this original person.

XXVI

THE COMÉDIE FRANÇAISE GOES TO LONDON

SHORTLY after, I came back to Paris. At the theatre they were preparing for a benefit performance for Bressant, who was about to retire from the stage. It was agreed that Mounet-Sully and I should play an act from *Othello*, by Jean Aicard. The theatre was well filled, and the audience in a good humour. After the song I was in bed as Desdemona, when suddenly I heard the public laugh, softly at first, and then irrepressibly. Othello had just come in, in the darkness, in his shirt or very little more, with a lantern in his hand, and gone to a door hidden in some drapery. The public, that impersonal unity has no hesitation in taking part in these unseemly manifestations, but each member of the audience, taken as a separate individual, would be ashamed to admit that he participated in them. But the ridicule thrown on this act by the exaggerated pantomime of the actor prevented the play being staged again, and it was only twenty years later that *Othello* as an entire play was produced at the Théâtre Français. I was then no longer there.

After having played Bérénice in *Mithridate* successfully, I reappeared in my *rôle* of the Queen in *Ruy Blas*. The play was as successful at the Théâtre Français as it had been at the Odéon, and the public was, if anything, still more favourable to me. Mounet-Sully played Ruy Blas. He was admirable in the part, and infinitely superior to Lafontaine, who had played it at the Odéon. Frédéric Febvre, very well costumed, rendered his part in a most interesting manner, but he was not so good as Geffroy, who was the most distinguished and the most terrifying Don Salluste that could be imagined.

My relations with Perrin were more and more strained.

He was pleased that I was successful, for the sake of the theatre ; he was happy at the magnificent receipts of *Ruy Blas ;* but he would have much preferred that it had been another than I who received all the applause. My independence, my horror of submission, even in appearance, annoyed him vastly.

One day my servant came to tell me that an elderly English-man was asking to see me so insistently that he thought it better to come and tell me, though I had given orders I was not to be disturbed.

" Send him away, and let me work in peace."

I was just commencing a picture which interested me very much. It represented a little girl, on Palm Sunday, carrying branches of palm. The little model who posed for me was a lovely Italian of eight years old. Suddenly she said to me :

" He's quarrelling—that Englishman ! "

As a matter of fact, in the ante-room there was a noise of voices rising higher and higher. Irritated, I rushed out, my palette in my hand, resolved to make the intruder flee. But just as I opened the door of my studio a tall man came so close to me that I drew back, and he came into the large room. His eyes were clear and piercing, his hair silvery white, and his beard carefully trimmed. He made his excuses very politely, admired my paintings, my sculpture, my " hall "—and this while I was in complete ignorance of his name. When at the end of ten minutes I begged him to sit down and tell me to what I owed the pleasure of his visit, he replied in a stilted voice with a strong accent :

" I am Mr. Jarrett, the *impresario.* I can make your fortune. Will you come to America ?

" Never ! " I exclaimed firmly. " Never ! "

" Oh well, don't get angry. Here is my address—don't lose it." Then at the moment he took leave he said :

" Ah ! you are going to London with the Comédie Française. Would you like to earn a lot of money in London ? "

" Yes. How ? "

" By playing in drawing-rooms. I can make a small fortune for you."

" Oh, I would be pleased—that is if I go to London, for I have not yet decided."

" Then will you sign a little contract to which we will add an additional clause ? "

And I signed a contract with this man, who inspired me with confidence at first sight—a confidence which he never betrayed.

The committee and M. Perrin had made an agreement with John Hollingshead, director of the Gaiety Theatre in London. Nobody had been consulted, and I thought that was a little too free and easy. So when they told me about this agreement, I said nothing.

Perrin rather anxiously took me aside :

" What are you turning over in your mind ? "

" I am turning over this : That I will not go to London in a situation inferior to anybody. For the entire term of my contract I intend to be a Sociétaire with one entire share in the profits."

This intention irritated the committee considerably. And the next day Perrin told me that my proposal was rejected.

" Well, I shall not go to London. That is all ! Nothing in my contract compels me to go."

The committee met again, and Got cried out, " Well, let her stay away ! She is a regular nuisance ! "

It was therefore decided that I should not go to London. But Hollingshead and Mayer, his partner, did not see things in this light, and they declared that the contract would not be binding if either Croizette, Mounet-Sully, or I did not go.

The agents, who had bought two hundred thousand francs' worth of tickets beforehand, also refused to regard the affair as binding on them if we did not go. Mayer came to see me in profound despair, and told me all about it.

" We shall have to break our contract with the Comédie if you don't come," he said, " for the business cannot go through."

Frightened at the consequences of my bad temper, I ran to see Perrin, and told him that after the consultation I had just had with Mayer I understood the involuntary injury I should be causing to the Théâtre Français and to my comrades, and I told him I was ready to go under any conditions.

The committee was holding a meeting. Perrin asked me to wait, and shortly after he came back to me. Croizette and I had been appointed Sociétaires with one entire share in the profits each, not only for London, but for always.

Everybody had done their duty. Perrin, very much touched, took both my hands and drew me to him.

" Oh, the good and untamable little creature ! "

We embraced, and peace was again concluded between us.
But it could not last long, for five days after this reconciliation,
about nine o'clock in the evening, M. Perrin was announced at
my house. I had some friends to dinner, so I went to receive
him in the hall. He held out to me a paper.

" Read that," said he.

And I read in an English newspaper, the *Times*, this paragraph :

DRAWING-ROOM COMEDIES OF MLLE. SARAH BERNHARDT,
UNDER THE MANAGEMENT OF SIR JULIUS BENEDICT.—" The
répertoire of Mlle. Sarah Bernhardt is composed of comedies,
proverbs, one-act plays, and monologues, written specially for
her and one or two artistes of the Comédie Française. These
comedies are played without accessories or scenery, and can be
adapted both in London and Paris to the *matinées* and *soirées*
of the best society. For all details and conditions please com-
municate with Mr. Jarrett (secretary of Mlle. Sarah Bernhardt)
at Her Majesty's Theatre."

As I was reading the last lines it dawned on me that Jarrett,
learning that I was certainly coming to London, had begun to
advertise me. I explained this frankly to Perrin.

" What objection is there," I said, " to my making use of my
evenings to earn money ? This business has been proposed to
me."

" I am not complaining—it's the committee."

" That is too bad ! " I cried, and calling for my secretary, I
said, " Give me Delaunay's letter that I gave you yesterday."

He brought it out of one of his numerous pockets and gave it
to Perrin to read.

" Would you care to come and play *La Nuit d'Octobre* at
Lady Dudley's on Thursday, June 5 ? We are offered 5000
francs for us two. Kind regards.—DELAUNAY."

" Let me have this letter," said the manager, visibly annoyed.

" No, I will not. But you may tell Delaunay that I spoke to
you about his offer."

For the next two or three days nothing was talked of in Paris
but the scandalous notice in the *Times*. The French were
then almost entirely ignorant of the habits and customs of the

English. At last all this talk annoyed me, and I begged Perrin to try and stop it, and the next day the following appeared in the *National* (May 29): "*Much Ado about Nothing.*—In friendly discussion it has been decided that outside the rehearsals and the performances of the Comédie Française each artiste is free to employ his time as he sees fit. There is therefore absolutely no truth at all in the pretended quarrel between the Comédie Française and Mlle. Sarah Bernhardt. This artiste has only acted strictly within her rights, which nobody attempts to limit, and all our artistes intend to benefit in the same manner. The manager of the Comédie Française asks only that the artistes who form this company do not give performances in a body."

This article came from the Comédie, and the members of the committee had taken advantage of it to advertise themselves a little, announcing that they also were ready to play in drawing-rooms, for the article was sent to Mayer with a request that it should appear in the English papers. It was Mayer himself who told me this.

All disputes being at an end, we commenced our preparations for departure.

I had been but once on the sea when it was decided that the artistes of the Comédie Française should go to London. The determined ignorance of the French with regard to all things foreign was much more pronounced in those days than it is at present. Therefore I had a very warm cloak made, as I had been assured that the crossing was icy cold even in the very middle of summer, and I believed this. On every side I was besieged with lozenges for sea-sickness, sedatives for headache, tissue paper to put down my back, little compress plasters to put on my diaphragm, and waterproof cork soles for my shoes, for it appeared that above all things I must not have cold feet. Oh, how droll and amusing it all was! I took everything, paid attention to all the recommendations, and believed everything I was told.

The most inconceivable thing of all, though, was the arrival, five minutes before the boat started, of an enormous wooden case. It was very light, and was held by a tall young man, who to-day is a most remarkable individual, possessing all orders and honours, a colossal fortune, and the most outrageous vanity. At that time he was a timid inventor, young, poor, and sad : he was always buried in books which treated of abstract questions, whilst of life he knew absolutely nothing. He had a great admiration for me, mingled with a trifle of awe. My little court had surnamed him " La Quenelle." He was long, vacillating, colourless, and really did resemble the thin roll of forcemeat in a *vol-au-vent*.

He came up to see me, his face more wan-looking even than usual. The boat was moving a little. My departure terrified him, and the wind caused him to plunge from right to left. He made a mysterious sign to me, and I followed him, accompanied by *mon petit Dame*, and leaving my friends, who were inclined to be ironical, behind. When I was seated he opened the case and took out an enormous life-belt invented by himself. I was perfectly astounded, for I was new to sea voyages, and the idea had never even occurred to me that we might be ship-wrecked during one hour's crossing. La Quenelle was by no means disconcerted, and he put the belt on himself in order to show me how it was used.

Nothing could have looked more foolish than this man, with his sad, serious face, putting on this apparatus. There were a dozen egg-sized bladders round the belt, eleven of which were filled with air and contained a piece of sugar. In the twelfth, a very small bladder, were ten drops of brandy. In the middle of the belt was a tiny cushion with a few pins on it.

" You understand," he said to me. " You fall in the water—paff!—you stay like this." Hereupon he pretended to sit down, rising and sinking with the movement of the waves, his two hands in front of him laid upon the imaginary sea, and his neck stretched like that of a tortoise in order to keep his head above water.

" You see, you have now been in the water for two hours," he explained, " and you want to get back your strength. You take a pin and prick an egg, like this. You take your lump of sugar and eat it; that is as good as a quarter of a pound of meat." He then threw the broken bladder overboard, and from the packing case brought out another, which he fastened to the life-belt. He had evidently thought of everything. I was petrified with amazement. A few of my friends had gathered round, hoping for one of La Quenelle's mad freaks, but they had never expected anything like this one.

M. Mayer, one of our *impresarii*, fearing a scandal of too absurd a kind, dispersed the people who were gathering round us. I did not know whether to be angry or to laugh, but the jeering, unjust speech of one of my friends roused my pity for this poor Quenelle. I thought of the hours he had spent in planning, combining, and then manufacturing his ridiculous machine. I was touched by the anxiety and affection which had prompted the invention of this life-saving apparatus, and I held out my hand to my poor Quenelle, saying, " Be off now, quickly; the boat is just going to start."

He kissed the hand held out to him in a friendly way, and hurried off. I then called my steward, Claude, and I said, " As soon as we are out of sight of land, throw that case and all it contains into the sea."

The departure of the boat was accompanied by shouts of " Hurrah! Au revoir! Success! Good luck! " There was a waving of hands, handkerchiefs floating in the air, and kisses thrown haphazard to every one.

But what was really fine, and a sight I shall never forget, was our landing at Folkestone. There were thousands of people there, and it was the first time I had ever heard the cry of " Vive Sarah Bernhardt! "

I turned my head and saw before me a pale young man, the ideal face of Hamlet. He presented me with a gardenia. I was destined to admire him later on as Hamlet played by Forbes Robertson. We passed on through a crowd offering us flowers and shaking hands, and I soon saw that I was more favoured than the others. This slightly embarrassed me, but I was delighted all the same. One of my comrades who was just near, and with whom I was not a favourite, said to me in a spiteful tone :

" They'll make you a carpet of flowers soon."

" Here is one! " exclaimed a young man, throwing an armful of lilies on the ground in front of me.

I stopped short, rather confused, not daring to walk on these white flowers, but the crowd pressing on behind compelled me to advance, and the poor lilies had to be trodden under foot.

" Hip, hip, hurrah! A cheer for Sarah Bernhardt! " shouted the turbulent young man.

His head was above all the other heads; he had luminous eyes and long hair, and looked like a German student. He was an English poet, though, and one of the greatest of the century, a poet who was a genius, but who was, alas! later tortured and finally vanquished by madness. It was Oscar Wilde.

The crowd responded to his appeal, and we reached our train amidst shouts of "Hip, hip, hurrah for Sarah Bernhardt! Hip, hip, hurrah for the French actors!"

When the train arrived at Charing Cross towards nine o'clock we were nearly an hour late. A feeling of sadness came over me. The weather was gloomy, and then, too, I thought we should have been greeted again on our arrival in London with more hurrahs. There were plenty of people, crowds of people, but none appeared to know us.

On reaching the station I had noticed that there was a handsome carpet laid down, and I thought it was for us. Oh, I was prepared for anything, as our reception at Folkestone had turned my head. The carpet, however, had been laid down for their Royal Highnesses the Prince and the Princess of Wales, who had just left for Paris.

This news disappointed me, and even annoyed me personally. I had been told that all London was quivering with excitement at the very idea of the visit of the Comédie Française, and I had found London extremely indifferent. The crowd was large and even dense, but cold.

"Why have the Prince and Princess gone away to-day?" I asked M. Mayer.

"Well, because they had decided beforehand about this visit to Paris," he replied.

"Oh, then they won't be here for our first night?" I continued.

"No. The Prince has taken a box for the season, for which he has paid four hundred pounds, but it will be used by the Duke of Connaught."

I was in despair. I don't know why, but I certainly was in despair, as I felt that everything was going wrong.

A footman led the way to my carriage, and I drove through London with a heavy heart. Everything looked dark and dismal, and when I reached the house, 77 Chester Square, I did not want to get out of my carriage.

The door of the house was wide open, though, and in the

brilliantly lighted hall I could see what looked like all the flowers on earth arranged in baskets, bouquets, and huge bunches. I got out of the carriage and entered the house in which I was to live for the next six weeks. All the branches seemed to be stretching out their flowers to me.

"Have you the cards that came with all these flowers?" I asked my man-servant.

"Yes," he replied. "I have put them together on a tray. All of them are from Paris, from Madame's friends there. This one is the only bouquet from here." He handed me an enormous one, and on the card with it I read the words, "Welcome!—Henry Irving."

I went all through the house, and it seemed to me very dismal-looking. I visited the garden, but the damp seemed to go through me, and my teeth chattered when I came in again. That night when I went to sleep my heart was heavy with foreboding, as though I were on the eve of some misfortune.

The following day was given up to receiving journalists. I wanted to see them all at the same time, but Mr. Jarrett objected to this. That man was a veritable advertising genius. I had no idea of it at that time. He had made me some very good offers for America, and although I had refused them, I nevertheless held a very high opinion of him, on account of his intelligence, his comic humour, and my need of being piloted in this new country.

"No," he said; "if you receive them all together, they will all be furious, and you will get some wretched articles. You must receive them one after the other."

Thirty-seven journalists came that day, and Jarrett insisted on my seeing every one of them. He stayed in the room and saved the situation when I said anything foolish. I spoke English very badly, and some of the men spoke French very badly. Jarrett translated my answers to them. I remember perfectly well that all of them began with, "Well, Mademoiselle, what do you think of London?"

I had arrived the previous evening at nine o'clock, and the first of these journalists asked me this question at ten in the morning. I had drawn my curtain on getting up, and all I knew of London was Chester Square, a small square of sombre verdure, in the midst of which was a black statue, and the horizon bounded by an ugly church.

I really could not answer the question, but Jarrett was quite prepared for this, and I learnt the following morning that I was most enthusiastic about the beauty of London, that I had already seen a number of the public buildings, &c. &c.

Towards five o'clock Hortense Damain arrived. She was a charming woman, and a favourite in London society. She had come to inform me that the Duchess of —— and Lady —— would call on me at half-past five.

"Oh, stay with me, then," I said to her. "You know how unsociable I am; I feel sure that I shall be stupid."

At the time fixed my visitors were announced. This was the first time I had come into contact with any members of the English aristocracy, and I have always had since a very pleasant memory of it.

Lady R—— was extremely beautiful, and the Duchess was so gracious, so distinguished, and so kind that I was very much touched by her visit.

A few minutes later Lord Dudley called. I knew him very well, as he had been introduced to me by Marshal Canrobert, one of my dearest friends. He asked me if I would care to have a ride the following morning, and he said he had a very nice lady's horse which was entirely at my service. I thanked him, but I wanted first to drive in Rotten Row.

At seven o'clock Hortense Damain came to fetch me to dine with her at the house of the Baroness M——. She had a very nice house in Prince's Gate. There were about twenty guests, among others the painter Millais. I had been told that the *cuisine* was very bad in England, but I thought this dinner perfect. I had been told that the English were cold and sedate : I found them charming and full of humour. Every one spoke French very well, and I was ashamed of my ignorance of the English language. After dinner there were recitations and music. I was touched by the gracefulness and tact of my hosts in not asking me to recite any poetry.

I was very much interested in observing the society in which I found myself. It did not in any way resemble a French gathering. The young girls seemed to be enjoying themselves on their own account, and enjoying themselves thoroughly.

They had not come there to find a husband. What surprised
me a little was the *décolleté* of ladies who were getting on
in years and to whom time had not been very merciful. I spoke
of this to Hortense Damain.

" It's frightful ! " I said.

" Yes, but it's chic."

She was very charming, my friend Hortense, but she troubled
about nothing that was not *chic*. She sent me the " *Chic* commandments " a few days before I left Paris :

Chester Square tu habiteras.	In Chester Square thou shalt live
Rotten Row tu monteras	In Rotten Row thou shalt ride
Le Parlement visiteras	Parliament thou shalt visit
Garden-parties fréquenteras	Garden parties thou shalt frequent,
Chaque visite tu rendras	Every visit thou shalt return
A chaque lettre tu repondras	Every letter thou shalt answer
Photographies tu signeras	Photographs thou shalt sign
Hortense Damain tu écouteras	To Hortense Damain thou shalt listen
Et tous ses conseils, les suivras.	And all her counsels thou shalt follow.

I laughed at these " commandments," but I soon realised that
under this jocular form she considered them as very serious and
important. Alas ! my poor friend had hit upon the wrong
person for her counsels. I detested paying visits, writing letters,
signing photographs, or following any one's advice. I adore
having people come to see me, and I detest going to see them.
I adore receiving letters, reading them, commenting on them,
but I detest writing them. I detest riding and driving in fre-
quented parts, and I adore lonely roads and solitary places.
I adore giving advice and I detest receiving it, and I never
follow at once any wise advice that is given me. It always
requires an effort of my will to recognise the justice of any
counsel, and then an effort of my intellect to be grateful for it :
at first, it simply annoys me.

Consequently, I paid no attention to Hortense Damain's
counsels, nor yet to Jarrett's ; and in this I made a great mistake,
for many people were vexed with me (in any other country
I should have made enemies). On that first visit to London
what a quantity of letters of invitation I received to which
I never replied ! How many charming women called upon me
and I never returned their calls. Then, too, how many times
I accepted invitations to dinner and never went after all, nor

did I even send a line of excuse. It is perfectly odious, I know ;
and yet I always accept with pleasure and intend to go, but
when the day comes I am tired perhaps, or want to have a
quiet time, or to be free from any obligation, and when I
am obliged to decide one way or another, the time has gone by
and it is too late to send word and too late to go. And so I
stay at home, dissatisfied with myself, with every one else and
with everything.

XXVII

LONDON LIFE—MY FIRST PERFORMANCE AT
THE GAIETY THEATRE

HOSPITALITY is a quality made up of primitive taste and
antique grandeur. The English are, in my opinion, the most
hospitable people on earth, and they are hospitable simply
and munificently. When an Englishman has opened his door
to you he never closes it again. He excuses your faults and
accepts your peculiarities. It is thanks to this broadness of
ideas that I have been for twenty-five years the beloved and
pampered artiste.

I was delighted with my first *soirée* in London, and I returned
home very gay and very much " anglomaniaised." I found
some of my friends there—Parisians who had just arrived—and
they were furious. My enthusiasm exasperated them, and we
sat up arguing until two in the morning.

The next day I went to Rotten Row. It was glorious
weather, and all Hyde Park seemed to be strewn with enormous
bouquets. There were the flower-beds wonderfully arranged by
the gardeners ; then there were the clusters of sunshades, blue,
pink, red, white, or yellow, which sheltered the light hats
covered with flowers under which shone the pretty faces of
children and women. Along the riding path there was an exciting
gallop of graceful thoroughbreds bearing along some hundreds
of horsewomen, slender, supple, and courageous ; then there were
men and children, the latter mounted on big Irish ponies.
There were other children, too, galloping along on Scotch
ponies with long, shaggy manes, the children's hair and the
manes of the horses streaming in the wind of their own speed.

The carriage road between the riding-track and the foot
passengers was filled with dog-carts, open carriages of various

kinds, mail-coaches, and very smart cabs. There were powdered
footmen, horses decorated with flowers, sportsmen driving,
ladies, too, driving admirable horses. All this elegance, this
essence of luxury, and this joy of life brought back to my
memory the vision of our Bois de Boulogne, so elegant and so
animated a few years before, when Napoleon III. used to drive
through on his *daumont*, nonchalant and smiling. Ah, how
beautiful it was in those days—our Bois de Boulogne, with the
officers caracoling in the Avenue des Acacias, admired by our
beautiful society women!

The joy of life was everywhere—the love of love enveloping
life with an infinite charm. I closed my eyes, and I felt a pang
at my heart as the awful recollections of 1870 crowded to my
brain. He was dead, our gentle Emperor, with his shrewd smile.
Dead, vanquished by the sword, betrayed by fortune, crushed
with grief.

The thread of life in Paris had been taken up again in all its
intenseness, but the life of elegance, of charm, and of luxury was
still shrouded in crape. Scarcely eight years had passed since
the war had struck down our soldiers, ruined our hopes, and
tarnished our glory. Three Presidents had already succeeded
each other. That wretched little Thiers, with his perverse
bourgeois soul, had worn his teeth out with nibbling at every
kind of Government—royalty under Louis Philippe, Empire
under Napoleon III., and the executive power of the French
Republic. He had never even thought of lifting our beloved
Paris up again, bowed down as she was under the weight of so
many ruins. He had been succeeded by MacMahon, a good,
brave man, but a cipher. Grévy had succeeded the Marshal,
but he was miserly, and considered all outlay unnecessary for
himself, for other people, and for the country. And so Paris
remained sad, nursing the leprosy that the Commune had communicated to her by the kiss of its fires. And our delightful
Bois de Boulogne still bore the traces of the injuries that the
national defence had inflicted on her. The Avenue des Acacias
was deserted.

I opened my eyes again. They were filled with tears, and
through their mist I caught a glimpse once more of the
triumphant vitality which surrounded me.

I wanted to return home at once, for I was acting that night for the first time, and I felt rather wretched and despairing. There were several persons awaiting me at my house in Chester Square, but I did not want to see any one. I took a cup of tea and went to the Gaiety Theatre, where we were to face the English public for the first time. I knew already that I had been elected the favourite, and the idea of this chilled me with terror, for I am what is known as a *traqueuse*. I am subject to the *trac* or stage fright, and I have it terribly. When I first appeared on the stage I was timid, but I never had this *trac*. I used to turn as red as a poppy when I happened to meet the eye of some spectator. I was ashamed of talking so loud before so many silent people. That was the effect of my cloistered life, but I had no feeling of fear. The first time I ever had the real sensation of *trac* or stage fright was in the month of January 1869, at the seventh or perhaps the eighth performance of *Le Passant*. The success of this little master-piece had been enormous, and my interpretation of the part of Zanetto had delighted the public, and particularly the students. When I went on the stage that day I was suddenly applauded by the whole house. I turned towards the Imperial box, thinking that the Emperor had just entered. But no ; the box was empty, and I realised then that all the bravos were for me. I was seized with a fit of nervous trembling, and my eyes smarted with tears that I had to keep back. Agar and I had five curtain calls, and on leaving the theatre the students ranged on each side gave me three cheers. On reaching home I flung myself into the arms of my blind grandmother, who was then living with me.

"What's the matter with you, my dear ? " she asked.

"It's all over with me, grandmother," I said. "They want to make a 'star' of me, and I haven't talent enough for that. You'll see they'll drag me down and finish me off with all their bravos."

My grandmother took my head in her hands, and I met the vacant look in her large light eyes fixed on me.

"You told me, my child, that you wanted to be the first in your profession, and when the opportunity comes to you, why, you are frightened. It seems to me that you are a very bad soldier."

I drove back my tears, and declared that I would bear up courageously against this success which had come to interfere

U

with my tranquillity, my heedlessness, and my " don't care-ism."
But from that time forth fear took possession of me, and
stage fright martyrised me.

It was under these conditions that I prepared for the second
act of *Phèdre*, in which I was to appear for the first time before
the English public. Three times over I put rouge on my cheeks,
blackened my eyes, and three times over I took it all off again
with a sponge. I thought I looked ugly, and it seemed to me I
was thinner than ever and not so tall. I closed my eyes to
listen to my voice. My special pitch is " *le bal*," which I
pronounce low down with the open *a*, " *le bâââl*," or take
high by dwelling on the *l*—" *le balll*." Ah, but there was no
doubt about it; my " *le bal* " neither sounded high nor low,
my voice was hoarse in the low notes and not clear in the
soprano. I cried with rage, and just then I was informed that the
second act of *Phèdre* was about to commence. This drove me
wild. I had not my veil on, nor my rings, and my cameo belt
was not fastened.

I began to murmur :
> " *Le voici !   Vers mon cœur tout mon sang se retire.*
>   *J'oublie en le voyant. . . .*"

That word " *j'oublie* " struck me with a new idea. What if I
did forget the words I had to say ? Why, yes. What was it I
had to say ? I did not know—I could not remember. What
was I to say after " *en le voyant* "?

No one answered me. Every one was alarmed at my nervous
state. I heard Got mumble, " She's going mad ! "

Mlle. Thénard, who was playing Œnone, my old nurse, said
to me, " Calm yourself. All the English have gone to Paris ;
there's no one in the house but Belgians."

This foolishly comic speech turned my thoughts in another
direction.

" How stupid you are ! " I said. " You know how frightened
I was at Brussels ! "

" Oh, all for nothing," she answered calmly. " There were
only English people in the theatre that day."

I had to go on the stage at once, and I could not even answer
her, but she had changed the current of my ideas. I still had
stage fright, but not the fright that paralyses, only the kind
that drives one wild. This is bad enough, but it is preferable

to the other sort. It makes one do too much, but at any rate one does something.

The whole house had applauded my arrival on the stage for a few seconds, and as I bent my head in acknowledgment I said within myself, " Yes—yes—you shall see. I'm going to give you my very blood—my life itself—my soul."

When I began my part, as I had lost my self-possession, I started on rather too high a note, and when once in full swing I could not get lower again—I simply could not stop. I suffered, I wept, I implored, I cried out ; and it was all real. My suffering was horrible ; my tears were flowing, scorching and bitter. I implored Hippolyte for the love which was killing me, and my arms stretched out to Mounet-Sully were the arms of Phèdre writhing in the cruel longing for his embrace. The inspiration had come..

When the curtain fell Mounet-Sully lifted me up inanimate and carried me to my dressing-room.

The public, unaware of what was happening, wanted me to appear again and bow. I too wanted to return and thank the public for its attention, its kindliness, and its emotion. I returned.

The following is what John Murray said in the *Gaulois* of June 5, 1879 :

" When, recalled with loud cries, Mlle. Bernhardt appeared, exhausted by her efforts and supported by Mounet-Sully, she received an ovation which I think is unique in the annals of the theatre in England."

The following morning the *Daily Telegraph* terminated its admirable criticism with these lines :

" Clearly Mlle. Sarah Bernhardt exerted every nerve and fibre, and her passion grew with the excitement of the spectators, for when, after a recall that could not be resisted, the curtain drew up, M. Mounet-Sully was seen supporting the exhausted figure of the actress, who had won her triumph only after tremendous physical exertion—and triumph it was, however short and sudden."

The *Standard* finished its article with these words :

" The subdued passion, repressed for a time, until at length it burst its bonds, and the despairing, heart-broken woman is revealed to Hippolyte, was shown with so vivid a reality that a scene of enthusiasm such as is rarely witnessed in a theatre followed the fall of the curtain.   Mlle. Sarah Bernhardt in the few minutes she was upon the stage (and coming on, it must be remembered, to plunge into the middle of a stirring tragedy) yet contrived to make an impression which will not soon be effaced from those who were present."

The *Morning Post* said :

" Very brief are the words spoken before Phèdre rushes into the room to commence tremblingly and nervously, with struggles which rend and tear and convulse the system, the secret of her shameful love.   As her passion mastered what remained of modesty or reserve in her nature, the woman sprang forward and recoiled again, with the movements of a panther, striving, as it seemed, to tear from her bosom the heart which stifled her with its unholy longings, until in the end, when, terrified at the horror her breathings have provoked in Hippolyte, she strove to pull his sword from its sheath and plunge it in her own breast, she fell back in complete and absolute collapse.   This exhibition, marvellous in beauty of pose, in febrile force, in intensity, and in purity of delivery, is the more remarkable as the passion had to be reached, so to speak, at a bound, no performance of the first act having roused the actress to the requisite heat.   It proved Mlle. Sarah Bernhardt worthy of her reputation, and shows what may be expected from her by the public which has eagerly expected her coming."

This London first night was decisive for my future.

XXVIII

MY PERFORMANCES IN LONDON—MY EXHIBITION—
MY WILD ANIMALS—TROUBLE WITH THE
COMÉDIE FRANÇAISE
'

My intense desire to win over the English public had caused
me to overtax my strength. I had done my utmost at the first
performance, and had not spared myself in the least. The
consequence was in the night I vomited blood in such an alarming way that a messenger was despatched to the French Embassy
in search of a physician. Dr. Vintras, who was at the head of
the French Hospital in London, found me lying on my bed,
exhausted and looking more dead than alive. He was afraid
that I should not recover, and requested that my family be sent
for. I made a gesture with my hand to the effect that it was
not necessary. As I could not speak, I wrote down with a pencil,
" Send for Dr. Parrot."

Dr. Vintras remained with me part of the night, putting
crushed ice between my lips every five minutes. At length
towards five in the morning the blood vomiting ceased, and,
thanks to a potion that the doctor gave me, I fell asleep.

We were to play *L'Etrangère* that night at the Gaiety, and,
as my *rôle* was not a very fatiguing one, I wanted to perform my
part *quand-même*.

Dr. Parrot arrived by the four o'clock boat, and refused cate-
gorically to give his consent. He had attended me from my
childhood. I really felt much better, and the feverishness
had left me. I wanted to get up, but to this Dr. Parrot
objected.

Presently Dr. Vintras and Mr. Mayer, the impresario of the
Comédie Française, were announced. Mr. Hollingshead, the
director of the Gaiety Theatre, was waiting in a carriage at the

door to know whether I was going to play in *L'Etrangère*, the piece announced on the bills. I asked Dr. Parrot to rejoin Dr. Vintras in the drawing-room, and I gave instructions for Mr. Mayer to be introduced into my room.

" I feel much better," I said to him very quickly. " I'm very weak still, but I will play. Hush!—don't say a word here. Tell Hollingshead, and wait for me in the smoking-room, but don't let any one else know."

I then got up and dressed very quickly. My maid helped me, and as she had guessed what my plan was, she was highly amused.

Wrapped in my cloak, with a lace fichu over my head, I joined Mayer in the smoking-room, and then we both got into his hansom.

" Come to me in an hour's time," I said in a low voice to my maid.

" Where are you going ? " asked Mayer, perfectly stupefied.

" To the theatre ! Quick—quick ! " I answered.

The cab started, and I then explained to him that if I had stayed at home, neither Dr. Parrot nor Dr. Vintras would have allowed me to perform.

" The die is cast now," I added, " and we shall see what happens."

When once I was at the theatre I took refuge in the manager's private office, in order to avoid Dr. Parrot's anger. I was very fond of him, and I knew how wrongly I was acting with regard to him, considering the inconvenience to which he had put himself in making the journey specially for me in response to my summons. I knew, though, how impossible it would have been to have made him understand that I felt really better, and that in risking my life I was really only risking what was my own to dispose of as I pleased.

Half an hour later my maid joined me. She brought with her a letter from Dr. Parrot, full of gentle reproaches and furious advice, finishing with a prescription in case of a relapse. He was leaving an hour later, and would not even come and shake hands with me. I felt quite sure, though, that we should make it all up again on my return. I then began to prepare for my *rôle* in *L'Etrangère*. While dressing I fainted three times, but I was determined to play *quand-même*.

The opium that I had taken in my potion made my head rather heavy. I arrived on the stage in a semi-conscious state, delighted with the applause I received. I walked along as though I were in a dream, and could scarcely distinguish my surroundings. The house itself I only saw through a luminous mist. My feet glided along without any effort on the carpet, and my voice sounded to me far away, very far away. I was in that delicious stupor that one experiences after chloroform, morphine, opium, or hasheesh.

The first act went off very well, but in the third act, just when I was about to tell the Duchesse de Septmonts (Croizette) all the troubles that I, Mrs. Clarkson, had gone through during my life, just as I should have commenced my interminable story, I could not remember anything. Croizette murmured my first phrase for me, but I could only see her lips move without hearing a word. I then said quite calmly:

"The reason I sent for you here, Madame, is because I wanted to tell you my reasons for acting as I have done. I have thought it over and have decided not to tell you them to-day."

Sophie Croizette gazed at me with a terrified look in her eyes. She then rose and left the stage, her lips trembling, and her eyes fixed on me all the time.

"What's the matter?" every one asked when she sank almost breathless into an arm-chair.

"Sarah has gone mad!" she exclaimed. "I assure you she has gone quite mad. She has cut out the whole of her scene with me."

"But how?" every one asked.

"She has cut out two hundred lines," said Croizette.

"But what for?" was the eager question.

"I don't know. She looks quite calm."

The whole of this conversation, which was repeated to me later on, took much less time than it does now to write it down. Coquelin had been told, and he now came on to the stage to finish the act. The curtain fell. I was stupefied and desperate afterwards on hearing all that people told me. I had not noticed that anything was wrong, and it seemed to me that I had played the whole of my part as usual, but I was really under the influence of the opium. There was very little for me to say

in the fifth act, and I went through that perfectly well. The
following day the accounts in the papers sounded the praises of
our company, but the piece itself was criticised. I was afraid at
first that my involuntary omission of the important scene in the
third act was one of the causes of the severity of the Press.
This was not so, though, as all the critics had read and re-read
the piece. They discussed the play itself, and did not mention
my slip of memory.

The *Figaro*, which was in a very bad humour with me just
then, had an article from which I quote the following extract:

" *L'Etrangère* is not a piece in accordance with the English
taste. Mlle. Croizette, however, was applauded enthusiastically,
and so were Coquelin and Febvre. Mlle. Sarah Bernhardt,
nervous as usual, lost her memory." (*Figaro*, June 3rd.)

He knew perfectly well, this worthy Mr. Johnson,[1] that I was
very ill. He had been to my house and seen Dr. Parrot; consequently he was aware that I was acting in spite of the Faculty
in the interests of the Comédie Française. The English public
had given me such proofs of appreciation that the Comédie was
rather affected by it, and the *Figaro*, which was at that time
the organ of the Théâtre Français, requested Johnson to modify
his praises of me. This he did the whole time that we were
in London.

My reason for telling about my loss of memory, which was
quite an unimportant incident in itself, is merely to prove to
authors how unnecessary it is to take the trouble of explaining
the characters of their creations. Alexandre Dumas was certainly anxious to give us the reasons which caused Mrs. Clarkson
to act as strangely as she did. He had created a person who was
extremely interesting and full of action as the play proceeds.
She reveals herself to the public, in the first act, by the lines
which Mrs. Clarkson says to Madame de Septmonts:

" I should be very glad, Madame, if you would call on me.
We could talk about one of your friends, Monsieur Gérard,
whom I love perhaps as much as you do, although he does not
perhaps care for me as he does for you."

That was quite enough to interest the public in these two
women. It was the eternal struggle of good and evil, the com-
bat between vice and virtue. But it evidently seemed rather

[1] T. Johnson, London correspondent of *Le Figaro*.

Painting of Sarah Bernhardt by Jules Bastien-Lepage (1879).

In travelling costume (1880).

commonplace to Dumas, ancient history, in fact, and he wanted to rejuvenate the old theme by trying to arrange for an orchestra with organ and banjo. The result he obtained was a fearful cacophony. He wrote a foolish piece, which might have been a beautiful one. The originality of his style, the loyalty of his ideas, and the brutality of his humour sufficed for rejuvenating old ideas which, in reality, are the eternal basis of tragedies, comedies, novels, pictures, poems, and pamphlets. It was love between vice and virtue. Among the spectators who saw the first performance of *L'Etrangère* in London, and there were quite as many French as English present, not one remarked that there was something wanting, and not one of them said that he had not understood the character.

I talked about it to a very learned Frenchman.

" Did you notice the gap in the third act ? " I asked him.

" No," he replied.

" In my big scene with Croizette ? "

" No."

" Well then, read what I left out," I insisted.

When he had read this he exclaimed :

" So much the better. It's very dull, all that story, and quite useless. I understand the character without all that rigmarole and that romantic history."

Later on, when I apologised to Dumas *fils* for the way in which I had cut down his play, he answered, " Oh, my dear child, when I write a play I think it is good, when I see it played I think it is stupid, and when any one tells it to me I think it is perfect, as the person always forgets half of it."

The performances given by the Comédie Française drew a crowd nightly to the Gaiety Theatre, and I remained the favourite. I mention this now with pride, but without any vanity. I was very happy and very grateful for my success, but my comrades had a grudge against me on account of it, and hostilities began in an underhand, treacherous way.

Mr. Jarrett, my adviser and agent, had assured me that I should be able to sell a few of my works, either my sculpture or paintings. I had therefore taken with me six pieces of sculpture and ten pictures, and I had an exhibition of them in Piccadilly. I sent out invitations, about a hundred in all.

His Royal Highness the Prince of Wales let me know that he

would come with the Princess of Wales. The English aristocracy and the celebrities of London came to the inauguration. I had only sent out a hundred invitations, but twelve hundred people arrived and were introduced to me. I was delighted, and enjoyed it all immensely.

Mr. Gladstone did me the great honour of talking to me for about ten minutes. With his genial mind he spoke of everything in a singularly gracious way. He asked me what impression the attacks of certain clergymen on the Comédie Française and the damnable profession of dramatic artistes had made on me. I answered that I considered our art quite as profitable, morally, as the sermons of Catholic and Protestant preachers.

"But will you tell me, Mademoiselle," he insisted, "what moral lesson you can draw from *Phèdre?*"

"Oh, Mr. Gladstone," I replied, "you surprise me. *Phèdre* is an ancient tragedy; the morality and customs of those times belong to perspective quite different from ours and different from the morality of our present society. And yet in that there is the punishment of the old nurse Œnone, who commits the atrocious crime of accusing an innocent person. The love of Phèdre is excusable on account of the fatality which hangs over her family and descends pitilessly upon her. In our times we should call that fatality atavism, for Phèdre was the daughter of Minos and Pasiphaë. As to Theseus, his verdict, against which there could be no appeal, was an arbitrary and monstrous act, and was punished by the death of that beloved son of his, who was the sole and last hope of his life. We ought never to do what is irreparable."

"Ah," said the Grand Old Man, "you are against capital punishment?"

"Yes, Mr. Gladstone."

"And quite right, Mademoiselle."

Frederic Leighton then joined us, and with great kindness complimented me on one of my pictures, representing a young girl holding some palms. This picture was bought by Prince Leopold.

My little exhibition was a great success, but I never thought that it was to be the cause of so much gossip and of so many cowardly side-thrusts, until finally it led to my rupture with the Comédie Française.

I had no pretensions either as a painter or a sculptress, and I exhibited my works for the sake of selling them, as I wanted to buy two little lions, and had not money enough. I sold the pictures for what they were worth—that is to say, at very modest prices.

Lady H—— bought my group *After the Storm*. It was smaller than the large group I had exhibited two years previously at the Paris Salon, and for which I had received a prize. The smaller group was in marble, and I had worked at it with the greatest care. I wanted to sell it for £160, but Lady H—— sent me £400, together with a charming note, which I venture to quote. It ran as follows:

" Do me the favour, Madame, of accepting the enclosed £400 for your admirable group, *After the Storm*. Will you also do me the honour of coming to lunch with me, and afterwards you shall choose for yourself the place where your piece of sculpture will have the best light.—ETHEL H."

This was Tuesday, and I was playing in *Zaïre* that evening, but Wednesday, Thursday, and Friday I was not acting. I had money enough now to buy my lions, so without saying a word at the theatre I started for Liverpool. I knew there was a big menagerie there, Cross's Zoo, and that I should find some lions for sale.

The journey was most amusing, as although I was travelling incognito, I was recognised all along the route and was made a great deal of.

Three gentlemen friends and Hortense Damain were with me, and it was a very lively little trip. I knew that I was not shirking my duties at the Comédie, as I was not to play again before Saturday, and this was only Wednesday.

We started in the morning at 10.30, and arrived at Liverpool about 2.30. We went at once to Cross's, but could not find the entrance to the house. We asked a shopkeeper at the corner of the street, and he pointed to a little door which we had already opened and closed twice, as we could not believe that was the entrance.

I had seen a large iron gateway with a wide courtyard beyond, and we were in front of a little door leading into quite a small, bare-looking room, where we found a little man.

" Mr. Cross ? " we said.

"That's my name," he replied.

"I want to buy some lions," I then said

He began to laugh, and then he asked:

"Do you really, Mademoiselle? Are you so fond of animals? I went to London last week to see the Comédie Française, and I saw you in *Hernani*."

"It wasn't from that you discovered that I like animals?" I said to him.

"No, it was a man who sells dogs in St. Andrew's Street who told me. He said you had bought two dogs from him, and that if it had not been for a gentleman who was with you, you would have bought five."

He told me all this in very bad French, but with a great deal of humour.

"Well, Mr. Cross," I said, "I want two lions to-day."

"I'll show you what I have," he replied, leading the way into the courtyard where the wild beasts were. Oh, what magnificent creatures they were! There were two superb African lions with shining coats and powerful-looking tails, which were beating the air. They had only just arrived and they were in perfect health, with plenty of courage for rebellion. They knew nothing of the resignation which is the dominating stigma of civilised beings.

"Oh, Mr. Cross," I said, "these are too big. I want some young lions!"

"I haven't any, Mademoiselle."

"Well, then, show me all your animals."

I saw the tigers, the leopards, the jackals, the cheetahs, the pumas, and I stopped in front of the elephants. I simply adore them, and I should have liked to have a dwarf elephant. That has always been one of my dreams, and perhaps some day I shall be able to realise it.

Cross had not any, though, so I bought a cheetah. It was quite young and very droll; it looked like a gargoyle on some castle of the Middle Ages. I also bought a dog-wolf, all white with a thick coat, fiery eyes, and spear-like teeth. He was terrifying to look at. Mr. Cross made me a present of six chameleons which belonged to a small breed and looked like lizards. He also gave me an admirable chameleon, a prehistoric, fabulous sort of animal. It was a veritable Chinese curiosity, and changed colour from pale green to dark bronze, at one minute slender and long like a lily leaf, and then all at once puffed out and thick-set like a toad. Its lorgnette eyes, like those of a lobster, were quite independent of each other. With its right eye it would look ahead and with its left eye it looked backwards. I was delighted and quite enthusiastic over this present. I named my chameleon " Cross-ci Cross-ça," in honour of Mr. Cross.

We returned to London with the cheetah in a cage, the dog-wolf in a leash, my six little chameleons in a box, and Cross-ci Cross-ça on my shoulder, fastened to a gold chain we had bought at a jeweller's.

I had not found any lions, but I was delighted all the same.

My servants were not as pleased as I was. There were already three dogs in the house : Minniccio, who had accompanied me from Paris; Bull and Fly, bought in London. Then there was my parrot Bizibouzou, and my monkey Darwin.

Madame Guérard screamed when she saw these new guests arrive. My steward hesitated to approach the dog-wolf, and it was all in vain that I assured them that my cheetah was not dangerous. No one would open the cage, and it was carried out into the garden. I asked for a hammer in order to open the door of the cage which had been nailed down, thus keeping the poor cheetah a prisoner. When my domestics heard me ask for the hammer they decided to open it themselves. Madame Guérard and the women servants watched from the windows. Presently the door burst open, and the cheetah, beside himself with joy, sprang like a tiger out of his cage, wild with liberty. He rushed at the trees and made straight for the dogs, who all four began to howl with terror. The parrot was excited, and uttered shrill cries ; and the monkey, shaking his cage about, gnashed his teeth to distraction. This concert in the silent square made the most prodigious effect. All the windows were opened, and more than twenty faces appeared above my garden wall, all of them inquisitive, alarmed, or furious. I was seized with a fit of uncontrollable laughter, and so was my friend Louise Abbema. Nittis the painter, who had come to call on me, was in the same state, and so was Gustave Doré, who had been waiting for me ever since two o'clock. Georges Deschamp, an amateur musician with a great deal of talent, tried to note down this Hofmannesque harmony, whilst my friend Georges Clairin, his back shaking with laughter, sketched the never-to-be-forgotten scene.

The next day in London the chief topic of conversation was the Bedlam that had been let loose at 77 Chester Square. So much was made of it that our *doyen*, M. Got, came to beg me not to make such a scandal, as it reflected on the Comédie Française. I listened to him in silence, and when he had finished I took his hands.

" Come with me and I will show you the scandal," I said. I led the way into the garden, followed by my visitor and friends.

" Let the cheetah out !" I said, standing on the steps like a captain ordering his men to take in a reef.

When the cheetah was free the same mad scene occurred again as on the previous day.

" You see, Monsieur le Doyen," I said, " this is my Bedlam."

" You are mad," he said, kissing me ; " but it certainly is irresistibly comic," and he laughed until the tears came when he saw all the heads appearing above the garden wall.

The hostilities continued, though, through scraps of gossip retailed by one person to another and from one set to another. The French Press took it up, and so did the English Press. In spite of my happy disposition and my contempt for ill-natured tales, I began to feel irritated. Injustice has always roused me to revolt, and injustice was certainly having its fling. I could not do a thing that was not watched and blamed.

One day I was complaining of this to Madeleine Brohan, whom I loved dearly. That adorable artiste took my face in her hands, and looking into my eyes, said :

" My poor dear, you can't do anything to prevent it. You are original without trying to be so. You have a dreadful head of hair that is naturally curly and rebellious, your slenderness is exaggerated, you have a natural harp in your throat, and all this makes of you a creature apart, which is a crime of high treason against all that is commonplace. That is what is the matter with you physically. Now for your moral defects. You cannot hide your thoughts, you cannot stoop to anything, you never accept any compromise, you will not lend yourself to any hypocrisy—and all that is a crime of high treason against society. How can you expect

under these conditious not to arouse jealousy, not to wound
people's susceptibilities, and not to make them spiteful ? If
you are discouraged because of these attacks, it will be all
over with you, as you will have no strength left to withstand
them.   In that case I advise you to brush your hair, to put oil
on it, and so make it lie as sleek as that of the famous Corsican ;
but even that would never do, for Napoleon had such sleek
hair that it was quite original.   Well, you might try to
brush your hair as smooth as Prudhon's,[1] then there would
be no risk for you.   I would advise you," she continued, " to
get a little stouter, and to let your voice break occasionally ;
then you would not annoy any one.   But if you wish to remain
yourself, my dear, prepare to mount on a little pedestal made of
calumny, scandal, injustice, adulation, flattery, lies, and truths.
When you are once upon it, though, do the right thing, and
cement it by your talent, your work, and your kindness.   All
the spiteful people who have unintentionally provided the first
materials for the edifice will kick it then, in hopes of destroying
it.   They will be powerless to do this, though, if you choose to
prevent them ; and that is just what I hope for you, my dear
Sarah, as you have an ambitious thirst for glory.   I cannot
understand that myself, as I only like rest and retirement."

I looked at her with envy, she was so beautiful : with her liquid
eyes, her face with its pure, restful lines, and her weary smile.
I wondered in an uneasy way if happiness were not rather in
this calm tranquillity, in the disdain of all things.   I asked her
gently if this were so, for I wanted to know ; and she told me
that the theatre bored her, that she had had so many disappointments.   She shuddered when she spoke of her marriage, and as
to her motherhood, that had only caused her sorrow.   Her love
affairs had left her with affections crushed and physically disabled.
The light seemed doomed to fade from her beautiful eyes, her
legs were swollen and could scarcely carry her.   She told me all
this in the same calm, half weary tone.

What had charmed me only a short time before chilled me to
the heart now, for her dislike to movement was caused by the
weakness of her eyes and her legs, and her delight in retirement
was only the love of that peace which was so necessary to her,
wounded as she was by the life she had lived.

---

[1] Prudhon was one of the artistes of the Théâtre Français.

The love of life, though, took possession of me more violently than ever. I thanked my dear friend, and profited by her advice. I armed myself for the struggle, preferring to die in the midst of the battle rather than to end my life regretting that it had been a failure. I made up my mind not to weep over the base things that were said about me, and not to suffer any more injustices. I made up my mind, too, to stand on the defensive, and very soon an occasion presented itself.

L'Etrangère was to be played for the second time at a *matinée*, June 21, 1879. The day before I had sent word to Mayer that I was not well, and that as I was playing in *Hernani* at night, I should be glad if he could change the play announced for the afternoon if possible. The advance booking, however, was more than £400, and the committee would not hear of it.

'Oh well," Got said to Mr. Mayer, " we must give the *rôle* to some one else if Sarah Bernhardt cannot play. There will be Croizette, Madeleine Brohan, Coquelin, Febvre, and myself in the cast, and, *que diable!* it seems to me that all of us together will make up for Mademoiselle Bernhardt."

Coquelin was requested to ask Lloyd to take my part, as she had played this *rôle* at the Comédie when I was ill. Lloyd was afraid to undertake it, though, and refused. It was decided to change the play, and *Tartufe* was given instead of *L'Etrangère*. Nearly all the public, however, asked to have their money refunded, and the receipts, which would have been about £500, only amounted to £84. All the spite and jealousy now broke loose, and the whole company of the Comédie, more particularly the men, with the exception of M. Worms, started a campaign against me. Francisque Sarcey, as drum-major, beat the measure with his terrible pen in his hand. The most foolish, slanderous, and stupid inventions and the most odious lies took their flight like a cloud of wild ducks, and swooped suddenly down upon all the newspapers that were against me. It was said that for a shilling any one might see me dressed as a man; that I smoked huge cigars, leaning on the balcony of my house; that at the various receptions where I gave one-act plays I took my maid with me to play a small part; that I practised fencing in my garden, dressed as a pierrot in white; and that when taking boxing lessons I had broken two teeth of my unfortunate professor.

Some of my friends advised me to take no notice of all these turpitudes, assuring me that the public could not possibly believe them. They were mistaken, though, for the public likes to believe bad things about any one, as these are always more amusing than the good things. I soon had a proof that the English public was beginning to believe what the French papers said. I received a letter from a tailor asking me if I would consent to wear a coat of his make when I appeared in masculine attire, and not only did he offer me this coat for nothing, but he was willing to pay me a hundred pounds if I would wear it. This man was an ill-bred person, but he was sincere. I received several boxes of cigars, and the boxing and fencing professors wrote to offer their services gratuitously. All this annoyed me to such a degree that I resolved to put an end to it. An article by Albert Wolff in the Paris *Figaro* caused me to take steps to cut matters short.

This is what I wrote in reply to the article in the *Figaro*, June 27, 1879 :

" ALBERT WOLFF, *Figaro*, Paris.

" And you, too, my dear Monsieur Wolff—you believe in such insanities ? Who can have been giving you such false information ? Yes, you are my friend, though, for in spite of all the infamies you have been told, you have still a little indulgence left. Well then, I give you my word of honour that I have never dressed as a man here in London. I did not even bring my sculptor costume with me. I give the most emphatic denial to this misrepresentation. I only went once to the exhibition which I organised, and that was on the opening day, for which I had only sent out a few private invitations, so that no one paid a shilling to see me. It is true that I have accepted some private engagements to act, but you know that I am one of the least remunerated members of the Comédie Française. I certainly have the right, therefore, to try to make up the difference. I have ten pictures and eight pieces of sculpture on exhibition. That, too, is quite true, but as I brought them over here to sell, really I must show them. As to the respect due to the House of Molière, dear Monsieur Wolff, I lay claim to keeping that in mind more than any one else, for I am absolutely incapable of inventing such calumnies for the sake of slaying one of its standard-bearers. And now, if the stupidities

x

invented about me have annoyed the Parisians, and if they have decided to receive me ungraciously on my return, I do not wish any one to be guilty of such baseness on my account, so I will send in my resignation to the Comédie Française. If the London public is tired of all this fuss and should be inclined to show me ill-will instead of the indulgence hitherto accorded me, I shall ask the Comédie to allow me to leave England, in order to spare our company the annoyance of seeing one of its members hooted at and hissed. I am sending you this letter by wire, as the consideration I have for public opinion gives me the right to commit this little folly, and I beg you, dear Monsieur Wolff, to accord to my letter the same honour as you did to the calumnies of my enemies.—With very kind regards,

" Yours sincerely,

" SARAH BERNHARDT."

This telegram caused much ink to flow. Whilst treating me as a spoiled child, people generally agreed that I was quite right. The Comédie was most amiable. Perrin, the manager, wrote me an affectionate letter begging me to give up my idea of leaving the company. The women were most friendly. Croizette came to see me, and putting her arms round me, said, " Tell me you won't do such a thing, my dear, foolish child! You won't really send in your resignation? In the first place; it would not be accepted, I can answer for that ! "

Mounet-Sully talked to me of art and of probity. His whole speech savoured of Protestantism. There are several Protestant pastors in his family, and this influenced him unconsciously. Delaunay, surnamed Father Candour, came solemnly to inform me of the bad impression my telegram had made. He told me that the Comédie Française was a Ministry ; that there was the Minister, the secretary, the sub-chiefs and the *employés*, and that each one must conform to the rules and bring in his share either of talent or work, and so on and so on. I saw Coquelin at the theatre in the evening. He came to me with outstretched hands.

" You know I can't compliment you," he said, " on your rash action, but with good luck we shall make you change your mind. When one has the good fortune and the honour of belonging to the Comédie Française, one must remain there until the end of one's career."

Frédéric Febvre pointed out to me that I ought to stay with the Comédie, because it would save money for me, and I was quite incapable of doing that myself.

" Believe me," he said, " when we are with the Comédie we must not leave ; it means our bread provided for us later on."

Got, our *doyen*, then approached me.

" Do you know what you are doing in sending in your resignation ? " he asked.

" No," I replied.

" Deserting."

" You are mistaken," I answered ; " I am not deserting : I am changing barracks."

Others then came to me, and they all gave me advice tinged by their own personality : Mounet as a seer or believer ; Delaunay prompted by his bureaucratic soul ; Coquelin as a politician blaming another person's ideas, but extolling them later on and putting them into practice for his own profit ; Febvre, a lover of respectability ; Got, as a selfish old growler understanding nothing but the orders of the powers that be and advancement as ordained on hierarchical lines. Worms said to me in his melancholy way :

" Will they be better towards you elsewhere ? "

Worms had the most dreamy soul and the most frank, straightforward character of any member of our illustrious company. I liked him immensely.

We were about to return to Paris, and I wanted to forget all these things for a time. I was in a hesitating mood. I postponed taking a definite decision. The stir that had been made about me, the good that had been said in my favour and the bad things written against me—all this combined had created in the artistic world an atmosphere of battle. When on the point of leaving for Paris some of my friends felt very anxious about the reception which I should get there.

The public is very much mistaken in imagining that the agitation made about celebrated artistes is in reality instigated by the persons concerned, and that they do it purposely. Irritated at seeing the same name constantly appearing on every occasion, the public declares that the artiste who is being either slandered

or pampered is an ardent lover of publicity. Alas! three times
over alas! We are victims of the said advertisement. Those
who know the joys and miseries of celebrity when they have
passed the age of forty know how to defend themselves. They
are at the beginning of a series of small worries, thunderbolts
hidden under flowers, but they know how to hold in check that
monster advertisement. It is a sort of octopus with innumer-
able tentacles. It throws out on the right and on the left,
in front and behind, its clammy arms, and gathers in through
its thousand little inhaling organs all the gossip and slander
and praise afloat, to spit out again at the public when it is
vomiting its black gall. But those who are caught in the
clutches of celebrity at the age of twenty know nothing. I
remember that the first time a reporter came to me I drew
myself up straight and was as red as a cock's-comb with joy. I
was just seventeen years old—I had been acting in a private house,
and had taken the part of Richelieu with immense success.
This gentleman came to call on me at home, and asked me first
one question and then another and then another. I answered
and chattered, and was wild with pride and excitement. He
took notes, and I kept looking at my mother. It seemed to me
that I was getting taller. I had to kiss my mother by way of
keeping my composure, and I hid my face on her shoulder to
hide my delight. Finally the gentleman rose, shook hands with
me, and then took his departure. I skipped about in the room
and began to turn round singing, *Trois petits pâtés, ma chemise
brûle,* when suddenly the door opened and the gentleman said
to mamma, " Oh, Madame, I forgot, this is the receipt for the
subscription to the journal. It is a mere nothing, only sixteen
francs a year." Mamma did not understand at first. As for
me, I stood still with my mouth open, unable to digest my
petits pâtés. Mamma then paid the sixteen francs, and in her
pity for me, as I was crying by that time, she stroked my hair
gently. Since then I have been delivered over to the monster,
bound hand and foot, and I have been and still am accused of
adoring advertisement. And to think that my first claims to
celebrity were my extraordinary thinness and delicate health.
I had scarcely made my *début* when epigrams, puns, jokes, and
caricatures concerning me were indulged in by every one to
their heart's content. Was it really for the sake of advertising

myself that I was so thin, so small, so weak ; and was it for this, too, that I remained in bed six months of the year, laid low by illness ?   My name became celebrated before I was myself.

On the first night of Louis Bouilhet's piece, *Mademoiselle Aïssé*, at the Odéon, Flaubert, who was an intimate friend of the author, introduced an *attaché* of the British Embassy to me.

" Oh, I have known you for some time, Mademoiselle," he said ; " you are the little stick with the sponge on the top."

This caricature of me had st appeared, and had been the delight of idle folks.   I was quite a young girl at that time, and nothing of that kind hurt me or troubled me.   In the first place, all the doctors had given me up, so that I was indifferent about things ; but all the doctors were mistaken, and twenty years later I had to fight against the monster.

XXIX

THE return of the Comédie to its home was an event, but
an event that was kept quiet.   Our departure from Paris had been
very lively and gay, and quite a public function.   Our return
was clandestine for many of the members, and for me among the
number.   It was a doleful return for those who had not been
appreciated, whilst those who had been failures were furious.

I had not been back home an hour when Perrin was
announced.   He began to reproach me gently about the little
care I took of my health.   He said I caused too much fuss to be
made about me.

"But," I exclaimed, "is it my fault if I am too thin? Is
it my fault, too, if my hair is too curly, and if I don't
think just as other people do?   Supposing that I took sufficient arsenic during a month to make me swell out like a
barrel, and supposing I were to shave my head like an Arab
and only answer, 'Yes' to everything you said, people would
declare I did it for advertisement."

"But, my dear child," answered Perrin, "there are people
who are neither fat nor thin, neither close shaven nor with
shocks of hair, and who answer 'Yes' and 'No.'"

I was simply petrified by the justice and reason of this remark,
and I understood the " because " of all the " whys" I had been
asking myself for some years.   There was no happy medium
about me ; I was " too much " and " too little," and I felt that
there was nothing to be done for this. I owned it to Perrin, and
told him that he was quite right.   He took advantage of my
mood to lecture me and advise me not to put in an appear-

ance at the opening ceremony that was soon to take place at the Comédie. He feared a cabal against me. Some people were rather excited, rightly or wrongly—a little of both, he added, in that shrewd and courteous way which was peculiar to him. I listened to him without interrupting, which slightly embarrassed him, for Perrin was an arguer but not an orator. When he had finished I said :

"You have told me too many things that excite me, Monsieur Perrin. I love a battle, and I shall appear at the ceremony. You see, I have already been warned about it. Here are three anonymous letters. Read this one; it is the nicest."

He unfolded the letter, which was perfumed with amber, and read as follows :

"My poor Skeleton,—You will do well not to show your horrible Jewish nose at the opening ceremony the day after to-morrow. I fear that it would serve as a target for all the potatoes that are now being cooked specially for you in your kind city of Paris. Have some paragraphs put in the papers to the effect that you have been spitting blood, and remain in bed and think over the consequence of excessive advertisement.

"A Subscriber."

Perrin pushed the letter away from him in disgust.

"Here are two more," I said ; "but they are so coarse that I will spare you. I shall go to the opening ceremony."

"Good !" replied Perrin. "There is a rehearsal to-morrow. Shall you come ?"

"I shall come," I answered.

The next day at the rehearsal not one of the artistes, man or woman, seemed to care about going on to the stage to bow with me. I must say, though, that they all showed nevertheless much good grace. I declared, however, that I would go on alone, although it was against the rule, for I thought I ought to face the ill humour and the cabal alone.

The house was crowded when the curtain rose.

The ceremony commenced in the midst of "Bravos !" The public was delighted to see its beloved artistes again. They advanced two by two, one on the right and the other on the left, holding the palm or the crown to be placed on the pedestal of Molière's bust. My turn came, and I advanced alone. I felt that

I was pale and then livid, with a will that was determined to conquer. I went forward slowly towards the footlights, but instead of bowing as my comrades had done, I stood up erect and gazed with my two eyes into all the eyes turning towards me. I had been warned of the battle, and I did not wish to provoke it, but I would not fly from it. I waited a second, and I felt the thrill and the emotion that ran through the house ; and then, suddenly stirred by an impulse of generous kindliness, the whole house burst into wild applause and shouts. The public, so beloved and so loving, was intoxicated with joy. That evening was certainly one of the finest triumphs of my whole career.

Some artistes were delighted, especially the women, for there is one thing to remark with regard to our art : the men are more jealous of the women than the women are amongst themselves. I have met with many enemies among male comedians, and with very few among actresses.

I think that the dramatic art is essentially feminine.

To paint one's face, to hide one's real feelings, to try to please and to endeavour to attract attention—these are all faults for which we blame women and for which great indulgence is shown. These same defects seem odious in a man. And yet the actor must endeavour to be as attractive as possible, even if he is obliged to have recourse to paint and to false beard and hair. He may be a Republican, and he must uphold with warmth and conviction Royalist theories. He may be a Conservative, and must maintain anarchist principles, if such be the good pleasure of the author.

At the Théâtre Français poor Maubant was a most advanced Radical, and his stature and handsome face doomed him to play the parts of kings, emperors, and tyrants. As long as the re-hearsals went on Charlemagne or Cæsar could be heard swearing at tyrants, cursing the conquerors, and claiming the hardest punishments for them. I thoroughly enjoyed this struggle between the man and the actor. Perhaps this perpetual abstrac-tion from himself gives the comedian a more feminine nature. However that may be, it is certain that the actor is jealous of the actress. The courtesy of the well-educated man vanishes before the footlights, and the comedian who in private life would render a service to a woman in any difficulty will pick a quarrel with her on the stage. He would risk his life to save her from any danger in the road, on the railway, or in a boat, but when once on the boards he will not do anything to help her out of a difficulty. If her memory should fail, or if she should make a false step, he would not hesitate to push her. I am going a long way, perhaps, but not so far as people may think. I have performed with some celebrated comedians who have played me some bad tricks. On the other hand, there are some actors who are admirable, and who are more men than comedians when on the stage. Pierre Berton, Worms, and Guitry are, and always will be, the most perfect models of friendly and protecting courtesy towards the woman comedian. I have played in a number of pieces with each of them, and, subject as I am to stage fright, I have always felt perfect confidence when acting with these three artistes. I knew that their intelligence was of a high order, that they had pity on me for my fright, and that they would be prepared for any nervous weaknesses caused by it. Pierre Berton and Worms, both of them very great artistes, left the stage in full artistic vigour and vital strength, Pierre Berton to devote himself to literature, and Worms—no one knows why. As to Guitry, much the youngest of the three, he is now the first artist on the French stage, for he is an admirable comedian and at the same time an artist, a very rare thing. I know very few artistes in France or in other countries with these two qualities combined. Henry Irving was an admirable artist, but not a comedian. Coquelin is an admirable comedian, but he is not an artist. Mounet-Sully has genius, which he sometimes places at the service of the artist and sometimes at the service of the comedian; but, on the other hand, he sometimes gives us exaggerations as artist and comedian which make lovers of beauty and truth gnash their teeth. Bartet is a perfect *comédienne* with a very delicate artistic sense. Réjane is the most comedian of comedians, and an artist when she wishes to be.

Eleonora Duse is more a comedian than an artist; she walks in paths that have been traced out by others; she does not imitate them, certainly not, for she plants flowers where there were trees, and trees where there were flowers; but she has never by her art made a single personage stand out identified by her name; she has not created a being or a vision which reminds one of herself. She puts on other people's gloves, but she puts them on inside out.   And all this she has done with infinite grace and with careless unconsciousness.   She is a great comedian, a very great comedian, but not a great artist.

Novelli is a comedian of the old school which did not trouble much about the artistic side.   He is perfect in laughter and tears.   Beatrice Patrick Campbell is especially an artist, and her talent is that of charm and thought : she execrates beaten paths ; she wants to create, and she creates.   Antoine is often betrayed by his own powers, for his voice is heavy and his general appearance rather ordinary.   As a comedian there is therefore often much to be desired, but he is always an artist without equal, and our art owes much to him in its evolution in the direction of truth.   Antoine, too, is not jealous of the actress.

XXX

MY DEPARTURE FROM THE COMÉDIE FRANAÇISE— PREPARATIONS FOR MY FIRST AMERICAN TOUR—ANOTHER VISIT TO LONDON

The days which followed the return of the Comédie to its own home were very trying for me. Our manager wanted to subdue me, and he tortured me with a thousand little pin-pricks which were much more painful for a nature like mine than so many stabs with a knife. (At least I imagine so, as I have never had any.) I became irritable, bad-tempered on the slightest provocation, and was in fact ill. I had always been gay, and now I was sad. My health, which had ever been feeble, was endangered by this state of chaos.

Perrin gave me the *rôle* of the *Aventurière* to study. I detested the piece, and did not like the part, and I considered the lines of *L'Aventurière* very bad poetry indeed. As I cannot dissimulate well, in a fit of temper I said this straight out to Emile Augier, and he avenged himself in a most discourteous way on the first opportunity that presented itself. This was on the occasion of my definite rupture with the Comédie Française, the day after the first performance of *L'Aventurière* on Saturday, April 17, 1880. I was not ready to play my part, and the proof of this was a letter I wrote to M. Perrin on April 14, 1880.

"I regret very much, my dear Monsieur Perrin," I said, "but I have such a sore throat that I cannot speak, and am obliged to stay in bed. Will you kindly excuse me? It was at that wretched Trocadéro that I took cold on Sunday. I am very much worried, as I know it will cause you inconvenience. Anyhow, I will be ready for Saturday, whatever happens. A thousand excuses and kind regards.

"Sarah Bernhardt."

I was able to play, as I had recovered from my sore throat, but I had not studied my part during the three days, as I could not speak. I had not been able to try on my costumes either, as I had been in bed all the time. On Friday I went to ask Perrin to put off the performance of *L'Aventurière* until the next week. He replied that it was impossible; that every seat was booked, and that the piece had to be played the following Tuesday for the subscription night. I let myself be persuaded to act, as I had confidence in my star.

" Oh," I said to myself, " I shall get through it all right."

I did not get through it, though, or rather I came through it very badly. My costume was a failure; it did not fit me. They had always jeered at me for my thinness, and in this dress I looked like an English tea-pot. My voice was still rather hoarse, which very much disconcerted me. I played the first part of the *rôle* very badly, and the second part rather better. At a certain moment during the scene of violence I was standing up resting my two hands on the table, on which there was a lighted candelabra. There was a cry raised in the house, for my hair was very near to the flame. The following day one of the papers said that, as I felt things were all going wrong, I wanted to set my hair on fire so that the piece should come to an end before I failed completely. That was certainly the very climax of stupidity. The Press did not praise me, and the Press was quite right. I had played badly, looked ugly, and been in a bad temper, but I considered that there was nevertheless a want of courtesy and indulgence with regard to me. Auguste Vitu, in the *Figaro* of April 18, 1880, finished his article with the phrase : " The new Clorinde (the Adventuress) in the last two acts made some gestures with her arms and movements of her body which one regrets to see taken from Virginie of *L'Assommoir* and introduced at the Comédie Française." The only fault which I never have had, which I never shall have, is vulgarity. That was an injustice and a determination to hurt my feelings. Vitu was no friend of mine, but I understood from this way of attacking me that petty hatreds were lifting up their rattlesnake heads. All the low-down, little viper world was crawling about under my flowers and my laurels. I had known what was going on for a long time, and sometimes I had heard rattling behind the scenes. I wanted to have the enjoyment of hearing them all rattle together, and so I threw my laurels and my flowers to the four winds of heaven. In the most abrupt way I broke the contract which bound me to the Comédie Française, and through that to Paris.

I shut myself up all the morning, and after endless discussions with myself I decided to send in my resignation to the Comédie. I therefore wrote to M. Perrin this letter :

"To THE DIRECTOR.

"You have compelled me to play when I was not ready. You have only allowed me eight rehearsals on the stage, and the play has been rehearsed in its entirety only three times. I was unwilling to appear before the public. You insisted absolutely. What I foresaw has happened. The result of the performance has surpassed my anticipations. A critic pretended that I played Virginie of *L'Assommoir* instead of Dona Clorinde of *L'Aventurière*. May Emile Augier and Zola absolve me! It is my first rebuff at the Comédie; it shall be my last. I warned you on the day of the dress rehearsal. You have gone too far. I keep my word. By the time you receive this letter I shall have left Paris. Will you kindly accept my immediate resignation, and believe me

"Yours sincerely,
"SARAH BERNHARDT."

In order that this resignation might not be refused at the committee meeting, I sent copies of my letter to the *Gaulois* and the *Figaro*, and it was published at the same time as M. Perrin received it.

Then, quite decided not to be influenced by anybody, I set off at once with my maid for Hâvre. I had left orders that no one was to be told where I was, and the first evening I was there I passed in strict incognito. But the next morning I was recognised, and telegrams were sent to Paris to that effect. I was besieged by reporters.

I took refuge at La Hêve, where I spent the whole day on the beach, in spite of the cold rain which fell unceasingly.

I went back to the Hôtel Frascati frozen, and in the night I was so feverish that Dr. Gibert was requested to call. Madame Guérard, who was sent for by my alarmed maid, came at once. I was feverish for two days. During this time the newspapers continued to pour out a flood of ink on paper. This turned to bitterness, and I was accused of the worst misdeeds. The committee sent a *huissier* to my hotel in the Avenue de Villiers, and this man declared that after having knocked three times at the door and having received no answer, he had left copy, &c. &c.

This man was lying. In the hotel there were my son and his tutor, my steward, the husband of my maid, my butler, the cook, the kitchen-maid, the second lady's maid, and five dogs; but it was all in vain that I protested against this minion of the law; it was useless.

The Comédie must, according to the rules, send me three summonses. This was not done, and a law-suit was commenced against me. It was lost in advance.

Maître Allou, the advocate of the Comédie Française, invented wicked little histories about me. He took pleasure in trying to make me ridiculous. He had a big file of letters from me to Perrin, letters which I had written in softer moments or in anger. Perrin had kept them all, even the shortest notes. I had kept none of his. The few letters from Perrin to myself which have been published were given by him from his letter-copy book. Of course, he only showed those which could inspire the public with an idea of his paternal kindness to me, &c. &c.

The pleading of Maître Allou was very successful: he claimed three hundred thousand francs damages, in addition to the confiscation for the benefit of the Comédie Française of the forty-three thousand francs which that theatre owed me.

Maître Barboux was my advocate. He was an intimate friend of Perrin. He defended me very indifferently. I was condemned to pay a hundred thousand francs to the Comédie Française and to lose the forty-three thousand francs which I had left with the management. I may say that I did not trouble much about this law-suit.

Three days after my resignation Jarrett called upon me. He proposed to me, for the third time, to make a contract for America. This time I lent an ear to his propositions. We had never spoken about terms, and this is what he proposed:

Five thousand francs for each performance and one-half of the receipts above fifteen thousand francs; that is to say, the day the receipts reached the sum of twenty thousand francs I should receive seven thousand five hundred francs. In addition, one thousand francs per week for my hotel bill; also a special Pullman car, on all railway journeys, containing a bedroom, a drawing-room with a piano, four beds for my staff, and two cooks to cook for me on the way. Mr. Jarrett was to have ten per cent. on all sums received by me.

I accepted everything. I was anxious to leave Paris. Jarrett immediately sent a telegram to Mr. Abbey, the great American *impresario*, and he landed on this side thirteen days later. I signed the contract made by Jarrett, which was discussed clause by clause with the American manager.

I was given, on signing the contract, one hundred thousand francs as advance payment for my expenses before departure. I was to play eight pieces : *Hernani*, *Phèdre*, *Adrienne Lecouvreur*, *Froufrou*, *La Dame aux Camélias*, *Le Sphinx*, *L'Etrangère*, and *La Princesse Georges*.

I ordered twenty-five modern dresses at Laferrière's, of whom I was then a customer.

At Baron's I ordered six costumes for *Adrienne Lecouvreur* and four costumes for *Hernani*. I ordered from a young theatre *costumier* named Lepaul my costume for *Phèdre*. These thirty-six costumes cost me sixty-one thousand francs ; but out of this my costume for *Phèdre* alone cost four thousand francs. The poor *artist-costumier* had embroidered it himself. It was a marvel. It was brought to me two days before my departure, and I cannot think of this moment without emotion. Irritated by long waiting, I was writing an angry letter to the *costumier* when he was announced. At first I received him very badly, but I found him looking so unwell, the poor man, that I made him sit down and asked how he came to be so ill.

" Yes, I am not at all well," he said in such a weak voice that I was quite upset. " I wanted to finish this dress, and I have worked at it three days and nights. But look how nice your costume is ! " And he spread it out with loving respect before me.

" Look ! " remarked Guérard, " a little spot ! "

" Ah, I pricked myself," answered the poor artist quickly.

But I had just caught sight of a drop of blood at the corner of his lips. He wiped it quickly away, so that it should not

fall on the pretty costume as the other little spot had done.
I gave the artist the four thousand francs, which he took with
trembling hands. He murmured some unintelligible words and
withdrew.

"Take away this costume, take it away!" I cried to *mon
petit Dame* and my maid. And I cried so much that I had the
hiccoughs all the evening. Nobody understood why I was
crying. But I reproached myself bitterly for having worried
the poor man. It was plain that he was dying. And by the
force of circumstances I had unwittingly forged the first link
of the chain of death which was dragging to the tomb this
youth of twenty-two—this artist with a future before him.

I would never wear this costume. It is still in its box,
yellowed with age. Its gold embroidery is tarnished by time,
and the little spot of blood has slightly eaten away the stuff.
As to the poor artist, I learnt of his death during my stay in
London in the month of May, for before leaving for America
I signed with Hollingshead and Mayer, the *impresarii* of the
Comédie, a contract which bound me to them from May 24
to June 24 (1880).

It was during this period that the the law-suit which the
Comédie Française brought against me was decided.

Maître Barboux did not consult me about anything, and my
success in London, which was achieved without the help of the
Comédie, irritated the committee, the Press, and the public.

Maître Allou in his pleadings pretended that the London
public had tired of me very quickly, and did not care to come to
the performances of the Comédie in which I appeared.

The following list gives the best possible denial to the
assertions of Maître Allou :

PERFORMANCES GIVEN BY THE COMÉDIE FRANÇAISE
AT THE GAIETY THEATRE

(The * indicates the pieces in which I appeared.)

1879.	Plays.	Receipts in Francs.
June 2.	Le Misanthrope (Prologue) ; Phèdre (Acte II.) ; Les Précieuses Ridicules	*13,080
„ 3.	L'Etrangère	*12,565
„ 4.	Le Fils naturel	9,300

1879.	Plays.	Receipts in Francs.
June 5.	Les Caprices de Marianne ; La Joie fait Peur	10,100
„ 6.	Le Menteur ; Le Médecin malgré lui	9,530
„ 7.	Le Marquis de Villemer	9,960
„ 7.	Tartuffe (matinée) ; La Joie fait Peur	8,700
„ 9.	Hernani	*13,600
„ 10.	Le Demi-monde	11,525
„ 11.	Mlle. de Belle-Isle ; Il faut qu'une porte soit ouverte ou fermée	10,420
„ 12.	Le Post-Scriptum ; Le Gendre de M. Poirier	10,445
„ 13.	Phèdre	*13,920
„ 14.	Le Luthier de Crémône ; Le Sphinx	*13,350
„ 14.	Le Misanthrope (matinée) ; Les Plaideurs	8,800
„ 16.	L'Ami Fritz	9,375
„ 17.	Zaïre ; Les Précieuses Ridicules	*13,075
„ 18.	Le Jeu de l'amour et du hasard ; Il ne faut jurer de rien	11,550
„ 18.	Le Demi-monde	12,160
„ 20.	Les Fourchambault	11,200
„ 21.	Hernani	*13,375
„ 21.	Tartufe (matinée) ; Il faut qu'une porte soit ouverte ou fermée	2,115
„ 23.	Gringoire ; On ne badine pas avec l'amour	11,080
„ 24.	Chez l'avocat ; Mlle. de la Seiglière	9,660
„ 25.	L'Etrangère (matinée)	*11,710
„ 25.	Le Barbier de Seville	9,180
„ 26.	Andromaque ; Les Plaideurs	*13,350
„ 27.	L'Avare ; L'Etincelle	11,775
„ 28.	Le Sphinx ; Le Dépit amoureux	*12,860
„ 28.	Hernani (matinée)	*13,730
„ 30.	Ruy-Blas	*13,660
July 1.	Mercadet ; L'Eté de la St. Martin	9,850
„ 2.	Ruy-Blas	*13,160
„ 3.	Le Mariage de Victorine ; Les Fourberies de Scapin	10,165
„ 4.	Les Femmes savantes ; L'Etincelle	11,960
„ 5.	Les Fourchambault	10,700
„ 5.	Phèdre (matinée) ; La Joie fait Peur	*14,265
„ 7.	Le Marquis de Villemer	10,565
„ 8.	L'Ami Fritz	11,005
„ 9.	Hernani	*14,275
„ 10.	Le Sphinx	*13,775
„ 11.	Philiberte ; L'Etourdi	11,500
„ 12.	Ruy-Blas	*12,660
„ 12.	Gringoire (matinée) ; Hernani (Acte V.) ; La Bénédiction ; Davenant ; L'Etincelle	*13,725
	Total receipts . . . . 492,150 francs	

The average of the receipts was about 11,715 francs. These figures show that, out of the forty-three performances given by the Comédie Française, the eighteen performances in which

I took part gave an average of 13,350 francs each, while the twenty-five other performances gave an average of 10,000 francs.

*   *   *   *   *

While I was in London I learned that I had lost my law-suit. "The Court—with its 'Inasmuch as,' 'Nevertheless,' &c.—declares hereby that Mlle. Sarah Bernhardt loses all the rights, privileges, and advantages, resulting to her profit from the engagement which she contracted with the company by authentic decree of March 24, 1875, and condemns her to pay to the plaintiff in his lawful quality the sum of one hundred thousand francs damages."

I gave my last performance in London the very day that the papers published this unjust verdict. I was applauded, and the public overwhelmed me with flowers.

I had taken with me Madame Devoyod, Mary Jullien, Kalb, my sister Jeanne, Pierre Berton, Train, Talbot, Dieudonné—all artistes of great repute.

I played all the pieces which I was to play in America.

Vitu, Sarcey, Lapommeraye had said so much against me that I was stupefied to learn from Mayer that they had arrived in London to be present at my performances.

I could no longer understand what it all meant. I thought that the Parisian journalists were leaving me in peace at last, and here were my worst enemies coming across the sea to see and hear me. Perhaps they were hoping—like the Englishman who followed the lion-tamer to see him devoured by his lions!

Vitu in the *Figaro* had finished one of his bitter articles with these words:

"But we have heard enough, surely, of Mlle. Sarah Bernhardt! Let her go abroad with her monotonous voice and her funereal fantasies! Here we have nothing new to learn from her talents or her caprices. . ."

Sarcey, in an equally bitter article, *à propos* of my resignation at the Comédie, had finished in these terms:

"There comes a time when naughty children must go to bed."

As to the amiable Lapommeraye, he had showered on my devoted head all the rumours that he had collected from all sides. But as they said he had no originality, he tried to show that he also could dip his pen in venom, and he had cried, "Pleasant journey!" And here they all came, these three, and

others with them. And the day following my first performance of *Adrienne Lecouvreur*, Auguste Vitu telegraphed to the
Figaro a long article, in which he criticised me in certain scenes,
regretting that I had not followed the example of Rachel, whom
I had never seen. And he finished his article thus :

" The sincerity of my admiration cannot be doubted when I
avow that in the fifth act Sarah Bernhardt rose to a height of
dramatic power, to a force of expression which could not be surpassed. She played the long and cruel scene in which Adrienne,
poisoned by the Duchesse de Bouillon, struggles against death
in her fearful agony, not only with immense talent, but with a
science of art which up to the present she has never revealed.
If the Parisian public had heard, or ever hears, Mlle. Sarah
Bernhardt cry out with the piercing accent which she put into
her words that evening, ' I will not die, I will not die ! ' it would
weep with her."

Sarcey finished an admirable critique with these words :
" She is prodigious ! "

And Lapommeraye, who had once more become amiable
begged me to go back to the Comédie, which was waiting for me,
which would kill the fatted calf on the return of its prodigal
child.

Sarcey, in his article in the *Temps*, consecrated five columns of
praises to me, and finished his article with these words :

" Nothing, nothing can ever take the place of this last act
of *Adrienne Lecouvreur* at the Comédie. Ah ! she should
have stayed at the Comédie. Yes, I come back to my
litany ! I cannot help it ! We shall lose as much as she will.
Yes, I know that we can say Mlle. Dudlay is left to us. Oh, she
will always stay with us ! I cannot help saying it. What a
pity ! What a pity ! "

And eight days after, on June 7, he wrote in his theatrical
feuilleton, on the first performance of *Froufrou* :

" I do not think that the emotion at any theatre has ever been
so profound. There are, in the dramatic art, exceptional times
when the artistes are transported out of themselves, carried above
themselves, and compelled to obey this inward ' demon ' (I
should have said ' god '), who whispered to Corneille his immortal verses.

" ' Well,' " said I to Mlle. Sarah Bernhardt, after the play :

' this is an evening which will open to you, if you wish, the doors of the Comédie Française. ' Do not speak of it,' said she, 'to me. We will not speak of it.' But what a pity! What a pity!"

My success in *Froufrou* was so marked that it filled the void left by Coquelin, who, after having signed, with the consent of Perrin, with Messrs. Mayer and Hollingshead, declared that he could not keep his engagements. It was a nasty *coup de Jarnac*, by which Perrin hoped to injure my London performances. He had previously sent Got to me to ask officially if I would not come back to the Comédie. He said I should be permitted to make my American tour, and that everything would be arranged on my return. But he should not have sent Got. He should have sent Worms or *le petit père Franchise*—Delaunay. The one might have persuaded me by his affectionate reasoning and the other by the falsity of arguments presented with such grace that it would have been difficult to refuse.

Got declared that I should be only too happy to come back to the Comédie on my return to America, "For you know," he added, "you know, my little one, that you will die in that country. And if you come back you will perhaps be only too glad to return to the Comédie Française, for you will be in a bad state of health, and it will take some time before you are right again. Believe me, sign, and it is not we who will benefit by it, but you!"

"I thank you," I answered, "but I prefer to choose my hospital myself on my return. And now you can go and leave me in peace." I fancy I said, "Get out!"

That evening he was present at a performance of *Froufrou*; he came to my dressing-room and said:

"You had better sign, believe me! And come back to commence with *Froufrou*! I promise you a happy return!"

I refused, and finished my performances in London without Coquelin.

The average of the receipts was nine thousand francs, and I left London with regret—I who had left it with so much pleasure the first time. But London is a city apart; its charm unveils little by little. The first impression for a Frenchman or woman is that of keen suffering, of mortal *ennui*. Those tall houses with sash windows without curtains; those ugly monu-

ANOTHER VISIT TO LONDON 341

ments, all in mourning with the dust and grime and black and greasy dirt; those flower-sellers at the corners of all the streets, with faces sad as the rain and bedraggled feathers in their hats and lamentable clothing; the black mud of the streets; the low sky; the funereal mirth of drunken women hanging on to men just as drunken; the wild dancing of dishevelled children round the street organs, as numerous as the omnibuses—all that caused twenty-five years ago an indefinite suffering to a Parisian. But little by little one finds that the profusion of the squares is restful to the eyes; that the beauty of the aristocratic ladies effaces the image of the flower-sellers. . . .

The constant movement of Hyde Park, and especially of Rotten Row, fills the heart with gaiety. The broad English hospitality, which is manifested from the first moment of making an acquaintance; the wit of the men, which compares favourably with the wit of Frenchmen; and their gallantry, much more respectful and therefore much more flattering, left no regrets in me for French gallantry.

But I prefer our pale mud to the London black mud, and our windows opening in the centre to the horrible sash windows. I find also that nothing marks more clearly the difference of character of the two nations than their respective windows. Ours open wide; the sun enters in our houses even to the heart of the dwelling; the air sweeps away all the dust and all the microbes. They shut in the same manner, simply as they open.

English windows open only half-way, either the top half or the bottom half. One may even have the pleasure of opening them a little at the top and a little at the bottom, but not at all in the middle. The sun cannot enter openly, nor the air. The window keeps its selfish and perfidious character. I hate the English windows. But now I love London and—is there any need to add?—its inhabitants.

Since my first visit I have returned there twenty-one times, and the public has always remained faithful and affectionate.

XXXI

A TOUR IN DENMARK—ROYAL FAMILIES—THE "TWENTY-EIGHT DAYS" OF SARAH BERNHARDT

AFTER this first test of my freedom I felt more sure of life than before. Although I was very weak of constitution, the possibility of doing as I wanted without hindrance and without control calmed my nervous system, and my health, which had been weakened by perpetual irritations and by excessive work, was improved. I reposed on the laurels which I had gathered myself, and I slept better. Sleeping better, I commenced to eat better. And great was the astonishment of my little court when they saw their idol come back from London round and rosy.

I remained several days in Paris; then I set out for Brussels. where I was to play *Adrienne Lecouvreur* and *Froufrou.*

The Belgian public—by which I mean the Brussels public—is the one most like our own. In Belgium I never feel that I am in a strange country. Our language is the language of the country; the horses and carriages are always in perfect taste; the fashionable women resemble our own fashionable women; *cocottes* abound; the hotels are as good as in Paris; the cab-horses are as poor; the newspapers are as spiteful. Brussels is gossiping Paris in miniature.

I played for the first time at the Théâtre de la Monnaie, and I felt uncomfortable in that immense and frigid house. But the benevolent enthusiasm of the public soon warmed me, and I shall never forget the four performances I gave there.

Then I set out for Copenhagen, where I was to give five performances at the Theatre Royal.

Our arrival, which doubtless was anxiously expected, really frightened me. More than two thousand persons who were assembled in the station when the train came in gave a hurrah

so terrible that I did not know what was happening. But when
M. de Fallesen, manager of the Theatre Royal, and the First
Chamberlain of the King entered my compartment, and begged
me to show myself at the window to gratify the curiosity of the
public, the hurrahs began again, and then I understood. But
a dreadful anxiety now took possession of me. I could never, I
was sure, rise to what was expected from me. My slender frame
would inspire disdain in those magnificent men and those
splendid and healthy women. I stepped out of the train so
diminished by comparison that I had the sensation of being
nothing more than a breath of air; and I saw the crowd, submissive to the police, divide into two compact lines, leaving a
wide path for my carriage. I passed slowly through this double
hedge of sympathetic sight-seers, who threw me flowers and kisses
and lifted their hats to me. In the course of my long career I
have had many triumphs, receptions, and ovations, but my
reception by the Danish people remains one of my most
cherished memories. The living hedge lasted till we reached
the Hôtel d'Angleterre, where I went in, after thanking once
more the sympathetic friends who surrounded me.

In the evening the King, the Queen, and their daughter, the
Princess of Wales, were present at the first performance of
Adrienne Lecouvreur.

This is what the *Figaro* of August 16, 1880, said :

" Sarah Bernhardt has played *Adrienne Lecouvreur* with a
tremendous success before a magnificent audience. The royal
family, the King and the Queen of the Hellenes, as well as
the Princess of Wales, were present at the performance. The
Queens threw their bouquets to the French artiste, amidst
applause. It was an unprecedented triumph. The public was
delirious. To-morrow *Froufrou* will be played."

The performance of *Froufrou* was equally successful. But as
I was only playing every other day, I wanted to visit Elsinore.
The King placed the royal steamer at my disposal for this little
journey.

I had invited all my company.

M. de Fallesen, the First Chamberlain, and manager of the
Theatre Royal, had ordered a magnificent lunch for us, and
accompanied by the principal notabilities of Denmark, we visited

Hamlet's tomb, the spring of Ophelia, and the castle of Marienlyst. Then we went over the castle of Kronborg. I regretted my visit to Elsinore. The reality did not come up to the expectation. The so-called tomb of Hamlet is represented by a small column, ugly and mournful-looking; there is little verdure, and the desolate sadness of deceit without beauty. They gave me a little water from the spring of Ophelia to drink, and the Baron de Fallesen broke the glass, without allowing any one else to drink from the spring.

I returned from this very ordinary journey feeling rather sad. Leaning against the side of the vessel, I watched the water gliding past, when I noticed a few rose petals on the surface. Carried by an invisible current, they were borne against the sides of the boat; then the petals increased to thousands, and in the mysterious sunset rose the melodious chant of the sons of the North. I looked up. In front of us, rocked on the water by the evening breeze, was a pretty boat with outspread sails; a score of young men, throwing handfuls of roses into the waters, which were carried to us by the little wavelets, were singing the marvellous legends of past centuries. And all that was for me : all those roses, all that love, all that musical poetry. And that setting sun was also for me. And in this fleeting moment, which brought all the beauty of life near to me, I felt myself very near to God.

The following day, at the close of the performance, the King sent for me to come into the royal box, and he decorated me with a very pretty Order of Merit adorned with diamonds. He kept me some time in his box, asking me about different things. I was presented to the Queen, and I noticed immediately that she was somewhat deaf. I was rather embarrassed, but the Queen of Greece came to my rescue. She was beautiful, but much less so than her lovely sister the Princess of Wales. Oh, that adorable and seductive face—with the eyes of a child of the North, and classic features of virginal purity, a long, supple neck that seemed made for queenly bows, a sweet and almost timid smile. The indefinable charm of this Princess made her so radiant that I saw nothing but her, and I went from the box leaving behind me, I fear, but a poor opinion of my intelligence with the royal couples of Denmark and Greece.

The evening before my departure I was invited to a grand

supper. Fallesen made a speech, and thanked us in a very charming manner for the "French week" which we had given in Denmark.

Robert Walt made a very cordial speech on behalf of the Press, very short but very sympathetic. Our Ambassador in a few courteous words thanked Robert Walt, and then, to the general surprise, Baron Magnus, the Prussian Minister, rose, and in a loud voice, turning to me, he said, "I drink to France, which gives us such great artistes! To France, la belle France, whom we all love so much!"

Hardly ten years had passed since the terrible war. French men and women were still suffering; their wounds were not healed.

Baron Magnus, a really amiable and charming man, had from the time of my arrival in Copenhagen sent me flowers with his card. I had sent back the flowers, and begged an *attaché* of the English Embassy, Sir Francis ——, I believe, to ask the German baron not to renew his gifts. The Baron laughed good-naturedly, and waited for me as I came out of my hotel. He came to me with outstretched hands, and spoke kindly and reasonable words. Everybody was looking at us, and I was embarrassed. It was evident that he was a kind man. I thanked him, touched in spite of myself by his frankness, and I went away quite undecided as to what I really felt. Twice he renewed his visit, but I did not receive him, but only bowed as I left my hotel. I was somewhat irritated at the tenacity of this amiable diplomatist. On the evening of the supper, when I saw him take the attitude of an orator, I felt myself grow pale. He had barely finished his little speech when I jumped to my feet and cried, "Let us drink to France, but to the whole of France, Monsieur l'Ambassadeur de Prusse!" I was nervous, sensational, and theatrical without intending it.

It was like a thunderbolt.

The orchestra of the court, which was placed in the upper gallery, began playing the "Marseillaise." At this time the Danes hated the Germans. The supper-room was suddenly deserted as if by enchantment.

I went up to my rooms, not wishing to be questioned. I had gone too far. Anger had made me say more than I intended. Baron Magnus did not deserve this thrust of mine. And also my instinct forewarned me of results to follow. I went to bed angry with myself, with the Baron, and with all the world.

About five o'clock in the morning I commenced to doze, when I was awakened by the growling of my dog. Then I heard some one knocking at the door of the *salon*. I called my maid, who woke her husband, and he went to open the door. An *attaché* from the French Embassy was waiting to speak to me on urgent business. I put on an ermine tea-gown and went to see the visitor.

"I beg you," he said, "to write a note immediately to explain that the words you said were not meant. The Baron Magnus, whom we all respect, is in a very awkward situation and we are all upset about it. Prince Bismarck is not to be trifled with, and it may be very serious for the Baron."

"Oh, I assure you, Monsieur, I am a hundredfold more unhappy about it than you, for the Baron is a good and charming man. He lacked political tact, and in this case it is excusable, because I am not a woman of politics. I was lacking in coolness. I would give my right hand to repair the ill."

"We don't ask you for so much as that, as it would spoil the beauty of your gestures!" (He was French, you see.) "Here is the rough copy of a letter. Will you take it, rewrite it, sign it, and everything will be at an end?"

But that was unacceptable. The wording of this letter gave twisted and rather cowardly explanations. I rejected it, and after several attempts to rewrite it I gave up in despair and did nothing.

Three hundred persons had been present at the supper, in addition to the royal orchestra and the attendants. Everybody had heard the amiable but awkward speech of the Baron. I had replied in a very excited manner. The public and the Press had all been witnesses of my *algarade;* we were the victims of our own foolishness, the Baron and myself. If such a thing were to happen at the present time I should not care a pin for public opinion, and I should even take pleasure in ridiculing myself in order to do justice to a brave and gallant man. But at that time I was very nervous and uncompromisingly patriotic. And also, perhaps, I thought I was some one of importance. Since then life has taught me that if one is to be famous it can only really become manifest after death. To-day I am going down the hill of life, and I regard gaily all the pedestals on which I have been lifted up, and there have been so many, so many of them that their fragments, broken by the same hands that had raised them, have made me a solid pillar, from which I look out on life, happy with what has been and attentive to what will be.

My stupid vanity had wounded one who meant no harm, and this incident has always left in me a feeling of remorse and chagrin.

I left Copenhagen amidst applause and the repeated cries of " Vive la France ! " From all the windows hung the French flag, fluttering in the breeze, and I felt that this was not only *for* me, but *against* Germany—I was sure of it.

Since then the Germans and the Danes are solidly united, and I am not certain that several Danes do not still bear me ill-will because of this incident of the Baron Magnus.

I came back to Paris to make final preparations for my journey to America. I was to set sail on October 15.

One day in August I was having a reception of all my friends, who came to see me in full force, because I was about to set out for a long journey.

Among the number were Girardin, Count Kapenist, Marshal Canrobert, Georges Clairin, Arthur Meyer, Duquesnel, the beautiful Augusta Holmes, Raymond de Montbel, Nordenskjold, O'Connor, and other friends. I chatted gaily, happy to be surrounded by so many kind and intellectual friends.

Girardin did all he could to persuade me not to undertake this journey to America. He had been the friend of Rachel, and told me the sad end of her journey.

Arthur Meyer was of opinion that I ought always to do what I thought best. The other friends discussed the subject. That admirable man, whom France will always worship, Canrobert, said how much he should miss and regret those intimate *causeries* at our five o'clock teas.

" But," said he, " we have not the right to try, in our affectionate selfishness, to hinder our young friend from doing all she can in the strife. She is of a combative nature."

" Ah yes ! " I cried. " Yes, I am born for strife, I feel it. Nothing pleases me like having to master a public, perhaps hostile, who have read and heard all that the Press has said

against me.   But I am sorry that I cannot play, not only
in Paris but in all France, my two big successes, *Adrienne* and
Froufrou."

"As to that, you can count on me!" exclaimed Félix
Duquesnel. "My dear Sarah, you had your first successes with
me, and it is with me that you will have your last. . . ."

Everybody protested, and I jumped up.

"Wait one moment," said he. "Last successes until you come
back from America! If you will consent, you can count on me
for everything. I will obtain, at any price, theatres in all the
large towns, and we will give twenty-five performances during the
month of September. As to financial arrangements, they will
be of the simplest : twenty-five performances—fifty thousand
francs. To-morrow I will give you one half of this sum, and
sign a contract with you, so that you will not have time to
change your mind."

I clapped my hands joyfully. All the friends who were there
begged Duquesnel to send them, as soon as possible, an itinerary
of the tour, for they all wanted to see me in the two plays in
which I had gained laurels in England, Belgium, and Denmark.

Duquesnel promised to send them the details of the tour, and
it was settled that their visits should be drawn by lot from a
little bag, and each town marked with the date and the name of
the play.

A week later Duquesnel, with whom I had signed a contract, returned with the tour mapped out and all the company
engaged. It was almost miraculous.

The performances were to commence on Saturday, September 4,
and there were to be twenty-five of them ; and the whole, including the day of departure and the day of return, was to last
twenty-eight days, which caused this tour to be called "The
twenty-eight days of Sarah Bernhardt," like the twenty-eight
days of a citizen who is obliged to accomplish his military
service.

The little tour was most successful, and I never enjoyed
myself more than during this artistic promenade. Duquesnel
organised excursions and *fêtes* outside the towns.

At first he had prepared, thinking to please me, some visits
to the sights of the towns. He had written beforehand from
Paris fixing dates and hours. The guardians of the different

museums, art galleries, &c., had offered to point out to me the finest objects in their collections, and the mayors had prepared visits to the churches and celebrated buildings.

When, on the eve of our departure, he showed us the heap of letters, each giving a most amiable affirmative, I shrieked.

I hate seeing public buildings and having them explained to me. I know most of the public sights of France, but I have visited them when I felt inclined and with my own chosen friends. As to the churches and other buildings, I find them very tiresome. I cannot help it—it really wearies me to see them.

I can admire their outline in passing, or when I see them silhouetted against the setting sun, that is all right, but further than that I will not go. The idea of entering these cold spaces, while some one explains their absurd and interminable history, of looking up at their ceilings with craning neck, of cramping my feet by walking unnaturally over highly waxed floors, of being obliged to admire the restoration of the left wing that they would have done better to let crumble to ruins ; to have some one express wonder at the depth of some moat which once upon a time used to be full of water, but is now as dry as the east wind—all that is so tiresome it makes me want to howl. From my earliest childhood I have always detested houses, castles, churches, towers, and all buildings higher than a mill. I love low buildings, farms, huts, and I positively adore mills, because these little buildings do not obstruct the horizon. I have nothing to say against the Pyramids, but I would a hundred times rather they had never been built.

I begged Duquesnel to send telegrams at once to all the notabilities who had been so obliging. We passed two hours over this task, and on September 3, I set out, free, joyful, and content.

My friends came to see me while I was on tour, in accordance with the lots they had drawn, and we had picnics by coach into the surrounding country from all the towns in which I played.

I came back to Paris on September 30, and had only just time to prepare for my journey to America. I had only been a week in Paris when I had a visit from M. Bertrand, who was then director of the Variétés. His brother was director of the Vaudeville in partnership with Raymond Deslandes.

I did not know Eugène Bertrand, but I received him at once, for we had mutual friends.

"What are you going to do when you come back from America?" he asked me, after we had exchanged greetings.

"I really don't know. Nothing. I have not thought of anything."

"Well, I have thought of something for you. And if you like to make your reappearance in Paris in a play of Victorien Sardou's, I will sign with you at once for the Vaudeville."

"Ah!" I cried. "The Vaudeville! What are you thinking of? Raymond Deslandes is the manager, and he hates me like poison because I ran away from the Gymnase the day following the first performance of his play *Un mari qui lance sa femme*. His play was ridiculous, and I was even more ridiculous than his play in the part of a young Russian lady addicted to dancing and eating sandwiches. That man will never engage me!"

He smiled. "My brother is the partner of Raymond Deslandes. My brother—to put it plainly—is myself. All the money put in the affair by us is mine. I am the sole master. What salary do you want?"

"But—— I really don't know."

"Will fifteen hundred francs per performance suit you?"

I looked at him in stupefaction, not quite sure if he was in his right mind.

"But, Monsieur, if I do not succeed you will lose money, and I cannot agree to that."

"Do not be afraid," he said. "I can assure you it will be a success—a colossal success. Will you sign? And I will also guarantee you fifty performances!"

"Oh no, never! I will sign willingly, for I admire the talent of Victorien Sardou, but I do not want any guarantee. Success will depend on Victorien Sardou, and after him on me. So I sign, and thank you for your confidence."

At my afternoon teas I showed the new contract to my friends, and they were all of opinion that luck was on my side in the matter of my resignation (from the Comédie Française).

I was to leave Paris in three days. My heart was sore at the idea of leaving France, for many sorrowful reasons. But in these Memoirs I have put on one side all that touches the inner part of my life. There is one family "me" which lives another life, and whose sensations, sorrows, joys, and griefs are born and die for a very small number of hearts.

But I felt the need of another atmosphere, of vaster space, of other skies.

I left my little boy with my uncle, who had five boys of his own. His wife was rather a strict Protestant, but kind, and my cousin Louise, their eldest daughter, was witty and highly intelligent. She promised me to be on the watch, and to let me know at once if there was anything I ought to know.

Up to the last moment people in Paris did not believe that I would really go. My health was so uncertain that it seemed folly to undertake such a journey. But when it became absolutely certain that I was going, there was a general concert of spiteful reproaches. The hue and cry of my enemies was in full swing. I have now under my eyes these specimens of insanity, calumnies, lies, and stupidities ; burlesque portraits, doleful pleasantries ; good-byes to the Darling, the Idol, the Star, the Zimm ! boum ! boum ! &c. &c. It was all so absolutely idiotic that I was confounded. I did not read the greater part of these articles, but my secretary had orders to cut them out and paste them in little note-books, whether favourable or unfavourable. It was my godfather who had commenced doing this when I entered the Conservatoire, and after his death I had it continued.

Happily, I find in these thousands of lines fine and noble words—words written by J. J. Weiss, Zola, Emile de Girardin, Jules Vallès, Jules Lemaître, &c. ; and beautiful verses full of grace and justice, signed Victor Hugo, François Coppée, Richepin, Haraucourt, Henri de Bornier, Catulle Mendès, Parodi, and later Edmond Rostand.

I neither could nor would suffer unduly from the calumnies and lies, but I confess that the kind appreciation and praises accorded me by the superior minds afforded me infinite joy.

XXXII

EXPERIENCES AND REFLECTIONS ON BOARD SHIP
FROM HÂVRE TO NEW YORK

THE ship which was to take me away to other hopes, other sensations, and other successes was named *L'Amérique*. It was the unlucky boat, the boat that was haunted by the gnome. All kinds of misfortunes, accidents, and storms had been its lot. It had been blockaded for months with its keel out of water. Its stern had been staved in by an Iceland boat, and it had foundered on the shores of Newfoundland, I believe, and been set afloat again. Another time fire had broken out on it right in the Hâvre roadstead, but no great damage was done. The poor boat had had a celebrated adventure which had made it ridiculous.

In 1876 or 1877 a new pumping system was adopted, and although this system had been in use by the English for a long time, it was quite unknown aboard French boats. The captain very wisely decided to have these pumps worked by his crew, so that in case of any danger the men should be ready to manipulate them easily.

The experiment had been going on for a few minutes when one of the men came to inform the captain that the hold of the ship was filling with water, and no one could discover the cause of it. " Go on pumping!" shouted the captain. " Hurry up! Pump away!" The pumps were worked frantically, and the result was that the hold filled entirely, and the captain was obliged to abandon the ship after seeing the passengers safely off in the boats. An English whaler met the ship two days after, tried the pumps, which worked admirably, but in the contrary way to that indicated by the French captain. This slight error cost the Compagnie Transatlantique £48,000 salvage

money, and when they wanted to run the ship again and passengers refused to go by it, they offered my *impresario*, Mr.
Abbey, excellent terms. He accepted them, and very intelligent he was, for, in spite of all prognostications, nothing further
happened to the boat.

I had hitherto travelled very little, and I was wild with
delight.

On October 15, 1880, at six o'clock in the morning, I entered
my cabin. It was a large one, and was hung with light red repp
embroidered with my initials. What a profusion of the letters
S. B.! Then there was a large brass bedstead brightly polished,
and flowers were everywhere. Adjoining mine was a very comfortable cabin for *mon petit Dame*, and leading out of that was one
for my maid and her husband. All the other persons in my
service were at the other end of the ship.

The sky was misty, the sea grey, with no horizon. I was on
my way over there, beyond that mist which seemed to unite the
sky and the water in a mysterious rampart.

The clearing of the deck for the departure upset every one
and everything. The rumbling of the machinery, the boatswain's call, the bell, the sobbing and the laughter, the
creaking of the ropes, the shrill shouting of the orders, the
terror of those who were only just in time to catch the boat,
the " Halloa!" "Look out!" of the men who were pitching
the packages from the quay into the hold, the sound of the
laughing waves breaking on the side of the boat, all this
mingled together made the most frightful uproar, tiring the
brain so that its own sensations were all vague and bewildered.
I was one of those who up to the last moment enjoyed the
good-byes, the hand-shakings, the plans about the return, and
the farewell kisses, and when it was all over flung themselves
sobbing on their beds.

For the next three days I was in utter despair, weeping bitter
tears, tears that scalded my cheeks. Then I began to get calm
again; my will-power triumphed over my grief. On the fourth
day I dressed at seven o'clock and went on deck to have some
fresh air. It was icy cold, and as I walked up and down I met
a lady dressed in black with a sad resigned face. The sea looked
gloomy and colourless, and there were no waves. Suddenly a
wild billow dashed so violently against the ship that we were

z

both thrown down. I immediately clutched hold of the leg of one of the benches, but the unfortunate lady was flung forward. Springing to my feet with a bound, I was just in time to seize hold of the skirt of her dress, and with the help of my maid and a sailor managed to prevent the poor woman from falling head first down the staircase. Very much hurt though she was, and a trifle confused, she thanked me in such a gentle dreamy voice that my heart began to beat with emotion.

" You might have been killed, Madame," I said, " down that horrible staircase."

" Yes," she answered, with a sigh of regret ; " but it was not God's will."

" Are you not Madame Hessler ? " she continued, looking earnestly at me.

" No, Madame," I answered ; " my name is Sarah Bernhardt." She stepped back and drawing herself up, her face very pale and her brows knitted, she said in a mournful voice, a voice that was scarcely audible, " I am the widow of President Lincoln."

I too stepped back, and a thrill of anguish ran through me, for I had just done this unhappy woman the only service that I ought not to have done her—I had saved her from death. Her husband had been assassinated by an actor, Booth, and it was an actress who had now prevented her from joining her beloved husband.

I went back again to my cabin and stayed there two days, for I had not the courage to meet the woman for whom I felt such sympathy and to whom I should never dare to speak again.

On the 22nd we were surprised by an abominable snowstorm. I was called up hurriedly by Captain Jouclas. I threw on a long ermine cloak and went on to the bridge. It was perfectly stupefying and at the same time fairy-like. The heavy flakes met each other with a thud in their mad waltzing provoked by the wind. The sky was suddenly veiled from us by all this whiteness which fell round us in avalanches, completely hiding the horizon. I was facing the sea, and as Captain Jouclas pointed out to me, we could not see a hundred yards in front of us. I then turned round and saw that the ship was as white as a sea-gull : the ropes, the cordage, the nettings, the port-holes, the shrouds, the boats, the deck, the sails, the ladders, the funnels, the ventilators, everything was white. The sea was

Boston. Women form the majority there. They are puritanical with intelligence, and independent with a certain grace. I passed between the two lines formed by this strange, courteous, and cold crowd, and just as I was about to get into my carriage a lady advanced towards me and said, "Welcome to Boston, Madame!"

"Welcome, Madame!" and she held out a soft little hand to me. (American women generally have charming hands and feet.) Other people now approached and smiled, and I had to shake hands with many of them.

I took a fancy to this city at once, but all the same I was furious for a moment when a reporter sprang on the steps of the carriage just as we were driving away. He was in a greater hurry and more audacious than any of the others, but he was certainly overstepping the limits, and I pushed the impolite fellow back angrily. Jarrett was prepared for this, and saved him by the collar of his coat; otherwise he would have fallen down on the pavement as he deserved.

"At what time will you come and get on the whale to-morrow?" this extraordinary personage asked. I gazed at him in bewilderment. He spoke French perfectly, and repeated his question.

"He's mad!" I said in a low voice to Jarrett.

"No, Madame; I am not mad, but I should like to know at what time you will come and get on the whale? It would be better perhaps to come this evening, for we are afraid it may die in the night, and it would be a pity for you not to come and pay it a visit while it still has breath."

He went on talking, and as he talked he half seated himself beside Jarrett, who was still holding him by the collar lest he should fall out of the carriage.

"But, Monsieur," I exclaimed, "what do you mean? What is all this about a whale?"

"Ah, Madame," he replied, "it is admirable, enormous. It is in the harbour basin, and there are men employed day and night to break the ice all round it."

He broke off suddenly, and standing on the carriage step he clutched the driver.

"Stop! Stop!" he called out. "Hi! Hi! Henry, come here! Here's Madame; here she is!"

black and the sky black. The ship alone was white, floating along in this immensity. There was a contest between the high funnel, spluttering forth with difficulty its smoke through the wind which was rushing wildly into its great mouth, and the prolonged shrieks of the siren. The contrast was so extraordinary between the virgin whiteness of this ship and the infernal uproar it made that it seemed to me as if I had before me an angel in a fit of hysterics.

On the evening of that strange day the doctor came to tell me of the birth of a child among the emigrants, in whom I was deeply interested. I went at once to the mother, and did all I could for the poor little creature who had just come into this world. Oh, the dismal moans in that dismal night in the midst of all that misery! Oh, that first strident cry of the child affirming its will to live in the midst of all these sufferings, of all these hardships, and of all these hopes! Everything was there mingled together in this human medley—men, women, children, rags and preserves, oranges and basins, heads of hair and bald pates, half open lips of young girls and tightly closed mouths of shrewish women, white caps and red handkerchiefs, hands stretched out in hope and fists clenched against adversity. I saw revolvers half concealed under the rags, knives in the men's belts. A sudden roll of the boat showed us the contents of a parcel that had fallen from the hands of a rascally-looking fellow with a very determined expression on his face, and a hatchet and a tomahawk fell to the ground. One of the sailors immediately seized the two weapons to take them to the purser. I shall never forget the scrutinising glance of the man; he had evidently made a mental note of the features of the sailor, and I breathed a fervent prayer that the two might never meet in a solitary place.

I remember now with remorse the horrible disgust that took possession of me when the doctor handed the child over to me to wash. That dirty little red, moving, sticky object was a human being. It had a soul, and would have thoughts! I felt quite sick, and I could never again look at that child, although I was afterwards its godmother, without living over again that first impression. When the young mother had fallen asleep I wanted to go back to my cabin. The doctor helped me, but the sea was so rough that we could scarcely walk at all among the packages and emigrants. Some of them who were crouching on the floor watched us silently as we tottered and stumbled along like drunkards. I was annoyed at being watched by those malevolent, mocking eyes. " I say, doctor," one of the men called out, " the sea water gets in the head like wine. You and your lady look as though you were coming back from a spree ! " An old woman clung to me as we passed : " Oh, Madame," she said, " shall we be shipwrecked with the boat rolling like this ? Oh God ! Oh God ! " A tall fellow with red hair and beard came forward and laid the poor old woman down again gently. " You can sleep in peace, mother," he said. " If we are shipwrecked I swear there shall be more saved down here than up above." He then came closer to me and continued in a defiant tone : " The rich folks—first-class—into the sea ! The emigrants and the second-class in the boats ! " As he uttered these words I heard a sly, stifled laugh from everywhere, in front of me, behind, at the side, and even from under my feet. It seemed to echo in the distance like the laughing behind the scenes on the stage. I drew nearer to the doctor, and he saw that I was uneasy.

" Nonsense," he said, laughing ; " we should defend ourselves."

" But how many *could* be saved," I asked, " in case we were really in danger ? "

" Two hundred—two hundred and fifty at the most, with all the boats out, if all arrived safely."

" But the purser told me that there were seven hundred and sixty emigrants," I insisted, " and there are only a hundred and twenty passengers. How many do you reckon with the officers, the crew, and the servants ? "

" A hundred and seventy," the doctor answered.

" Then there are a thousand and fifty on board, and you can only save two hundred and fifty ? "

" Yes."

" Well then, I can understand the hatred of these emigrants, whom you take on board like cattle and treat like negroes. They are absolutely certain that in case of danger they would be sacrificed ! "

" But we should save them when their turn came."

I glanced with horror at the man who was talking to me. He looked honest and straightforward and he evidently meant what he said. And so all these poor creatures who had been disappointed in life and badly treated by society would have no right to life until after *we* were saved—we, the more favoured ones! Oh, how I understood now the rascally-looking fellow, with his hatchet and tomahawk! How thoroughly I approved at that moment of the revolvers and the knives hidden in the belts. Yes, he was quite right, the tall, red-haired fellow. We want the first places, always the first places. And so we should have the first places in the water.

" Well, are you satisfied ? " asked the captain, who was just coming out of his cabin. " Has it gone off all right ? "

" Yes, captain," I answered ; " but I am horrified."

Jouclas stepped back in surprise.

" Good Heavens, what has horrified you ? " he asked.

" The way in which you treat your passengers——"

He tried to put in a word, but I continued :

" Why—you expose us in case of a shipwreck——"

" We never have a shipwreck."

" Good. In case of a fire, then——"

" We never have a fire——"

" Good ! In case of sinking——"

" I give in," he said, laughing. " To what do we expose you, though, Madame ? "

" To the very worst of deaths : to a blow on the head with an axe, to a dagger thrust in our back, or merely to be flung into the water——"

He attempted to speak, but again I continued :

" There are seven hundred and fifty emigrants below, and there are scarcely three hundred of us, counting first-class passengers and the crew. You have boats which might save two hundred persons, and even that is doubtful——"

" Well ? "

" Well, what about the emigrants ? "

" We should save them before the crew."

" But after us ? "

" Yes, after you."

" And you fancy that they would let you do it ? "

" We have guns with which to keep them in order."

" Guns—guns for women and children ? "

" No ; the women and children would take their turn first."

" But that is idiotic ! " I exclaimed ; " it is perfectly absurd !
Why save women and children if you are going to make widows
and orphans of them ?   And do you believe that all those
young men would resign themselves to their fate because of your
guns ?   There are more of them than there are of you, and they
are armed.   Life owes them their revenge, and they have the
same right that we have to defend themselves in such moments.
They have the courage of those who have nothing to lose and
everything to gain in the struggle.   In my opinion it is iniquitous
and infamous that you should expose us to certain death and
them to an obligatory and perfectly justified crime."

The captain tried to speak, but again I persisted :

" Without going as far as a shipwreck, only fancy if we were
to be tossed about for months on a raging sea. This has happened,
and might happen again. You cannot possibly have food enough
on board for a thousand people during two or three months."

" No, certainly not," put in the purser dryly.   He was a very
amiable man, but very touchy.

" Well then, what should you do ? " I asked.

" What would *you* do ? " asked the captain, highly amused at
the annoyed expression on the purser's face.

" I—oh, I should have a ship for emigrants and a ship for
passengers, and I think that would be only just."

" Yes, but it would be ruinous."

" No ; the one for wealthy people would be a steamer like this,
and the one for emigrants a sailing vessel."

" But that too would be unjust, Madame, for the steamer
would go more quickly than the sailing boat."

" That would not matter at all," I argued.   " Wealthy people
are always in a hurry, and the poor never are.   And then, considering what is awaiting them in the land to which they are
going——"

" It is the Promised Land."

" Oh, poor things ! poor things ! with their Promised Land !
Dakota or Colorado. . . .   In the day-time they have the sun
which makes their brains boil, scorches the ground, dries up the
springs, and brings forth endless numbers of mosquitoes to sting
their bodies and try their patience. The Promised Land ! . . .
At night they have the terrible cold to make their eyes smart, to
stiffen their. joints and ruin their lungs. The Promised Land !

It is just death in some out-of-the-world place after fruitless appeals to the justice of their fellow countrymen. They will breathe their life out in a sob or in a terrible curse of hatred. God will have mercy on them though, for it is piteous to think that all these poor creatures are delivered over, with their feet bound by suffering and their hands bound by hope, to the slave-drivers who trade in white slaves. And when I think that the money is in the purser's cash-box which the slave-driver has paid for the transport of all these poor creatures! Money that has been collected by rough hands or trembling fingers. Poor money economised, copper by copper, tear by tear. When I think of all this it makes me wish that we could be shipwrecked, that *we* could be all killed and all of them saved."

With these words I hurried away to my cabin to have a good cry, for I was seized with a great love for humanity and intense grief that I could do nothing, absolutely nothing!

The following morning I woke late, as I had not fallen asleep until very late. My cabin was full of visitors, and they were all holding small parcels half concealed. I rubbed my sleepy eyes, and could not quite understand the meaning of this invasion.

" My dear Sarah," said Madame Guérard, coming to me and kissing me, " don't imagine that this day, your *fête* day, could be forgotten by those who love you."

" Oh," I exclaimed, " is it the 23rd ? "

" Yes, and here is the first of the remembrances from the absent ones."

My eyes filled with tears, and it was through a mist that I saw the portrait of that young being more precious to me than anything else in the world, with a few words in his own handwriting. Then there were some presents from friends—pieces of work from humble admirers. My little godson of the previous evening was brought to me in a basket, with oranges, apples, and tangerines all round him. He had a golden star on his forehead, a star cut out of some gold paper in which chocolate had been wrapped. My maid Félicie, and Claude her husband, who were most devoted to me, had prepared some very ingenious little surprises. Presently there was a knock at my door, and on my calling out " Come in ! " I saw, to my surprise,

three sailors carrying a superb bouquet, which they presented to
me in the name of the whole crew.

I was wild with admiration, and wanted to know how they
had managed to keep the flowers in such good condition.

It was an enormous bouquet, but when I took it in my hands
I let it fall to the ground in an uncontrollable fit of laughter.
The flowers were all cut out of vegetables, but so perfectly done
that the illusion was complete at a little distance.   Magnificent
roses were cut out of carrots, camellias out of turnips, small
radishes had furnished sprays of rose-buds stuck on to long leeks
dyed green, and all these relieved by carrot leaves artistically
arranged to imitate the grassy plants used for elegant bouquets.
The stalks were tied together with a bow of tri-coloured ribbon.
One of the sailors made a very touching little speech on behalf
of his comrades, who wished to thank me for a trifling service
rendered.   I shook hands cordially and thanked them heartily,
and this was the signal for a little concert that had been organised
in the cabin of *mon petit Dame*.   There had been a private
rehearsal with two violins and a flute, so that for the next hour
I was lulled by the most delightful music, which transported me
to my own dear ones, to my home, which seemed so distant from
me at that moment.

This little *fête*, which was almost a domestic one, together
with the music, had evoked the tender and restful side of my
life, and the tears that all this called forth fell without grief,
bitterness, or regret.   I wept simply because I was deeply moved,
and I was tired, nervous, and weary, and had a longing for rest
and peace.   I fell asleep in the midst of my tears, sighs, and
sobs.

XXXIII

ARRIVAL IN NEW YORK—AMERICAN REPORTERS—THE
CUSTOM HOUSE—PERFORMANCES IN NEW YORK—
A VISIT TO EDISON AT MENLO PARK

FINALLY the ship arrived on October 27, at half-past six in
the morning. I was asleep, worn out by three days and nights
of wild storms. My maid had some difficulty in rousing me. I
could not believe that we had arrived, and I wanted to go on
sleeping until the last minute. I had to give in to the evidence,
however, as the screw had stopped, and I heard a sound of dull
thuds echoing in the distance. I put my head out of my port-
hole, and saw some men endeavouring to make a passage for us
through the river. The Hudson was frozen hard, and the heavy
vessel could only advance with the aid of pick-axes cutting away
the blocks of ice.

This sudden arrival delighted me, and everything seemed to
be transformed in a minute. I forgot all my discomforts and
the weariness of the twelve days' crossing. The sun was rising,
pale but rose-tinted, dispersing the mists and shining over the
ice, which, thanks to the efforts of our pioneers, was splintered
into a thousand luminous pieces. I had entered the New World
in the midst of a display of ice-fireworks. It was fairy-like and
somewhat crazy, but it seemed to me that it must be a good
omen.

I am so superstitious that if I had arrived when there was no
sunshine I should have been wretched and most anxious until
after my first performance. It is a perfect torture to be superstitious to this degree, and, unfortunately for me, I am ten times
more so now than I was in those days, for besides the superstitions of my own country, I have, thanks to my travels, added to
my stock all the superstitions of the other countries. I know

them all now, and in any critical moment of my life they all rise
up in armed legions, for or against me. I cannot walk a single
step or make any movement or gesture, sit down, go out, look
at the sky or the ground, without finding some reason for hope
or for despair, until at last, exasperated by the trammels put
upon my actions by my thought, I defy all my superstitions and
just act as I want to act. Delighted, then, with what seemed to
me to be a good omen, I began to dress gleefully.

Mr. Jarrett had just knocked at my door.

" Do please be ready as soon as possible, Madame," he said,
" for there are several boats, with the French colours flying, that
have come out to meet you."

I glanced in the direction of my port-hole, and saw a steamer,
the deck of which was black with people, and then two other
small boats no less laden than the first one.

The sun lighted up all these French flags, and my heart began
to beat more quickly.

I had been without any news for twelve days, as, in spite of
all the efforts of our good captain, L'Amerique had taken twelve
days for the journey.

A man had just come on deck, and I rushed towards him with
outstretched hands, unable to utter a single word.

He gave me a packet of telegrams. I did not see any one
present, and I heard no sound. I wanted to know something.
And among all the telegrams I was searching first for one, just
one name. At last I had it, the telegram I had waited for,
feared and hoped to receive, signed Maurice. Here it was at
last. I closed my eyes for a second, and during that time I
saw all that was dear to me and felt the infinite sweetness of it
all.

When I opened my eyes again I was slightly embarrassed, for
I was surrounded by a crowd of unknown people, all of them
silent and indulgent, but evidently very curious. Wishing to go
away, I took Mr. Jarrett's arm and went to the saloon. As soon
as I entered the first notes of the Marseillaise rang out, and our
Consul spoke a few words of welcome and handed me some
flowers. A group representing the French colony presented me
with a friendly address. Then M. Mercier, the editor of the
Courrier des Etats Unis, made a speech, as witty as it was
kindly. It was a thoroughly French speech. Then came the

terrible moment of introductions. Oh, what a tiring time that was! My mind was kept at a tension to catch the names. Mr. Pemb——, Madame Harth——, with the *h* aspirated. With great difficulty I grasped the first syllable, and the second finished in a confusion of muffled vowels and hissing consonants. By the time the twentieth name was pronounced I had given up listening; I simply kept on with my little *risorius de Santorini*, half closed my eyes, held out mechanically the arm at the end of which was the hand that had to shake and be shaken. I replied all the time: "*Combien je suis charmée, Madame. . . . Oh! Certainement . . . Oh oui! . . . Oh non! . . . Ah! . . . Oh! . . . Oh! . . .*" I was getting dazed, idiotic — worn out with standing. I had only one idea, and that was to get my rings off the fingers that were swelling with the repeated grips they were enduring. My eyes were getting larger and larger with terror as they gazed at the door through which the crowd continued to stream in my direction. There were still the names of all these peeple to hear and all these hands to shake. My *risorius de Santorini* must still go on working more than fifty times. I could feel the beads of perspiration standing out under my hair, and I began to get terribly nervous. My teeth chattered and I commenced stammering: "*Oh, Madame! . . . Oh! . . . Je suis cha —— cha ——*" I really could not go on any longer. I felt that I should get angry or burst out crying—in fact, that I was about to make myself ridiculous. I decided therefore to faint. I made a movement with my hand as though it wanted to continue but could not. I opened my mouth, closed my eyes, and fell gently into Jarrett's arms. "Quick! Air! . . . A doctor! . . . Poor thing. . . . How pale she is! Take her hat off! . . . Loosen her corset! . . . She doesn't wear one. Unfasten her dress! . . ." I was terrified, but Félicie was called up in haste, and *mon petit Dame* would not allow any *deshabillage*. The doctor came back with a bottle of ether. Félicie seized the bottle.

"Oh no, doctor—not ether! When Madame is quite well the odour of ether will make her faint."

This was quite true, and I thought it was time to come to my senses again. The reporters were arriving, and there were more than twenty of them; but Jarrett, who was very much affected,

asked them to go to the Albemarle Hotel, where I was to put up.
I saw each of the reporters take Jarrett aside, and when I asked
him what the secret was of all these " asides," he answered
phlegmatically, " I have made an appointment with them for
one o'clock. There will be a fresh one every ten minutes." I
looked at him, petrified with astonishment. He met my anxious
gaze and said :

" *Ah oui ; il était nécessaire.*"

On arriving at the Albemarle Hotel I felt tired and nervous,
and wanted to be left quite alone. I hurried away at once to
my room in the suite that had been engaged for me, and
fastened the doors. There was neither lock nor bolt on one of
them, but I pushed a piece of furniture against it, and then
refused emphatically to open it. There were about fifty people
waiting in the drawing-room, but I had that feeling of awful
weariness which makes one ready to go to the most violent
extremes for the sake of an hour's repose. I wanted to lie
down on the rug, cross my arms, throw my head back, and close
my eyes. I did not want to talk any more, and I did not want
to have to smile or look at any one. I threw myself down
on the floor, and was deaf to the knocks on my door and to
Jarrett's supplications. I did not want to argue the matter, so
I did not utter a word. I heard the murmur of grumbling
voices, and Jarrett's words tactfully persuading the visitors to
stay. I heard the rustle of paper being pushed under the door,
and Madame Guérard whispering to Jarrett, who was furious.

" You don't know her, Monsieur Jarrett," I heard her say.
" If she thought you were forcing the door open, against which
she has pushed the furniture, she would jump out of the
window ! "

Then I heard Félicie talking to a French lady who was
insisting on seeing me.

" It is quite impossible," she was saying. " Madame would
be quite hysterical. She needs an hour's rest, and every one
must wait ! "

For some little time I could hear a confused murmur which
seemed to get farther away, and then I fell into a delicious
sleep, laughing to myself as I went off, for my good temper
returned as I pictured the angry, nonplussed expression on the
faces of my visitors.

I woke in an hour's time, for I have the precious gift of being able to sleep ten minutes, a quarter of an hour, or an hour, just as I like, and I then wake up quite peacefully without a shake at the time I choose to rouse up. Nothing does me so much good as this rest to body and mind, decided upon and regulated merely by my will.

Very often when among my intimate friends I have lain down on the bear-skin hearth-rug in front of the fire, telling every one to go on talking, and to take no notice of me. I have then slept perhaps for an hour, and on waking have found two or three new-comers in the room, who, not wishing to disturb me. have taken part in the general conversation whilst waiting until I should wake up and they could present their respects to me. Even now I lie down on the huge wide sofa in the little Empire *salon* which leads into my dressing-room, and I sleep whilst waiting for the friends and artistes with whom I have made appointments to be ushered in. When I open my eyes I see the faces of my kind friends, who shake hands cordially, delighted that I should have had some rest. My mind is then tranquil, and I am ready to listen to all the beautiful ideas proposed to me, or to decline the absurdities submitted to me without being ungracious.

I woke up then at the Albemarle Hotel an hour later, and found myself lying on the rug. I opened the door of my room, and discovered my dear Guérard and my faithful Félicie seated on a trunk.

" Are there any people there still ? " I asked.

" Oh, Madame, there are about a hundred now," answered Félicie.

" Help me to take my things off then quickly," I said, " and find me a white dress."

In about five minutes I was ready, and I felt that I looked nice from head to foot. I went into the drawing-room where all these unknown persons were waiting. Jarrett came forward to meet me, but on seeing me well dressed and with a smiling face he postponed the sermon that he wanted to preach to me.

I should like to introduce Jarrett to my readers, for he was a most extraordinary man. He was then about sixty-five or seventy years of age. He was tall, with a face like King Agamemnon, framed by the most beautiful silver-white hair I

have ever seen on a man's head.   His eyes were of so pale a blue
that when they lighted up with anger he looked as though he
were blind.   When he was calm and tranquil, admiring nature,
his face was really handsome, but when gay and animated his
upper lip showed his teeth and curled up in a most ferocious
sniff, and his grins seemed to be caused by the drawing up of his
pointed ears, which were always moving as though on the watch
for prey.

He was a terrible man, extremely intelligent ; but from childhood he must have been fighting with the world, and he had the
most profound contempt for all mankind.   Although he must
have suffered a great deal himself, he had no pity for others who
suffered.   He always said that every man was armed for his own
defence.   He pitied women ; did not care for them, but was
always ready to help them.   He was very rich and very economical, but not miserly.

"I made my way in life," he often said to me, "by the aid of
two weapons : honesty and a revolver.   In business honesty is
the most terrible weapon a man can use against rascals and crafty
people.   The former don't know what it is and the latter don't
believe in it ; while the revolver is an admirable invention for
compelling scoundrels to keep their word."

He used to tell me about wonderful and terrifying adventures.

He had a deep scar under his right eye.   During a violent
discussion about a contract to be signed for Jenny Lind, the
celebrated singer, Jarrett said to his interlocutor, pointing at the
same time to his right eye : "Look at that eye, sir.   It is now
reading in your mind all that you are not saying."

"It doesn't know how to read, then, for it never foresaw that,"
said the other, firing his revolver at Jarrett's right eye.

"A bad shot, sir," replied Jarrett.   "This is the way to take
aim for effectually closing an eye."

And he put a ball between the two eyes of the other man, who
fell down dead.

When Jarrett told this story his lip curled up and his two
incisors appeared to be crunching the words with delight, and
his bursts of stifled laughter sounded like the snapping of his
jaws.   He was an upright, honest man, though, and I liked him
very much, and I like what I remember of him.

My first impression was a joyful one, and I clapped my hands

with delight as I entered the drawing-room, which I had not yet
seen. The busts of Racine, Molière, and Victor Hugo were on
pedestals surrounded with flowers. All round the large room
were sofas laden with cushions, and, to remind me of my home
in Paris, there were tall palms stretching out their branches over
the sofas. Jarrett introduced Knoedler, who had suggested this
piece of gallantry. He was a very charming man. I shook
hands with him, and we were friends from that time forth.

The visitors soon went away, but the reporters remained.
They were all seated, some of them on the arms of the chairs,
others on the cushions. One of them had crouched down tailor-
fashion on a bear-skin. and was leaning back against the steam
heater. He was pale and thin, and coughed a great deal. I
went towards him, and had just opened my lips to speak to him,
although I was rather shocked that he did not rise, when he
addressed me in a bass voice.

" Which is your favourite *rôle*, Madame ? " he asked.

" That is no concern of yours," I answered, turning my back
on him. In doing so I knocked against another reporter, who
was more polite.

" What do you eat when you wake in the morning, Madame ? "
he inquired.

I was about to reply to him as I had done to the first one, but
Jarrett, who had had difficulty in appeasing the anger of the
crouching man, answered quickly for me, " Oatmeal." I did not
know what that dish was, but the ferocious reporter continued
his questions.

" And what do you eat during the day ? "

" Mussels."

He wrote down phlegmatically, " Mussels during the day."

I moved towards the door, and a female reporter in a tailor-
made skirt, with her hair cut short, asked me in a clear, sweet
voice, " Are you a Jewess-Catholic-Protestant-Mohammedan-
Buddhist-Atheist-Zoroaster-Theist-or-Deist ? " I stood still, rooted
to the spot in bewilderment. She had said all that in a breath,
accenting the syllables haphazard, and making of the whole one
word so wildly incoherent that my impression was that I was not
in safety near this strange, gentle person. I must have looked
uneasy, and as my eyes fell on an elderly lady who was talking
gaily to a little group of people, she came to my rescue, saying

in very good French, " This young lady is asking you, Madame, whether you are of the Jewish religion or whether you are a Catholic, a Protestant, a Mohammedan, a Buddhist, an Atheist, a Zoroastrian, a Theist, or a Deist."

I sank down on a couch.

" Oh, Heavens ! " I exclaimed, " will it be like this in all the cities I visit ? "

" Oh no," answered Jarrett placidly ; " your interviews will be wired throughout America."

" What about the mussels ? " I thought to myself, and then in an absent-minded way I answered, " I am a Catholic, Mademoiselle."

" A Roman Catholic, or do you belong to the Orthodox Church ? " she asked.

I jumped up from my seat, for she bored me beyond en-durance, and a very young man then approached timidly.

" Will you allow me to finish my sketch, Madame ? " he asked.

I remained standing, my profile turned towards him at his request.   When he had finished I asked to see what he had done, and, perfectly unabashed, he handed me his horrible drawing of a skeleton with a curly wig.   I tore the sketch up and threw it at him, but the following day that horror appeared in the papers, with a disagreeable inscription beneath it. Fortunately I was able to speak seriously about my art with a few honest and intelligent journalists, but twenty-five years ago reporters' paragraphs were more appreciated in America than serious articles, and the public, very much less literary then than at present, always seemed ready to echo the turpitudes invented by reporters hard up for copy. I should think that no creature in the world, since the invention of reporting, has ever had as much to endure as I had during that first tour. The basest calumnies were circulated by my enemies long before I arrived in America, there was all the treachery of the friends of the Comédie, and even of my own admirers, who hoped that I should not succeed on my tour, so that I might re-turn more quickly to the fold, humiliated, calmed down, and subdued.   Then there were the exaggerated announcements invented by my *impresario* Abbey and my representative Jarrett.   These announcements were often outrageous and always ridiculous; but I did not know their real source until long afterwards, when it was too late—much too late—to undeceive the public, who were fully persuaded that I was the instigator of all these inventions. I therefore did not attempt to undeceive them. It matters very little to me whether people believe one thing or another.

Life is short, even for those who live a long time, and we must live for the few who know and appreciate us, who judge and absolve us, and for whom we have the same affection and indulgence. The rest I look upon as a mere crowd, lively or sad, loyal or corrupt, from whom there is nothing to be expected but fleeting emotions, either pleasant or unpleasant, which leave no trace behind them. We ought to hate very rarely, as it is too fatiguing; remain indifferent to a great deal, forgive often and never forget. Forgiving does not mean forgetting—at least, it does not with me. I will not mention here any of the outrageous and infamous attacks that were made upon me, as it would be doing too great an honour to the wretched people who were responsible for them, from beginning to end dipping their pen in the gall of their own souls. All I can say is that nothing kills but death, and that any one who wishes to defend himself or herself from slander can do it. For that one must live. It is not given to every one to be able to do it, but it depends on the will of God, who sees and judges.

I took two days' rest before going to the theatre, for I could feel the movement of the ship all the time: my head was dizzy, and it seemed to me as though the ceiling moved up and down. The twelve days on the sea had quite upset my health. I sent a line to the stage manager, telling him that we would rehearse on Wednesday, and on that day, as soon as luncheon was over, I went to Booth's Theatre, where our performances were to take place. At the stage-door I saw a compact, swaying crowd, very much animated and gesticulating. These strange-looking individuals did not belong to the world of actors. They were not reporters either, for I knew them too well, alas! to be mistaken in them. They were not there out of curiosity either, these people, for they seemed too much occupied, and then, too, there were only men. When my carriage drew up, one of them rushed

2 A

forward to the door of it and then returned to the swaying
crowd. "Here she is! Here she is!" I heard, and then all these
common men, with their white neckties and questionable-looking
hands, with their coats flying open, and trousers the knees of
which were worn and dirty-looking, crowded behind me into
the narrow passage leading to the staircase. I did not feel very
easy in my mind, and I mounted the stairs rapidly. Several
persons were waiting for me at the top : Mr. Abbey, Jarrett, and
also some reporters, two gentlemen and a charming and most
distinguished woman, whose friendship I have kept ever since,
although she does not care much for French people. I saw
Mr. Abbey, who was usually very dignified and cold, advance in
the most gracious and courteous way to one of the men who
were following me. They raised their hats to each other, and,
followed by the strange and brutal-looking regiment, they
advanced towards the centre of the stage.

I then saw the strangest of sights. In the middle of the
stage were my forty-two trunks. In obedience to a sign,
twenty of the men came forward, and placing themselves each
one between two trunks, with a quick movement with their
right and left hands they took the covers off the trunks on the
right and left of them. Jarrett, with frowns and an unpleasant
grin, held out my keys to them. He had asked me that morning
for my keys for the Customs.

"Oh, it's nothing," he said ; "don't be uneasy," and the
way in which my luggage had always been respected in other
countries had given me perfect confidence about it.

The principal personage of the ugly group came towards me,
accompanied by Abbey, and Jarrett explained things to me.
The man was an official from the American Custom-house.

The Custom-house is an abominable institution in every
country, but worse in America than anywhere else. I was
prepared for all this, and was most affable to the tormentor of a
traveller's patience. He raised the melon which served him for
a hat, and without taking his cigar out of his mouth made some
incomprehensible remark to me. He then turned to his regiment
of men, made an abrupt sign with his hand, and uttered some
word of command, whereupon the forty dirty hands of these
twenty men proceeded to forage among my velvets, satins, and
laces. I rushed forward to save my poor dresses from such out-

rageous violation, and I ordered the lady of our company who
had charge of the costumes to lift my gowns out one at a time,
which she accordingly did, aided by my maid, who was in tears
at the small amount of respect shown by these boors to all my
beautiful, fragile things. Two ladies had just arrived, very
noisy and businesslike. One of them was short and stout: her
nose seemed to begin at the roots of her hair; she had round,
placid-looking eyes, and a mouth like a snout; her arms she was
hiding timidly behind her heavy flabby bust, and her ungainly
knees seemed to come straight out of her groin. She looked
like a seated cow. Her companion was like a terrapin, with her
little black evil-looking head at the end of a neck which was too
long and very stringy. She kept shooting it out of her boa
and drawing it back with the most incredible rapidity. The
rest of her body bulged out flat. These two delightful persons
were the dressmakers sent for by the Custom-house to value
my costumes. They glanced at me in a furtive way, and gave
a little bow full of bitterness and jealous rage at the sight of
my dresses; and I was quite aware that two more enemies had
now come upon the scene. These two odious shrews began to
chatter and argue, pawing and crumpling my dresses and cloaks
at the same time. They kept exclaiming in the most emphatic
way, "Oh, how beautiful! What magnificence! What luxury!
All our customers will want gowns like these, and we shall never
be able to make them! It will be the ruin of all the American
dressmakers." They were working up the judges into a state of
excitement for this chiffon court-martial. They kept lamenting,
then going into raptures and asking for "justice" against
foreign invasion. The ugly band of men nodded their heads in
approval, and spat on the ground to affirm their independence.
Suddenly the Terrapin turned on one of the inquisitors:

"Oh, isn't it beautiful? Show it! show it!" she exclaimed,
seizing on a dress all embroidered with pearls, which I wore in
La Dame aux Camélias.

"This dress is worth at least ten thousand dollars," she said;
and then, coming up to me, she asked, "How much did you pay
for that dress, Madame?"

I ground my teeth together and would not answer, for just at
that moment I should have enjoyed seeing the Terrapin in one
of the saucepans in the Albemarle Hotel kitchen. It was nearly

half-past five, and my feet were frozen. I was half dead, too, with fatigue and suppressed anger. The rest of the examination was postponed until the next day, and the ugly band of men offered to put everything back in the trunks, but I objected to that. I sent out for five hundred yards of blue tarletan to cover over the mountain of dresses, hats, cloaks, shoes, laces, linen, stockings, furs, gloves, &c. &c. They then made me take my oath to remove nothing, for they had such charming confidence in me, and I left my steward there in charge. He was the husband of Félicie, my maid, and a bed was put up for him on the stage. I was so nervous and upset that I wanted to go somewhere far away, to have some fresh air, and to stay out for a long time. A friend offered to take me to see Brooklyn Bridge.

"That masterpiece of American genius will make you forget the petty miseries of our red tape affairs," he said gently, and so we set out for Brooklyn Bridge.

Oh, that bridge! It is insane, admirable, imposing; and it makes one feel proud. Yes, one is proud to be a human being when one realises that a brain has created and suspended in the air, fifty yards from the ground, that fearful thing which bears a dozen trains filled with passengers, ten or twelve tramcars, a hundred cabs, carriages, and carts, and thousands of foot passengers; and all that moving along together amidst the uproar of the music of the metals—clanging, clashing, grating, and groaning under the enormous weight of people and things. The movement of the air caused by this frightful tempestuous coming and going caused me to feel giddy and stopped my breath.

I made a sign for the carriage to stand still, and I closed my eyes. I then had a strange, undefinable sensation of universal chaos. I opened my eyes again when my brain was a little more tranquil, and I saw New York stretching out along the river, wearing its night ornaments, which glittered as much through its dress with thousands of electric lights as the firmament with its tunic of stars.

I returned to the hotel reconciled with this great nation.

I went to sleep, tired in body but rested in mind, and had such delightful dreams that I was in a good humour the following day. I adore dreams, and my sad, unhappy days are those which follow dreamless nights.

My great grief is that I cannot choose my dreams. How

many times I have done all in my power at the end of a happy day to make myself dream a continuation of it. How many times I have called up the faces of those I love just before falling asleep; but my thoughts wander and carry me off elsewhere, and I prefer that a hundred times over to the absolute negation of thought.

When I am asleep my body has an infinite sense of enjoyment, but it is torture to me for my thoughts to slumber.

My vital forces rebel against such negation of life. I am quite willing to die once for all, but I object to slight deaths such as those of which one has the sensation on dreamless nights. When I awoke my maid told me that Jarrett was waiting for me to go to the theatre so that the valuation of my costumes could be terminated. I sent word to Jarrett that I had seen quite enough of the regiment from the Custom-house, and I asked him to finish everything without me, as Madame Guérard would be there. During the next two days the Terrapin, the Seated Cow, and the Black Band made notes for the Custom-house, took sketches for the papers and patterns of my dresses for customers. I began to get impatient, as we ought to have been rehearsing. Finally, I was told on Thursday morning that the business was over, and that I could not have my trunks until I had paid twenty-eight thousand francs for duty. I was seized with such a violent fit of laughing that poor Abbey, who had been terrified, caught it from me, and even Jarrett showed his cruel teeth.

" My dear Abbey," I exclaimed, " arrange as you like about it, but I must make my *début* on Monday the 8th of November, and to-day is Thursday. I shall be at the theatre on Monday to dress. See that I have my trunks, for there was nothing about the Custom-house in my contract. I will pay half, though, of what you have to give."

The twenty-eight thousand francs were handed over to an attorney who made a claim in my name on the Board of Customs. My trunks were left with me, thanks to this payment, and the rehearsals commenced at Booth's Theatre.

On Monday, November 8, at 8.30, the curtain rose for the first performance of *Adrienne Lecouvreur*. The house was crowded, and the seats, which had been sold to the highest bidders and then sold by them again, had fetched exorbitant prices. I was awaited with impatience and curiosity, but not with any sympathy. There were no young girls present, as the piece was too immoral. Poor Adrienne Lecouvreur!

The audience was very polite to the artistes of my company, but rather impatient to see the strange person who had been described to them.

In the play the curtain falls at the end of the first act without Adrienne having appeared. A person in the house, very much annoyed, asked to see Mr. Henry Abbey. "I want my money back," he said, " as la Bernhardt is not in every act." Abbey refused to return the money to the extraordinary individual, and as the curtain was going up he hurried back to take possession of his seat again. My appearance was greeted by several rounds of applause, which I believe had been paid for in advance by Abbey and Jarrett. I commenced, and the sweetness of my voice in the fable of the " Two Pigeons" worked the miracle. The whole house this time burst out into hurrahs. A current of sympathy was established between the public and myself. Instead of the hysterical skeleton that had been announced to them, they had before them a very frail-looking creature with a sweet voice. The fourth act was applauded, and Adrienne's rebellion against the Princesse de Bouillon stirred the whole house. Finally in the fifth act, when the unfortunate artiste is dying, poisoned by her rival, there was quite a manifestation, and every one was deeply moved. At the end of the third act all the young men were sent off by the ladies to find all the musicians they could get together, and to my surprise and delight on arriving at my hotel a charming serenade was played for me while I was at supper. The crowd had assembled under my windows at the Albemarle Hotel, and I was obliged to go out on to the balcony several times to bow and to thank this public, which I had been told I should find cold and prejudiced against me. From the bottom of my heart I also thanked all my detractors and slanderers, as it was through them that I had had the pleasure of fighting, with the certainty of conquering. The victory was all the more enjoyable as I had not dared to hope for it.

I gave twenty-seven performances in New York. The plays were *Adrienne Lecouvreur, Froufrou, Hernani, La Dame aux Camélias, Le Sphinx,* and *L'Etrangère.* The average receipts were 20,342 francs for each performance, including *matinées*. The last performance was given on Saturday, December 4, as a *matinée*, for my company had to leave that night for Boston, and I had reserved the evening to go to Mr. Edison's at Menlo Park, where I had a reception worthy of fairyland.

Oh, that *matinée* of Saturday, December 4! I can never forget it. When I got to the theatre to dress it was mid-day, for the *matinée* was to commence at half-past one. My carriage stopped, not being able to get along, for the street was filled by ladies, sitting on chairs which they had borrowed from the neighbouring shops, or on folding seats which they had brought themselves. The play was *La Dame aux Camélias*. I had to get out of my carriage and walk about twenty-five yards on foot in order to get to the stage door. It took me twenty-five minutes to do it. People shook my hands and begged me to come back. One lady took off her brooch and pinned it in my mantle—a modest brooch of amethysts surrounded by fine pearls, but certainly for the giver the brooch had its value. I was stopped at every step. One lady pulled out her note-book and begged me to write my name. The idea took like lightning. Small boys under the care of their parents wanted me to write my name on their cuffs. My arms were full of small bouquets which had been pushed into my hands. I felt behind me some one tugging at the feather in my hat. I turned round sharply. A woman with a pair of scissors in her hand had tried to cut off a lock of my hair, but she only succeeded in cutting the feather out of my hat. In vain Jarrett signalled and shouted. I could not get along. They sent for the police, who delivered me, but without any ceremony either for my admirers or for myself. Those policemen were real brutes, and they made me very angry. I played *La Dame aux Camélias*, and I counted seventeen calls after the third act and twenty-nine after the fifth. In consequence of the cheering and calls the play had lasted an hour longer than usual, and I was half dead with fatigue. I was just about to go to my carriage to get back to my hotel, when Jarrett came to tell me that there were more than 50,000 people waiting outside. I fell back on a chair, tired and disheartened.

"Oh, I will wait till the crowd has dispersed. I am tired out I can do no more,"

But Henry Abbey had an inspiration of genius.

"Come," said he to my sister. "Put on Madame's hat and boa and take my arm. And take also these bouquets—give me what you cannot carry. And now we will go to your sister's carriage and make our bow."

He said all this in English, and Jarrett translated it to my sister, who willingly accepted her part in this little comedy. During this time Jarrett and I got into Abbey's carriage, which was stationed in front of the theatre where no one was waiting. And it was fortunate we took this course, for my sister only got back to the Albemarle Hotel an hour later, very tired, but very much amused. Her resemblance to myself, my hat, my boa, and the darkness of night had been the accomplices of the little comedy which we had offered to my enthusiastic public.

We had to set out at nine o'clock for Menlo Park. We had to dress in travelling costume, for the following day we were to leave for Boston, and my trunks were leaving the same day with my company, which preceded me by several hours.

Our meal was, as usual, very bad, for in those days in America the food was unspeakably awful. At ten o'clock we took the train—a pretty special train, all decorated with flowers and banners, which they had been kind enough to prepare for me. But it was a painful journey all the same, for at every moment we had to pull up to allow another train to pass or an engine to manœuvre, or to wait to pass over the points. It was two o'clock in the morning when the train at last reached the station of Menlo Park, the residence of Thomas Edison.

It was a very dark night, and the snow was falling silently in heavy flakes. A carriage was waiting, and the one lamp of this carriage served to light up the whole station, for orders had been given that the electric lights should be put out. I found my way with the help of Jarrett and some of my friends who had accompanied us from New York. The intense cold froze the snow as it fell, and we walked over veritable blocks of sharp, jagged ice, which crackled under our feet. Behind the first carriage was another heavier one, with only one horse and no lamp. There was room for five or six persons to crowd into this. We were ten in all. Jarrett, Abbey, my sister, and I took our places in the first one, leaving the others to get into the second. We looked like a band of conspirators. The dark night,

the two mysterious carriages, the silence caused by the icy coldness, the way in which we were muffled in our furs, and our
anxious expression as we glanced around us—all this made our
visit to the celebrated Edison resemble a scene out of an
operetta.

The carriage rolled along, sinking deep into the snow and
jolting terribly; the jolts made us dread every instant some
tragi-comic accident.

I cannot tell how long we had been rolling along, for, lulled by
the movement of the carriage and buried in my warm furs, I was
quietly dozing, when a formidable " Hip, hip, hurrah ! " made us
all jump, my travelling companions, the coachman, the horse,
and I. As quick as thought the whole country was suddenly
illuminated. Under the trees, on the trees, among the bushes,
along the garden walks, lights flashed forth triumphantly.

The wheels of the carriage turned a few more times, and then
drew up at the house of the famous Thomas Edison. A group
of people awaited us on the verandah—four men, two ladies,
and a young girl. My heart began to beat quickly as I
wondered which of these men was Edison. I had never seen
his photograph, and I had the greatest admiration for his genial
brain. I sprang out of the carriage, and the dazzling electric
light made it seem like day-time to us. I took the bouquet which
Mrs. Edison offered me, and thanked her for it, but all the time
I was endeavouring to discover which of these was the great
man.

They all four advanced towards me, but I noticed the flush
that came into the face of one of them, and it was so evident
from the expression of his blue eyes that he was intensely bored
that I guessed this was Edison. I felt confused and embarrassed
myself, for I knew very well that I was causing inconvenience to
this man by my visit. He of course imagined that it was due
to the idle curiosity of a foreigner eager to court publicity. He
was no doubt thinking of the interviewing in store for him the
following day, and of the stupidities he would be made to utter.
He was suffering beforehand at the idea of the ignorant
questions I should ask him, of all the explanations he would
out of politeness be obliged to give me, and at that moment
Thomas Edison took a dislike to me. His wonderful blue eyes,
more luminous than his incandescent lamps, enabled me to read

his thoughts. I immediately understood that he must be won over, and my combative instinct had recourse to all my powers of fascination in order to vanquish this delightful but bashful *savant*. I made such an effort, and succeeded so well that half an hour later we were the best of friends.

I followed him about quickly, climbing up staircases as narrow and steep as ladders, crossing bridges suspended in the air above veritable furnaces, and he explained everything to me. I understood all, and I admired him more and more, for he was so simple and charming, this king of light.

As we were leaning over a slightly unsteady bridge above the terrible abyss, in which immense wheels encased in wide thongs were turning, whirling about, and rumbling, he gave various orders in a clear voice, and light then burst forth on all sides, sometimes in sputtering greenish jets, sometimes in quick flashes, or in serpentine trails like streams of fire. I looked at this man of medium size, with rather a large head and a noble-looking profile, and I thought of Napoleon I. There is certainly a great physical resemblance between these two men, and I am sure that one compartment of their brain would be found to be identical. Of course I do not compare their genius. The one was destructive and the other creative, but whilst I execrate battles I adore victories, and in spite of his errors I have raised an altar in my heart to that god of glory, Napoleon! I therefore looked at Edison thoughtfully, for he reminded me of the great man who was dead. The deafening sound of the machinery, the dazzling rapidity of the changes of light, all that together made my head whirl, and forgetting where I was, I leaned for support on the slight balustrade which separated me from the abyss beneath. I was so unconscious of all danger that before I had recovered from my surprise Edison had helped me into an adjoining room and installed me in an arm-chair without my realising how it had all happened. He told me afterwards that I had turned dizzy.

After having done the honours of his telephonic discovery and of his astonishing phonograph, Edison offered me his arm and took me to the dining-room, where I found his family assembled. I was very tired, and did justice to the supper that had been so hospitably prepared for us.

I left Menlo Park at four o'clock in the morning, and the

time the country round, the roads and the station were all lighted up *à giorno*, by the thousands of lamps of my kind host. What a strange power of suggestion the darkness has! I thought I had travelled a long way that night, and it seemed to me that the roads were impracticable. It proved to be quite a short distance, and the roads were charming, although they were now covered with snow. Imagination had played a great part during the journey to Edison's house, but reality played a much greater one during the same journey back to the station. I was enthusiastic in my admiration of the inventions of this man, and I was charmed with his timid graciousness and perfect courtesy, and with his profound love of Shakespeare.

XXXIV

AT BOSTON—STORY OF THE WHALE

THE next day, or rather that same day, for it was then four in the morning, I started with my company for Boston. Mr. Abbey, my *impresario*, had arranged for me to have a delightful " car," but it was nothing like the wonderful Pullman car that I was to have from Philadelphia for continuing my tour. I was very much pleased with this one, nevertheless. In the middle of it there was a real bed, large and comfortable, on a brass bedstead. Then there were an arm-chair, a pretty dressing-table, a basket tied up with ribbons for my dog, and flowers everywhere, but flowers without an overpowering perfume. In the car adjoining mine were my own servants, who were also very comfortable. I went to bed feeling thoroughly satisfied, and woke up at Boston.

A large crowd was assembled at the station. There were reporters and curious men and women—a public decidedly more interested than friendly, not badly intentioned, but by no means enthusiastic. Public opinion in New York had been greatly occupied with me during the past month. I had been so much criticised and glorified. Calumnies of all kinds, stupid and disgusting, foolish and odious, had been circulated about me. Some people blamed and others admired the disdain with which I had treated these turpitudes, but every one knew that I had won in the end and that I had triumphed over all and everything. Boston knew, too, that clergymen had preached from their pulpits saying that I had been sent by the Old World to corrupt the New World, that my art was an inspiration from hell, &c. &c. Every one knew all this, but the public wanted to see for itself. Boston belongs especially to the women. Tradition says that it was a woman who first set foot in

The carriage drew up, and without any further ceremony he jumped down and pushed into my landau a little man, square all over, who was wearing a fur cap pulled down over his eyes, and an enormous diamond in his cravat. He was the strangest type of the old-fashioned Yankee. He did not speak a word of French, but he took his seat calmly by Jarrett, whilst the reporter remained half sitting and half hanging on to the vehicle. There had been three of us when we started from the station, and we were five when we reached the Hotel Vendome. There were a great many people awaiting my arrival, and I was quite ashamed of my new companion. He talked in a loud voice, laughed, coughed, spat, addressed every one, and gave every one invitations. All the people seemed to be delighted. A little girl threw her arms round her father's neck, exclaiming, "Oh yes, papa ; do please let us go ! "

"Well, but we must ask Madame," he replied, and he came up to me in the most polite and courteous manner. "Will you kindly allow us to join your party when you go to see the whale to-morrow ? " he asked.

"But, Monsieur," I answered, delighted to have to do with a gentleman once more, "I have no idea what all this means. For the last quarter of an hour this reporter and that extraordinary man have been talking about a whale. They declare authoritatively that I must go and pay it a visit, and I know absolutely nothing about it all. These two gentlemen took my carriage by storm ; installed themselves in it without my permission, and, as you see, are giving invitations in my name to people I do not know, asking them to go with me to a place about which I know nothing, for the purpose of paying a visit to a whale which is to be introduced to me, and which is waiting impatiently to die in peace."

The kindly disposed gentleman signed to his daughter to come with us, and, accompanied by them, and by Jarrett and Madame Guérard, I went up in a lift to the door of my suite of rooms. I found my apartments hung with valuable pictures and full of magnificent statues. I felt rather disturbed in my mind, for among these objects of art were two or three very rare and beautiful things, which I knew must have cost an exorbitant price. I was afraid lest any of them should be stolen, and I spoke of my fear to the proprietor of the hotel.

" Mr. X., to whom the knick-knacks belong," he answered, " wished you to have them to look at as long as you are here, Mademoiselle; and when I expressed my anxiety about them to him, just as you have done to me, he merely remarked that 'it was all the same to him.' As to the pictures, they belong to two wealthy Bostonians." There was among them a superb Millet, which I should very much have liked to own.

After expressing my gratitude and admiring these treasures, I asked for an explanation of the story of the whale, and Mr. Max Gordon, the father of the little girl, translated for me what the little man in the fur cap had said. It appeared that he owned several fishing-boats, which he sent out cod-fishing for his own benefit. One of these boats had captured an enormous whale, which still had two harpoons in it. The poor creature was thoroughly exhausted with its struggles, and only a few miles distant along the coast, so it had been easy to capture it and bring it in triumph to Henry Smith, the owner of the boats. It was difficult to say by what freak of fancy and by what turn of the imagination this man had arrived at associating in his mind the idea of the whale and my name as a source of wealth. I could not understand it, but the fact remained that he insisted in such a droll way, and so authoritatively and energetically, that the following morning at seven o'clock fifty of us assembled, in spite of the icy cold rain, on the quay.

Mr. Gordon had given orders that his mail coach with four beautiful horses should be in readiness. He drove himself, and his daughter, Jarrett, my sister, Madame Guérard, and another elderly lady, whose name I have forgotten, were with us. Seven other carriages followed. It was all very amusing indeed.

On our arrival at the quay we were received by this comic Henry, shaggy-looking this time from head to foot, and his hands encased in fingerless woollen gloves. Only his eyes and his huge diamond shone out from his furs. I walked along the quay, very much amused and interested. There were a few idlers looking on also, and alas!—three times over alas!—there were reporters.

Henry's shaggy paw then seized my hand, and he drew me along with him quickly to the steps.

I only just escaped breaking my neck at least a dozen times. He pushed me along, made me stumble down the ten steps of the basin, and I next found myself on the back of the whale. They assured me that it still breathed, but I should not like to affirm that it really did; but the splashing of the water breaking its eddy against the poor creature caused it to oscillate slightly. Then, too, it was covered with glazed frost, and twice I fell down full length on its spine. I laugh about it now, but I was furious then.

Every one around me insisted, however, on my pulling a piece of whalebone from the blade of the poor captured creature, one of those little bones which are used for women's corsets. I did not like to do this, as I feared to cause it suffering, and I was sorry for the poor thing, as three of us—Henry, the little Gordon girl, and I—had been skating about on its back for the last ten minutes. Finally I decided to do it. I pulled out the little whale bone, and went up the steps again, holding my poor trophy in my hand. I felt nervous and flustered, and every one surrounded me.

I was annoyed with this Henry Smith. I did not want to return to the coach, as I thought I could hide bad temper better in one of the huge, gloomy-looking landaus which followed, but the charming Miss Gordon asked me so sweetly why I would not ride with them that I felt my anger melt away before the child's smiling face.

"Would you like to drive?" her father asked me, and I accepted with pleasure.

Jarrett immediately proceeded to get down from the coach as quickly as his age and corpulence would allow him.

"If you are going to drive I prefer getting down," he said, and he took a seat in another carriage. I changed places boldly with Mr. Gordon in order to drive, and we had not gone a hundred yards before I had let the horses make for a chemist's shop along the quay and got the coach itself up on to the footpath, so that if it had not been for the quickness and energy of Mr. Gordon we should all have been killed. On arriving at the hotel I went to bed, and stayed there until it was time for the theatre in the evening. We played *Hernani* that night to a full house.

The seats had been sold to the highest bidders, and considerable prices were obtained for them. We gave fifteen performances at Boston, at an average of nineteen thousand francs for each performance. I was sorry to leave that city, as I had spent two charming weeks there, my mind all the time on the alert when holding conversations with the Boston women. They are Puritans from the crown of the head to the sole of the foot, but they are indulgent, and there is no bitterness about their Puritanism. What struck me most about the women of Boston was the harmony of their gestures and the softness of their voices. Brought up among the severest and harshest of traditions, the Bostonian race seems to me to be the most refined and the most mysterious of all the American races.

As the women are in the majority in Boston, many of the young girls remain unmarried. All their vital forces which they cannot expend in love and in maternity they employ in fortifying and making supple the beauty of their body by means of exercise and sports, without losing any of their grace. All the reserves of heart are expended in intellectuality. They adore music, the stage, literature, painting, and poetry. They know everything and understand everything, are chaste and reserved, and neither laugh nor talk very loud.

They are as far removed from the Latin race as the North Pole is from the South Pole, but they are interesting, delightful, and captivating.

It was therefore with a rather heavy heart that I left Boston for New Haven, and to my great surprise, on arriving at the hotel there I found Henry Smith the famous whale man.

" Oh, Heavens ! " I exclaimed, flinging myself into an armchair, " what does this man want now with me ? "

I was not left in ignorance very long, for the most infernal noise of brass instruments, drums, trumpets, and, I should think, saucepans, drew me to the window. I saw an immense carriage surrounded by an escort of negroes dressed as minstrels. On this carriage was an abominable, monstrous coloured advertisement representing me standing on the whale, tearing away its blade while it struggled to defend itself.

Some sandwich-men followed with posters on which were written the following words :

"Come and see
the enormous cetacean
which
Sarah Bernhardt
killed
by tearing out its whalebone for her corsets.
These are made by Madame Lily Noe,
who lives," etc. etc.

Some of the other sandwich-men carried posters with these
words :

"The whale is just as flourishing (*sic*) as
when it was alive !

It has five hundred dollars' worth of salt in its stomach,
and every day the ice upon which it is resting is
renewed at a cost of one hundred dollars ! "

My face turned more livid than that of a corpse, and my teeth
chattered with fury on seeing this.

Henry Smith advanced towards me, and I struck him in my
anger, and then rushed away to my room, where I sobbed with
vexation, disgust, and utter weariness.

I wanted to start back to Europe at once, but Jarrett showed
me my contract. I then wanted to take steps to have this
odious exhibition stopped, and in order to calm me I was promised that this should be done, but in reality nothing was done
at all.

Two days later I was at Hartford, and the same whale was
there. It continued its tour as I continued mine.

They gave it more salt and renewed its ice, and it went on its
way, so that I came across it everywhere. I took proceedings
about it, but in every State I was obliged to begin all over again,
as the law varied in the different States. And every time I
arrived at a fresh hotel I found there an immense bouquet
awaiting me, with the horrible card of the showman of the whale.
I threw his flowers on the ground and trampled on them, and
much as I love flowers, I had a horror of these. Jarrett went to
see the man and begged him not to send me any more bouquets,
but it was all of no use, as it was the man's way of avenging the
box on the ears I had given him. Then too he could not understand

my anger. He was making any amount of money, and had even proposed that I should accept a percentage of the receipts. Ah, I would willingly have killed that execrable Smith, for he was poisoning my life. I could see nothing else in all the different cities I visited, and I used to shut my eyes to go from the hotel to the theatre. When I heard the minstrels I used to fly into a rage and turn green with anger. Fortunately I was able to rest when once I reached Montreal, where I was not followed by this show. I should certainly have been ill if it had continued, as I saw nothing but that, I could think of nothing else, and my very dreams were about it. It haunted me; it was an obsession and a perpetual nightmare. When I left Hartford, Jarrett swore to me that Smith would not be at Montreal, as he had been taken suddenly ill. I strongly suspected that Jarrett had found a way of administering to him some violent kind of medicine which had stopped his journeying for the time. I felt sure of this, as the ferocious gentleman laughed so heartily *en route*, but anyhow I was infinitely grateful to him for ridding me of the man for the present.

XXXV

MONTREAL'S GRAND RECEPTION—THE POET FRECHETTE—
AN ESCAPADE ON THE ST. LAWRENCE RIVER

AT last we arrived at Montreal.

For a long time, ever since my earliest childhood, I had
dreamed about Canada. I had always heard my godfather
regret, with considerable fury, the surrender of that territory by
France to England.

I had heard him enumerate, without very clearly understanding
them, the pecuniary advantages of Canada, the immense fortune
that lay in its lands, &c., and that country had seemed to my
imagination the far-off promised land.

Awakened some considerable time before by the strident
whistle of the engine, I asked what time it was. Eleven o'clock
in the evening, I was informed. We were within fifteen minutes
of the station. The sky was black and smooth, like a steel
shield. Lanterns placed at distant intervals caught the whiteness of the snow heaped up there for how many days? The
train stopped suddenly, and then started again with such a slow
and timid movement that I fancied that there might be a possibility of its running off the rails. But a deadened sound, growing louder every second, fell upon my attentive ears. This sound
soon resolved itself into music—and it was in the midst of
a formidable "Hurrah! long live France!" shouted by ten
thousand throats, strengthened by an orchestra playing the
"Marseillaise" with a frenzied fury, that we made our entry
into Montreal.

The place where the train stopped in those days was very
narrow. A somewhat high bank served as a rampart for the
slight platform of the station.

Standing on the small step of my carriage, I looked with

emotion upon the strange spectacle I had before me. The bank was packed with bears holding lanterns. There were hundreds and hundreds of them. In the narrow space between the bank and the train, which had come to a stop, there were more bears, large and small, and I wondered with terror how I should manage to reach my sleigh.

Jarrett and Abbey caused the crowd to make way, and I got out. But a deputy, whose name I cannot make out on my notes (what commendation for my writing!)—a deputy advanced towards me and handed me an address signed by the notabilities of the city. I returned thanks as best I could, and took the magnificent bouquet of flowers that was tendered in the name of the signatories to the address. When I lifted the flowers to my face in order to smell them I hurt myself slightly with their pretty petals, which were frozen by the cold.

However, I began myself to feel both arms and legs were getting benumbed. The cold crept over my whole body. That night, it appears, was one of the coldest that had been experienced for many years past.

The women who had come to be present at the arrival of the French company had been compelled to withdraw into the interior of the station, with the exception of Mrs. Jos. Doutre, who handed me a bouquet of rare flowers and gave me a kiss. The temperature was twenty-two degrees below zero. I whispered low to Jarrett, "Let us continue our journey; I am turning into ice. In ten minutes I shall not be able to move a step."

Jarrett repeated my words to Abbey, who applied to the Chief of Police. The latter gave orders in English, and another police officer repeated them in French. And we were able to proceed for a few yards. But the main station was still some way off. The crowd grew bigger, and at one time I felt as though I were about to faint. I took courage, however, holding or rather hanging on to the arms of Jarrett and Abbey. Every minute I thought I should fall, for the platform was like a mirror.

We were obliged, however, to stay further progress. A hundred lanterns, held aloft by a hundred students' hands, suddenly lit up the place.

A tall young man separated himself from the group and came straight towards me, holding a wide unrolled piece of paper, and in a loud voice declaimed :

A SARAH BERNHARDT.

Salut, Sarah ! salut, charmante dona Sol !
Lorsque ton pied mignon vient fouler notre sol,
    Notre sol tout couvert de givre,
Est-ce frisson d'orgueil ou d'amour ? je ne sais ;
Mais nous sentons courir dans notre sang français
    Quelque chose qui nous enivre !

Femme vaillante au cœur saturé d'idéal,
Puisque tu n'as pas craint notre ciel boréal,
    Ni redouté nos froids sévères.
Merci !   De l'âpre hiver pour longtemps prisonniers,
Nous rêvons à ta vue aux rayons printaniers
    Qui font fleurir les primevères !

Oui, c'est au doux printemps que tu nous fais rêver !
Oiseau des pays bleus, lorsque tu viens braver
    L'horreur de nos saisons perfides,
Aux clairs rayonnements d'un chaud soleil de mai,
Nous croyons voir, du fond d'un bosquet parfumé,
    Surgir la reine des sylphides.

Mais non : de floréal ni du blond messidor,
Tu n es pas, O Sarah, la fée aux ailes d'or
    Qui vient répandre l'ambroisie ;
Nous saluons en toi l'artiste radieux
Qui sut cueillir d'assaut dans le jardin des dieux
    Toutes les fleurs de poesie !

Que sous ta main la toile anime son réseau ;
Que le paros brillant vive sous ton ciseau,
    Ou l'argile sous ton doigt rose ;
Que sur la scène, au bruit délirant des bravos,
En types toujours vrais, quoique toujours nouveaux,
    Ton talent se métamorphose ;

Soit que, peintre admirable ou sculpteur souverain,
Toi-même oses ravir la muse au front serein,
    A ta sourire toujours prête ;
Soit qu'aux mille vivats de la foule à genoux,
Des grands maîtres anciens ou modernes, pour nous
    Ta voix se fasse l'interprète ;

Des bords de la Tamise aux bords du Saint-Laurent,
Qu'il soit enfant du peuple ou brille au premier rang,
    Laissant glapir la calomnie,
Tour à tour par ton œuvre et ta grâce enchanté
Chacun courbe le front devant la majesté
    De ton universel génie !

Salut donc, O Sarah ! salut, O dona Sol !
Lorsque ton pied mignon vient fouler notre sol,
    Te montrer de l'indifférence
Serait à notre sang nous-mêmes faire affront ;
Car l'étoile qui luit la plus belle à ton front,
    C'est encore celle de la France !

                            LOUIS FRÉCHETTE.

He read very well, it is true ; but those lines, read at a temperature of twenty-two degrees of cold to a poor woman dumfounded through listening to a frenzied " Marseillaise," stunned by the mad hurrahs from ten thousand throats delirious with patriotic fervour, were more than my strength could bear.

I made superhuman efforts at resistance, but was overwhelmed with fatigue. Everything appeared to be turning round in a mad farandole. I felt myself raised from the ground, and heard a voice which seemed to come from far away, " Make room for our French lady ! " Then I heard nothing further, and only recovered my senses in my room at the Hotel Windsor.

My sister Jeanne had become separated from me by the movement of the crowd. But the poet Fréchette, a Franco-Canadian, acted as escort, and brought her several minutes later, safe and sound, but trembling on my account, and this is what she told me. " Just imagine. When the crowd was pressing against you, seized with terror on seeing your head fall back with closed eyes on to Abbey's shoulder," I shouted out, ' Help ! My sister is being killed.' I had become mad. A man of enormous size, who had followed us for a long time, worked his elbows and hips to make the enthusiastic but over-excited mob give way, with a quick movement placed himself before you just in time to prevent you from falling. The man, whose face I could not see on account of its being hidden beneath a fur cap, the ear flaps of which covered almost his entire face, raised you up as though you had been a flower, and held forth to the crowd in English. I did not understand anything he said, but the Canadians were struck with it, for the pushing ceased, and the crowd separated into two compact files in order to let you pass through. I can assure you that it made me feel quite impressed to see you, so slender, with your head back, and the whole of your poor frame borne at arm's length by that Hercules. I followed as fast as I could, but having caught my foot in the flounce of my skirt, I had to stop for a second, and that second was enough to separate us completely. The crowd, having closed up after your passage, formed an impenetrable barrier. I can assure you, dear sister, that I felt anything but at ease, and it was M. Fréchette who saved me."

I shook the hand of that worthy gentleman, and thanked him this time as well as I could for his fine poem ; then I spoke to him of other poems of his, a volume of which I had obtained at New York, for alas ! to my shame I must acknowledge it, I knew nothing about Fréchette up to the time of my departure from France, and yet he was already known a little in Paris.

He was very much touched with the several lines I dwelt upon as the finest of his work. He thanked me. We remained friends.

The day following, nine o'clock had hardly struck when a card was sent up to me on which were written these words, " He who had the joy of saving you, Madame, begs that your kindness will grant him a moment's interview." I directed that the man should be shown into the drawing-room, and after notifying Jarrett, went to waken my sister. " Come with me," I said. She slipped on a Chinese dressing-gown, and we went in the direction of the large, the immense drawing-room of my suite, for a bicycle would have been necessary to traverse without fatigue the entire length of my rooms, drawing-room, dining-room and bedroom. On opening the door I was struck by the beauty of the man who was before me. He was very tall, with wide shoulders, small head, a hard look, hair thick and curly, tanned complexion. The man was fine-looking, but seemed uneasy. He blushed slightly on seeing me. I expressed my gratitude, and asked to be excused for my foolish weakness. I received joyfully the bouquet of violets he handed me. On taking leave he said in a low voice, " If you ever hear who I am, swear that you will only think of the slight service I have rendered you." At that moment Jarrett entered. His face was pale, as he walked towards the stranger and spoke to him in English. I could, however, catch the words, " detective . . . door . . . assassination . . . impossibility . . . New Orleans." The stranger's sunburnt complexion became chalky, his nostrils quivered as he glanced towards the door. Then, as flight appeared impossible, he looked at Jarrett and in a peremptory tone, as cold as flint, said, "Well!" as he went towards the door. My hands, which had opened under the stupor, let fall his bouquet, which he picked up whilst looking at me with a supplicating and appealing air. I understood, and said to him in a loud tone of voice, "I swear to it, Monsieur." The man disappeared with his flowers. I heard the uproar of people behind the door and of the crowd in the street. I did not wish to listen to anything further.

When my sister, of a romantic and foolish turn of mind, wished to tell me about the horrible thing, I closed my ears.

Four months afterwards, when an attempt was made to read aloud to me an account of his death by hanging, I refused to hear anything about it. And now after twenty-six years have passed and I know, I only wish to remember the service rendered and my pledged word.

This incident left me somewhat sad. The anger of the Bishop of Montreal was necessary to enable me to regain my good humour. That prelate, after holding forth in the pulpit against the immorality of French literature, forbade his flock to go the theatre. He spoke violently and spitefully against modern France. As to Scribe's play (*Adrienne Lecouvreur*), he tore it into shreds, as it were, declaiming against the immoral love of the *comédienne* and of the hero and against the adulterous love of the Princesse de Bouillon. But the truth showed itself in spite of all, and he cried out, with fury intensified by outrage : " In this infamous lucubration of French authors there is a court abbé, who, thanks to the unbounded licentiousness of his expressions, constitutes a direct insult to the clergy." Finally he pronounced an anathema against Scribe, who was already dead, against Legouvé, against me, and against all my company. The result was that crowds came from everywhere, and the four performances, *Adrienne Lecouvreur*, *Froufrou*, *La Dame aux Camélias* (matinée), and *Hernani* had a colossal success and brought in fabulous receipts.

I was invited by the poet Fréchette and a banker whose name I do not remember to pay a visit to the Iroquois. I accepted with joy, and went there accompanied by my sister, Jarrett, and Angelo, who was always ready for a dangerous excursion. I felt in safety in the presence of this artiste, full of bravery and composure, and gifted with herculean strength. The only thing he lacked to make him perfect was talent.   He had none then, and never did have any.

The St. Lawrence river was frozen over almost entirely ; we crossed it in a carriage along a route indicated by two rows of branches fixed in the ice.   We had four carriages.   The distance between Caughnanwaga and Montreal was five kilometres.

This visit to the Iroquois was deliciously enchanting.   I was introduced to the chief, father, and mayor of the Iroquois tribes.   Alas ! this former chief, son of " Big White Eagle," surnamed during his childhood " Sun of the Nights," now clothed in sorry European rags, was selling liquor, thread, needles, flax, pork fat, chocolate, &c.   All that remained of his mad rovings through the old wild forests—when he roamed naked over a land free of all allegiance—was the stupor of the bull held prisoner by the horns.   It is true he also sold brandy, and that he quenched his thirst, as did all of them, at that source of forgetfulness.

Sun of the Nights introduced me to his daughter, a girl of eighteen to twenty years of age, insipid, and devoid of beauty and grace.

She sat down at the piano and played a tune that was popular at the time—I do not remember what.   I was in a hurry to leave the store, the home of these two victims of civilisation.

I visited Caughnanwaga, but found no pleasure in it.   The same compression of the throat, the same retrospective anguish, caused me to revolt against man's cowardice which hid under the name of civilisation the most unjust and most protected of crimes.

I returned to Montreal somewhat sad and tired.   The success of our four performances was extraordinary, but what gave them a special charm in my eyes was the infernal and joyous noise made by the students.   The doors of the theatre were opened every day one hour in advance for them.   They then arranged matters to suit themselves.   Most of them were gifted with magnificent voices.   They separated into groups according to the requirements of the songs they wished to sing.   They then prepared, by means of a strong string worked by a pulley, the aerial route that was to be followed by the flower-bedecked baskets which descended from their paradise to where I was,

They tied ribbons round the necks of doves bearing sonnets and good wishes.

These flowers and birds were sent off during the "calls," and by a happy disposition of the strings the flowers fell at my feet, the doves flew where their astonishment led them; and every evening these messages of grace and beauty were repeated. I experienced considerable emotion the first evening. The Marquis of Lorne, son-in-law of Queen Victoria, Governor of Canada, was of royal punctuality. The students knew it. The house was noisy and quivering. Through an opening in the curtain I gazed on the composition of this assembly. All of a sudden a silence came over it without any outward reason for it, and the "Marseillaise" was sung by three hundred warm young male voices. With a courtesy full of grandeur the Governor stood up at the first notes of our national hymn. The whole house was on its feet in a second, and the magnificent anthem echoed in our hearts like a call from the mother-country. I do not believe I ever heard the "Marseillaise" sung with keener emotion and unanimity. As soon as it was over, the plaudits of the crowd broke out three times over; then, upon a sharp gesture from the Governor, the band played "God save the Queen."

I never saw a prouder or more dignified gesture than that of the Marquis of Lorne when he motioned to the conductor of the orchestra. He was quite willing to allow these sons of submissive Frenchmen to feel a regret, perhaps even a flickering hope. The first on his feet, he listened to that fine plaint with respect, but he smothered its last echo beneath the English National Anthem.

Being an Englishman, he was incontestably right in doing so.

I gave for the last performance, on December 25, Christmas Day, *Hernani*.

The Bishop of Montreal again thundered against me, against Scribe and Legouvé, and the poor artistes who had come with me, who could not help it. I do not know whether he did not even threaten to excommunicate all of us, living and dead. Lovers of France and French art, in order to reply to his abusive attack, unyoked my horses, and my sleigh was almost carried by an immense crowd, among which were the deputies and notabilities of the city.

One has only to consult the daily papers of that period to

realise the crushing effect caused by such a triumphant return to my hotel.

The day following, Sunday, I went at seven o'clock in the morning, in company with Jarrett and my sister, for a promenade on the banks of the St. Lawrence river. At a given moment I ordered the carriage to stop, with the object of walking a little way.

My sister laughingly said, " What if we climb on to that large piece of ice that seems ready to crack ? "

No sooner thought of than done.

And behold both of us walking on the ice, trying to break it loose! All of a sudden a loud shout from Jarrett made us understand that we had succeeded. As a matter of fact, our ice barque was already floating free in the narrow channel of the river that remained always open on account of the force of the current. My sister and I sat down, for the piece of ice rocked about in every direction, making both of us laugh inordinately. Jarrett's cries caused people to gather. Men armed with boat-hooks endeavoured to stop our progress, but it was not easy, for the edges of the channel were too friable to bear the weight of a man. Ropes were thrown out to us. We caught hold of one of them with our four hands, but the sudden pull of the men in drawing us towards them cast our raft so suddenly against the ice edges that it broke in two, and we remained, full of fear this time, on one small part of our skiff. I laughed no longer, for we were beginning to travel somewhat fast, and the channel was opening out in width. But in one of the turns it made we were fortunately squeezed in between two immense blocks, and to this fact we owed being able to escape with our lives.

The men who had followed our very rapid ride with real courage climbed on to the blocks. A harpoon was thrown with marvellous skill on to our icy wreck so as to retain us in our position, for the current, rather strong underneath, might have caused us to move. A ladder was brought and planted against one of the large blocks ; its steps afforded us means of delivery. My sister was the first to climb up, and I followed, somewhat ashamed at our ridiculous escapade.

During the length of time required to regain the bank the carriage, with Jarrett in it, was able to rejoin us. He was pallid, not from fear of the danger I had undergone, but at the idea that if I died the tour would come to an end.   He said to me quite seriously, " If you had lost your life, Madame, you would have been dishonest, for you would have broken your contract of your own free will."

We had just enough time to get to the station, where the train was ready to take me to Springfield.

An immense crowd was waiting, and it was with the same cry of love, underlined with *au revoirs*, that the Canadian public wished us good-bye.

XXXVI

SPRINGFIELD—BALTIMORE—PHILADELPHIA—CHICAGO—
ADVENTURES BETWEEN ST. LOUIS AND CINCINNATI
—CAPITAL PUNISHMENT

AFTER our immense and noisy success at Montreal, we were
somewhat surprised with the icy welcome of the public at
Springfield.

We played *La Dame aux Camélias*—in America *Camille*,
why, no one was ever able to tell me. This play, which the
public rushed to see in crowds, shocked the over-strained Puritanism of the small American towns. The critics of the large
cities discussed this modern Magdalene. But those of the small
towns began by throwing stones at her. This stilted reserve on
the part of the public, prejudiced against the impurity of
Marguerite Gautier, we met with from time to time in the
small cities. Springfield at that time had barely thirty thousand
inhabitants.

During the day I passed at Springfield I called at a gun-
smith's to purchase a rifle. The salesman showed me into a long
and very narrow courtyard, where I tried several shots. On
turning round I was surprised and confused to see two gentlemen
taking an interest in my shooting. I wished to withdraw at
once, but one of them came up to me :

" Would you like, Madame, to come and fire off a cannon ? " I
almost fell to the ground with surprise, and did not reply for a
second. Then I said, " Yes, I would."

An appointment was made with my strange questioner, who
was the director of the Colt gun factory. An hour afterwards I
went to the rendezvous.

More than thirty people who had been hastily invited were
there already. It got on my nerves a trifle. I fired off the

newly invented quick-firing cannon. It amused me very much without procuring me any emotion, and that evening, after the icy performance, we left for Baltimore with a vertiginous rush, the play having finished later than the hour fixed for the departure of the train. It was necessary to catch it up at any cost. The three enormous carriages that made up my special train went off under full steam. With two engines, we bounded over the metals and dropped again, thanks to some miracle.

We finally succeeded in catching up the express, which knew we were on its track, having been warned by telegram. It made a short stop, just long enough to couple us to it anyhow, and in that way we reached Baltimore, where I stayed four days and gave five performances.

Two things struck me in that city : the deadly cold in the hotels and the theatre, and the loveliness of the women.

I felt a profound sadness at Baltimore, for I spent the 1st of January far from everything that was dear to me. I wept all night, and underwent that moment of discouragement that makes one wish for death.

Our success, however, had been colossal in that charming city, which I left with regret to go to Philadelphia, where we were to remain a week.

That handsome city I do not care for. I received an enthusiastic welcome there, in spite of a change of programme the first evening. Two artistes having missed the train, we could not play *Adrienne Lecouvreur*, and I had to replace it by *Phèdre*, the only piece in which the absentees could be replaced. The receipts averaged twenty thousand francs for the seven performances given in six days. My sojourn was saddened by a letter announcing the death of my friend Gustave Flaubert, the writer who had the beauty of our language at heart.

From Philadelphia we proceeded to Chicago.

At the station I was received by a deputation of Chicago ladies, and a bouquet of rare flowers was handed to me by a delightful young lady, Madame Lily B.

Jarrett then led me into one of the rooms of the station, where the French delegates were waiting.

A very short but highly emotional speech from our Consul spread confidence and friendly feelings among every one, and after having returned heartfelt thanks, I was preparing to leave the station, when I stopped stupefied—and it seems that my features assumed such an intense expression of suffering that everybody ran towards me to offer assistance.

But a sudden anger electrified all my being, and I walked straight towards the horrible vision that had just appeared before me—the whale man! He was alive, that terrible Smith! —enveloped in furs, with diamonds on all of his fingers. He was there with a bouquet in his hand, the wretched brute! I refused the flowers and repulsed him with all my strength, increased tenfold by anger, and a flood of confused words escaped from my pallid lips. But this scene charmed him, for it was repeated and spread about, magnified, and the whale had more visitors than ever.

I went to the Palmer House, one of the most magnificent hotels of that day, whose proprietor, Mr. Potter-Palmer, was a perfect gentleman, courteous, kind, and generous, for he filled the immense apartment I occupied with the rarest flowers, and taxed his ingenuity in order to have my meals cooked and served in the French style, a difficult matter in those days.

We were to remain a fortnight in Chicago. Our success exceeded all expectations. These two weeks seemed to me the most agreeable days I had had since my arrival in America. First of all, there was the vitality of the city in which men pass each other without ever stopping, with knitted brows, with one thought in mind, "the end to attain." They move on and on, never turning for a cry or prudent warning. What takes place behind them matters little. They do not wish to know why a cry is raised, and they have no time to be prudent: " the end to attain " awaits them.

Women here, as everywhere else in America, do not work, but they do not stroll about the streets, as in other cities: they walk quickly; they also are in a hurry to seek amusement. During the day time I went some distance into the surrounding country in order not to meet the sandwich-men advertising the whale.

One day I went to the pigs' slaughter-house. Ah, what a dreadful and magnificent sight! There were three of us, my sister, myself, and an Englishman, a friend of mine.

On arrival we saw hundreds of pigs hurrying, bunched together, grunting and snorting, along a small narrow raised bridge. Our carriage passed under this bridge, and stopped before a group of men who were waiting for us. The manager of the stock-yards received us and led the way to the special slaughter-houses. On entering into the immense shed, which is dimly lighted by windows with greasy and ruddy panes, an abominable smell gets into your throat, a smell that only leaves one several days afterwards. A sanguinary mist rises everywhere, like a light cloud floating on the side of a mountain and lit up by the setting sun. An infernal hubbub drums itself into your brain : the almost human cries of the pigs being slaughtered, the violent strokes of the hatchets lopping off the limbs, the repeated shouts of the " ripper," who with a superb and sweeping gesture lifts the heavy hatchet, and with one stroke opens from top to bottom the unfortunate, quivering animal hung on a hook. During the terror of the moment one hears the con-tinuous grating of the revolving razor which in one second removes the bristles from the trunk thrown to it by the machine that has cut off the four legs ; the whistle of the escaping steam from the hot water in which the head of the animal is scalded ; the rippling of the water that is constantly renewed ; the cascade of the waste water ; the rumbling of the small trains carrying under wide arches trucks loaded with hams, sausages, &c., and the whistling of the engines warning one of the danger of their approach, which in this spot of terrible massacre seems to be the perpetual knell of wretched agonies.

Nothing was more Hoffmanesque than this slaughter of pigs at the period I am speaking about, for since then a sentiment of humanity has crept, although still somewhat timidly, into this temple of porcine hecatombs.

I returned from this visit quite ill. That evening I played in *Phèdre*. I went on to the stage quite unnerved, and trying to do everything to get rid of the horrible vision of the stock-yard. I threw myself heart and soul into my *rôle*, so much so that at the end of the fourth act I absolutely fainted on the stage.

On the day of my last performance a magnificent collar of camellias in diamonds was handed me on behalf of the ladies of Chicago. I left that city fond of everything in it : its people ; its lake, as big as a small inland sea ; its audiences, who were so enthusiastic ; everything, everything—except its stock-yards.

I did not even bear any ill-will towards the Bishop, who also, as

2 c

had happened in other cities, had denounced my art and French literature. By the violence of his sermons he had, as a matter of fact, advertised us so well that Mr. Abbey, the manager, wrote the following letter to him :

"Your Grace ——, Whenever I visit your city, I am accustomed to spend four hundred dollars in advertising. But as you have done the advertising for me, I send you two hundred dollars for your poor.

"HENRY ABBEY."

We left Chicago to go to St. Louis, where we arrived after having covered 283 miles in fourteen hours.

In the drawing-room of my car, Abbey and Jarrett showed me the statement of the sixty-two performances that had been given since our arrival. The gross receipts were $227,459, that is to say, 1,137,295 francs, an average of 18,343 francs per performance. This gave me great pleasure on Henry Abbey's account, for he had lost all he had in his previous tour with an admirable troup of opera artistes, and greater pleasure still on my own account, as I was to receive a good share of the takings.

We stayed at St. Louis all the week, from January 24 to 31. I must admit that this city, which was specially French, was less to my liking than the other American cities, as it was dirty and the hotels were not very comfortable. Since then St. Louis has made great strides, but it was the Germans who planted there the bulb of progress. At the time of which I speak, the year 1881, the city was repulsively dirty. In those days, alas ! we were not great at colonising, and all the cities where French influence preponderated were poor and behind the times. I was bored to death at St. Louis, and I wanted to leave the place at once, after paying an indemnity to the manager, but Jarrett, the upright man, the stern man of duty, the ferocious man, said to me, holding my contract in his hand :

"No, Madame ; you must stay. You can die of *ennui* here if you like, but stay you must."

By way of entertaining me he took me to a celebrated grotto where we were to see some millions of fish without eyes. The light had never penetrated into this grotto, and as the first fish who lived there had no use for their eyes, their descendants had

no eyes at all. We went to see this grotto. It was a long way
off. We went down and groped our way to the grotto very
cautiously, on all fours like cats. The road seemed to me
interminable, but at last the guide told us that we had arrived
at our destination. We were able to stand upright again, as
the grotto itself was higher. I could see nothing, but I heard
a match being struck, and the guide then lighted a small lantern.
Just in front of me, nearly at my feet, was a rather deep natural
basin. "You see," remarked our guide phlegmatically, "that
is the pond, but just at present there is no water in it; neither
are there any fish. You must come again in three months'
time."

Jarrett made such a fearful grimace that I was seized with an
uncontrollable fit of laughter, of that kind of laughter which
borders on madness. I was suffocated with it, and I choked
and laughed till the tears came. I then went down into the
basin of the pond in search of a relic of some kind, a little
skeleton of a dead fish, or anything, no matter what. There
was nothing to be found, though—absolutely nothing. We
had to return on all fours, as we came. I made Jarrett
go first, and the sight of his big back in his fur coat and
of him walking on hands and feet, grumbling and swearing as
he went, gave me such delight that I no longer regretted anything, and I gave ten dollars to the guide for his ineffable
surprise.

We returned to the hotel, and I was informed that a jeweller
had been waiting for me more than two hours. "A jeweller!"
I exclaimed; "but I have no intention of buying any jewellery.
I have too much as it is." Jarrett, however, winked at Abbey,
who was there as we entered. I saw at once that there was
some understanding between the jeweller and my two *impresarii*. I was told that my ornaments needed cleaning,
that the jeweller would undertake to make them look like new,
repair them if they required it, and in a word exhibit them.
I rebelled, but it was of no use. Jarrett assured me that the
ladies of St. Louis were particularly fond of shows of this kind.
He said it would be an excellent advertisement; that my
jewellery was very much tarnished, that several stones were
missing, and that this man would replace them for nothing,
"What a saving!" he added. "Just think of it!"

I gave up, for discussions of that kind bore me to death, and two days later the ladies of St. Louis went to admire my ornaments in this jeweller's show-cases under a blaze of light.   Poor Madame Guérard, who also went to see them, came back horrified.

"They have added to your things," she said, "sixteen pairs of ear-rings, two necklaces, and thirty rings ; a lorgnette studded with diamonds and rubies, a gold cigarette-holder set with turquoises ; a small pipe, the amber mouthpiece of which is encircled with diamond stars ; sixteen bracelets, a tooth-pick studded with sapphires, a pair of spectacles with gold mounts ending with small acorns of pearls.

"They must have been made specially," said poor Guérard, "for there can't be any one who would wear such glasses, and, on them were written the words, 'Spectacles which Madame Sarah Bernhardt wears when she is at home.' "

I certainly thought that this was exceeding all the limits allowed to advertisement.   To make me smoke pipes and wear spectacles was going rather too far, and I got into my carriage and drove at once to the jeweller's.   I arrived just in time to find the place closed.   It was five o'clock on Saturday afternoon ; the lights were out, and everything was dark and silent.   I returned to the hotel, and spoke to Jarrett of my annoyance.   "What does it all matter, Madame ?" he said tranquilly.   "So many girls wear spectacles ; and as to the pipe, the jeweller tells me he has received five orders from it, and that it is going to be quite the fashion.   Anyhow, it is of no use worrying about the matter, as the exhibition is now over.   Your jewellery will be returned to-night, and we leave here the day after to-morrow."

That evening the jeweller returned all the objects I had lent him, and they had been polished and repaired so that they looked quite new.   He had included with them a gold cigarette-holder set with turquoises, the very one that had been on view.   I simply could not make that man understand anything, and my anger cooled down when confronted by his pleasant manner and his joy.

This advertisement, though, came very near costing me my life.   Tempted by this huge quantity of jewellery, the greater part of which did not belong to me, a little band of sharpers planned to rob me, believing that they would find all these valuables in the large hand-bag which my steward always carried.

On Sunday, January 30, we left St. Louis at eight o'clock in the morning for Cincinnati.   I was in my magnificently appointed Pullman car, and I had requested that the car should be put at the end of [our special train, so that from the platform I might enjoy the beauty of the landscape, which passes before one like a continually changing living panorama.

We had scarcely been more than ten minutes *en route* when the guard suddenly stooped down and looked over the little balcony. He then drew back quickly, and his face turned pale. Seizing my hand, he said in a very excited tone in English, " Please go inside, Madame! "   I understood that we were in danger of some kind. He pulled the alarm signal, made a sign to another guard, and before the train had quite come to a standstill the two men sprang down and disappeared under the train.

The guard had fired a revolver in order to attract every one's attention, and Jarrett, Abbey, and the artistes hurried out into the narrow corridor.   I found myself in the midst of them, and to our stupefaction we saw the two guards dragging out from underneath my compartment a man armed to the teeth.   With a revolver held to his temple on either side, he decided to confess the truth of the matter.

The jeweller's exhibition had excited the envy of all the gangs of thieves, and this man had been despatched by an organised band at St. Louis to relieve me of my jewellery.

He was to unhook my carriage from the rest of the train between St. Louis and Cincinnati, at a certain spot known as the " Little Incline."

As this was to be done during the night, and as my carriage was the last, the thing was comparatively easy, since it was only a question of lifting the enormous hook and drawing it out of the link.

The man, a veritable giant, was fastened on to my carriage. We examined his apparatus, and found that it merely consisted of very thick wide straps of leather about half a yard wide By means of these he was secured firmly to the underpart of the train, with his hands perfectly free.   The courage and the *sang-*

froid of that man were admirable. He told us that seven armed men were waiting for us at the Little Incline, and that they certainly would not have injured us if we had not attempted to resist, for all they wanted was my jewellery and the money which the secretary carried (two thousand three hundred dollars). Oh, he knew everything; he knew every one's name, and he gabbled on in bad French, " Oh, as for you, Madame, we should not have done you any harm, in spite of your pretty little revolver. We should even have let you keep it."

And so this man and his gang knew that the secretary slept at my end of the train, and that he was not to be dreaded much (poor Chatterton!); that he had with him two thousand three hundred dollars, and that I had a very prettily chased revolver, ornamented with cats-eyes. The man was firmly bound and taken in charge by the two guards, and the train was then backed into St. Louis; we had only started a quarter of an hour before. The police were informed, and they sent us five detectives. A goods train which should have departed half an hour before us was sent on ahead of us. Eight detectives travelled on this goods train, and received orders to get out at the Little Incline. Our giant was handed over to the police authorities, but I was promised that he should be dealt with mercifully on account of the confession he had made. Later on I learnt that this promise had been kept, as the man was sent back to his native country, Ireland.

From this time forth my compartment was always placed between two others every night. In the day-time I was allowed to have my carriage at the end on condition that I would agree to have on the platform an armed detective whom I was to pay, by the way, for his services. Our dinner was very gay, and every one was rather excited. As to the guard who had discovered the giant hidden under the train, Abbey and I had rewarded him so lavishly that he was intoxicated, and kept coming on every occasion to kiss my hand and weep his drunkard's tears, repeating all the time, " I saved the French lady; I'm a gentleman."

When finally we approached the Little Incline, it was dark. The engine-driver wanted to rush along at full speed, but we had not gone five miles when crackers exploded under the wheels and we were obliged to slacken our pace. We wondered what new danger there was awaiting us, and we began to feel anxious.

The women were nervous, and some of them were in tears. We went along slowly, peering into the darkness, trying to make out the form of a man or of several men by the light of each cracker. Abbey suggested going at full speed, because these crackers had been placed along the line by the bandits, who had probably thought of some way of stopping the train in case their giant did not succeed in unhooking the carriage. The engine-driver refused to go more quickly, declaring that these crackers were signals placed there by the railway company, and that he could not risk every one's life on a mere supposition. The man was quite right, and he was certainly very brave.

" We can certainly settle a handful of ruffians," he said, " but I could not answer for any one's life if the train went off the lines, clashed into or collided with something, or went over a precipice."

We continued therefore to go slowly. The lights had been turned off in the car, so that we might see as much as possible without being seen ourselves. We had tried to keep the truth from the artistes, except from three men whom I had sent for to my carriage. The artistes really had nothing to fear from the robbers, as I was the only person at whom they were aiming. To avoid all unnecessary questions and evasive answers, we sent the secretary to tell them that as there was some obstruction on the line, the train had to go slowly. They were also told that one of the gas-pipes had to be repaired before we could have the light again. The communication was then cut between my car and the rest of the train. We had been going along like this for ten minutes perhaps when everything was suddenly lighted up by a fire, and we saw a gang of railway-men hastening towards us. It makes me shudder now when I think how nearly these poor fellows escaped being killed. Our nerves had been in such a state of tension for several hours that we imagined at first that these men were the wretched friends of the giant. Some one fired at them, and if it had not been for our plucky engine-driver calling out to them to stop, with the addition of a terrible oath, two or three of these poor men would have been wounded. I too had seized my revolver, but before I could have drawn out the ramrod which serves as a cog to prevent it from going off, any one would have had time to seize me, bind me, and kill me a hundred times over.

And still any time I go to a place where I think there is danger, I invariably take my pistol with me, for it is a pistol, and not a revolver. I always call it a revolver, but in reality it is a pistol, and a very old-fashioned make too, with this ramrod and the trigger so hard to pull that I have to use my other hand as well. I am not a bad shot, for a woman, provided that I may take my time, but this is not very easy when one wants to fire at a robber. And yet I always have my pistol with me; it is here on my table, and I can see it as I write. It is in its case, which is rather too narrow, so that it requires a certain amount of strength and patience to pull it out. If an assassin should arrive at this particular moment I should first have to unfasten the case, which is not an easy matter, then to get the pistol out, pull out the ramrod, which is rather too firm, and press the trigger with both hands. And yet, in spite of all this, the human animal is so strange that this ridiculously useless little object here before me seems to me an admirable protection. And nervous and timid as I am, alas! I feel quite safe when I am near to this little friend of mine, who must roar with laughter inside the little case out of which I can scarcely drag it.

Well, everything was now explained to us. The goods train which had started before us ran off the line, but no great damage was done, and no one was killed. The St. Louis band of robbers had arranged everything, and had prepared to have this little accident two miles from the Little Incline, in case their comrade crouching under my car had not been able to unhook it. The train had left the rails, but when the wretches rushed forward, believing that it was mine, they found themselves surrounded by the band of detectives. It seems that they fought like demons. One of them was killed on the spot, two more wounded, and the remainder taken prisoners. A few days later the chief of this little band was hanged. He was a Belgian, named Albert Wirbyn, twenty-five years of age.

I did all in my power to save him, for it seemed to me that unintentionally I had been the instigator of his evil plan.

If Abbey and Jarrett had not been so rabid for advertisement, if they had not added more than six hundred thousand francs' worth of jewellery to mine, this man, this wretched youth, would not perhaps have had the stupid idea of robbing me. Who can say what schemes had floated through the mind of the poor fellow, who was perhaps half-starved, or perhaps excited by a clever, inventive brain? Perhaps when he stopped and looked at the jeweller's window he said to himself: "There is jewellery there worth a million francs. If it were all mine I would sell it and go back to Belgium. What joy I could give to my poor mother, who is blinding herself with work by gaslight, and I could help my sister to get married." Or perhaps he was an inventor, and he thought to himself: "Ah, if only I had the money which that jewellery represents I could bring out my invention myself, instead of selling my patent to some highly esteemed rascal, who will buy it from me for a crust of bread. What would it matter to the artiste. Ah, if only I had the money!" Ah, if I had the money!—perhaps the poor fellow cried with rage to think of all this wealth belonging to one person. Perhaps the idea of crime germinated in this way in a mind which had hitherto been pure. Ah, who can tell to what hope may give birth in a young mind? At first it may be only a beautiful dream, but this may end in a mad desire to realise the dream. To steal the goods of another person is certainly not right, but this should not be punished by death—it certainly should not. To kill a man of twenty-five years of age is a much greater crime than to steal jewellery even by force, and a society which bands together in order to wield the sword of Justice is much more cowardly when it kills than the man who robs and kills quite alone, at his own risk and peril. Oh, what tears I wept for that man, whom I did not know at all—who was a rascal or perhaps a hero! He was perhaps a man of weak intellect who had turned thief, but he was only twenty-five years of age, and he had a right to live.

How I hate capital punishment! It is a relic of cowardly barbarism, and it is a disgrace for civilised countries still to have their guillotines and scaffolds. Every human being has a moment when his heart is easily touched, when the tears of grief will flow; and those tears may fecundate a generous thought which might lead to repentance.

I would not for the whole world be one of those who condemn a man to death. And yet many of them are good, upright men, who when they return to their families are affectionate to their wives, and reprove their children for breaking a doll's head.

I have seen four executions, one in London, one in Spain, and two in Paris.

In London the method is hanging, and this seems to me more hideous, more repugnant, more weird than any other death. The victim was a young man of about thirty, with a strong, self-willed looking face. I only saw him a second, and he shrugged his shoulders as he glanced at me, his eyes expressing his contempt for my curiosity. At that moment I felt that individual's ideas were very much superior to mine, and the condemned man seemed to me greater than all who were there. It was, perhaps, because he was nearer than we all were to the great mystery. I can see him now smile as they covered his face with the hood, while, as for me, I rushed away completely upset.

In Madrid I saw a man garrotted, and the barbarity of this torture terrified me for weeks after. He was accused of having killed his mother, but no real proof seemed to have been brought forward against the wretched man. And he cried out, when they were holding him down on his seat before putting the garrotte on him, " Mother, I shall soon be with you, and you will tell them all, in my presence, that they have lied."

These words were uttered in Spanish, in a voice that vibrated with earnestness. They were translated for me by an *attaché* to the British Embassy, with whom I had gone to see the hideous sight. The wretched man cried out in such a sincere, heart-rending tone of voice that it was impossible for him not to have been innocent, and this was the opinion of all those who were with me.

The two other executions which I witnessed were at the Place de la Roquette, Paris. The first was that of a young medical student, who with the help of one of his friends had killed an old woman who sold newspapers. It was a stupid, odious crime, but the man was more mad than criminal. He was more than ordinarily intelligent, and had passed his examinations at an earlier age than is usual. He had worked too hard, and it had affected his brain. He ought to have been allowed to rest, to have been treated as an invalid, cured in mind and body, and then returned to his scientific pursuits. He was a young man quite above the average as regards intellect. I can see him now, pale and haggard, with a dreamy, far-away look in his eyes, an expression of infinite sadness. I know, of course, that he had killed a poor, defenceless old woman. That was certainly odious, but he was only twenty-three years old, and his mind was disordered through study and overwork, too much ambition, and the habit of cutting off arms and legs and dissecting the dead bodies of women and children. All this does not excuse the man's abominable deed, but it had all contributed to unhinge his moral sense, which was perhaps already in a wavering state, thanks to study, poverty, or atavism. I consider that a crime of high treason against humanity was committed in taking the life of a man of intellect, who, when once he had recovered his reason, might have rendered great service to science and to humanity.

The last execution at which I was present was that of Vaillant, the anarchist. He was an energetic man, and at the same time mild and gentle, with very advanced ideas, but not much more advanced than those of men who have since risen to power.

My theatre at that time was the Renaissance, and he often applied to me for free seats, as he was too poor to pay for the luxuries of art. Ah, poverty, what a sorry counsellor art thou, and how tolerant we ought to be to those who have to endure misery!

One day Vaillant came to see me in my dressing-room at the theatre. I was playing Lorenzaccio, and he said to me: "Ah, that Florentine was an anarchist just as I am, but he killed the tyrant and not tyranny. That is not the way I shall go to work."

A few days later he threw a bomb in a public building, the Chamber of Deputies. The poor fellow was not as successful as the Florentine, whom he seemed to despise, for he did not kill any one, and did no real harm except to his own cause.

I said I should like to know when he was to be executed, and the night before, a friend of mine came to the theatre and told me that the execution was to take place the following day, Monday, at seven in the morning.

I started after the performance, and went to the Rue Merlin, at the corner of the Rue de la Roquette. The streets were still very animated, as that Sunday was Dimanche Gras (Shrove Sunday). People were singing, laughing, and dancing everywhere. I waited all night, and as I was not allowed to enter the prison, I sat on the balcony of a first floor flat which I had engaged. The cold darkness of the night in its immensity seemed to enwrap me in sadness. I did not feel the cold, for my blood was flowing rapidly through my veins. The hours passed slowly, the hours which rang out in the distance, *L'heure est morte. Vive l'heure!* I heard a vague, muffled sound of footsteps, whispering, and of wood which creaked heavily, but I did not know what these strange, mysterious sounds were until day began to break. I saw that the scaffold was there. A man came to extinguish the lamps on the Place de la Roquette, and an anæmic-looking sky spread its pale light over us. The crowd began to collect gradually, but remained in compact groups, and circulation in the streets was interrupted. Every now and then a man, looking quite indifferent, but evidently in a hurry, pushed aside the crowd, presented a card to a policeman, and then disappeared under the porch of the prison. I counted more than ten of these men : they were journalists. Presently the military guard appeared suddenly on the spot, and took up its position around the melancholy-looking pedestal. The usual number of the guard had been doubled for this occasion, as some anarchist plot was feared. On a given signal swords were drawn and the prison door opened.

Vaillant appeared, looking very pale, but energetic and brave. He cried out in a manly voice, with perfect assurance, "*Vive l'anarchie!*" There was not a single cry in response to his. He was seized and thrown back over the slab. The knife fell with a muffled sound. The body tottered, and in a second the scaffold was taken away, the place swept ; the crowds were allowed to move. They rushed forward to the place of execution, gazing down on the ground for a spot of blood which was not to be seen, sniffing in the air for any odour of the drama which had just been enacted.

There were women, children, old men, all joking there on the very spot where a man had just expired in the most supreme agony. And that man had made himself the apostle of this populace ; that man had claimed for this teeming crowd all kinds of liberties, all kinds of privileges and rights.

I was thickly veiled so that I could not be recognised, and accompanied by a friend as escort.

I mingled with the crowd, and it made me sick at heart and

desperate.   There was not a word of gratitude to this man, not a murmur of vengeance nor of revolt.

I felt inclined to cry out : " Brutes that you are !   Kneel down and kiss the stones that the blood of this poor madman has stained for your sakes, for you, because he believed in you."

But before I had time for this a street urchin was calling out, " Buy the last moments of Vaillant !   Buy, buy !"

Oh, poor Vaillant !   His headless body was then being taken to Clamart, and the crowds for whom he had wept, worked, and died were now going quietly away, indifferent and bored. Poor Vaillant !   His ideas were exaggerated ones, but they were generous.

XXXVII

NEW ORLEANS AND OTHER AMERICAN CITIES—
A VISIT TO THE FALLS OF NIAGARA

WE arrived at Cincinnati safe and sound. We gave three performances there, and set off once more for New Orleans.

Now, I thought, we shall have some sunshine and we shall be able to warm our poor limbs, which were stiffened with three months of mortal cold. We shall be able to open our windows and breathe fresh air instead of the suffocating and anæmia-giving steam heat. I fell asleep, and dreams of warmth and sweet scents lulled me in my slumber. A knock roused me suddenly, and my dog with ears erect sniffed at the door, but as he did not growl, I knew it was some one of our party. I opened the door, and Jarrett, followed by Abbey, made signs to me not to speak. Jarrett came in on tip-toe, and closed the door again.

"Well, what is it now?" I asked.

"Why," replied Jarrett, "the incessant rain during the last twelve days has swollen the water to such a height that the bridge of boats across the bay here is liable to give way under the terrible pressure of the water. Do you hear the awful storm of wind that is now blowing? If we go back by the other route it will require three or four days."

I was furious. Three or four days, and to go back to the snow again! Ah no! I felt I must have sunshine.

"Why can we not pass? Oh, Heavens! what shall we do?" I exclaimed.

"Well, the engine-driver is here. He thinks that he might get across; but he has only just married, and he will try the crossing on condition that you give him two thousand five hundred dollars, which he will at once send to Mobile, where his

father and wife live. If we get safely to the other side he will
give you back this money, but if not it will belong to his
family."

I must confess that I was stupefied with admiration for this
plucky man. His daring excited me, and I exclaimed :

" Yes, certainly. Give him the money, and let us cross."

As I have said, I generally travelled by special train. This
one was made up of only three carriages and the engine. I
never doubted for a moment as to the success of this foolish and
criminal attempt, and I did not tell any one about it except my
sister, my beloved Guérard, and my faithful Félicie and her
husband Claude. The comedian Angelo, who was sleeping in
Jarrett's berth on this journey, knew of it, but he was courageous,
and had faith in his star. The money was handed over to the
engine-driver, who sent it off to Mobile. It was only just as we
were actually starting that I had the vision of the responsibility
I had taken upon myself, for it was risking without their consent
the lives of thirty-two persons. It was too late then to do
anything : the train had started, and at a terrific speed it
touched the bridge of boats. I had taken my seat on the platform, and the bridge bent and swayed like a hammock under
the dizzy speed of our wild course. When we were half way
across it gave way so much that my sister grasped my arm and
whispered, " Ah, we are drowning ! " She closed her eyes and
clutched me nervously, but was quite brave. I certainly imagined
as she did that the supreme moment had arrived ; and abominable
as it was, I never for a second thought of all those who were full
of confidence and life, whom I was sacrificing, whom I was killing.
My only thought was of a dear little face which would soon be
in mourning for me. And to think that we take about within us
our most terrible enemy, thought, and that it is continually at
variance with our deeds. It rises up at times, terrible, perfidious, and we try to drive it away without success. We do
not, thanks to God, invariably obey it ; but it pursues us,
torments us, makes us suffer. How often the most evil thoughts
assail us, and what battles we have to fight in order to drive
away these children of our brain ! Anger, ambition, revenge
give birth to the most detestable thoughts, which make us
blush with shame as we should at some horrible blemish. And
yet they are not ours, for we have not evoked them ; but they

defile us nevertheless, and leave us in despair at not being masters of our own heart, mind, and body.

My last minute was not inscribed, though, for that day in the book of destiny. The train pulled itself together, and, half leaping and half rolling along, we arrived on the other side of the water. Behind us we heard a terrible noise, a column of water falling back like a huge sheaf. The bridge had given way! For more than a week the trains from the east and the north could not run over this route.

I left the money to our brave engine-driver, but my conscience was by no means tranquil, and for a long time my sleep was disturbed by the most frightful nightmares; and when any of the artistes spoke to me of their child, their mother, or their husband, whom they longed to see once more, I felt myself turn pale; a thrill of deep emotion went through me, and I had the deepest pity for my own self.

When getting out of the train I was more dead than alive from retrospective emotion. I had to submit to receiving a most friendly though fatiguing deputation of my compatriots. Then, loaded with flowers, I climbed into the carriage that was to take me to the hotel. The roads were rivers, and we were on an elevated spot. The lower part of the city, the coachman explained to us in French, with a strong Marseilles accent, was inundated up to the tops of the houses. Hundreds of negroes had been drowned. " Ah, *bagasse* ! " he cried, as he whipped up his horses.

At that period the hotels in New Orleans were squalid—dirty, uncomfortable, black with cockroaches, and as soon as the candles were lighted the bedrooms became filled with large mosquitoes that buzzed round and fell on one's shoulder, sticking in one's hair. Oh, I shudder still when I think of it !

At the same time as our company, there was at New Orleans an opera company, the " star " of which was a charming woman, Emilie Ambre, who at one time came very near being Queen of Holland. The country was poor, like all the other American districts where the French were to be found preponderating.

The opera did very poor business, and we did not do excellently either. Six performances would have been ample in that city : we gave eight.

Nevertheless, my sojourn pleased me immensely.

An infinite charm was evolved from it. All these people, so different, black and white, had smiling faces. All the women were graceful. The shops were attractive from the cheerfulness of their windows. The open-air traders under the arcades challenged one another with joyful flashes of wit. The sun, however, did not show itself once. But these people had the sun within themselves.

I could not understand why boats were not used. The horses had water up to their hams, and it would have been impossible even to get into a carriage if the pavements had not been a metre high and occasionally more.

Floods being as frequent as the years, it would be of no use to think of banking up the river or arm of the sea. But circulation was made easy by the high pavements and small movable bridges. The dark children amused themselves catching crayfish in the streams. (Where did they come from?) And they sold them to passers-by.

Now and again we would see a whole family of water serpents speed by. They swept along, with raised head and undulating body, like long starry sapphires.

I went down towards the lower part of the town. The sight was heartrending. All the cabins of the coloured inhabitants had fallen into the muddy waters. They were there in hundreds, squatting upon these moving wrecks, with eyes burning from fever. Their white teeth chattered with hunger. Right and left, everywhere, were dead bodies with swollen stomachs floating about, knocking up against the wooden piles. Many ladies were distributing food, endeavouring to lead away these unfortunate creatures. No. They would stay where they were. With a blissful smile they would reply, "The water go away. House be found. Me begin again." And the women would slowly nod their heads in token of assent. Several alligators had shown themselves, brought up by the tide. Two children had disappeared.

One child of fourteen years of age had just been carried off to the hospital with his foot cut clean off at the ankle by one of these marine monsters. His family were howling with fury. They wished to keep the youngster with them. The negro quack doctor pretended that he could have cured him in two days, and that the white "quacks" would leave him for a month in bed.

2 D

I left this city with regret, for it resembled no other city I had visited up to then. We were really surprised to find that none of our party were missing—they had gone through, so they said, various dangers. The hair-dresser alone, a man called Ibé, could not recover his equilibrium, having become half mad from fear the second day of our arrival. At the theatre he generally slept in the trunk in which he stored his wigs. However strange it may seem, the fact is quite true. The first night everything passed off as usual, but during the second night he woke up the whole neigbourhood by his shrieks. The unfortunate fellow had got off soundly to sleep, when he woke up with a feeling that his mattress, which lay suspended over his collection of wigs, was being raised by some inconceivable movements. He thought that some cat or dog had got into the trunk, and he lifted up the feeble rampart. Two serpents were either quarrelling or making love to each other—he could not say which ; two serpents of a size sufficient to terrify the people whom the shouts of the poor Figaro had caused to gather round.

He was still very pale when I saw him embark on board the boat that was to take us to our train. I called him, and begged he would relate to me the Odyssey of his terrible night. As he told me the story he pointed to his big leg: "They were as thick as that, Madame. Yes, like that——" And he quaked with fear as he recalled the dreadful girth of the reptiles. I thought that they were about one quarter as thick as his leg, and that would have been enough to justify his fright, for the serpents in question were not inoffensive water-snakes that bite out of pure viciousness, but have no venom fangs.

We reached Mobile somewhat late in the day.

We had stopped at that city on our way to New Orleans, and I had had a real attack of nerves caused by the "cheek" of the inhabitants, who, in spite of the lateness of the hour, had got up a deputation to wait upon me. I was dead with fatigue, and was dropping off to sleep in my bed in the car. I therefore energetically declined to see anybody. But these people knocked at my windows, sang round about my carriage, and finally exasperated me. I quickly threw up one of the windows and emptied a jug of water on their heads. Women and men, amongst whom were several journalists, were inundated. Their fury was great.

I was returning to that city, preceded by the above story, embellished in their favour by the drenched reporters. But on the other hand, there were others who had been more courteous, and had refused to go and disturb a lady at such an unearthly hour of the night. These latter were in the majority, and took up my defence.

It was therefore in this warlike atmosphere that I appeared before the public of Mobile. I wanted, however, to justify the good opinion of my defenders and confound my detractors.

Yes, but a sprite who had decided otherwise was there.

Mobile was a city that was generally quite disdained by *impresarii*. There was only one theatre. It had been let to the tragedian Barrett, who was to appear six days after me. All that remained was a miserable place, so small that I know of nothing that can be compared to it. We were playing *La Dame aux Camélias*. When Marguerite Gautier orders supper to be served, the servants who were to bring in the table ready laid tried to get it in through the door. But this was impossible. Nothing could be more comical than to see those unfortunate servants adopt every expedient.

The public laughed. Among the laughter of the spectators was one that became contagious. A negro of twelve or fifteen, who had got in somehow, was standing on a chair, and with his two hands holding on to his knees, his body bent, head forward, mouth open, he was laughing with such a shrill and piercing tone, and with such even continuity, that I caught it too. I had to go out while a portion of the back scenery was being removed to allow the table to be brought in.

I returned somewhat composed, but still under the domination of suppressed laughter. We were sitting round the table, and the supper was drawing to a close as usual. But just as the servants were entering to remove the table, one of them caught the scenery, which had been badly adjusted by the scene-shifters in their haste, and the whole back scene fell on our heads. As the scenery was nearly all made of paper in those days, it did not fall on our heads and remain there, but round our necks, and we had to remain in that position without being able to move. Our heads having gone through the paper, our appearance was most comical and ridiculous. The young nigger's laughter started again more piercing than ever, and this time my suppressed laughter ended in a crisis that left me without any strength.

The money paid for admission was returned to the public. It exceeded fifteen thousand francs.

This city was an unlucky one for me, and came very near proving fatal during the third visit I paid to it, as I will narrate in the second volume of these Memoirs.

That very night we left Mobile for Atlanta, where, after playing *La Dame aux Camélias*, we left again the same evening for Nashville.

We stayed an entire day at Memphis, and gave two performances there.

At one in the morning we left for Louisville. During the journey from Memphis to Louisville we were awakened by the sound of a fight, by oaths and cries. I opened the door of my railway carriage, and recognised the voices. Jarrett came out at the same time. We went towards the spot whence the noise came—to the small platform, where the two combatants, Captain Hayné and Marcus Mayer, were fighting with revolvers in their hands. Marcus Mayer's eye was out of its orbit, and blood covered the face of Captain Hayné. I threw myself without a moment's reflection between the two madmen, who, with that brutal but delightful courtesy of North Americans, stopped their fight.

We were beginning the dizzy round of the smaller towns, arriving at three, four, and sometimes six o'clock in the evening, and leaving immediately after the play. I only left my car to go to the theatre, and returned as soon as the play was over to retire to my elegant but diminutive bedroom. I sleep well on the railway. I felt an immense pleasure travelling in that way at high speed, sitting outside on the small platform, or rather reclining in a rocking-chair, gazing on the ever-changing spectacle of American plains and forests that passed before me. Without stopping we went through Louisville, Cincinnati for the second time, Columbus, Dayton, Indianapolis, St. Joseph, where one gets the best beer in the world, and where, when I was obliged to go to an hotel on account of repairs to one of the wheels of the car, a drunken dancer at a big ball given in the hotel seized me in the corridor leading to my room. This brutal fellow caught hold of me just as I was getting out of the elevator, and dragged me off with cries like those of a wild animal finding its prey after five days of enforced hunger. My dog, mad with excitement on hearing me scream, bit his legs severely, and that aroused the drunken man to the point of fury. It was with the greatest difficulty that I was delivered from the clutches of this demoniac. Supper was served. What a supper! Fortunately the beer was light both in colour and consistency, and enabled me to swallow the dreadful things that were served up.

The ball lasted all night, accompanied by revolver shots.

We left for Leavenworth, Quincy, Springfield, but not the Springfield in Massachusetts—the one in Illinois.

During the journey from Springfield to Chicago we were stopped by the snow in the middle of the night.

The sharp and deep groanings of the locomotive had already awakened me. I summoned my faithful Claude, and learned that we were to stop and wait for help.

Aided by my Félicie, I dressed in haste and tried to descend, but it was impossible. The snow was as high as the platform of the car. I remained wrapped up in furs, contemplating the magnificent night. The sky was hard, implacable, without a star, but all the same translucid. Lights extended as far as the eye could see along the rails before me, for I had taken refuge on the rear platform. These lights were to warn the trains that followed. Four of these came up, and stopped when the first fog-signals went off beneath their wheels, then crept slowly forward to the first light, where a man who was stationed there explained the incident. The same lights were lit immediately for the following train. as far off as possible, and a man, proceeding beyond the lights, placed detonators on the metals. Each train that arrived followed that course.

We were blocked by the snow. The idea came to me of lighting the kitchen fire, and I thus got sufficient boiling water to melt the top coating of snow on the side where I wanted to alight. Having done this, Claude and our coloured servants got down and cleared away a small portion as well as they could.

I was at last able to descend myself, and I tried to remove the snow to one side. My sister and I finished by throwing snowballs at each other, and the *melée* became general. Abbey, Jarrett, the secretary, and several of the artistes joined in, and we were warmed by this small battle with white cannon-balls.

When dawn appeared we were to be seen firing a revolver and Colt rifle at a target made from a champagne case. A distant sound, deadened by the cotton-wool of the snow, at length made us realise that help was approaching. As a matter of fact, two engines, with men who had shovels, hooks, and spades, were coming at full speed from the opposite direction. They were obliged to slow down on getting to within one kilometre of where we were, and the men began clearing the way before them. They finally succeeded in reaching us, but we were obliged to go back and take the western route. The unfortunate artistes, who had counted on getting breakfast in Chicago, which we ought to have reached at eleven o'clock, were lamenting, for with the new itinerary that we were forced to follow we could not reach Milwaukee before half-past one. There we were to give a *matinée* at two o'clock—*La Dame aux Camélias*. I therefore had the best lunch I could get prepared, and my servants carried it to my company, the members of which showed themselves very grateful.

The performance only began at three, and finished at half-past six o'clock ; we started again at eight with *Froufrou.*

Immediately after the play we left for Grand Rapids, Detroit, Cleveland, and Pittsburg, in which latter city I was to meet an American friend of mine who was to help me to realise one of my dreams—at least, I fancied so. In partnership with his brother, my friend was the owner of large steel works and several petroleum wells. I had known him in Paris, and had met him again at New York, where he offered to conduct me to Buffalo, so that I could visit or rather he could initiate me into the Falls of Niagara, for which he entertained a lover's passion. Frequently he would start off quite unexpectedly like a madman and take a rest at a place just near the Niagara Falls. The deafening sound of the cataracts seemed like music after the hard, hammering, strident noise of the forges at work on the iron, and the limpidity of the silvery cascades rested his eyes and refreshed his lungs, saturated as they were with petroleum and smoke.

My friend's buggy, drawn by two magnificent horses, took us along in a bewildering whirlwind of mud splashing over us and snow blinding us. It had been raining for a week, and Pittsburg in 1881 was not what it is at present, although it was a city

which impressed one on account of its commercial genius. The
black mud ran along the streets, and everywhere in the sky rose
huge patches of thick, black, opaque smoke; but there was a
certain grandeur about it all, for work was king there. Trains
ran through the streets laden with barrels of petroleum or
piled as high as possible with charcoal and coal. That fine
river, the Ohio, carried along with it steamers, barges, loads of
timber fastened together and forming enormous rafts, which
floated down the river alone, to be stopped on the way by the
owner for whom they were destined. The timber is marked, and
no one else thinks of taking it. I am told that the wood is not
conveyed in this way now, which is a pity.

The carriage took us along through streets and squares in the
midst of railways, under the enervating vibration of the electric
wires, which ran like furrows across the sky. We crossed a
bridge which shook under the light weight of the buggy. It was
a suspension bridge. Finally we drew up at my friend's home.
He introduced his brother to me, a charming man, but very cold
and correct, and so quiet that I was astonished.

"My poor brother is deaf," said my companion, after I had
been exerting myself for five minutes to talk to him in my
gentlest voice. I looked at this poor millionaire, who was
living in the most extraordinary noise, and who could not hear
even the faintest echo of the outrageous uproar. He could not
hear anything at all, and I wondered whether he was to be
envied or pitied. I was then taken to visit his incandescent
ovens and his vats in a state of ebullition. I went into a room
where some steel discs were cooling, which looked like so many
setting suns.

The heat from them seemed to scorch my lungs, and I felt as
though my hair would take fire.

We then went down a long, narrow road through which small
trains were running to and fro. Some of those trains were laden
with incandescent metals which made the atmosphere iridescent
as they passed. We walked in single file along the narrow passage
reserved for foot passengers between the rails. I did not feel at
all safe, and my heart began to beat fast. Blown first one way
then the other by the wind from the two trains coming in
opposite directions and passing each other, I drew my skirts
closely round me so that they should not be caught. Perched

on my high heels, at every step I took I was afraid of slipping
on this narrow, greasy, coal-strewn pavement.

To sum up briefly, it was a very unpleasant moment, and very
delighted I was to come to the end of that interminable street,
which led to an enormous field stretching away as far as the eye
could see.   There were rails lying all about here, which men
were polishing and filing, &c.   I had had quite enough, though,
and I asked to be allowed to go back and rest.   So we all three
returned to the house.

On arriving there, valets arrayed in livery opened the doors,
took our furs, walking on tip-toe as they moved about.   There
was silence everywhere, and I wondered why, as it seemed to me
incomprehensible.   My friend's brother scarcely spoke at all,
and when he did his voice was so low that I had great difficulty
in understanding him.   When we asked him any question by
gesticulating we had to listen most attentively to catch his reply,
and I noticed that an almost imperceptible smile lighted up
for an instant his stony face.   I understood very soon that this
man hated humanity, and that he avenged himself in his own
way for his infirmity.

Lunch had been prepared for us in the winter conservatory, a
nook of magnificent verdure and flowers.   We had just taken
our seats at the table when the songs of a thousand birds burst
forth like a veritable fanfare.   Underneath some large leaves,
whole families of canaries were imprisoned by invisible nets.
They were everywhere, up in the air, down below, under my
chair, on the table behind me, all over the place.   I tried to
quiet this shrill uproar by shaking my napkin and speaking in
a loud voice, but the little feathered tribe began to sing in a
maddening way.   The deaf man was leaning back in a rocking-
chair, and I noticed that his face had lighted up.   He laughed
aloud in an evil, spiteful manner.   Just as my own temper was
getting the better of me a feeling of pity and indulgence came
into my heart for this man, whose vengeance seemed to me as
pathetic as it was puerile.   Promptly deciding to make the best
of my host's spitefulness, and assisted by his brother, I took my
tea into the hall at the other end of the conservatory.   I was
nearly dead with fatigue, and when my friend proposed that I
should go with him to see his petroleum wells, a few miles out
of the city, I gazed at him with such a scared, hopeless expres-

sion that he begged me in the most friendly and polite way to forgive him.

It was five o'clock and quite dusk, and I wanted to go back to my hotel. My host asked if I would allow him to take me back by the hills. The road was rather longer, but I should be able to have a bird's eye view of Pittsburg, and he assured me that it was quite worth while. We started off in the buggy with two fresh horses, and a few minutes later I had the wildest dream. It seemed to me that he was Pluto, the god of the infernal regions, and I was Proserpine. We were travelling through our empire at a quick trot, drawn by our winged horses. All round us we could see fire and flames. The blood-red sky was blurred with long black trails that looked like widows' veils. The ground was covered with long arms of iron stretched heavenwards in a supreme imprecation. These arms threw forth smoke, flames, or sparks, which fell again in a shower of stars. The buggy carried us on up the hills, and the cold froze our limbs while the fires excited our brains. It was then that my friend told me of his love for the Niagara Falls. He spoke of them more like a lover than an admirer, and told me he liked to go to them alone. He said, though, that for me he would make an exception. He spoke of the rapids with such intense passion that I felt rather uneasy, and began to wonder whether the man was not mad. I grew alarmed, for he was driving along over the very verge of the precipice, jumping the stone heaps. I glanced at him sideways : his face was calm, but his under-lip twitched slightly ; and I had noticed this particularly with his deaf brother, also.

By this time I was quite nervous. The cold and the fires, this demoniacal drive, the sound of the anvil ringing out mournful chimes which seemed to come from under the earth, and then the deep forge whistle sounding like a desperate cry rending the silence of the night ; the chimney-stacks too, with their worn-out lungs spitting forth their smoke with a perpetual death-rattle, and the wind which had just risen twisting the streaks of smoke into spirals which it sent up towards the sky or beat down all at once on to us, all this wild dance of the natural and the human elements, affected my whole nervous system so that it was quite time for me to get back to the hotel. I sprang out of the carriage quickly on arriving, and arranged to see my friend at Buffalo, but, alas! I was never to see him again. He took cold that very day, and could not meet me there; and the following year I heard that he had been dashed against the rocks when trying to navigate a boat in the rapids. He died of his passion,—for his passion.

At the hotel all the artistes were awaiting me, as I had forgotten we were to have a rehearsal of *La Princesse Georges* at half-past four. I noticed a face that was unknown to me among the members of our company, and on making inquiries about this person found that he was an illustrator who had come with an introduction from Jarrett. He asked to be allowed to make a few sketches of me, and after giving orders that he should be taken to a seat, I did not trouble any more about him. We had to hurry through the rehearsal in order to be at the theatre in time for the performance of *Froufrou*, which we were giving that night. The rehearsal was accordingly rushed and gabbled through, so that it was soon over, and the stranger took his departure, refusing to let me look at his sketches on the plea that he wanted to touch them up before showing them. My joy was great the following day when Jarrett arrived at my hotel perfectly furious, holding in his hand the principal newspaper of Pittsburg, in which our illustrator, who turned out to be a journalist, had written an article giving at full length an account of the dress rehearsal of *Froufrou*! " In the play of *Froufrou*," wrote this delightful imbecile, "there is only one scene of any importance, and that is the one between the two sisters. Madame Sarah Bernhardt did not impress me greatly, and as to the artistes of the Comédie Francaise, I considered they were mediocre. The costumes were not very fine, and in the ball scene the men did not wear dress suits."

Jarrett was wild with rage and I was wild with joy. He knew my horror of reporters, and he had introduced this one in an underhand way, hoping to get a good advertisement out of it. The journalist imagined that we were having a dress rehearsal of *Froufrou*, and we were merely rehearsing Alexandre Dumas's *Princesse Georges* for the sake of refreshing our memory. He had mistaken the scene between Princesse Georges and the Comtesse de Terremonde for the scene in the third act between the two sisters in *Froufrou*. We were all of us wearing our travelling costumes, and he was surprised at not seeing the men in dress coats and the women in evening dress. What fun this was for our company and for all the town, and I may add what a subject it furnished for the jokes of all the rival newspapers.

I had to play two days at Pittsburg, and then go on to Bradford, Erie, Toronto, and arrive at Buffalo on Sunday. It was my intention to give all the members of my company a day's outing at Niagara Falls, but Abbey too wanted to invite them. We had a discussion on the subject, and it was extremely animated. He was very dictatorial, and so was I, and we both preferred giving the whole thing up rather than yield to each other. Jarrett, however, pointed out the fact to us that this course would deprive the artistes of a little festivity about which they heard a great deal and to which they were looking forward. We therefore gave in finally, and in order to settle the matter we agreed to share the outlay between us. The artistes accepted our invitation with the most charming good grace, and we took the train for Buffalo, where we arrived at ten minutes past six in the morning. We had telegraphed beforehand for carriages and coffee to be in readiness, and to have food provided for us, as it is simply madness for thirty-two persons to arrive on a Sunday in such towns as these without giving notice of such an event. We had a special train going at full speed over the lines, which were entirely clear on Sundays, and it was decorated with festoons of flowers. The younger artistes were as delighted as children; those who had already seen everything before told about it; then there was the eloquence of those who had heard of it, &c. &c.; and all this, together with the little bouquets of flowers distributed among the women and the cigars and cigarettes presented to the men, made every one good-humoured, so that all appeared to be happy. The carriages met our train and took us to the Hotel d'Angleterre, which had been kept open for us. There were flowers everywhere, and any number of small tables upon which were coffee, chocolate, or tea. Every table was soon surrounded with guests. I had my sister, Abbey, Jarrett, and the principal artistes at my table. The meal was of short duration and very gay and animated. We then went to the Falls, and I remained more than an hour on the balcony hollowed out of the rock. My eyes filled with tears as I stood there, for I was deeply moved by the splendour of the sight. A radiant sun made the air around us iridescent. There were rainbows everywhere, lighting up the atmosphere with their soft silvery colours. The pendants of hard ice hanging down along the rocks on each side looked like enormous jewels. I was sorry to leave this balcony. We went down in narrow cages which glided gently into a tube arranged in the cleft of the enormous rock. We arrived in this way under the American Falls. They were there almost over our heads, sprinkling us with their blue, pink, and mauve drops. In front of us, protecting us from the Falls, was a heap of icicles forming quite a little mountain. We climbed over this to the best of our ability. My heavy fur mantle tired me, and about half way down I took it off and let it slip over the side of the ice mountain, to take it again when I reached the bottom. I was wearing a dress of white cloth with a satin blouse, and every one screamed with surprise on seeing me. Abbey took off his overcoat and threw it over my shoulders. I shook this off quickly, and Abbey's coat went to join my fur cloak below. The poor *impresario's* face looked very blank. As he had taken a fair number of cocktails, he staggered, fell down on the ice, got up, and immediately fell again, to the amusement of every one. I was not at all cold, as I never am when out of doors. I only feel the cold inside houses when I am inactive.

Finally we arrived at the highest point of the ice, and the cataract was really most threatening. We were covered by the impalpable mist, which rises in the midst of the tumultuous noise. I gazed at it all, bewildered and fascinated by the rapid movement of the water, which looked like a wide curtain of silver, unfolding itself to be dashed violently into a rebounding, splashing heap with a noise unlike any sound I had ever heard. I very easily turn dizzy, and I know very well that if I had been alone I should have remained there for ever with my eyes fixed on the sheet of water hurrying along at full speed, my mind lulled by the fascinating sound, and my limbs numbed by the treacherous cold which encircled us. I had to be dragged away, but I am soon myself again when confronted by an obstacle.

We had to go down again, and this was not as easy as it had been to climb up. I took the walking-stick belonging to one of my friends, and then sat down on the ice. By putting the stick under my legs I was able to slide down to the bottom. All the others imitated me, and it was a comical sight to see thirty-two people descending the ice-hill in this way. There were several somersaults and collisions, and plenty of laughter. A quarter of an hour later we were all at the hotel, where luncheon had been ordered.

We were all cold and hungry; it was warm inside the hotel, and the meal smelt good. When luncheon was over the landlord of the hotel asked me to go into a small drawing-room, where a surprise awaited me. On entering I saw on a table, protected under a long glass box, the Niagara Falls in miniature, with the rocks looking like pebbles. A large glass represented the sheet of water, and glass threads represented the Falls. Here and there was some foliage of a hard, crude green. Standing up on a little hillock of ice was a figure intended for me. It was enough to make any one howl with horror, for it was all so hideous. I managed to raise a broad smile for the benefit of the hotel keeper by way of congratulating him on his good taste, but I was petrified on recognising the man-servant of my friends the Th—— brothers of Pittsburg. They had sent this monstrous caricature of the most beautiful thing in the world.

I read the letter which their domestic handed me, and all my disdain melted away. They had gone to so much trouble in order to explain what they wanted me to understand, and they were so delighted at the idea of giving me any pleasure.

I dismissed the valet, after giving him a letter for his masters, and I asked the hotel keeper to send the work of art to Paris, packed carefully. I hoped that it might arrive in fragments.

The thought of it haunted me, though, and I wondered how my friend's passion for the Falls could be reconciled with the idea of such a gift. Whilst admitting that his imaginative mind might have hoped to be able to carry out his idea, how was it that he was not indignant at the sight of this grotesque imitation? How had he dared to send it to me? How was it that my friend loved the Falls, and what had he understood of their marvellous grandeur? Since his death I have questioned my own memory of him a hundred times, but all in vain. He died for them, tossed about in their waters, killed by their caresses; and I cannot think that he could ever have seen how beautiful they really were. Fortunately I was called away, as the carriage was there and every one waiting for me. The horses started off with us, trotting in that weary way peculiar to tourists' horses.

When we arrived on the Canadian shore we had to go underground and array ourselves in black or yellow mackintoshes. We looked like so many heavy, dumpy sailors who were wearing these garments for the first time. There were two large cells to shelter us, one for the women and the other for the men. Every one undressed more or less in the midst of wild confusion, and making a little package of our clothes, we gave this into the keeping of the woman in charge. With the mackintosh hood drawn tightly under the chin, hiding the hair entirely, an enormous blouse much too wide covering the whole body, fur boots with roughed soles to avoid broken legs and heads, and immense mackintosh breeches in zouave style, the prettiest and slenderest woman was at once transformed into a huge, cumbersome, awkward bear. An iron-tipped cudgel to carry in the hand completed this becoming costume. I looked more ridiculous than the others, for I would not cover my hair, and in the most pretentious way I had fastened some roses into my mackintosh blouse. The women went into raptures on seeing me. " How pretty she looks like that ! " they exclaimed. " She always finds a way to be *chic, quand-même !* " The men kissed my bear's paw in the most gallant way, bowing low and saying in low tones : " Always and *quand-même* the queen, the fairy, the goddess, the divinity," &c. &c. And I went along, purring with content and quite satisfied with myself, until, as I passed by the counter where the girl who gives the tickets was sitting, I caught sight of myself in the glass. I looked enormous and ridiculous with my roses pinned in, and the curly locks of hair forming a kind of peak to my clumsy hood. I appeared to be stouter than all the others, because of the silver belt I was wearing round my waist, as this drew up the hard folds of the mackintosh round my hips. My thin face was nearly covered by my hair, which was flattened down by my hood. My eyes could not be seen, and only my mouth served to show that this barrel was a human being. Furious with myself for my pretentious coquetry, and ashamed of my own weakness in having been so content with the pitiful, insincere flattery of people who were making fun of me, I decided to remain as I was as a punishment for my stupid vanity. There were a number of strangers among us, who nudged each other, pointing to me and laughing slyly at my absurd get-up, and this was only what I deserved.

We went down the flight of steps cut in the block of ice in order to get underneath the Canadian Falls. The sight there was most strange and extraordinary. Above me I saw an immense cupola of ice hanging over in space, attached only on one side to the rock. From this cupola thousands of icicles of the most varied shapes were hanging. There were dragons, arrows, crosses, laughing faces, sorrowful faces, hands with six fingers, deformed feet, incomplete human bodies, and women's long locks of hair. In fact, with the help of the imagination and by fixing the gaze when looking with half-shut eyes, the illusion is complete, and in less time than it takes to describe all this one can evoke all the pictures of nature and of our dreams, all the wild conceptions of a diseased mind, or the realities of a reflective brain.

In front of us were small steeples of ice, some of them proud and erect, standing out against the sky, others ravaged by the wind which gnaws the ice, looking like minarets ready for the muezzin. On the right a cascade was rushing down as noisily as on the other side, but the sun had commenced its descent towards the west, and everything was tinged with a rosy hue. The water splashed over us, and we were suddenly covered with small silvery waves which when shaken slightly stiffened against our mackintoshes. It was a shoal of very small fish which had had the misfortune to be driven into the current, and which had come to die in the dazzling brilliancy of the setting sun. On the other side there was a small block which looked like a rhinoceros entering the water.

"I should love to mount on that!" I exclaimed.

"Yes, but it is impossible," replied one of my friends.

"Oh, as to that, nothing is impossible," I said. "There is only the risk; the crevice to be covered is not a yard long."

"No, but it is deep," remarked an artiste who was with us.

"Well," I said, "my dog is just dead. We will bet a dog—and if I win I am to choose my dog—that I go."

Abbey was fetched immediately, but he only arrived in time to see me on the block. I came very near falling into the crevice, and when I was on the back of the rhinoceros I could not stand up. It was as smooth and transparent as artificial ice. I sat down on its back, holding on to the little hump, and I declared that if no one came to fetch me I should stay where I was, as I had not the courage to move a step on this slippery back; and then, too, it seemed to me as though it moved slightly. I began to lose my self-possession. I felt dizzy, but I had won my dog. My excitement was over, and I was seized with fright. Every one gazed at me in a bewildered way, and that increased my terror. My sister went into hysterics, and my dear Guérard groaned in a heartrending way, "Oh heavens, my dear Sarah, oh heavens!" An artist was making sketches; fortunately the members of our company had gone up again in order to go and see the Rapids. Abbey besought me to return; poor Jarrett besought me. But I felt dizzy, and I could not and would not cross again. Angelo then sprang across the crevice, and remaining there, called for a plank of wood and a hatchet.

"Bravo! bravo!" I exclaimed from the back of my rhinoceros.

The plank was brought. It was an old, black-looking piece of wood, and I glanced at it suspiciously. The hatchet cut into the tail of my rhinoceros, and the plank was fixed firmly by Angelo on my side and held by Abbey, Jarrett, and Claude on the other side. I let myself slide over the crupper of my rhinoceros, and I then started, not without terror, along the rotten plank of wood, which was so narrow that I was obliged to put one foot in front of the other, the heel over the toe. I returned in a very feverish state to the hotel, and the artist brought me the droll sketches he had taken.

After a light luncheon I was to start again by the train, which had been waiting for us twenty minutes. All the others had taken their seats some time before. I was leaving without having seen the rapids in which my poor Pittsburg friend met his death.

XXXVIII

THE RETURN TO FRANCE—THE WELCOME
AT HÂVRE

OUR great voyage was drawing towards its close. I say great voyage, for it was my first one. It had lasted seven months. The voyages I have since undertaken were always from eleven to sixteen months.

From Buffalo we went to Rochester, Utica, Syracuse, Albany, Troy, Worcester, Providence, Newark, making a short stay in Washington, an admirable city, but one which at that time had a sadness about it that affected one's nerves. It was the last large city I visited.

After two admirable performances there and a supper at the Embassy, we left for Baltimore, Philadelphia, and New York, where our tour was to come to a close. In that city I gave a grand professional *matinée* at the general demand of the actors and actresses of New York. The piece chosen was *La Princesse Georges*.

Oh, what a fine and never-to-be-forgotten performance! Everything was applauded by the artistes. Nothing escaped the particular state of mind of that audience made up of actors and actresses, painters and sculptors. At the end of the play a gold hair-comb was handed to me, on which were engraved the names of a great number of persons present. From Salvini I received a pretty casket of lapis, and from Mary Anderson, at that time in the striking beauty of her nineteen years, a small medal bearing a forget-me-not in turquoises. In my dressing-room I counted one hundred and thirty bouquets.

That evening we gave our last performance with *La Dame aux Camélias*. I had to return and bow to the public fourteen times.

2 E

Then I had a moment's stupefaction, for in the tempest of cries and bravos I heard a shrill cry shouted by thousands of mouths, which I did not in the least understand. After each " call " I asked in the wings what the meaning of the word was that struck on my ears like a dreadful sneeze, beginning again time after time. Jarrett appeared and enlightened me. " They are calling for a speech." I looked at him, abashed. " Yes, they want you to make a little speech."

" Ah no! " I exclaimed, as I again went on the stage to make a bow. " No." And in making my bow to the public I murmured, " I cannot speak. But I can tell you : Thank you, with all my heart ! "

It was in the midst of a thunder of applause, underscored with " Hip, hip, hurrah ! *Vive la France !* " that I left the theatre.

On Wednesday, May 4, I embarked on the same Transatlantic steamer, the *America*, the phantom vessel to which my journey had brought good luck. But it had no longer the same commander. The new one's name was Santelli. He was as little and fair-complexioned as his predecessor was big and dark. But he was as charming, and a nice conversationist.

Commander Jowclas blew his brains out after losing heavily at play.

My cabin had been newly fitted up, and this time the woodwork had been covered in sky-blue material. On boarding the steamer I turned towards the friendly crowd and threw them a last adieu. " *Au revoir !* " they shouted back.

I then went towards my cabin. Standing at the door, in an elegant iron-grey suit, wearing pointed shoes, hat in the latest style, and dog-skin gloves, stood Henry Smith, the showman of whales. I gave a cry like that of a wild beast. He kept his joyful smile, and held out a jewel casket, which I took with the object of throwing it into the sea through the open port-hole. But Jarrett caught hold of my arm and took possession of the casket, which he opened. " It is magnificent ! " he exclaimed, but I had closed my eyes. I stopped up my ears and cried out to the man, " Go away ! you knave ! you brute ! Go away ! I hope you will die under atrocious suffering ! Go away ! "

I half opened my eyes. He had gone. Jarrett wanted to

THE RETURN TO FRANCE 435

talk to me about the present. I would not hear anything about it.

"Ah, for God's sake, Mr. Jarrett, leave me alone! Since this jewel is so fine, give it to your daughter, and do not speak to me about it any more." And he did so.

The evening before my departure from America I had received a long cablegram, signed Grosos, president of the Life Saving Society at Hâvre, asking me to give upon my arrival a performance, the proceeds of which would be distributed among the families of the society of Life Savers. I accepted with unspeakable joy.

On regaining my native land, I should assist in drying tears.

After the decks had been cleared for departure, our ship moved slowly off, and we left New York on Thursday the 5th of May.

Detesting sea travelling as I usually do, I set out this time with a light heart and smiling face, disdainful of the horrible discomfort caused by the voyage.

We had not left New York forty-eight hours when the vessel stopped. I sprang out of my berth, and was soon on deck, fearing some accident to our *Phantom*, as we had nick-named the ship. In front of us a French boat had raised, lowered, and again raised its small flags. The captain, who had given the replies to these signals, sent for me, and explained to me the working and the orthography of the signals. I could not remember anything he told me, I must confess to my shame. A small boat was lowered from the ship opposite us, and two sailors and a young man very poorly dressed and with a pale face embarked. Our captain had the steps lowered, the small boat was hailed, and the young man, escorted by two sailors, came on deck. One of them handed a letter to the officer who was waiting at the top of the steps. He read it, and looking at the young man he said quietly, "Follow me!" The small boat and the sailors returned to the ship, the boat was hoisted, the whistle shrieked, and after the usual salute the two ships continued their way. The unfortunate young man was brought before the captain. I went away, after asking the captain to tell me later on what was the meaning of it all, unless it should prove to be something which had to be kept secret.

The captain came himself and told me the little story. The

young man was a poor artist, a wood-engraver, who had managed to slip on to a steamer bound for New York. He had not a sou of money for his passage, as he had not even been able to pay for an emigrant's ticket. He had hoped to get through without being noticed, hiding under the bales of various kinds. He had, however, been taken ill, and it was this illness which had betrayed him. Shivering with cold and feverish, he had talked aloud in his sleep, uttering the most incoherent words. He was taken into the infirmary, and when there he had confessed everything. The captain undertook to make him accept what I sent him for his journey to America. The story soon spread, and other passengers made a collection, so that the young engraver found himself very soon in possession of a fortune of twelve hundred francs. Three days later he brought me a little wooden box, manufactured, carved, and engraved by him. This little box is now nearly full of petals of flowers, for every year on May 7 I received a small bouquet of flowers with these words, always the same ones, year after year, " Gratitude and devotion." I always put the petals of the flowers into the little box, but for the last seven years I have not received any. Is it forgetfulness or death which has caused the artist to discontinue this graceful little token of gratitude ? I have no idea, but the sight of the box always gives me a vague feeling of sadness, as forgetfulness and death are the most faithful companions of the human being. Forgetfulness takes up its abode in our mind, in our heart, while death is always present laying traps for us, watching all we do, and jeering gaily when sleep closes our eyes, for we give it then the illusion of what it knows will some day be a reality.

Apart from the above incident, nothing particular happened during the voyage. I spent every night on deck gazing at the horizon, hoping to draw towards me that land on which were my loved ones. I turned in towards morning, and slept all day to kill the time.

The steamers in those days did not perform the crossing with the same speed as they do nowadays. The hours seemed to me to be wickedly long. I was so impatient to land that I called for the doctor and asked him to send me to sleep for eighteen hours. He gave me twelve hours sleep with a strong dose of chloral, and I felt stronger and calmer for affronting the shock of happiness.

Santelli had promised that we should arrive on the evening of the 14th. I was ready, and had been walking up and down distractedly for an hour when an officer came to ask whether I would not go on to the bridge with the commander, who was waiting for me.

With my sister I went up in haste, and soon understood from the embarrassed circumlocutions of the amiable Santelli that we were too far off to hope to make the harbour that night.

I began to cry. I thought we should never arrive. I imagined that the sprite was going to triumph, and I wept those tears that were like a brook that runs on and on without ceasing.

The commander did what he could to bring me to a rational state of mind. I descended from the bridge with both body and soul like limp rags.

I lay down on a deck-chair, and when dawn came was benumbed and sleepy.

It was five in the morning. We were still twenty miles from land. The sun, however, began joyously to brighten up the small white clouds, light as snowflakes. The remembrance of my young beloved one gave me courage again. I ran towards my cabin. I spent a long while over my toilet in order to kill time.

At seven o'clock I made inquiries of the captain.

"We are twelve miles off," he said. "In two hours we shall land."

"You swear to it?"

"Yes, I swear." I returned on deck, where, leaning on the bulwark, I scanned the distance. A small steamer appeared on the horizon. I saw it without looking at it, expecting every minute to hear a cry from over there, over there. . . .

All at once I noticed masses of little white flags being waved on the small steamer. I got my glasses—and then let them fall with a joyous cry that left me without any strength, without breath. I wanted to speak: I could not. My face, it appears, became so pale that it frightened the people who were about me. My sister Jeanne wept as she waved her arms towards the distance.

They wanted to make me sit down. I would not. Hanging on to the bulwarks, I smell the salts that are thrust under my nose. I allow friendly hands to wipe my temples, but I am gazing over there whence the vessel is coming. Over there lies my happiness! my joy! my life! my everything! dearer than everything!

The *Diamond* (the vessel's name) comes near. A bridge of love is formed between the small and the large ship, a bridge formed of the beatings of our hearts, under the weight of the kisses that have been kept back for so many days. Then comes the reaction that takes place in our tears, when the small boats, coming up to the large vessel, allow the impatient ones to climb up the rope ladders and throw themselves into outstretched arms.

The *America* is invaded. Every one is there, my dear and faithful friends. They have accompanied my young son Maurice. Ah, what a delicious time! Answers get ahead of questions. Laughter is mingled with tears. Hands are pressed, lips are kissed, only to begin over again. One is never tired of this repetition of tender affection. During this time our ship is moving. The *Diamond* has disappeared, carrying away the mails. The farther we advance, the more small boats we meet; they are decked with flags, ploughing the sea. There are a hundred of them. And more are coming. . . .

"Is it a public holiday?" I asked Georges Boyer, the correspondent of the *Figaro*, who with some friends had come to meet me.

"Oh yes, Madame, a great *fête* day to-day at Hâvre, for they are expecting the return of a fairy who left seven months ago."

"Is it really in my honour that all these pretty boats have spread their wings and beflagged their masts? Ah, how happy I am!" We are now alongside the jetty. There are perhaps twenty thousand people there, who cry out, "*Vive* Sarah Bernhardt!"

I was dumfounded. I did not expect any triumphant return. I was well aware that the performance to be given for the Life Saving Society had won the hearts of the people of Hâvre, but now I learnt that trains had come from Paris, packed with people, to welcome my return. . . .

I feel my pulse. It is me. I am not dreaming.

The boat stops opposite a red velvet tent, and an invisible orchestra strikes up an air from *Le Châlet*, "*Arrêtons-nous ici*."

I smile at this quite French childishness. I get off and walk through the midst of a hedge of smiling, kind faces of sailors, who offer me flowers.

Within the tent all the life-savers are waiting for me, wearing on their broad chests the medals they have so well deserved.

M. Grosos, the president, reads to me the following address :

" MADAME,—As President, I have the honour to present to you a delegation from the Life Saving Society of Hâvre, come to welcome you and express their gratitude for the sympathy you have so warmly worded in your transatlantic despatch.

" We have also come to congratulate you on the immense success that you have met with at every place you have visited during your adventurous journey. You have now achieved in two worlds an incontestable popularity and artistic celebrity; and your marvellous talent, added to your personal charms, has affirmed abroad that France is always the land of art and the birthplace of elegance and beauty.

" A distant echo of the words you spoke in Denmark, evoking a deep and sad memory, still strikes on our ears. It repeats that your heart is as French as your talent, for in the midst of the feverish and burning successes on the stage you have never forgotten to unite your patriotism to your artistic triumphs.

" Our life-savers have charged me with expressing to you their admiration for the charming benefactress whose generous hand has spontaneously stretched itself out towards their poor but noble society. They wish to offer you these flowers, gathered from the soil of the mother-country, on the land of France, where you will find them everywhere under your feet. They are worthy that you should accept them with favour, for they are presented to you by the bravest and most loyal of our life-savers."

It is said that my reply was very eloquent, but I cannot affirm that that reply was really made by me. I had lived for several hours in a state of over-excitement from successive emotions. I had taken no food, had no sleep. My heart had not ceased to beat a moving and joyous refrain. My brain had been filled with a thousand facts that had been piled up for seven months and narrated in two hours. This triumphant reception, which I was far from expecting after what had happened just before my departure, after having been so badly treated by the Paris Press, after the incidents of my journey, which had been always badly interpreted by several French papers—all these coincidences were of such different proportions that they seemed hardly credible.

The performance furnished a fruitful harvest for the life-savers. As for me, I played *La Dame aux Camélias* for the first time in France.

I was really inspired. I affirm that those who were present at that performance experienced the quintessence of what my personal art can give.

I spent the night at my place at Ste. Adresse. The day following I left for Paris.

A most flattering ovation was waiting for me on my arrival. Then, three days afterwards, installed in my little mansion in the Avenue de Villiers, I received Victorien Sardou, in order to hear him read his magnificent piece, *Fédora*.

What a great artiste! What an admirable actor! What a marvellous author!

He read that play to me right off, playing every *rôle*, giving me in one second the vision of what I should do.

"Ah!" I exclaimed, after the reading was over. "Ah, dear Master! Thanks for this beautiful part! Thanks for the fine lesson you have just given me."

That night left me without sleep, for I wished to catch a glimpse in the darkness of the small star in which I had faith.

I saw it as dawn was breaking, and fell asleep thinking over the new era that it was going to light up.

*   *   *   *   *

My artistic journey had lasted seven months. I had visited fifty cities, and given 156 performances, as follows :

La Dame aux Camélias	65	performances
Adrienne Lecouvreur	17	,,
Froufrou	41	,,
La Princesse Georges . . .	3	,,
Hernani	14	,,
L'Etrangère	3	,,
Phèdre	6	,,
Le Sphinx	7	
Total receipts	2,667,600	francs
Average receipts . . .	17,100	,,

I conclude the first volume of my souvenirs here, for this is really the first halting-place of my life, the real starting-point of my physical and moral being.

I had run away from the Comédie Française, from Paris, from France, from my family, and from my friends.

I had thought of having a wild ride across mountains, seas, and space, and I came back in love with the vast horizon, but calmed down by the feeling of responsibility which for seven months had been weighing on my shoulders.

The terrible Jarrett, with his implacable and cruel wisdom, had tamed my wild nature by a constant appeal to my probity.

In those few months my mind had matured and the brusqueness of my will was softened.

My life, which I thought at first was to be so short, seemed now likely to be very, very long, and that gave me a great mischievous delight whenever I thought of the infernal displeasure of my enemies.

I resolved to live. I resolved to be the great artiste that I longed to be.

And from the time of this return I gave myself entirely up to my life.

INDEX

2 F